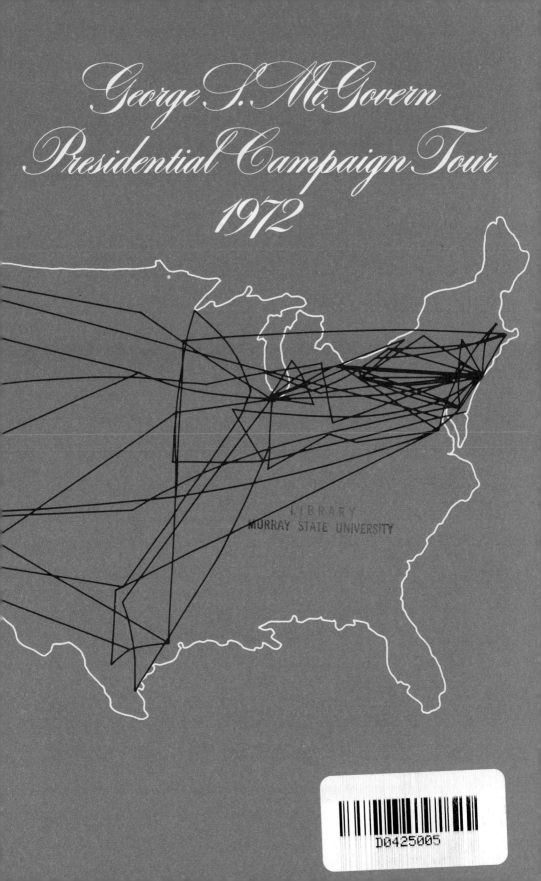

George S. McGovern
Presidential Campaign Tour
1972

Right from the Start
A Chronicle of the McGovern Campaign

Gary Warren Hart

Right from the Start
A Chronicle of the McGovern Campaign

QUADRANGLE/THE NEW YORK TIMES BOOK COMPANY

For the McGovern Army

Count where man's glory most begins and ends,
And say my glory was I had such friends.

CONTENTS

PREFACE

This is a book about Senator George McGovern's campaign for the Presidency of the United States—right from the start—the people, the events, the decisions, the successes, the failures.

It is really two separate stories. The first—and far and away the more fascinating—is the story of the nomination—how George McGovern captured control of the Democratic Party. This is a long story, covering more than two years. It involves one of the most profound upsets in the history of American politics. Attorney Edward Bennett Williams even suggested that the book be entitled "Heist" and that it focus only on this first part.

But when the McGovern campaign is mentioned to most people they immediately think of the events between McGovern's nomination and—for us—the unfortunate election outcome. Those events compose the second story—the general election race—and cover scarcely more than 90 days in the fall of 1972.

Because the first story is not only the longer and the more interesting, but probably also historically the more important, much of this book is concerned with it.

President John Kennedy popularized a saying which heads the final section of this book: "Victory has a thousand fathers, but defeat is an orphan." That pretty well sums it up. This book is not an exposé or a search for villians. For our defeat, as President Kennedy also said, there is blame enough to go around. This is not to say that personal differences involving difficult and controversial campaign decisions are avoided or glossed over. To the degree they are significant to these two stories, they are included.

In large part, this is the story of my experience inside the McGovern Presidential campaign as its first full-time staff member. If this book has a single purpose, it is to share that experience with the reader, to give as accurate an account as possible of how a Presidential campaign evolves and, on a day-to-day, personal basis, what it is really like. I have not made a systematic effort to include the views of everyone who played an important role. I did consult with a number of people who may have had a better opportunity than I to observe particular events, and have included their observations, with appropriate attribution. Since this is more a personal journal than an exhaustive history, I do not claim to be detached. But I have tried to be fair.

There may be those surprised, and perhaps disappointed, that the candidate, Senator McGovern, is not more thoroughly analyzed and his point of view more completely presented in every instance. This was not done for two reasons. First, much of the time I was not with him and cannot speak for his reaction to each event. This fact may itself surprise some people, but contrary to some political mythology, a campaign cannot and should not be run from the candidate's side. Second, it would be grossly presumptuous of me to try to speak for McGovern or present his interpretation of his own campaign. He is an articulate and direct man who has had, and presumably will have, much to say about the events surrounding his candidacy. He does not need me as an interpreter.

At heart, this is a book about people, about that incredible band that I think I was first to call the McGovern Army. They were, in Ruskin's phrase, the soldiers of the plowshare. They believed in a man and they believed in their cause, the effort to move this nation out of its rut of narrowness and fear and away from leaders who do not trust their own people. Adopting a project with about as much initial chance of success as moving Birnam wood to Dunsinane, they brought their cause to the very gates of power before being beaten back. To the degree that I may presume to speak for their motivation, I can only refer to a line from Aristotle:

A likely impossibility is always preferable
to an unconvincing possibility.

It is to these people that this story is dedicated, because they are the people who created it. I wish to thank the several dozen of them who willingly helped refresh my recollection and supplement my notes and records. Of special help was my campaign assistant, Marcia Johnston, whose ability to recall moods and atmospheres was invaluable and whose great good humor kept us both sane through some very trying times. About George McGovern I can only say, he is the finest man I have ever met in politics. I owe him a great deal for providing me an opportunity to contribute to a process in which I believe so strongly.

And finally I must thank Lee, Andrea, and John, who sacrificed as much as anyone for this cause.

G. W. H.

Denver, Colorado
March, 1973

Right from the Start
A Chronicle of the McGovern Campaign

PART I

Jimmie the Greek and the Impossible Dream
(March, 1970, to January, 1971)

"I've decided to make this race for the Presidency, and I'd like to have your help. I have as good a chance as anyone to get the nomination, and if I can get the Democratic nomination, I can beat Nixon. And besides, I would make a better President than anyone else around." Thus spoke Senator George McGovern. The place: a private meeting room, Stapleton International Airport, Denver, Colorado. The time: Sunday morning, March 22, 1970.

I was not surprised by his decision to run. Since his brief 18-day campaign for the Democratic Presidential nomination in 1968 following the assassination of Senator Robert Kennedy, Senator McGovern had maintained a highly visible leadership profile through his chairmanship of the Democratic Commission of Party Reform (the so-called McGovern Commission) and his continuing outspoken advocacy of an immediate end to the Vietnam war. I was impressed by the depth of his determination and self-confidence and surprised by his offer to me to play an important role in the Presidential campaign, because he knew practically nothing about me, and because I was not well known in national political circles.

Senator McGovern had come to Denver the previous day, March 21, to deliver the annual Jefferson-Jackson Day address for the Colorado Democratic Party. Significantly, his speech was entitled, "Come Home, America," the first public statement of the theme that was to dominate both the nomination and general-election races. I had never met him before, but through a series of minor accidents, I was contacted by his office to arrange his one-day visit to Denver—including meetings with the editors of *The Denver Post* and *The Rocky Mountain News,* a television talk-show taping, an airport press conference, brief introductions to state party leaders, and finally the Sunday morning breakfast with a majority of the 1968 delegates to the Democratic Convention in Chicago, most of whom had worked for Senator Robert Kennedy or Senator Eugene McCarthy. At this breakfast, Senator McGovern made the offer that eventually brought me into his Presidential campaign as its director and first full-time staff member.

The political climate during this period was heavily conditioned by the events of Chappaquiddick. Some political analysts believed that those

3

events had stopped Kennedy from active pursuit of the nomination, but had not ruled him out of consideration. Many felt that the 1972 Democratic nomination was his for the asking. However, in a casual conversation some months after my initial meeting with McGovern, he confessed, to my amazement, that he had already decided to run for President even if it mean competing with his close friend Ted Kennedy for the nomination.

With Kennedy not actively seeking the nomination, attention had turned in 1969 and early 1970 to Senator Edmund Muskie. He had moved somewhat tentatively and cautiously to cultivate a front-runner image, but was obviously trying not to emerge too visibly too soon. Speculation among columnists and reporters, party officials, and others who concern themselves with politics year-round also began to focus on other Senators, including Birch Bayh, Harold Hughes, Henry Jackson, Hubert Humphrey, Fred Harris—none of whom went out of his way to discourage such speculation—and to a somewhat lesser degree on Mayor John Lindsay.

But Muskie was considered by all the man to beat and by many to be unbeatable—even at this early date. For those who were not enthralled by a Muskie nomination, or who merely reveled in political gossip and speculation, a more romantic, charismatic, "dark-horse" figure was sought, thus giving some credence to a Lindsay, Hughes, or Harris candidacy, or the continued mongering of the Kennedy rumor.

In those early spring days of 1970, and for almost two years thereafter, the universal political judgment, the "smart" political money, on McGovern was something like this: He is a nice man, decent, honest, perhaps even courageous; he says what he thinks and is right on the issues before any of the others. *But* he can't win. He is from a small midwestern state; he has no money; he has no standing in the polls; he doesn't have the backing of organized labor or any substantial element of the Democratic Party or any of the constituent elements of the traditional Democratic coalition. Worse still, he is a "one-issue candidate"—the war—and that issue will be gone by 1972. But above all, *he does not have charisma.*

In short, no one who was anyone gave George McGovern even the ghost of a chance to become the Presidential nominee of the Democratic Party in 1972. But on March 22, 1970, I was struck by that combination of determination and self-confidence; McGovern impressed me as a man who seriously considered himself a possible President of the United States, and probably a very good one.

In response to a recruitment offer from the Senator, I outlined the difficulties of closing down my Denver law office and suggested as a compromise that I might help in the organization of the Western states, using my office as a base of operations. We agreed that this would be explored more fully a couple of weeks later in Washington.

In Washington on business on April 6, 1970, I delivered a proposal to the Senator outlining a Western campaign organizational effort, the substance of which was as follows:

First, using my own law office as a base, I propose to identify potential McGovern supporters in each of the 24 states West of the Mississippi. These key supporters will be selected from McGovern delegates to the 1968 Convention, strong party leaders who have otherwise indicated an interest in your candidacy, and word-of-mouth recommendations.

Second, once an initial pool of names is available, I will begin a program of personal contacts throughout the Western states designed to select key organizational leaders, encourage support among state party leaders and workers, and generally read the political climate in each state. These contacts will initially be personal and can be supplemented and maintained by telephone and additional visits later.

Third, the primary goal of this organizational effort will be the selection of a coordinator in each state. In each case this should be a person committed to a McGovern candidacy who has the dedication, experience, and personal manner required to organize the state efficiently without alienation of the established party structure. The secondary goal will be the identification and solicitation of potential 1972 Convention delegates. Both these operations should be carried out, at least through 1970, on a low-key basis and both should produce extensive card files which can be used throughout the campaign. Our files should also contain a detailed analysis of the political situation in each state which should become the basis for allocation of financial and candidate resources.

At a quiet corner of the Rotunda restaurant on Capitol Hill, McGovern repeated his request that I come back to Washington to direct the national effort. He restated his firm intention to seek the nomination and win the Presidency and his conviction that he could defeat the other Democratic contenders in the field, including Senator Muskie.

In our discussion, we arrived at a fundamental agreement which was to have a profound effect upon the entire two-and-a-half-year campaign: that McGovern's natural base within the Democratic Party was its liberal wing and, more specifically, those forces which shaped and supported the Kennedy and McCarthy candidacies in 1968; that he could and should harness and control those forces to obtain the nomination without necessarily alienating the Party establishment and that, in fact, he should try to bridge the gap between the liberals and the regulars before the 1972 Convention. Professor Richard Wade, an early McGovern advisor and campaign theorist, later identified this as the left-centrist strategy.

During the evening the Senator reiterated his intention to continue his outspoken opposition to the Vietnam war. But he acknowledged the need to broaden his issue base to demonstrate competence and foresight on other matters of widespread voter concern, such as unemployment, inflation, wasteful military spending, and social injustice, and to become a principal party spokesman against ill-advised Nixon policies.

His attitude was positive and eager. He felt that his position on the war would continue to distinguish him from his likely opponents for the nomination, none of whom had demonstrated particular leadership on this matter. He strongly ratified my conviction that fundamental political organizational principles could make the difference in obtaining the nomination, and that he certainly could not win the nomination without having a superior national field organization. On that note, we agreed that we should immediately begin translating my Western states organizational proposal into action.

The date was Tuesday, April 7, 1970—two years to the day from the time we would score a stunning upset victory in the Wisconsin primary and open the gates to the eventual Democratic nomination for the Presidency.

The first opportunity for McGovern and Muskie to share a purely political platform came in Salt Lake City on April 18, 1970, at the annual Western States Democratic Conference. Muskie was scheduled to deliver the principal address at the Saturday night dinner and McGovern to speak at the delegate's luncheon that day. A West-coast network camera crew and correspondent were on hand, along with Wally Turner, *The New York Times'* San Francisco bureau chief. Carl Luebsdorf of the Associated Press Washington bureau covered the conference as the first competitive appearance by two major Democratic Presidential contenders before a live and influential party gathering. In those days it was flattering enough just to receive recognition that the Senator was a contender.

The Senator's visit included a number of private meetings with party leaders from Western states. During this trip, and for months thereafter, these discussions went according to a script preordained by political ritual and the prevailing circumstances:

McGovern: "Bill (or Harriet), I know you have been active in the Democratic Party in (name of state) for quite a while now, and although it seems like a long way off, I'd be interested in your thoughts and the thoughts of the people back in your state on this 1972 Presidential race." (Interpretation: "Who are you for?")

Party Leader: "Well, Senator, we haven't really given it much thought yet, but most of the people I've talked to would like to have Teddy back in, but if he won't run they think we ought to unite early behind the strongest candidate and get this guy Nixon out." (Interpretation: "If we could get Kennedy, we wouldn't have to go through all this, but since we probably can't, me and my boys are going to try like hell to lock up our state early for Muskie.")

McGovern: "I couldn't agree with you more on beating Nixon and I would like to help do that. I've been giving some thought to getting into this race for the nomination myself, and I would be interested in your views on how I might go about building support in your state." (Interpretation: "Wait a minute. This race isn't over yet.")

Party Leader: "Well, Senator, I think you're going to have to talk about some other issues besides the war. Now I know how strongly you feel about it—I feel the same way myself—but you have to show you are for some other basic Democratic issues and that you have support from some regular Democrats and not just the peace people." (Interpretation: "You better quit harping on the war fast and get some people like me next to you instead of those crazies from the Chicago convention.")

McGovern: "Thanks for your time, Bill (or Harriet). If I make this race, I'm going to run hard and stay in all the way, so I hope you'll keep an open mind and not assume anyone has it locked up this early." (Interpretation: "If you go for Muskie early, I'll run right over you.")

Party Leader: "Good to see you, Senator. Good luck." (Interpretation: "Hmmm. I wonder. . . ?")

By most unbiased estimates, the Muskie dinner speech was a qualified disaster. Overly long, overly serious, and overly dull, it managed to put two elderly Idaho delegates near me to sleep. It was significant only as a portent of a continuing plague on the Muskie candidacy. The candidate's innate caution and extremely reserved demeanor did more than prevent him from naturally challenging and inspiring the large numbers of followers needed for a successful campaign—it actually seemed to discourage such evidence of enthusiasm and personal commitment.

Although Muskie received the most coverage, I carried away from that conference an overwhelming conviction that he could be defeated for the nomination. On the flight from Denver to Salt Lake City I stated to Leonard "Buzz" Larsen of *The Denver Post* and Dick Tucker of *The Rocky Mountain News* my belief that McGovern could get the Democratic nomination and be the next President, and my decision to take out considerable time beginning that spring to organize the West for him. I unfolded an airline route map and described, state by state, how the territory might be organized, how many delegates we could get, and the portion of the number needed to nominate that the Western contribution represented. It would have been hard to determine which of the two was the more skeptical, but their collective decency prevented them from telling me directly how insane they considered me to be. It would be much later before they would begin to change their minds—or have a reason to.

MAY, 1970

I set about organizing three information systems for each of the 24 Western states: first, a card file of supporters and potential supporters; second, lists of Democratic Party officials and elected officials, from United

States Senators and Governors to state legislators; third, statistics relating to registration and voting patterns in recent national elections, including, where applicable, information on voting behavior in Presidential primaries.

It soon became apparent that personal contacts were needed in every state to provide names and some degree of sophisticated political analysis of people and state parties, so by early May, 1970, I planned a trip to Washington, Oregon, and California to stir up interest and support and to gather information.

In Seattle, I contacted Mike Ryherd, chairman of the King County (Seattle) Democratic Party, who had excellent contacts among both Kennedy and McCarthy supporters. Like many others to follow, Mike seemed startled to receive a call in 1970 on behalf of a McGovern Presidential bid, but he quickly agreed to brief me on the political situation in the state of Washington and to collect a group of 1968 Kennedy and McCarthy leaders to discuss a McGovern candidacy. At a meeting with that group I explained that I was eager to identify people in Washington who would be willing to begin to organize the state for McGovern. Two kinds of questions were thrown at me: About other candidates (Isn't someone like Bayh or Lindsay more charismatic? What is Kennedy going to do?) and about McGovern (Is he really serious? Is he committed to the race all the way?). Questions like these were to be asked in similar meetings thousands of times over the next two years. I tried to assure the group both that McGovern was unflinchingly committed to the race right through to the convention and that he, more than any other possible liberal candidate, stood for the kind of issues that had motivated millions to work for and support John and Robert Kennedy, Adlai Stevenson, and Eugene McCarthy. This first organizational effort brought to the surface the attitude that was to predominate throughout this political period— "We want someone who is progressive on the key domestic and foreign problems, but also *someone who can win!*"

The net effect of the session was to identify four basic types of people:

• those who were completely burned out from their 1968 experience and who had decided that politics was futile;

• those who were looking for a man on a white horse, a "charismatic" leader who could ignite and inspire broadbased public support almost overnight and sweep dramatically into the White House to cure the nation's ills;

• those who genuinely liked McGovern and admired his outspoken, rather unconventional approach to politics and political issues, but who could not convince themselves that the country was ready for an essentially honest, decent man;

• those who were enthusiastic and signed on immediately, delighted that McGovern had decided to run.

Although this last group more often than not consisted of younger people, they were quite often our most effective organizers; they did not suffer from the bitternesses and scars of their seniors who were veterans of assassinations, disappointments, double-crosses, and the shock of political battles.

From Washington, I moved on to Oregon to repeat the process. There my initial contacts were with Jerry Robinson, a Portland lawyer and a knowledgeable political activist, and Bill McCoy, Multnomah County (Portland) Democratic chairman. Both agreed that the Oregon political picture was cloudy, and that a residue of political bitterness between Kennedy and McCarthy supporters remained from the divisive 1968 Presidential primary. Robinson advised against reliance on established party figures, or others who had led previous campaigns, for leadership in a future McGovern effort in Oregon.

We eventually developed a new cadre of campaign leadership in states with established liberal traditions or liberal control of the state party apparatus, as in Oregon. Although such states should have been our natural bases of strength, too often liberals there had developed complex enmities, friendships, and cabals, and we had to maneuver through these intricate relationships. As a result, we spent far more time in states such as California, New York, Wisconsin, Oregon, and Massachusetts—where our greatest resources and natural strength should have existed, but where we had to sort out jurisdictional and leadership squabbles—than in states where the liberal elements of the Democratic Party were small and embattled.

After visiting briefly with Blaine Whipple, Democratic National Committeeman from Oregon and chairman of the state's successful 1968 McCarthy primary effort ("I'm not sure George has the kind of charisma it takes to get a campaign off the ground," Blaine told me—but he later became our Oregon state chairman), and making a number of courtesy calls suggested by Robinson, I moved on to the toughest and most important state—California.

I spent the 21st and 22nd of May in San Francisco, the 25th in San Diego, and the 26th in Los Angeles, mostly sitting in hotel rooms making phone calls that went something like this:

Hart (to secretary, maid, receptionist, or child): "Hello. Is Mr. (or Mrs.)
_____ there?"

Answerer: "May I say who's calling?"

Hart: "Mr. Hart, calling on behalf of Senator McGovern."

Long pause. Confused whispering in background. Potential supporter or political figure comes on the line.

Hart: "Mr. _____, this is Gary Hart. I'm an attorney from Denver and I am in California briefly to contact a number of people such as yourself concerning possible support for a Presidential candidacy by Senator McGovern in 1972. I wonder what your reaction to such an idea might be."

Mr. _____: Long pause, seeming confusion. "Ahhh, I'm sorry. What was your name again?" "Hart; ahh, well, Mr. Hart, you are interested in uh, who was it again? . . . ah, President? . . . in 1972. Ah, that's next time, isn't it? Well, ha, ha, it seems like we just finished with the last time, doesn't it? Well, I don't know, I really haven't had a chance to think much about it. Looks right now like Ed Muskie will probably get it, at least most of the people I've talked to think so. That fellow Bayh was out here a short time ago. He's a go-getter. Well, McGovern, huh, I don't know much about him, but come to think about it, he sure did a good job speaking to our delegation at the 1968 convention. A lot of people still talk about how impressive he was there. I guess if he decides to run we'll have to pay some attention to him."

The uniform reaction seemed to be profound shock that anyone was giving serious thought to Presidential politics so early, compounded by disbelief that someone was in the state from outside promoting McGovern (that made it serious), and a degree of condescension for someone supporting a one-issue, non-charismatic candidate ("that's all right, young fellow, you stay right in there").

My instincts told me from the outset that the nomination would be won or lost here in California. Though I later called it Armageddon, it was impossible for me then to realize the symbolic importance the battle there would assume in the historic transition of power in the Democratic Party in 1972. California was now the largest state and had the largest number of delegates to the 1972 Democratic Convention—271 as it turned out. Even though, as chairman of the Democratic Reform Commission, McGovern had opposed "winner-take-all" primaries, the full Commission had voted to permit them through 1972. California's was such a primary, with the winner taking the full slate of delegates into the convention.

California's primary came next to last in the series of more than 20, followed only by New York's. But it was simple to calculate, even in the spring of 1970, that no more than two or three candidates would survive to see California and that the winner there would carry great momentum into the final, New York contest. With all that was at stake in California, it was certain that any candidate still in the race by early June would make his final all-out effort in that Disneyland of politics.

Most of the calls in California were to potential McGovern supporters whose names had been supplied by John Anderson, a San Francisco lawyer who had been a Kennedy advance man in 1968. But a substantial number also went to those who had been 1968 delegates to the Democratic convention. Since Robert Kennedy had won the California primary that year, most of the California delegation went to Chicago still morally committed to him. During the convention, the California delegation was the only one before which Humphrey, McCarthy, and McGovern appeared together. By almost all accounts, McGovern was forceful, articulate, and triumphant. His biographer, Robert Anson, said "he carried the day." That appearance continued to have a substantial impact on those 1968 delegates and their political friends almost two years later, and helped in the creation of a small political beachhead from that initial May 1970 organizing trip.

Having completed dozens of calls to potential supporters and political figures in California, I headed back to Denver to collect and catalog names and information and to prepare a report for the McGovern campaign headquarters. It was not until two weeks later that I discovered there was no national McGovern-for-President headquarters.

JUNE, 1970

The first indication that something was amiss came with a phone call from Senator McGovern asking me to join him on a trip to Hanover, New Hampshire, where he was to receive an honorary degree from Dartmouth. He suggested that it would provide an excellent chance to explore the state politically in preparation for a decision on entering that primary. The basic proposition was sound, but what puzzled me greatly was the reason for my being asked to help scout an Eastern state. During the more than two months in which I had been helping to set up the basic campaign structure and organization, I had presumed that there existed in Washington some kind of national political staff operation. If it did, why was I being asked to make a New Hampshire scouting trip? If it didn't, what was I doing free-lancing around in the West as if I were part of a large, national scheme?

A day before the Senator and I were scheduled to leave for New Hampshire, I returned to Washington to arrange some fall campaign trips for him on behalf of candidates for higher office in the West. Since I had assumed that *someone* was responsible for creating such a political travel schedule, I was mildly dumbfounded when Pat Donovan, the Senator's secretary, opened the red day book containing the Senator's future commitments and found nothing but blank pages for September and October of 1970. After talking to Pat and others on the Senate staff, it became clear that no long-range, coherent planning for a Presidential campaign was taking place on a national basis. Immediately, the efforts I had been making in the West seemed isolated, detached, and unrelated to any grander plan. It didn't make such sense to run a campaign for the Presidency in an area limited to half the geography of the country and a third of the total delegate votes needed to nominate.

Apparently, McGovern had been having similar thoughts. We left at noon Friday, June 12th, for New Hampshire. After take-off, I said: "Senator, everywhere I have traveled in the Western states I was urged to have you come out there this fall and campaign for other Democratic candidates. But I can't seem to find the national political staff which handles such arrangements. I don't even know who I am supposed to be reporting to."

"I know," he said. "That's why I wanted you to come with me on this trip, so we could discuss those problems." He repeated the offer made when we first met in Denver several weeks earlier—come back to Washington and help set up a national campaign operation. We discussed the idea at some length on the flight and I agreed to give an answer by the end of the New Hampshire weekend.

We were met at the West Lebanon, New Hampshire, airport by a lone student and driven the several miles into Hanover in an ancient, semi-enclosed jeep with the next Presidential nominee of the Democratic Party in the front seat and his future campaign manager rattling around on top of the luggage. Somehow this did not conform to my preconceptions of a Presidential campaign; where were the jubilant crowds, the banners and balloons, the eager supporters pressing to get closer to the great man? And most of all where were the limousines?

That evening we met with a number of Democratic leaders at the home of Charles Officer, former Congressional candidate. The group included Joe Grandmaison, former state president of the Young Democrats and, at 27, the most astute young politician in New Hampshire. Two highly significant facts emerged from that two-hour session: first, Muskie did *not* have this symbolic, neighboring primary state automatically locked-up; second, a potential political base did exist for another candidate willing to work hard in the state.

The consensus of the group was that Muskie possessed a strong natural advantage in being a New Englander, that as the senior elected Democrat from the northern New England area he had often appeared before and supported the New Hampshire Democratic Party, and that he had developed a reservoir of goodwill, respect, and friendship over the years, largely as a result of these efforts and his 1968 Vice-Presidential race. Nevertheless, there was a noticeable lack of enthusiasm even in this room full of prominent state Democrats for the man from Maine, and most of them suggested the same circumstances prevailed statewide among Democrats.

There were many references to the 1968 McCarthy effort in the state as illustrative of what a well-organized, citizen-based campaign could do for a candidate who would make an exhaustive effort to meet as many voters as possible. Grandmaison emphasized the importance of making as many personal contacts in as many small local meetings as possible.

Politically, the state was analyzed for us as follows:

• the very conservative towns constituting a third of the state north of Concord (even McCarthy, however, had done well in some of these towns as a result of such simple devices as playing hockey in Berlin);

• the very conservative mill town and "Queen City," Manchester, where approximately 35 percent of the state's Democrats lived and voted and where the influence of the fiercely demagogic, right-wing *Manchester Union Leader* was believed to be great. Its editor, William Loeb, was unalterably opposed to men like McGovern, and even loved to refer to the Maine Senator as "Moscow Muskie";

• the emerging Democratic communities of Portsmouth, Somersworth, and Dover, most susceptible to Muskie influence because of their proximity to Maine along the eastern border;

• the most natural enclaves of McGovern strength—the campus communities of Hanover, home of Dartmouth, and Durham, site of the University of New Hampshire (the prospect of basing a campaign on volunteers from these areas drew a contemptuous snort from Grandmaison, who suggested that if we intended to rely heavily for workers on the Hanover liberals and Dartmouth students the Senator might as well stay in South Dakota and save the trouble);

• and, most interesting, the southeast crescent, running from the coastal communities near Rye on the east over past Nashua on the west, an area that was dominated by Boston media and that included new, younger middle-income families, many of whom worked in the greater Boston area.

This kind of sophisticated analysis made New Hampshire a much more complex, intricate and challenging arena than my simplistic notions about taciturn, craggy Yankees sitting in rocking chairs muttering "ayup" would have had it. No commitments were sought and none were offered at the meeting at Officer's house, but it was an important beginning.

McGovern was clearly intrigued with the possibility of running in the New Hampshire primary in early 1972. He privately stated a thesis to me that was to dominate his thinking for the next 20 months: "You know, this state reminds me a lot of South Dakota. A lot of small towns, and the people are pretty conservative, but they will vote for a man who says what he believes and who personally goes out and asks for their vote. I bet I could slip up here on weekends and walk up and down the main streets shaking hands and get a lot of support by 1972." I suggested that the strong New Hampshire pride in courtesy to strangers might work in

his favor, causing large numbers of voters to give him special consideration to demonstrate they were not prejudiced toward Muskie because of
his New England background. The more we discussed the possibilities,
the more intriguing they became.

On Saturday, June 13th, the Senator addressed over 2,000 Dartmouth
students and parents, blistering the Nixon administration's failure to terminate United States military involvement in Southeast Asia. It was obvious that he had no intention of sacrificing this, his favorite theme for the
Presidential effort, even in this key primary, but conservative, state.

On the charter flight back to New York the next afternoon, I suggested
to the Senator a solution to the organizational stalemate. I would maintain my law office in Denver, tending to clients and commitments on the
weekends, and would commute to Washington each week through the
summer to accomplish three tasks: create the nucleus of a national political staff, develop a fall travel schedule on behalf of Democratic candidates, and systematize the growing lists and card files of actual and
potential supporters. By mid or late August we would reach a mutual
decision as to whether I should assume full-time command of the campaign. This interim arrangement was meant to give the Senator a chance
to form a first-hand judgment of my capabilities and to permit me to
close down my law practice gradually if I decided to move to Washington
full-time. The Senator readily agreed to this proposal and within a few
days the twelve exhausting weeks of long-distance commuting began.

Initially, the prospects for organizing a Presidential campaign from
scratch seemed overwhelming. There was no guide-book or set of rules.
There were few advisors around to suggest the way. There was despair
at ever having the resources and staff to mount a serious national effort.
Nevertheless, each problem was confronted as it arose and the elementary
steps were taken. Considerable time was required at first just to sort
through and respond to a substantial number of speaking invitations for
the summer and fall which had begun to flow in as a result of the Senator's continued leadership in opposition to the war and increased recognition as a potential candidate.

Help soon arrived. During June, McGovern made two staff additions,
Yancey Martin, former military officer and deputy director of the Minorities Division of the Democratic National Committee, and Richard G.
"Rick" Stearns, former staff member of the Commission on Party Reform
and Rhodes scholar. Yancey—big, handsome, fierce-looking but affable—
was, throughout the nomination race, our principal staff contact with the
leadership of the black community. His lack of tolerance for the day-to-
day details of organization was more than made up for by his wit, charm,
and ability to convert unconcerned or uncommitted local black leaders

around the country. Rick was a student of the delegate-selection process and procedures used by all 50 state Democratic parties and he had a profound understanding of the party reform guidelines promulgated by the Reform Commission. In addition, he possessed a technical proficiency in grassroots political organization, particularly in non-primary or caucus states. Rick immediately began compiling political data, statistics, dates, names, and other pertinent information into state books, beginning with the states the Senator would be visiting that fall.

J U L Y , 1 9 7 0

To crystalize some early McGovern support in New Mexico, and to get a campaign organization started, I went to Albuquerque, meeting on July 12th with about 20 Chicano or Spanish-American community action leaders. Rather unsuccessfully, I tried to explain why, in the summer of 1970, a Presidential candidate cared about their support. Like countless numbers of local minority leaders around the country, they had all heard endless promises of assistance and understanding from Anglo candidates from President down to sheriff and were understandably suspicious, particularly of a candidate such as McGovern about whom they knew so little. It was monumentally frustrating to try to enlist the support of people struggling on the fringe of society for a political system which had so often and so hypocritically betrayed them.

The following day, I lunched at the Sandia Corporation, outside Albuquerque, with a small group of engineers who had successfully labored for McCarthy in 1968. Most of this group later joined us. In the afternoon I went north to Santa Fe where I tried again, this time for two dozen local political activists, to describe the scenario leading to a McGovern victory. Late that night, with the initial New Mexico work wrapped up, and battling what was becoming a constant companion—fatigue—I drove back to Albuquerque to catch an early-morning plane to Washington.

Wednesday, July 15th, marked the first important milestone of the McGovern Presidential campaign—the opening of our first office, our national headquarters at 201 Maryland Avenue, N.E., in Washington. The Senator had located the space during one of his luncheon strolls around Capitol Hill. It was ideal for a beginning, the first floor of a corner townhouse, within sight of the Capitol, and one block from the Senator's Office in the Old Senate Office Building. At 6 o'clock that evening Rick Stearns and I, accompanied by Kate Douglas, the first McGovern volunteer, carried three cardboard boxes of files down the street to the new office to inaugurate, with monumental inauspicion, the McGovern campaign for the Presidency of the United States. Halfway down the block, through the heat and perspiration, I indicated my disappointment at the lack of fanfare for such a momentous occasion: "I always thought Theodore White covered events like this." Two years from that night, July 15, 1970, George McGovern would be the Presidential nominee of the Democratic Party.

In midmorning on the 25th of July a small group gathered at "Cedar Point," the McGovern farm near St. Michaels, on Maryland's eastern shore, for what turned out to be a highly significant strategy meeting. The group consisted of the Senator, Eleanor McGovern, Professor Richard Wade, Rick Stearns, George Cunningham, Pat Donovan, and myself. Wade had organized in New York for John Kennedy in 1960 and, while teaching at the University of Chicago, helped lead Robert Kennedy's 1968 effort in Illinois. Together with Pierre Salinger and a few others from the Kennedy campaign, he provided leadership for the 18-day McGovern race going into the 1968 Chicago Convention. He maintained his contacts with McGovern as a consultant to the Reform Commission. Wade, was above all a pragmatic politician, and he managed, in advising the Senator, to bridge the traditional gap between academe and the world of practical politics.

Seated in the comfortable, informal living room of the farmhouse, we began, following an agenda I had prepared, with a discussion of general campaign strategy, focusing on the timing of the candidacy announcement, a question which had plagued the Senator for months. The alternatives were: first, to announce shortly after the debate on the McGovern-Hatfield amendment to end the war in late August or early September; second, to announce sometime later in the fall, but prior to the November elections; third, to announce shortly after the elections.

Responding to a question from Wade concerning the importance of an early announcement, the Senator said that for a year and a half he had sensed, more than any time since he had been in public life, a widespread need for leadership, particularly among activists in the Democratic Party. There was no Adlai Stevenson as titular head of the party-in-opposition. Obviously, the forum of the White House did not exist for the Democrats, and Congressional leadership had never been sufficient to provide the kind of dynamic, moral leadership that was badly needed in times of prevalent public apathy and disenchantment. Finally, the national party organization was floundering in debt and traditionally had been unable to challenge and lift rank-and-file Democrats. Therefore, concluded the Senator, the first Democratic leader to announce "loudly and clearly" his intention to seek the nomination would receive broad-based support from those who were desperate to have a spokesman against the Nixon administration.

At that time, McGovern was convinced that anyone who waited beyond November 15th to announce would be the second man in the race. He was disturbed that Muskie had received considerable press notice for opening a national office—even though he had a 1970 re-election race—while our headquarters had opened to conspicuous inattention like an unknown, unheralded off-Broadway play. He was further convinced that other contenders from the liberal wing of the Democratic Party would begin to emerge shortly and that Lindsay, then a Republican, would switch parties and move quickly to consolidate support as a new, "charismatic" candidate, perhaps by campaigning for Jesse Unruh for Governor in California, Adlai Stevenson for Senator in Illinois, and Arthur Goldberg for Governor in New York.

Several problems were raised concerning an early announcement. Wade argued that the Senator would have to complete as much of the work of the Reform Commission as possible and resign as its chairman prior to this announcement; to stay on as an announced candidate would make the reform effort seem too self-serving and would jeopardize its chances for success. That would take some time. I also outlined the many problems a pre-election announcement would cause for the crucial fall campaign schedule. Candidates for whom he was to stump in 1970 would conclude that he was primarily piggy-backing on their campaigns in an effort to further his own candidacy. Those candidates would be put on the spot by the local press as to whether they supported McGovern for President. Finally, in an effort to put the announcement off until after November, I speculated that the considerable press coverage of an announcement, to test the seriousness of a McGovern candidacy, would concentrate on organizational strength, the experience, caliber, and depth of the staff, and the kind of citizens and politicians who might announce support for a McGovern candidacy. Our three-man political staff was certainly unprepared to handle the incredible burden of a full-fledged Presidential campaign and it would take weeks, if not months, to prepare for the close public scrutiny that an announced candidate could expect.

We decided to build up our national network of supporters, get additional exposure speaking in the fall for other candidates, and postpone the announcement of candidacy until after the elections, perhaps making it as early as November 10th.

The Senator was always concerned about the element of boredom in such a long campaign and asked all of us to be alert to imaginative events he might schedule to prevent people from being turned off to his constant public exposure. As it turned out, the Senator's boredom threshold proved to be lower than the public's and he tired much more often of the set public rallies, speeches, and receptions than did the people who turned out to meet him. "Can't we do something besides all these speeches and receptions?" he used to plead. "I think people get tired of those same old things." What he meant was, he was tired of the same old thing. Most of the people who turned out to see McGovern in 1970, '71, and early '72 were getting their initial impression of him and the appearances were therefore both interesting to them and important to the campaign.

Nevertheless, McGovern's basic instincts proved sound—the American voters were looking for courage, boldness, and imagination in their leaders, and were bored with politics-as-usual. We discussed, in the international arena, the possibility of a lengthy meeting with Willy Brandt to discuss a more meaningful role for NATO, or being the first American political leader inside the People's Republic of China. Domestically, we considered meetings with police officials on police reform and visits to veterans hospitals, nursing homes, prisons, and mental institutions to lay the foundation for creative solutions to the social problems existing within these institutions.

We then discussed other possible candidates, the Senator feeling that Humphrey, Muskie, and Bayh all shared essentially the same views on the important issues, but that eventually Humphrey would try to out-maneuver Muskie by making him appear too conservative. We further discussed the possibility of a fourth-party effort, led perhaps by Lindsay, Ramsey Clark, or John Gardner. One of McGovern's clear strengths, it was concluded, was his ability to pre-empt such an effort by present-ing the necessity for change in the political system at least as well as any of these others, combined with his commitment to the Democratic Party. He would provide a legitimate candidacy for the disenchanted but was clearly committed to the Democratic Party and would never lead a splinter, fourth-party movement. This would be a strong argu-ment in his favor with the party polls—his ability to reconcile dissident and regular elements in the party. From this, all present concurred in the so-called left-centrist strategy: co-opt the left, precluding the possibility of other liberal candidates, and, at the same time, make the campaign open and acceptable to party regulars. The issues, together with early organizational activity, would help nail down the left, but the most convincing argument for the party regulars, the center, would be or-ganizational strength—victories in the middle and later primaries and superior numbers of people in the caucuses in the non-primary states.

We agreed that we would enter primaries in New Hampshire, West Virginia, Wisconsin, Nebraska, Oregon, California, South Dakota, and New Mexico. Four of these—Wisconsin, Nebraska, Oregon, and New Mexico—were "ballot designation states," in which all the candidates' names were placed on the ballot automatically. In addition, New York,

Maryland, Pennsylvania, and Massachusetts were considered as states to enter. We agreed to give later consideration to Ohio and Illinois—the latter being a constant favorite of McGovern's—and to abandon Rhode Island, where we felt that insurgency stood little chance of success against entrenched old-line leadership.

With the analyses of these states began a mild, but constant, difference of opinion between the Senator and myself, as much instinctive as reasoned. McGovern was inclined to run in almost every primary that came up—later there would be Florida and North Carolina, Tennessee and Michigan; I leaned toward a strategy throughout the early and middle primaries of picking and choosing, entering only for a particular purpose, to eliminate a particular contender—strike and retreat, guerrilla warfare. We would have only limited resources throughout the nomination race and could be out-gunned by better-financed candidates running in primary after primary. I didn't think infantry had much chance against tanks and heavy guns.

We concluded the two days of planning with a much-too-limited discussion of campaign financing in which we agreed that the Senator should leave money-raising entirely to a committee. This proved to be an illusion and a farce; money would continue to be a constant source of conflict and irritation, for the Senator and for everyone else in the campaign.

In the weeks following the Cedar Point meeting we turned our attention to organization. From the outset, I believed strongly in a decentralized campaign structure. My limited experience in national campaigns had led me to distrust and dislike the traditional organizational approach of headquartering key staff members in Washington and sending them out into the states to instruct and command the less politically sophisticated local supporters. Conflict between national staff and local supporters in Presidential campaigns is legendary. We also assumed that our campaign would not be adequately financed until we demonstrated substantial political strength, which wouldn't be until well into the primary races in 1972. Therefore, we would rely heavily on citizen volunteers and would need their good favor to accomplish all the tasks that needed to be done to prepare for the primaries and caucuses.

The principle upon which we relied—the principle of a decentralized campaign organization—is one innovation that will have a profound and lasting influence on American politics. Our earliest staff selections were field organizers who lived and worked in the key states, rather than traveling to and from Washington. Because these field organizers were members of the national staff and drew their salaries from Washington, they would participate in policy decisions affecting the campaign in the states for which they were responsible. But because they worked and lived in those states, they would be part of the local effort and would not be "outsiders" whose direction of the state campaigns would automatically alienate the local workers.

Our original plan was to create five geographical regions containing roughly ten states each. Each region would have as its nucleus one or more key primary states and would be under the organizational direction of a regional coordinator. For these positions we looked for people who were identified in some way with the region, young but experienced in field organization, mobile (therefore probably single), capable of motivating volunteer workers, determined, tireless, and accustomed to, or able to grow accustomed to, a spartan life. Above all, we wanted people who believed that McGovern could and should get the Democratic nomination and be President. Political reality also played a part—older, experienced regulars were not clambering to get aboard the McGovern bandwagon. All these factors and qualifications narrowed down the field considerably, especially in the late summer of 1970.

Nevertheless, our first effort to find a regional coordinator, for the Midwest, proved to be stunningly successful. Gene Pokorny had been an itinerant field organizer for McCarthy in that area and had met Rick Stearns in 1968. Rick recommended Gene, if he were available, as "the best in the business." In early August, 1970, a telephone search located Gene in Utica, New York, on his way home to Howells, Nebraska, after a disenchanting year of graduate work at Harvard and several frustrating weeks working on an ill-conceived Senate campaign in Rhode Island. After a few skeptical questions, Gene agreed to interrupt his Westward migration for a quick trip to Washington to discuss the McGovern candidacy.

Appearing five years younger than his 24 years, Gene wore horn-rimmed glasses, short hair, and conventional ivy-league clothes and had a Midwestern twang heavier than the candidate's. After about fifteen minutes of his intensive questions about our plans for capturing the nomination, it became apparent that despite his boyish appearance he was a hard-bitten and practical veteran of political wars. Many months later, Chris Lydon of *The New York Times* quoted me as saying that Gene had "a revolutionary's mind in Henry Aldrich's body." (Gene, successfully avenging himself while underscoring the brevity of a generation gap, queried a day later on the phone: "Who the hell is Henry Aldrich?")

Gene had been badly burned in the McCarthy campaign, along with countless others, by what appeared to be a failure of resolve on the candidate's part in the closing, crucial days of that 1968 nomination effort. It soured him on liberal candidates and liberal campaigns peopled by high-minded, well-motivated types who preferred principle to victory and who became catatonic at the prospect of governing. He was primarily concerned with these two questions: Did McGovern intend to stay in the race and fight to the finish? Was his campaign going to be run by tough, pragmatic politicians who were smart enough to figure out the price of victory and determined enough to pay it? I assured him the answer to both questions was strongly affirmative. After a brief session with the Senator, Gene headed on to Nebraska to think it over. Within a few days he signed on and, as the fourth member of the political staff, helped advance the strenuous and chaotic fall schedule. Thereafter he began to ride circuit in the Midwest: Minnesota, Wisconsin, Iowa, Nebraska, Missouri, Kansas, Oklahoma, and Texas. He was based in Wisconsin, and, after getting campaign organizations established in the other states, concentrated most of his efforts on that state and Nebraska in preparation for those two crucial primaries in 1972.

AUGUST, 1970

I made the first of several early exploratory trips into New Hampshire, principally to observe the fall campaigns, get better acquainted with the state's key political leaders, and begin the long, slow process of developing the nucleus of a campaign organization. I talked at length with Harry Makris, the state Democratic chairman, who made valuable suggestions of more liberally inclined Democrats who should be contacted on McGovern's behalf, making plain the truth of the political axiom that people want to be asked for their support and will not always volunteer automatically simply because they like the candidate or agree with his positions. Among other names suggested was that of Bill Dunfey, one of five brothers well-known in New England for having built a family-operated seafood stand into a hotel and restaurant empire. Bill, the most politically active of the brothers, had been an early and loyal supporter of the Kennedy brothers and was widely considered to be "the" Kennedy contact in northern New England. He was hospitable but non-committal, reserving his options (along with many others) for an eventual Kennedy entrance into the 1972 race.

David Hoeh, an early 1968 McCarthy supporter, had strongly urged that we make every effort to pick up check lists of registered Democrats for our later canvassing, mailing, and phoning work. (This was one of the most difficult tasks the McCarthyites had faced, since the check lists are kept only by the town clerks, often disorganized or un-cooperative, in the many small towns throughout the state.) Leaving Bill Dunfey, I started on a mad dash in search of the precious check lists in Hampton, Dover, Somersworth, Manchester, Nashua, Concord, then back to Manchester. I got what I was after. Early the next morning I ran out of gas during a frantic drive to Boston but, juggling suitcases, briefcases, newspapers, and roll after roll of the precious check lists, I managed to scramble aboard a Washington-bound plane just before it started to roll. I still don't know whether I checked in the rented car.

Back in Washington that afternoon, Thursday, August 13th, I summarized our progress for the Senator: in seven weeks we had almost completed plans for a post-Labor Day, twenty-state travel schedule for Democratic candidates, opened a national headquarters, assembled a six-person political staff, laid long-range strategic plans to be followed throughout the nomination race, and begun the tedious process of computerizing the tens of thousands of names of potential supporters. The last task was under the direction of Jeff Smith, a droll and highly competent 24-year-old member of the Senate staff who had joined McGovern in 1968 after organizing South Dakota Indian reservations for Robert Kennedy and whose near-photographic memory retained much of the detail of those thousands of index cards.

I indicated that I was prepared to move to Washington and assume full-time control over and responsibility for the campaign if the Senator still wanted me to. He was complimentary toward our initial accomplishments and reaffirmed the original offer he made in the spring: I would be in command of the campaign and, although we hoped that highly qualified people would come along as we picked up steam and showed promise, he saw no reason why I would later have to take a secondary leadership role. He wanted a younger man, new to the political scene, who could work with the young people of the country, but who also understood party regulars and who could deal reasonably with them without alienating them. We were agreed. On August 31st, having moved to Washington, I assumed official full-time control of the McGovern campaign as its director.

It was not an easy decision. On the one hand, it meant abandoning a law practice in which I had made a substantial financial investment, which had taken a year to develop and which was just beginning to be profitable. On the other hand, playing a key role in a Presidential campaign was obviously the kind of experience that rarely repeats itself in a lifetime. It would be an experience for which most people active in politics would sacrifice a great deal. My political instincts told me that Muskie did not have the race locked up. I felt especially strongly about this after my initial trips to California and New Hampshire. The base for a McGovern campaign definitely existed and, if we did our work properly, there was no doubt in my mind that we could win. Finally, there was McGovern himself. He had the indefinable and politically irreplaceable ability to command commitment, even devotion, among a great variety of people; he unquestionably deserved the reputation for political courage that his outspoken leadership against the Vietnam war and against hunger in America and for reform of the Democratic Party's rules and procedures had won; and he was undoubtedly one of the most human leaders on the national political scene. In short, it was impossible not to like him and difficult not to want to help him. Obviously these considerations had to outweigh personal difficulties. There are times when a man is bound to follow through on his convictions about the importance of the democratic process and the kind of country he wants his children to grow up in. That is what the McGovern campaign became for me; I couldn't walk away from it.

SEPTEMBER, 1970

After two months of scheduling and planning, we went on the road on Labor Day, September 7th, for 60 days of travel, starting in Phoenix. At the invitation of the Arizona Democratic Chairman, Herb Ely, the Senator was to inaugurate a series of "unity dinners" featuring national party leaders. Upon his arrival, local reporters asked the Senator the inevitable questions about his own candidacy, questions that were to be repeated throughout the fall: Was he going to run? (He was certainly giving it some thought.) Did he want to make an announcement statement? (No, he was out on behalf of the Democratic Party and its candidates and was primarily concerned with getting them elected in 1970.) Did he intend to announce fairly early? (Well, let's wait until after the 1970 elections to see about that.)

During a pre-dinner reception I made my way through the Arizona Democratic leadership in search of future campaign support, concentrating primarily upon those who had led the Kennedy and McCarthy efforts in the state.

Later that night I took a call to the Senator's suite from an obviously deranged, fanatic who made some rambling threats. It triggered what was to be a continuing concern about the possibility of an attempt on the Senator's life. McGovern routinely received more than his share of written threats, which were referred to the FBI or Secret Service. He was outspoken and controversial. He had a fairly strong identification with the Kennedy family and could be considered a target for whatever warped minds still conspired against that troubled clan. More and more, he was receiving attention as a potential Presidential candidate, thus increasing his visibility. And, most importantly, we were now embarked on an intensive, 60-day travel schedule which would involve considerable crowd exposure.

Yancey, Rick, Gene, and I simultaneously and without discussion soon found ourselves staying very close to the Senator in public gatherings, ostensibly taking names of potential supporters, but increasingly watching with an extremely critical eye those who approached him. It was a subtle but inescapable paranoia. After a day of speeches and public appearances, we would return to our hotel exhausted, not really realizing the tension involved in the subconscious instinct to examine every approaching eye for some unidentifiable gleam or stare or sign, watching every hand being drawn from every pocket, tensing the leg to leap or the arm to strike. (I later came to have great respect for the physical endurance as well as the overall professionalism of the Secret Service agents assigned to the Senator.) There are countless people now abroad in the land who met McGovern in the fall of 1970 or throughout 1971 who are unaware how close they came to being leaped upon by a zealous McGovern staff member who thought he had detected some quirk, some blink, some pocket bulge, some strange mannerism.

During the next few weeks the Senator completed a swing through New England, appearing for former Governor Phil Hoff in his campaign for the Senate in Vermont, for Reverend Joe Duffy, a Unitarian minister who was the Democratic nominee for the Senate in Connecticut, and then on to New York City for appearances for Dick Ottinger running for the Senate. Ottinger earned the respect of many original McGovern supporters when, in 1971, he became one of the first political figures in the country to demonstrate courage and loyalty by his endorsement of the fledgling McGovern candidacy; most of the candidates for whom the Senator campaigned in 1970 later endorsed and supported some other Presidential contender.

Besides public appearances with and on behalf of candidates for higher office, McGovern headed a direct-mail fund-raising appeal called "Campaign 70." Several mailings went out over his signature to liberal contributor lists seeking funds for Democratic candidates to the United States Senate, both incumbents and challengers, who would be favorably inclined toward progressive legislation. The appeal raised over a million dollars, which was allocated by a small committee including former Senator Paul Douglas and others. Had so-called political observers and commentators been looking for early clues to an eventual McGovern upset nomination victory, they might well have taken serious note of the profound strength of the McGovern name to raise substantial sums through the mails. "Campaign 70" (and thus the Senator) proved to be a substantial contributor to the 1970 Senate campaign efforts in Connecticut, Vermont, Indiana, Michigan, Nebraska, New Jersey, Ohio, Oregon, Tennessee, California, Illinois, Utah, Minnesota, and North Dakota.

Later in September the Senator made a swing through central New Jersey for incumbent Senator Harrison Williams, Jr., and several congressional candidates. During these fall weeks, in almost every appearance, whether reception, dinner, auditorium speech, or outdoor rally, the crowds were sizable, warm, and enthusiastic. On the 26th of September we went to Philadelphia for an intensive day of campaigning that started with the usual airport press conference, went across town to a television interview, then to lunch in a hotel room where the Senator was surrounded by local candidates, political reporters squeezing in personal interviews, still cameramen, old friends, and early—excessively eager and not always sensible—supporters.

These meals, lunches or dinners, were shown as hour stops on the formal schedule, to be eaten in private and combined with rest, but they invariably were reduced to cold, half-eaten, spectator-ridden twenty-minute invitations to indigestion. It is incredible how many people seem to enjoy watching a candidate, like a caged bear or lion, eat a meal, or who end up eating half the meal themselves as a result of the candidate's generosity or frustration at being watched.

Staff members close to Presidential candidates get bad reputations because they are the ones who must ultimately turn people away from access to the candidate. In every city there are: old friends of the Senator or his family, former school teachers (George McGovern must have had thousands of former school teachers), former constituents from South Dakota, people who met him somewhere before, well-wishers and supporters, applicants for campaign jobs, people with ideas for a speech or an important campaign strategy, candidates for local office, former office-holders, haters and crazies. But they can't all get in one small hotel room or car, and someone has to shut the door. This problem was compounded by McGovern himself, a warm and friendly human being who finds it difficult to anger well-meaning people and who often invited a number of those he met during the day to join him later in his hotel room. Occasionally, we would return from an exhausting day of campaigning, an hour and a half behind schedule, to find a dozen or more people in or around his suite dutifully waiting his return and the promised nightcap.

During the day of campaigning in Philadelphia, Police Chief Frank Rizzo—who later successfully ran for Mayor—provided full security from the time we landed until we departed from the Philadelphia airport. His men were professional and efficient: Rizzo was reported to have said that he wasn't going to have any politicians shot in his city, no matter who they were.

On the way to a dinner in suburban Bucks County, we stopped in the community of Feasterville, Pennsylvania, on behalf of Dr. Arthur Hennessey, university professor, Congressional candidate for that district (almost hopeless for a Democratic candidate), and local McGovern enthusiast. Dr. Hennessey had been instrumental in arranging the McGovern schedule of appearances in and around Philadelphia that day. The stop at his headquarters in the small Feasterville shopping center was pure political Americana. Seventy-five to a hundred souls—Hennessey workers, McGovern faithfuls, local politicians, and curious onlookers—had been waiting patiently during much of the blazing hot afternoon, entertained by Jimmy Ream and the "Joy Boys," who served in the Feasterville area as a loose cross between Lawrence Welk and the Beatles, with just a slice of the Grateful Dead thrown in. Upon our arrival, the "Joy Boys" serenaded us at some length while the patient Senator, probably having undergone similar experiences a thousand times in South Dakota, sipped the watery punch and tapped his foot. I suggested to Hennessey several times that we put the Senator on for a few words and then escape to the dinner for which we were already late. But every time Hennessey moved forward to capture the mike, a lank-haired youth announced yet another hit tune. Finally Hennessey prevailed and, gaining control of the sound system, delivered himself of a combined stump speech for his own election and effusive introduction of George McGovern. Ultimately, the Senator was permitted to make his brief remarks, and, after shaking hands all around, got into the car to head for the dinner in Bucks County.

The dinner, attended by a record 1000 loyal Democrats, was a great success; the Senator gave an exceptionally good, highly partisan speech, mixing standard end-the-war admonitions with criticisms of Nixon economic polices and domestic failures and ending with the "Come Home America" theme. The occasion was also a political coup for us. Our pre-trip intelligence on the state revealed a continuing rift between gubernatorial candidate Milton Shapp and State Auditor Bob Casey, who had opposed Shapp in Democratic primaries both times he had run for Governor. In a number of areas the Pennsylvania Democratic Party was split into Shapp and Casey supporters. Shapp badly needed the cooperation of the Casey followers to win the governorship. The Casey people, feeling strongly that 1970 should have been Casey's turn to run, were not satisfied that Shapp had been as conciliatory toward Casey as the situation demanded. Sizing all this up, we saw an opportunity to demonstrate the theme, discussed in July at Cedar Point, of party unity and McGovern as conciliator.

After many phone calls between our Washington headquarters, Shapp headquarters in Philadelphia, and the Casey office in Harrisburg, Casey agreed as a personal favor to McGovern, to attend the Bucks County dinner and introduce the Senator, whom he admired, even though it meant sharing the platform for the first time since the bitter primary with his old opponent Milton Shapp. The reconciliation went off smoothly, with the state press corps taking hundreds of pictures of Shapp, Mc-Govern, and Casey, engaged in the symbolic handshakes before the dinner. Shapp was pleased to have Casey's public support, Casey eased back into the role of loyal Democrat, and McGovern got the credit, at least in the minds of some observers, as the healer, reconciler, and party unifier.

O C T O B E R ,   1 9 7 0

The pace quickened even more; the Senator campaigned in almost a dozen states.

On the 10th, we went to South Bend, Indiana, for a Notre Dame speech. Then, late in the afternoon, we flew from South Bend to Gary, where the Senator was the featured speaker at a huge, 3,000-person dinner kicking off the re-election campaign of Mayor Richard Hatcher. The Mayor had laid on an incredible security force for the six or seven hours the Senator was in town; we were met at the Gary airport by Mayor Hatcher and his aides, motorcycle patrolmen in front and behind, car-loads of uniformed police officials and plainclothes city detectives, and a special force of private guards hired for the occasion. We moved around Gary that night at speeds up to 70 miles per hour with what seemed like every siren in the city turned on. Mayor Hatcher was a highly mobile and most gracious host.

Yancey Martin had advanced the trip for us and, while the Senator was receiving a long line of well-wishers before dinner, noticed a young black man approaching in a line that contained mostly middle-aged civil servants. "Give him the shake," Yancey whispered quickly to Mc-Govern. When the young man extended his hand, the Senator gave him a firm black-power grip, leaving the man wide-eyed, open-mouthed, and muttering as he walked away, "Hey, man, far out!"

Dick Wade, until his move to New York, our principal contact in Illinois, had arranged for the Senator to present on the next day, October 11th, the annual Robert F. Kennedy scholarships to deserving students from the Chicago area.

After a brief rest in the afternoon, we attended a reception at the elegant North Shore home of prominent Democrat Kenneth Montgomery to raise funds for the Senate campaign of Adlai Stevenson III. The Senator recalled for the guests the role Stevenson's father had played in his own political life and suggested the younger Stevenson had every chance of equaling his father's contribution, particularly if those present would empty their pockets to get him elected.

My conversations at that event and the questions asked were repeated endlessly throughout the fall: Yes, the Senator would probably make the Presidential race. No, I didn't think Muskie had it locked up. I had talked to people for months all across the country and they weren't sold. No, Teddy won't run. Yes, Bayh isn't ready. Yes, Lindsay would probably switch but it really didn't matter. No, believe it or not, I wouldn't be surprised if Humphrey jumped back in again—you know, the old fire-horse syndrome, the bell rings and off you go. But most of all, watch McGovern! He is the best man and we are going to win! Sowing seeds of doubt, here and there.

That night McGovern was the keynote speaker at the annual spaghetti dinner for State Senator Tony Scariano, a very popular state legislator from Chicago's South side. Jammed into the second floor of a hall designed to hold 300 were about 750 people with another one or two hundred watching on closed-circuit television downstairs. It proved to be one of the better political events we attended all fall with the garrulous, back-thumping host, Scariano, leading the way up and down the narrow space between the long tables, calling everyone by his first name, kissing the ladies, patting the children, uncorking chianti, laughing, joking, keeping the already lively crowd on its toes. Master of ceremonies was Mike Royko, Chicago's premier political columnist and later author of "Boss," the bestseller about Mayor Daley. Royko kept the place broken up with his comments on and introductions of politicians. Introducing Stevenson, he began: "Next we have Adlai. You all know Adlai. You can't miss him the way he dresses." (Stevenson was beginning to develop a reputation as a more than casual dresser. Sitting at the tiny, crowded head table, even more rumpled than usual, and sensing what was coming, he buried his head in his hands and his face sank lower toward his spaghetti as Royko bore in.) "Yes, good old Adlai. He's taking those comparisons to his father too seriously. His Dad campaigned with holes in his shoes, and last week Adlai addressed a women's group with a hole in his pants." (It was true.) "But I'm glad to report that Adlai is reforming. He went out this week and bought another suit. That gives him one to work in and one to sleep in."

The Senator's speeches during the many appearances in the fall of 1970 concentrated primarily on ending the war in Southeast Asia, the wastefulness and uselessness of that effort and its costs to our society here at home, the extravagant defense budget loaded with unnecessary and often outmoded weapons systems, the continuing need for social justice for traditionally oppressed minority groups, the need to begin the complicated conversion from a wartime to a peacetime economy, and the problems of reforming all of our social institutions, not just the political parties, to make them more responsive to human needs. The demand for broad-based tax reform, the controversial welfare reform proposal, and the alternative defense budget were not introduced into the campaign and into the Senator's speeches until 1971 and 1972.

McGovern ended almost every formal speech during this early period with an exhortation to the country to return to the traditional values which made it great, the respect for personal liberty, the right not to be harassed by one's government, the appreciation for the worth and rights of the individual, the guarantees of freedom of speech and the press, and the need to re-establish in some meaningful way the checks-and-balances system established by the Constitution. He was constantly frustrated by Congress', and particularly the Senate's, impotence to affect or effect foreign policy, especially as related to military commitments in places like Laos and Cambodia which served merely to sink us more deeply into the Southeast Asian quagmire. He often said publicly and privately that a major factor in his decision to seek the Presidency was his bitter conclusion that there was little he could do as an individual Senator, or little that the Senate itself could do, to terminate our involvement in Vietnam, that the war would be ended only by a President genuinely committed to ending it. Sometime during 1971 he began to make the commitment that if he were elected President he would end the war, withdraw all American troops and secure the release of the American prisoners of war within 90 days after his inauguration. The futility of the war obsessed him and, I am convinced, was a constant motivating force, together with his sincere and deeply felt conviction that he would be a good President.

The magnitude of the personal investment required by a political campaign taxes the imagination, and that magnitude increases in direct proportion to the importance of the office being sought. The higher the stakes, the higher the entrance fee. To become President of the United States you have to want it almost more than anything else in the world. You must possess the dedication of a martyr, the determination of a marathon runner, the stamina of a football linebacker, the precision of a heart surgeon, and the fortitude of a guerrilla commando. In terms of sheer desire, Eisenhower may have been an exception, but the trail is strewn with those who prove the rule: Goldwater, Rockefeller, Romney, Symington, McCarthy, and Stevenson in 1960. Those who had it—Truman, Roosevelt, Kennedy, Johnson, and Nixon—ultimately won. To seek the Presidency is, in short, one of the most demanding undertakings known to man. If motivation is lacking, the other attributes don't matter. George McGovern had that motivation, and its strength was constantly tested.

On we went through October, 1970, the pre-dawn of the campaign. Everywhere the Senator traveled the purposes were several: to help the party, to seek the election of its candidates, to raise funds for campaigns, to promote party unity and reconciliation, and to concentrate public attention on the key issues which distinguished the Democrats from the Republicans. Also important were the driving personal campaign considerations: to identify existing supporters and recruit potential supporters, to scrutinize possible McGovern campaign leaders in the states, to evaluate volunteer advance people, to gather political intelligence (what political figures were moving toward what potential Presidential candidate, who was approached to contribute to whom, what national party leaders were traveling around and to whom were they talking), and most importantly to begin the slow, careful process of building, one person at a time, campaign organizations in all fifty states.

This was also a baptism by fire for our meager national political staff— Stearns, Martin, Pokorny, and myself. During this period we were all simultaneously and constantly political operatives and organizers, schedulers and advancemen, personal aides to the Senator, luggage-handlers and ticket-arrangers, fund-raisers, name-gatherers, bodyguards, follow-up agents (whose duties included writing the indispensable thank-you notes), drivers, negotiators, magicians, and medicinemen. To accommodate to the extensive fall travel schedule, we worked out an intricate, leap-frogging set of advance assignments, with one staff member ahead of the Senator by a day or two, picking him up as he arrived in a particular city, where the staff member previously with him would fly on a city or two ahead to help set up the necessary arrangements.

Our primary responsibilities, aside from the logistical details, were to ensure a smooth schedule for the Senator, protecting him from as much of the endless nonsense as possible, and projecting as well as we could the impression of a smooth, well-oiled, experienced, political juggernaut. Thus we existed for many months in two worlds: the real world of mistakes, missed airplanes, unworkable schedules, lost luggage, disappearing reception committees, deserted shopping centers where rallies were supposed to be going on, and nights with four hours of sleep, and the unreal world of a large, powerful, national McGovern political operation staffed by seasoned organizers and experienced advancemen, computer-smooth scheduling, flawless logistical planning, monolithic efficiency, and enviable strength. Happily, during those months we were into and out of towns so fast—like smooth-talking drummers of a previous century— that the illusion was seldom penetrated.

I have never known the degree to which the Senator himself was aware of the near-disasters which our meager manpower resources constantly courted in the lean days. If he knew, he never mentioned it. Most of the time, I am convinced, he was unaware of how thinly we were stretched, how overly extended his political staff was. Reminiscing on those days later, I compared the travels of 1970 to a Laurel and Hardy movie where the fat one walked through a door and the roof collapsed on the thin one an unfortunate step behind him.

On October 18th, McGovern appeared with Humphrey, who was campaigning to regain his Senate seat, and addressed the World Affairs conference at McAllister College, where the former Vice President had been lecturing since the 1968 election. The Senator, an old friend and former neighbor of the Humphreys in Washington, stayed at the Humphrey home near the campus. He later told me that, although he was exhausted and wanted to get a good night's sleep in preparation for several days of strenuous campaigning on the West Coast, he and Humphrey sat in the kitchen until 3 A.M. discussing the political outlook for 1972. McGovern apparently was candid about his own intentions and preparations, indicating that he was seriously considering the race and would probably be making an early announcement. He acknowledged the high-risk character of our campaign—that it necessitated taking the lead on many new issues, forcing the other candidates out of positions of neutrality and compromise—but he also pointed out that we were building a national political organization to maximize our turn-out in the primaries and press the natural advantage of an insurgent candidate in non-primary states.

Humphrey outlined his own plans as winning back his Senate seat with as large a margin as possible that November and then occupying a position as senior Democratic stateman and spokesman in the Senate. He indicated that he had no long-range plans to seek the nomination in 1972, but would not rule out the possibility if the other leading contenders faded during the race. He suggested that this was a clear possibility in the case of one or two of them for whom he did not have particularly high regard. Humphrey apparently left open the chance for his own entry into the race if no clear front-runner or leadership emerged mid-way through the primary circuit. This seemed to rule out a head-on McGovern-Humphrey clash, since both agreed that if McGovern were to make it, he would have to show strength in the early primaries to stimulate the political and financial support needed for later primary contests.

There was certainly nothing in the brief description of the congenial conversation which the Senator gave me to suggest that either man foresaw the nomination race narrowing down to a struggle between the two of them, culminating in the destructive California primary confrontation, and the bitter struggle for the California delegation that continued into the convention.

The Senator traveled from Minnesota to California to campaign on behalf of Congressional candidates Don Edwards and Ron Dellums, in the San Francisco Bay area, and on behalf of Jesse Unruh, former Speaker of the California House and 1970 candidate for Governor against Ronald Reagan. All went well, except that the schedule, as always in California, became extremely complicated and crowded. Campaigning in California has a style and character all its own. Whatever the factors that make California a unique state—climate, topography, mobility, leisure-oriented life-style, media and movie influence, celebrity involvement, casualness, and informality combined with speed and tension—all seem to condition politics there, and outsiders must constantly adjust to these factors or risk a relationship to the voters about as pertinent as that of a man from another planet.

On October 22nd the Senator flew to Oregon, where he campaigned for Bob Stroub, Democratic candidate for Governor, speaking at Portland State College and in Eugene, site of the University of Oregon campus. The following day it was New Mexico and another full day of campaigning, and then on Saturday, the 24th, Colorado. Gene Pokorny had been the New Mexico advance man and Rick Stearns the Oregon man; both flew to Colorado, where I was the advance man. Yancey Martin met us in the airport, also having come in from California on his return to Washington. There we were, the Senator and almost all of his national political staff. Days, meals, hotels, receptions, faces, and names, had melted together in a monstrous blur. We were exhausted and trying to summon the energy to complete the remaining two or three stops.

The Senator, understandably, began to argue for a cancellation of his appearance the following night at a dinner in central Michigan. It was an event that had been negotiated over a course of weeks; the Democratic leadership in the area was adamant concerning the Senator's attendance. Ads had run, hundreds of tickets had been sold and numerous dignitaries notified. Although the Senator kept resisting, the event had taken on a life of its own and disaster threatened any future aspirations for McGovern in Michigan if he did not keep what the local party people felt was an ironclad commitment to speak at the dinner.

McGovern groused about "all this racing around the country." More and more he was beginning to feel that what was needed was a major speech by a leading Democrat responding to the harsh and divisive rhetoric of Spiro Agnew and the attacks Nixon was beginning to level at the Democratic-controlled Congress for creating all the nation's ills, including prolonging the war. The Senator stated several times: "If I just had a chance to take some time off and think, I know I could figure out what is missing. I keep thinking someone ought to make a major speech responding to all this nonsense the Republicans are putting out." We assured him that after Michigan there were only two more appearances before the election and he would have more time to sort out his uneasiness. Finally, much against his will, he acceded to his staff's demands and kept the Michigan appointments.

For the next several days this continued to preoccupy the Senator—this nagging concern about the failure of a Democratic leader to respond fully and dramatically to the increasingly hostile Nixon rhetoric. A number of times he considered going on television "to show what a phony" Nixon was. "You can't be President of the United States," McGovern said, "and use issues like busing to inflame people and throw a smokescreen around the real problems that have torn the country apart."

This theme kept running through his mind just before the 1970 elections. On Halloween, addressing the West Virginia Young Democrats convention in Charleston, he spoke about "Nixon's goblins"—that the war was ending (even though bombing of the North increased in direct ratio to the number of troops withdrawn and the only thing changing was the color of the bodies), that "forced, mass busing" was evil (but no alternative plan to solve the social problem had been suggested), that the Democrats were responsible for the nation's economic ills (even though inflation and unemployment were increasing under the Nixon administration), and that unrest at home was due to permissiveness and required more "law and order" (although crime statistics showed an increase under the Nixon administration). These and other themes, the Senator felt, desperately needed to be exposed as bluntly and forcefully as possible in some national forum.

The same idea had been occurring to others in Washington. During the last week of October, and even as the Senator spoke in West Virginia, plans were underway to purchase fifteen minutes of prime time television on election eve for a response to the Nixon administration. The speaker would be Senator Edmund Muskie and the net effect would be the single biggest boost the Muskie Presidential candidacy would receive. The idea for it apparently occurred to several people simultaneously, and initially seemed to spring from the same motivation as McGovern—not to let the President and Vice President go unanswered. In selecting a spokesman, however, those who conceived the idea settled on Muskie as much by elimination as by design. Muskie had been on the 1968 Democratic ticket and was considered by many to be still a legitimate spokesman for the party. Any consideration given to McGovern seems to have been confined to lumping him together with many other possible Presidential contenders, the selection of any one of whom was viewed as opening a political hornet's nest. Most importantly, the search for the tens of thousands of dollars necessary to pay for the telecast inevitably led to Muskie financiers. Much of the "smart," that is to say, committed, Democratic money in those early days was going to Senator Muskie. He was alternating with Kennedy for leadership in the polls and was widely perceived by the experts as the odds-on frontrunner for the nomination.

The evolution of the idea caused a great deal of intramural bickering among the party leaders considered potential candidates and their various camps of supporters. The objections were twofold: Who in the party had the arbitrary authority to select one individual, Muskie or anyone else, as *the* representative for all Democrats against the administration? And wasn't this whole idea just an effort to brighten Muskie's Presidential star? In the hours before the speech, charges and counter-charges were tossed about like darts in a darkened pub. We received reports that funds were being solicited from our contributors with the representation that the program had McGovern's full endorsement and support. Other Democratic leaders were embittered by what seemed to them to be a blatant power-play designed to put Muskie forward as the inevitable Democratic opponent to Nixon.

The speech, delivered on the eve of the 1970 elections, was right on target and in sharp contrast with a poorly produced, technically inferior, raspy old-Nixon performance taped in an Arizonia airport hangar. Muskie, in what was obviously his metier, calmly, deliberately, and thoughtfully performed surgery on the Nixon political mythology, shaming the President and Vice President, making them seem shabby, harsh, and divisive. McGovern greatly admired his colleague's presentation, but at the same time realized the tremendous boost it gave the Muskie candidacy and, thus, the difficulties it heaped on our already-burdened campaign.

He was extremely unhappy with his staff, which had run him at an exhausting pace all around the country for 60 days when his own instincts told him exactly what was called for. His arch-rival had finally stepped in at the appropriate moment to collect all the credit that, in retrospect, was there for the taking. From later comments it became evident that the Senator considered this one of the biggest mistakes we made in the entire nomination campaign.

I saw (perhaps rationalized) the situation much differently. It would have been much more difficult for us to raise the considerable amount of money necessary for the telecast. The same arguments would have been raised against McGovern as were raised against Muskie—that he was guilty of anointing himself party spokesman. And finally, we accomplished a great deal, very quietly and very subtly, during the fall travels in terms of laying a political base, identifying key supporters, and beginning the construction of a national political organization. We made many political contacts which later proved indispensable.

Nevertheless, the Senator felt the Muskie speech was a major setback and, at the time, I tended to agree with him. This experience made a significant impact on me. Thereafter I would defer almost completely to judgments the Senator felt strongly about based upon his own political instincts. Major questions of this sort occurred only rarely. But the 1970 Muskie speech led me to conclude that the Senator's judgment should be respected almost unquestionably when he was as strongly convinced about something as he was in this instance.

NOVEMBER AND DECEMBER, 1970

ELECTION NIGHT, NOVEMBER 3, 1970. We stayed up until the early hours of the morning calling Democratic candidates, successful or unsuccessful, but concentrating on the unsuccessful ones, on the theory, put forward by Dick Wade, that losers are more grateful because no one else calls to console them.

The following day the Senator left for ten days in the Virgin Islands to recuperate and draft a statement announcing his candidacy for the Presidency. Thus, Phase I of the McGovern campaign came to a close.

November and December seem, especially in retrospect, to be lost months. Two specific things happened: we gave a great deal of thought to money, and we made plans for the Senator's announcement of candidacy. In politics, the subject of money is consuming and disturbing. Consuming because, whatever some high-minded idealists may say, politics is a machine that runs on money; disturbing because it colors almost every major decision in a campaign—not only the organizational or structural decisions (how much will it cost?), but also the candidate's issues and positions (My God, he can't say that. It will turn off all the big contributors!).

Our financial needs in 1970 and early 1971 were relatively modest, at least by national campaign standards. Our beginning budget in the summer of 1970 was about $3,000 or $4,000 per month, increasing by the end of the year to $7,000 or $8,000. This included salaries for fewer than half a dozen people, rent for headquarters space, office supplies and phones, and travel for the candidate and the staff. In the late fall of 1970, I gave the Senator a memorandum estimating that continuing our operations merely at that level for the first year would cost approximately $100,000. In addition, if we implemented my proposal for five regional coordinators in the field to cover 26 key states we would need another

$100,000 for the year. But we all knew there is no such thing as a Presidential campaign that levels off at a certain point. A political campaign is like a national economy—it either grows or dies. Unlike other endeavors fueled by money, however, a campaign is almost impossible to budget accurately, primarily because there is no way of knowing how much will be raised. Consequently, throughout the campaign I would produce long-range and short-range budgets and give them to the fund-raisers, who used them as goals. As funds became available, we met the fixed budget requirements—office, phones and equipment, salaries, and travel—and if additional money was still available it was sent into the field for increased staff and headquarters. It was not until late in 1971 that we had to worry about the monumental costs of producing television spots, buying TV time and making other use of media for the early primary states.

The McGovern Presidential campaign was more fortunate than most in respect to predictability of income. After the direct-mail fund-raising effort got underway in 1971, following the announcement of candidacy, the experts responsible for this extremely successful program made accurate projections of the amount of money we could expect to raise. Meantime, the modest needs of 1970 and early 1971 were met by individual contributions. A friend might give enough to cover the salary needed by a new staff member, another might provide rent money. The Senator himself invested some income he received from his extensive lecture tour. One way or another, usually item-by-item, our meager early needs were met.

In an operation that small, it is much easier to interest a potential contributor in paying for a specific item such as an individual's salary than in contributing to the general treasury. This came to be known later as the "stained-glass window" concept of fund-raising, based on the principle that people are more inclined to make large contributions for things they can actually see and touch, their very own part of the campaign walking around live right in front of them. I even had the idea at one point of producing a campaign catalog for contributors. At fund-raising dinners, receptions, and cocktail parties, the catalog would be distributed, the pitch would be made, and people would be invited to "buy" specific items or projects. "How about your very own Gene Pokorny, or a full-page ad in *The New York Times,* or fifteen minutes of Senator McGovern on prime time television, or a headquarters in Madison, Wisconsin. For those with more modest means, a billboard outside Omaha, or 10,000 McGovern for President buttons or bumper strips, or transportation for student canvassers?" It is an interesting idea, and someone may do it in 1976. After all, if you sell enough stained-glass windows, pretty soon you have a cathedral.

From the beginning the campaign's finance chairman was Henry Kimelman, who met the Senator at the 1968 Democratic convention. Kimelman's friendship with McGovern expanded during 1968 and 1969, and the two discussed the possibility of a Presidential campaign a number of times during this period. In the fall of 1969, Kimelman hosted a small dinner at his home in Washington to enable the Senator to discuss this idea more fully with friends and advisors such as Senator Abraham Ribicoff; the Udall brothers, Stewart and Morris; media consultant Charles Guggenheim; Fred Dutton, an imaginative Kennedy advisor; Washington attorney Mike Feldman; McCarthy campaign manager Blair Clark; Allard Lowenstein, and others. Little apparently came out of the dinner, except a few thoughtful memos. When the campaign got underway in the summer of 1970, the Senator turned to Kimelman to help provide seed money. By the time the primary campaigns began in earnest in 1972, Henry was spending the better part of each day attempting to raise campaign funds and watchdogging expenditures.

The financial strictures in the beginning could have been worse (although it is often difficult to imagine how). The work on basic issues, the substantive research and the speech-writing were done almost entirely by the Senate staff throughout the nomination race. Not until almost the end of the primary circuit were additional research and writing staff members employed on the campaign staff. John Holum, the Senator's legislative assistant, became the principal speech-writer, tackling farm-related matters domestically as well as the defense budget and the Southeast Asian war. The original press secretary for the campaign was Gordon Weil, an international economist, who joined the Senate staff in 1970. Additional support was provided by other members of the Senate staff, particularly clerical and technical help in handling of mail and computerization of names and mailing lists.

It had become painfully apparent to me during our travels that fall that much of our inadequacy was traceable to the lack of staff resources; I repeatedly pointed this out to Henry in the closing weeks of 1970 and occasionally brought the matter to the Senator's attention—particularly when he would mention a report of the effectiveness of the staff of Senator Bayh or another of his presumed opponents. Although he had Senate staff resources no greater than McGovern's, Muskie had already begun to build a large national political staff devoted primarily to issues research, and Bayh had substantially reinforced his already sizable Senate staff to accommodate his extensive travels. The Bayh operation seemed to outnumber us almost three or four to one, and it used to cause me considerable annoyance when the smoothness and efficiency of their political operation received special attention, particularly since it usually led to a comment from McGovern that he hoped we could tighten up our operation to compete with the others. My response consistently was, "We need to hire more people." But we did not have the money, and consequently limped into 1971 terribly short-handed.

I was bothered, as I had been at the Cedar Point meeting in the summer, by the approaching candidacy announcement. It was obvious by late October that we could not carry out the steps leading up to the announcement by mid-November and it had, therefore, been postponed until a yet unselected date early in 1971. The purpose of the early announcement, among other things, was to generate support and enthusiasm for the McGovern candidacy long before other contenders were publicly committed to the race. Inevitably, this support would take the form of offers of help, pleas for approval to begin to set up local and state campaign operations, advice, invitations for speaking engagements, suggestions, speeches, questions and, most significantly, *mail* and job applications. We were still woefully unprepared to handle that kind of response, not to mention another round of national travel, perhaps to last until the early spring, of the sort that we had just survived that fall. It all led to one thing, hiring more people to help both in Washington, handling the increased load of calls and mail, and around the country, harnessing the organizational energies the announcement of candidacy would, we hoped, trigger. I sat at my headquarters desk many nights wondering how it could all be done.

I never once had any questions or doubts about *what* had to be done, what it would take to organize the country for the nomination and election of a President. But there were countless times when I wondered *how*—where those needed millions of dollars would come from. We knew the people were there—both the tens of thousands of volunteers and the dozens of political organizers it would take to lead them. Our concern was the money to hire those organizers, to open storefront headquarters, to pay for telephone deposits, to print millions of pieces of literature, to buy the stationery to answer the letters, to buy postage stamps.

Early in the fall we had already begun to receive invaluable help from volunteers in Washington, the forerunners of the McGovern army. Most of them would, when salaries were available, become full-time staff members, but they all worked just as hard and faithfully unpaid as they did when they were later salaried. One of the first full-time McGovern volunteers was Marcia Johnston, a young teacher who decided in the fall of 1970 that helping McGovern was more important than teaching school (or earning money); her great patience and sense of the absurd qualified her to be the principal director of what eventually was to become a host of other volunteers and then, throughout the crucial months of 1972, my assistant. Jan Gunnison, another early volunteer, became Rick Stearns' assistant. Her husband soon mustered out of the Army and joined the McGovern army and together, in 1972, they handled much of the logistics for the Senator's traveling party. (Smiling, always cheerful, and adolescent-looking, the Gunnisons became known as the Bobsey twins or Hansel and Gretel.) Then came Joe Daly, with casual dress, full mane and beard, whose strong convictions regarding the screwed-up condition of the world ordinarily received only muttered utterance; for months he handled the tedious and unenviable task of sorting the incoming mail without complaint and with little pay. Joe occasionally said the only thing he wanted out of his investment of two years of his life in the campaign was the pleasure of walking—just once—through the private gates to the White House past the uniformed guard, appearing as he did to be a member of the cast of "Hair," without question or challenge. And on they came, many dozens of others, often more than we could possibly find room for, the backbone of the McGovern campaign.

The detailed preparations for the announcement of candidacy began shortly after the fall elections. Almost all of our staff efforts during December and early January were directed toward this event and its immediate follow-up. On December 1st the second major planning session of the campaign was held at Henry Kimelman's home in Washington. For this discussion, we assembled Gene Pokorny from the Midwest, Stearns, Martin, Jeff Smith, and myself from the campaign staff, Cunningham, Weil, and Holum from the Senate staff, and, as advisors, Mike Feldman, Joe Dolan, former assistant to Robert Kennedy and now a Denver businessman, Charles Guggenheim for media advice, and John Douglas, later to be named Chairman of the National Citizens Committee. The Senator attended for about two hours in the middle of the all-day session. The political staff presented a comprehensive, updated version of the state-by-state strategy blocked out during the Cedar Point meeting in July, complete with 1971 travel proposal, allocating the campaign's most precious commodity, the Senator's time, almost day by day. We also presented plans to fill out the complement of regional organizers as early in the year as possible, analyzing each region for its strengths and weaknesses. We discussed, preliminarily, the states where initial organizational support in the form of key, effective people had emerged during the previous six months.

During this rather lengthy, and perhaps somewhat boring, background strategy briefing, Charles Guggenheim broke in: "Listen! I don't give a damn what the staff is or isn't doing. I don't have to waste my time listening to this kind of nonsense. Unless you people figure out a way to beat Harold Hughes in New Hampshire, you might as well all go home, because this campaign isn't going anywhere! It doesn't seem to me that anyone has done any real thinking about how to present Senator McGovern on television in such a way as to make people more inclined to vote for him than someone else. Until you do that, all this organizational stuff

STUART BRATESMAN

Gene Pokorny on the line for George McGovern.

doesn't mean anything." Most of us were so stunned and unfamiliar with Charles' blunt style that we didn't respond. The answer, however, was obvious. If we developed the strongest and most effective political organization around the country, including in New Hampshire, then we could pre-empt later entries into the race, particularly the other liberals, such as Hughes, who would be banking on an early McGovern failure. Political organization, especially maximizing volunteer support, was the least expensive and wisest investment of early campaign resources.

In any case, production of a media program in 1971 seemed to make no sense whatsoever. Considerable thought had to be given, and soon, to the themes and issues that set McGovern apart from other candidates and that would make him the strongest contender against President Nixon. Some of that thinking, of which Charles was unaware, had already been done; nevertheless, Charles' admonition was essentially well taken and his entrance into the campaign later in 1971 on a more or less full-time basis was a welcome addition to the creative side of our campaign.

The Senator responded to Charles' outburst with a rather philosophical discourse summarizing the perspective into which he had cast the campaign effort over the past few weeks. It was, he said, to be an effort that, win or lose, would leave the country a better place, that would challenge the minds and spirits of the concerned voters, that would open the door of the Democratic Party to widespread citizen participation, and that would, most importantly, be an uplifting and challenging experience for each of us who participated in it. He read several passages from a thoughtful, lengthy memorandum he had done regarding the long-term implications of the campaign and the attitude of all those who were deeply involved in it. At best it was poetic and moving and revealed great depth and concern on the part of its author. At worst it was an invitation to expect defeat and to look for the true meaning of political activism in participation rather than in victory. It was certainly not intended as the latter, but to someone like Joe Dolan, steeped in the Kennedy/Lombardi school of politics/football ("winning isn't everything, but losing isn't anything"), it was too much. "Senator," Dolan said, "don't ever talk about losing this election; don't even think about it. It's devastating to morale if you talk to your supporters about some other goal besides winning—they don't understand the subtleties and they'll think you're Gene McCarthy or something. It's all right to work these things out in your own mind, or even with some of your closest advisors, but never, never talk about them with anyone else."

In mid-December we selected Monday, January 18th, 1971, as the date for the formal announcement of the Senator's candidacy for the Presidency. Gordon Weil began preparing a scenario of events connected with the announcement, particularly as they related to the press, Rick Stearns started compiling the names of all political figures who should receive advance notice of the announcement, and Jeff Smith and I started the tedious process of preparing a massive mailing. The idea of using a letter to announce a candidacy for President was first raised during the July meeting at Cedar Point by Dick Wade. I had suggested at that time that the traditional press conference seemed undramatic and conventional, that since we had some time to think about it, we should come up with some unique, attention-getting method, perhaps something with historical overtones or precedence. Wade mentioned that Thomas Jefferson had announced his intention to seek the Presidency by sending letters to newspaper editors, handwritten of course. That rang a bell and the idea of sending an announcement letter dominated our thinking throughout the fall.

Our original plans were to distribute the letter personally over the weekend prior to January 18th to editors of leading newspapers around the country. It soon became apparent, however, that the major wire services would pick up copies of the letter from newsrooms and distribute it immediately. This would place the announcement on radio and television prior to publication in the newspapers and the unique effect of the letter announcement would be lost. This led to a modification of the original plan; we would mail the letter to all those on the McGovern mailing list— now almost a quarter of a million people. The text, together with an announcement statement, would be released to the press on the 18th.

As amateurs in the highly sophisticated world of massive direct-mail contacts, we fumblingly began the complex process of piecing together the numerous elements. Most important, tens of thousands of names had to be transferred from cards, lists, and tapes to some sort of computer tape, a process that turned out to be horrendously complicated. The primary burden fell on Jeff Smith who, toward late December, seemed to slip farther and farther beneath tons of tapes, cards, and printing problems. Finally, as the entire project threatened to slide out of the grasp of all of us, Yancey Martin suggested we contact Morris Dees, an acquaintance of his from Montgomery, Alabama, who knew something about direct mail. In the judgment of many, including myself, Morris was one of the very few bona fide geniuses involved in the McGovern campaign and, on more than one occasion, probably its saviour.

As a student at the University of Alabama Morris discovered that money could be made selling birthday cakes for students by sending letters to their parents and that well-written letters sent to the right recipients and promoting the right product, cause, or project could elicit profitable responses. Following his graduation from law school, where he took a great interest in civil rights problems, Morris developed a direct-mail firm based in Montgomery. Within ten years the business became the largest direct-mail firm outside New York and Chicago; Morris sold it to a national corporation and became a farmer and public-interest lawyer in the Montgomery area, pioneering on the frontiers of civil liberties. All this made him a prominent, but not particularly popular, member of his community.

Our call for help brought Morris and his former business partner to Washington to analyze the announcement mailing. After his partner left, Morris took charge of the entire mailing. His experience with suppliers, printers, and mailing firms permitted Morris, in his modest, unassuming way, to prepare the quarter-of-a-million-piece mailing in a few days— a project that had threatened to take the entire campaign staff weeks. What is more, Morris converted the announcement letter into a fund-raising appeal, pointing out that it made no sense to spend tens of thousands of dollars for the letter without seriously attempting to solicit at least enough funds to pay for the mailing. He calculated that with only an average response we might be able to raise enough money to finance the early stages of the campaign in 1971.

After the Senator prepared a draft of the proposed announcement letter in early January, Morris introduced another key member of the direct-mail team, Tom Collins, a specialist in mail advertising campaigns and a 1968 McCarthy delegate. They both proposed the novel idea that the letter might indeed be a rather long one, relying on the axiom of their trade that it isn't how much you say, but what you say and how you say it, that counts. (As the letter grew and grew and more copy was added, Morris constantly had to reassure me, the skeptical novice, by referring to the most successful direct-mail advertisement in the history of the business, a letter promoting Mercedes-Benz automobiles that ran almost two dozen pages.) We were told that people would read a long letter if it were well-written, informative, and challenging, particularly since no one had ever announced his candidacy for the Presidency in quite this manner. The Senator's final draft was seven letter-sized pages long. In the meantime Rick Stearns completed plans for advance calls or notes to go to key political leaders and supporters immediately before the announcement itself, and Gordon Weil coordinated the timing of events, which now included a statewide telecast by the Senator to his South Dakota constituents. As with most consequential productions of this sort, frantic last-minute details and problems were monumental. Over $20,000 had to be raised to buy postage stamps; the letters, printed in New York, were assembled, inserted, sealed, and stamped in Chicago, then trucked to Washington to be mailed (Morris explained that a

Washington postmark was important). They were to have been flown to Washington, but the weather grounded the planes, and as it was, one of the trucks was lost for a day and a half, causing widespread heart palpitations.

Starting about midnight, January 15th, the letters were deposited, West Coast first, with the drop being completed the night of the 16th. On Monday, January 18th, the Senator and Eleanor McGovern appeared on South Dakota television. The Senator stated the reasons for his candidacy simply and eloquently:

I seek the presidency because I believe deeply in the American promise and can no longer accept the diminishing of that promise. . . . Thoughtful Americans understand that the highest patriotism is not a blind acceptance of official policy, but a love of one's country deep enough to call her to a higher standard . . . we must undertake a re-examination of our ideas, institutions and the actual conditions of our lives which is as fundamental as the discussions of the founding fathers two centuries ago. . . .

A public figure today can perform no greater service than to lay bare the proven malfunctions of our society, try honestly to confront our problems in all their complexity, and stimulate the search for solutions. This is my intention in this campaign.

The kind of campaign I intend to run will rest on candor and reason; it will be rooted not in the manipulation of our fears and divisions, but in a national dialogue on mutual respect and common hope.

The people are not centrist or liberal or conservative. Rather, they seek a way out of the wilderness. But if we who seek their trust, trust them; if we try to evoke the "better angels of our nature," the people will find their own way. We are the children of those who built a great and free nation. And we are no less than that. We must now decide whether our courage and imagination are equal to our talents. If they are, as I believe, then future generations will continue to love America, not simply because it is theirs, but for what it has become—for what, indeed, we have made it.

The next morning, January 19th, at 11 A.M., the Senator held the traditional announcement press conference in a Capitol caucus room. The reporters' questions set the tone for the next 14 or 15 months: Wasn't he a candidate whose only issue was the war? And what would he do when President Nixon ended the war shortly? What support could he point to among party regulars? How did he expect to get the nomination when he came from South Dakota and had no money? Didn't he think Senator Muskie had it all locked up anyway? How did he expect to dispel the overwhelming suspicion that he was merely a stalking-horse for Ted Kennedy? Where was the evidence of support by organized labor? Wasn't he much too liberal to get the nomination?

If I had possessed both foresight and ready cash, I could have made a great deal of money that day laying bets on a McGovern nomination with the assembled press corps at *very* favorable odds.

For reasons that are still unclear to me, newspapers and news magazines about this time began to carry stories in which the Las Vegas oddsmaker "Jimmie the Greek" rated the various Democratic leaders' chances of winning the party's nomination for President. His earliest chart had McGovern at 500 to 1. Printing Jimmie the Greek on American politics was graduation day for the Peter Principle. A year and a half away from a convention is no time to start making book. As your seasoned nine-year-old canvasser can tell you—too many things can happen, situations change, and, according to Murphy's law, if the worst possible thing can happen, it will. Nevertheless, papers and magazines must be filled up and Jimmie the Greek bumbled on for the next year and a half. John Peter Zenger died for your newspaper editor's sins.

After eight months or more of preparation, the campaign was now publicly underway and the small but watertight McGovern ark had been launched (Titanic allusions would be reserved by reporters for the later Muskie campaign), but in what weather?

The obstacles were obvious. Muskie was believed to have solid and widespread support among party regulars, party officials at the state and local levels—the people who carry the water for the donkey. Largely because of this, he was also assumed to have substantial committed financial support, certainly enough to protect him from concern about this energy-draining subject. The Muskie candidacy was continually buoyed by the reservoir of goodwill developed during the 1968 general election and replenished by the 1970 election-eve television speech. What negative Muskie speculation occurred centered upon his weakening in the homestretch, and the possibility of his giving way to the more charismatic Kennedy. For month after month, most political commentators were incapable of resisting the seductiveness of a potential Kennedy candidacy—filling column after column with the cyclical, half-whispered speculation—"it is widely believed that," or "knowledgeable observers think," or "party leaders are said to be urging." It was cyclical because the press speculation encouraged political speculation, which in turn led to more press speculation, which in turn, etc. Those who reported that Senator Kennedy was not promoting this speculation were largely accurate. He is human, and political, enough to enjoy continued consideration as a potential President of the United States, but during this period he was genuinely discouraging public conjecture. Even though the Kennedy gossip did open a viable threat to the Muskie candidacy, it also had an adverse effect on our efforts. It led many to conclude that McGovern's fortunes were inextricably intertwined with Kennedy's, that Kennedy would immediately and automatically swallow up the McGovern campaign if he entered, that McGovern's candidacy, in effect, was hostage to the Kennedy will, and would disappear at his pleasure.

Humphrey was scarcely a factor as the McGovern candidacy was born. It was widely assumed that his participation as a candidate in national politics was precluded by his age and 1968 defeat. Yet the Democratic Party throughout much of the United States is still in the hands of fairly entrenched conservative forces and older politicians, some of whom at one time may—like Humphrey—have led the charge for reform, for liberal legislation, for change, but for whom time had made change a threat. For many of these politicians Hubert Humphrey was a champion of caution. But Humphrey is, withal, an ambitious man with influential friends, and he had come to doubt the determination of Muskie, his former running mate. McGovern voiced his prophetic opinion at Cedar Point in July, 1970—his old friend Humphrey had more guile, cunning, and political grit than Muskie and might well outflank the Maine Lincoln before it was all over. Several of us concluded that Humphrey could well emerge the Phoenix of the old guard in 1972.

Then there were the dark horses and "charismatic" horses—Harold Hughes of Iowa with the awesome bass voice, the massive door-filling frame, the romantic alcoholic-truck driver past (one of his earliest, most talented supporters used to say: "I could see him on the back of a flat-bed truck in some little town in Florida with his coat off, sweat under his arms, and his belly hanging out, converting those red-necked Wallacite farmers with speeches about taxes, jobs, and the screwing they're getting from the establishment!"); Birch Bayh of Indiana, young and energetic, with a carefully promoted identification with the Kennedys (he had been in that plane crash with Ted, after all), whose incessant bounding about the country led to so many jokes about running into Birch Bayh at every airport in the land; the Mayor of New York, John Lindsay, an erstwhile Republican whose youth (he is, in fact, the same age as McGovern), presumed Kennedy style (they must mean John, with whom there are, in fact, very few similarities), and "charisma" made him the darling of the magazine feature writers easily bored with the nitty-gritty tedium of real politics; John Gardner, Henry Jackson, Ramsey Clark, a clutch of newly elected Southern Governors. On and on went the list.

McGovern's liabilities had by now been widely discussed: he was a "one-issue candidate" from a nowhere state, with no financial backing; not well known, practically below freezing on the political poll thermometer, with no visible support from organized labor; too much identified with the liberal-left, practically anti-charismatic, and saddled with party reform. All in all, a losing cause.

For the smart money, his campaign was at best, an unrealistic, idealistic crusade by a faithful few and, at worst, a farce. "Quixotic? That's what it is. Pretty soon they're going to start playing 'The Impossible Dream' down at that damn telephone booth they call a national headquarters. Better listen to Jimmie the Greek—those are the boys that lay out the smart money and they're not taken in by that nonsense. Jimmie the Greek, he don't know nothin' about no impossible dreams."

PART II

From the Declaration of Independence to Valley Forge

(January, 1971, to January, 1972)

During the twelve or thirteen months between McGovern's announcement and the beginning of the intensive primary campaigning in early 1972, the McGovern army bivouacked around the country, using the entire year of 1971 to build, organize, and gain strength, and riding out the political storms caused, during that wintery period, by the entry and departure of various Democratic rivals. It was a difficult time for the campaign, marked by the increasing financial starvation caused by demands for expansion and preparation for the primaries, very limited funds, and the absence of any tangible signs of success or progress from the endless weeks of tedious work. There was almost no way to judge whether we were following the correct strategy or carrying out the proper tactical operations. Indeed, almost every outward sign indicated failure. The Harris and Gallup polls moved not one bit—once or twice they dipped a point. Few substantial contributors joined the campaign and few experienced political figures came to our aid. Other campaigns received more attention from the media; our campaign was criticized as dull and unimaginative.

Our goals throughout 1971 were several: to create a viable campaign organization in each of the primary states previously targeted as important; to begin organizing the non-primary states where we felt we could elect McGovern delegates through the caucus procedure; to develop a systematic travel schedule for the Senator in the key cities and states, permitting him to become better known, recruit additional supporters, and define the issues for 1972; to begin preparation of electronic and print media programs; to build an issues research and speech-writing capability using volunteer experts as much as possible; to raise enough funds to sustain one or two early primary states, by expanding the direct-mail operation as far as it would go; finally, and most importantly, to allocate our relatively meager resources so carefully and wisely that we would get the most effective use of our dollars and man-hours and not be forced out of the race before we had a real chance in 1972.

As important as each of these goals was, we could succeed at each of them and still fail in the final effort if we lacked the most essential and least tangible ingredient—that indefinable something that enables one candidate to elicit votes and support where other candidates fail. The real test in 1971 was of the candidate, George McGovern, his tenacity, his energy, and his ability to communicate and inspire.

The candidate, particularly in times of great fatigue, was occasionally disinclined to appreciate the importance of his own presence in the key primary states. Although he almost always followed the schedules we prepared for him, there were times when he considered trips useless and unproductive. Since he was not, and could not be, in touch with the day-to-day organizational effort, he tended to overestimate the degree to which he was known to most Democrats and underestimate the role he had to play in converting talented organizational people to his cause.

In each state these people exist. They are rare. But if one knows what to look for, they can be found. The characteristics of a good political organizer are universal—efficient, low-key, persistent, methodical, durable (mentally and physically), orderly to the point of compulsion. Since there are so few people with all these characteristics, capable organizers are sought for all sorts of projects and causes. They are overly extended and therefore extremely reluctant to commit their time. Often, too, their causes fail, and thus they become increasingly more cautious about "getting involved." Most of them have worked for too many candidates who were fakes, phonies, or bumblers, which leads them to want to meet and form a sense of a new candidate who seeks their support and their energies.

All of this meant that the Senator was required to travel extensively in 1971 for two reasons: to help convert these key people personally in many states to form the nucleus or infra-structure of a campaign in the state, and, later, to make the many public and media appearances required to recruit large numbers of volunteers necessary to provide manpower for the grassroots campaign in the state later on.

Two days before Christmas, 1970, we delivered to the Senator a 16-page travel schedule for the coming year. Based upon an elaborate political analysis, it ranked the states in five categories for purposes of allocating the candidate's time, and called for 91 days of travel, or one day out of four given to campaigning, with an average of four trips a month.

In analyzing each state, we considered, along with other factors, its political traditions. Does it usually vote Democrat or Republican? Does it have a tendency toward liberalism or conservatism? What kind of state-wide officials—Senators, Governors, Congressmen—have been chosen in the last few elections? What are the issues that have received the most attention recently, for example busing, property taxes, education? Does there seem to be much activity or enthusiasm for other candidates? Does any other candidate have a particular advantage because of geography, national heritage, or some other factor? How much money can be raised in the state to help finance a campaign? What style of campaigning seems to be most effective—handshaking? media? canvassing? What is the condition of the Democratic Party in the state? And, if the purpose is to run in a primary, are there subsidiary advantages to entering the race even if we cannot win?

Once all these factors were weighed and the states placed in some kind of relationship to each other, it became possible to make meaningful decisions about the candidate's schedule, the amount of money to be budgeted for each state, and the number and caliber of staff members to send in.

The highest priority states, with the number of 1971 campaign days allocated to each, were: California (7 days), Oregon (6), Wisconsin (6), New Hampshire (6), Nebraska (5), and West Virginia (5). Of these, West Virginia was the only one we eventually chose not to officially enter, and New Hampshire the only one we didn't win. Each state was to be visited four times during the year. The initial campaign visit was to include one large public event or speech which would get wide media coverage, an informal discussion or rap sessions with a cross section of people to get a feel for the political constituency and their concerns, a private meeting with the state party leadership, a private meeting with the liberal/progressive organizers and leaders in the state (if they were not party leaders also), small private meetings with selected interest groups such as labor councils, minority groups, or farm associations, interviews with local television stations, and interviews with boards of editors of leading papers.

The second-rank states were Connecticut, Ohio, New Jersey, New York, Pennsylvania, Michigan, Minnesota, Missouri, Illinois, and New Mexico. We eventually won primaries in three of these, barely missing an upset in Ohio, and got substantial numbers of delegates from all the rest except Missouri. These states were to be visited three days during 1971, one day each on three separate occasions.

The third-rank states were to receive two visits of one day each during the year. They were Colorado, Massachusetts, Maryland, Texas, North Carolina, Kentucky, Florida, and Kansas. Fourth-ranked states, to be visited one day each, were Arizona, Delaware, Georgia, Indiana, Iowa, Mississippi, North Dakota, Oklahoma, Tennessee, Utah, Vermont, Virginia, Washington, and Wyoming. The stop in these states was to be built around one central political event as the rationale for campaigning in the state. Suggestions were made for cities to be visited on each trip into a state, and for the particular congressional districts or political jurisdictions where the most emphasis should be placed.

For the remaining states—those in the fifth rank—the policy adopted was one of benign neglect.

This 12-month travel schedule reflected the political analysis we had done of the entire country. If our analysis and consequent strategy had been wrong, or if we had failed to plan the careful allocation of our resources, I do not believe McGovern could have won the Democratic nomination. The winding, torturous political road of 1971 and 1972 is littered with the wreckage of campaigns (a number of which had many advantages over us) which failed in both respects.

Financial decisions were more difficult than scheduling decisions. Early in 1971 I prepared a functional budget for our national campaign which broke all expenditures down into six categories: national operations (headquarters, national staff, overhead, etc.); candidate activities (scheduling, travel, advance costs); field operations (regional coordinators, organizers, offices, travel); political intelligence, which later became the delegate information system (staff); promotional activities (materials, preliminary radio and television); and direct mail (costs of preparing mailings). With some minor adjustments later, this remained the basic budget structure throughout the campaign. Amounts budgeted for each of these functions were always sliced to the bone. But even then there was seldom enough to keep each operation running efficiently and decisions had to be made constantly about which vital function to cut further.

Our organizational operations in the field in early 1971 remained quite modest, expanding gradually from Pokorny holding down the Midwest, to a New England coordinator, then an industrial states coordinator, then a Northwest coordinator, and eventually field offices springing up in these areas. By the latter part of 1971, monthly budgets were being submitted by the field organizers for the key primary states—New Hampshire, Wisconsin, Nebraska, Oregon, California, and New York.

JANUARY, 1971

Based primarily on the understanding reached at Cedar Point in mid-1970 and on later informal discussions involving the Senator, Rick Stearns, and myself, a long-range plan had evolved by the spring of 1971 for capturing the nomination. It was based on three premises.

1. The Democratic nomination results more from a struggle between the two ideological wings of the party, the liberals and conservatives, than it does from some amorphous consensus. The nomination in an open process will inevitably go to those who work hardest for it, and people are not motivated to work who have no strong convictions.

2. The 1972 nomination process will be an open one for two reasons: first, the party reform guidelines, recommended by the Commission on Party Reform and already adopted by a large number of states, will

become the official procedures of the party; second, after the bitterly divisive experience of 1968, the threat of a splinter fourth political party, ensuring the re-election of Richard Nixon, will be substantial if the process for selection of delegates and nomination of the candidate is closed or rigged.

3. The activists in the Democratic Party, those who work hardest in an election year, are usually the liberals. This is not a value judgment, but a fact of political life, tracing, in recent times, from Stevenson to John Kennedy to McCarthy and Robert Kennedy, and, eventually, to George McGovern. (This is exactly the opposite of the Republican Party, whose ideologically motivated, activist wing is conservative.)

These premises led to the inevitable conclusion and the key to the 1972 Democratic nomination: the delegate selection process will be open; a nomination race will be essentially ideological with the "center" playing very little role; whoever becomes the leader of the traditional liberal wing will have a natural advantage because it is a broader, more effective base than its conservative counterpart. Therefore, if McGovern becomes the leader of the liberal wing of the Democratic Party, and if we organize as much of the party as possible, he will become its nominee. Now, in retrospect, it seems fairly elementary. But in 1970 and early 1971, it was creative analysis.

To capture the unchallenged leadership of the progressive Democrats, our reasoning continued, McGovern had to continue to speak out on the major issues of the times, particularly the cessation of our military involvement in Southeast Asia, the need for social justice and equality, and the need for a more enlightened foreign policy, especially toward the Communist countries. This presented little problem because the Senator had developed a reputation for leadership on the war issue and progressive stands on most other issues and was not known for trimming under pressure.

The early announcement had emphasized the Senator's courage in submitting his candidacy to public scrutiny over a long period of time and his candor in telling the people exactly what he was up to instead of playing the traditional political game of "drafts." Now, we concluded, it was important for him to perpetuate the impression of courage and candor, of not being calculating and "political" by picking and choosing the most favorable primaries. That meant he had to enter some tough ones early, especially New Hampshire, even though the prospects of success were slim, not only to demonstrate courage but also to make it difficult for other candidates, particularly other liberals, to form a beachhead early. At the same time, some selection of primaries had to take place simply because we did not have the financial resources and manpower to run in every primary.

I felt there would be three categories of candidates or potential candidates who might compete for the liberal/progressive/activist constituency: those who might also start early and try to duplicate our grassroots organizational efforts, those who might enter the early and middle primaries against us, and those who would count on the early demise of McGovern and stay out awaiting the call to pick up the banner and inherit whatever structure remained.

Least troublesome was this last group, since we always knew we had to demonstrate some strength early to muster enough political and financial support to continue in the race. If we didn't succeed, then others, of course, had the right to pick up what pieces they could. The first category, the other potential early starters who would also emphasize organization, was somewhat more troublesome in that we would be competing for the same manpower and experience—that small pool of talented organizers and dedicated volunteers. But again, it was a fair contest and if we worked harder than anyone else we could squeeze some other contenders out of the race before the primaries began merely by absorbing the best people and constructing the most effective political operation state by state.

But most bothersome was the second category of possible liberal competitors. The threat of one or more other candidates competing for our votes in a primary, especially a crucial early primary like New Hampshire where the potential voting base is limited to begin with, caused us considerable concern. There was nothing to prevent a Lindsay, for example, from storing up money and staff for one dramatic push in an early primary that, even if unsuccessful, might result in a split liberal constituency in the state, and a smashing victory for a more conservative opponent. And there was no way we could influence that kind of decision. If a candidate was determined to make that one big dice-roll and run a media-blitz campaign even a superior pre-primary organizational effort on our part would not be sufficient to persuade him otherwise. We had no choice during 1971 but to make every effort to consolidate liberal support around the country and ride out the storm.

Shortly after the announcement and while we were working out our strategy, the advance guard of the really crazy people began to appear. We had seen signs of their coming much earlier. Their prophet might well have been the man from a little town in Alabama who appeared in our office in 1970 with a proposal to solicit the support of every truck driver in the country. All he wanted was for us to help him buy a tractor-trailer rig to drive around the country with "McGOVERN" emblazoned across the sides; he would stop in every truck stop in America to talk about McGovern for President and get other truck drivers to join him in what eventually would become a mammoth caravan. His request for $30,000 or $40,000 came at a time when the entire campaign staff of six had no assurance that salaries would be available next week.

But he was merely the forerunner of an endless merry band: The Rockville, Maryland, housewife who insisted on singing all twelve verses of her original campaign fight song, "On, McGovern," over the telephone; the sincere and persistent small-town volunteer fireman who felt that the entire campaign hinged upon McGovern's advocating a national program of firefighting based on the use of some novel nozzle or chemical fog or steam or something; the earnest, misguided young promoter who wanted to be the filter through which all contacts and communications between the Senator and his campaign passed, who viewed the whole operation (with more foresight than the more literal-minded among us) as some off-spring of Barnum & Bailey and who concocted one bizarre publicity gimmick after another for keeping McGovern in the headlines (and in trouble).

There were enough characters in that weird parade to populate a dozen Faulkner novels: people with dead-certain, undeniable proof that one candidate was a transvestite and another was a thief and another chased girls or boys or whatever; people who believed that elections, and probably history, turned upon some masterstroke, some phrase, some idea, some song, some word, some syllable—some *one thing* that if only the candidate would do or say would suddenly, dramatically convince all mankind that this man was its saviour. On they came in ranks too numerous to count, with crack-brained schemes too mind-boggling to describe, certain that they could provide the miracle that would lead to victory if only they could get past the unimaginative louts who stood between them and the candidate.

The weekend following the announcement, the Senator began his campaign in California, the state that was, in the judgment of some, to mark the watershed of the McGovern campaign in 1972. He delivered the keynote speech at the dinner for the state democratic convention in Sacramento, preceded by Senator Muskie at the delegates luncheon, and followed by Senator Bayh, who addressed the convention itself.

The three principal speeches were judged, weighed, and evaluated in lobbies, bars, and hallways by groups of delegates who resembled judges at a high school oratorical contest. McGovern scored on content, conviction, and force, Bayh on style and emotion; Muskie remained the frontrunner for the nomination in spite of his speech. The suites of the candidates or candidates-to-be resembled doctors' offices in a retirement community during the two-day convention, with individuals or groups whose support was being sought ushered in by eager but harried staff members for a brief visit with one of the Senators. Often people were lined up far down the hallways as schedules eroded and appointments fell further behind. But the entire operation eventually turned out to be very profitable for us.

The most eventful occurrence of this first post-announcement West Coast trip was a speech the Senator delivered on Sunday night January 24th, 1971, at the University of the Pacific in Stockton. The text was a thorough and detailed analysis of United States policy toward the People's Republic of China, together with a proposed ten-point revision of that policy to conform to current political realities. Primarily, the Senator proposed that the United States grant diplomatic recognition to the People's Republic, welcome its admission to the United Nations and begin the development of trade programs of non-strategic goods and products. It soon became clear to the 1,500 or more students and townspeople in the school auditorium that this was not a routine campaign speech or some idle thoughts on a minor foreign policy issue. McGovern was obviously using this forum to announce a bold, controversial, and politically risky program for relating to the world's largest nation. The real question was what the immediate response of this Stockton audience, drawn from an area of the state not recognized for its liberalism, would be. Several members of the national press corps who had traveled to California to cover Muskie's appearance were induced to travel to Stockton with us to cover the speech. Their presence increased the risk of an early campaign disaster if the reception were hostile. After initial enthusiasm over the Senator's introductory remarks condemning the Nixon administration's unproductive Southeast Asian policies, the crowd settled into an awesome 30-minute silence for the remainder of the address.

Matters were complicated further by the appearance, midway through the speech, of a half dozen or more marginal student types bearing black flags of anarchy. Rumors on campus had it that they intended to trash the place. Staff members present, Weil, Martin, Stearns, and myself, took up positions along the outside aisles, front and back, and prepared to do serious combat with the anarchists when they made their move. Tension grew as the black-flag boys shuffled back and forth across the back of the hall, feinting and dodging like red-dogging linebackers. Finally, after endless minutes of this charade, something refrigerated their ardor (I doubt that it was our presence; we didn't look fierce enough to do serious damage or straight enough to be Secret Service) and they retreated.

The Senator ended his detailed China proposal and sat down. Seconds seemed to tick until, finally, the crowd rose spontaneously and applauded for minutes. The Senator seemed pleasantly startled and the staff was overjoyed.

It was, in many respects, one of the most remarkable events of the entire campaign. McGovern had once again made the bold move that many of his colleagues wanted to make, but dared not. Within days of launching a Presidential campaign, he had delivered a forceful, controversial, and innovative foreign policy statement that was bound to evoke ripples of response for months to come. And he had chosen not New Haven or Cambridge, but Stockton, California, as the forum. The excitement of the audience at having witnessed this speech was a tribute both to McGovern's courage and foresight in reading the mood of the people of the country on this issue accurately, and to the basic intelligence of the audience itself.

The speech had even greater ramifications politically. Realizing that the McGovern candidacy was indeed a high-risk venture, we readily accepted the Senator's judgment that the so-called "centrist" candidates were vulnerable to a very honest and direct tactic: force the issues; don't let the race be decided on personalities or image or "charisma"; make the other candidates take stands on controversial and important subjects.

The concept was both simple and sound. Periodically, McGovern would deliver a heavy speech or answer a tough question at a press conference. His position on the controversial subject would eventually receive relatively wide coverage. Then the press would be constrained to question other real or potential candidates on the subject to determine primarily whether this was a matter upon which various contenders disagreed and was, therefore, a real campaign issue that the press and the voters could sink their respective teeth into. The other candidates would be faced with the tough choice of agreeing with McGovern, thus making him look imaginative and leaderlike, or avoiding the matter or taking a hesitant stand, thus making themselves appear cautious and political. Finally, the strategy of voluntarily bringing difficult problems to the surface and providing imaginative answers permitted the Senator to control the course and direction of the campaign; he could determine, to a large degree, the boundaries of the campaign arena; he could define the issues upon which the nomination, and perhaps the general election, would be decided.

This strategy was not a political gimmick. It was an approach to campaigning for public office that had suited McGovern for years in South Dakota and still suited his approach to the national issues of the day. It was also the kind of campaign which would do most to enlighten the electorate, to lift the level of public debate and to prevent the 1972 election from being merely a battle of media technicians.

As it turned out, the Senator had even more adventurous ideas in mind. He had mentioned to me earlier that he would like to be first American public figure inside mainland China and casually asked my judgment. At the time, it was a stunning proposal. I suggested that it would obviously help confirm his qualifications in the field of foreign affairs and provide fantastic public exposure, but I wondered whether it might not also give ammunition to those who considered his attitudes toward our policies in Southeast Asia unpatriotic already. He indicated that he was sure someone was going to get into China fairly soon and he wanted to be the one. It was clear, he said, that all our attitudes about China had to change, that the possibilities of substantial trade between the United States and China were so great that someone had to take the lead and start breaking down the barriers.

In the audience in Stockton was the wife of Edgar Snow, probably the foremost American journalist writing on Chinese affairs, who was in China at that time (he has since died). The Senator asked me before his speech to find Mrs. Snow in the audience and arrange a brief, private meeting between them following his address. During that meeting the Senator discussed with Mrs. Snow the possibility of getting her husband's assistance in obtaining the necessary approval from the Chinese government to enter the country. His efforts continued very quietly for the next several months, with little tangible results, until July 15, 1971, when Nixon made his startling announcement that, in fact, *he* was going to China. McGovern's reaction to that announcement was one of frustration, the same kind he had felt with the Muskie election-eve television speech; he seemed fated to imagine dramatic strokes that other men had an opportunity to carry out.

The Nixon China announcement was one of a number of periodic reminders that the ultimate opponent was indeed the incumbent President. All that has preceded in this account of the McGovern campaign might give the impression that we were fixated on the task of defeating other Democrats for the nomination. The fact is that anyone seeking the Presidency of the United States must engage in two distinct campaigns, the nomination race and the general election race.

It is a mistake to refer to this accomplishment or that mistake of "the campaign" without specifying which campaign. As will later become apparent, the McGovern nomination campaign was materially different in many respects from the McGovern general election campaign. They must be considered and judged separately.

The most obvious difference between them is their duration. The nomination campaign lasted more than two years, the general election campaign scarcely 90 days. The nomination campaign for us was guerrilla warfare—scattered, ragtag troops, minutemen, roving bands of citizen volunteers, the people of Russia plaguing and harassing Napoleon's élite corps. The general election campaign was heavy artillery, panzer divisions, massive, clanking movements of cumbersome weapons, mechanized, unwieldly warfare. One campaign was a lifetime that seems, in retrospect, a brief, brilliant moment. The other lasted only days but now seems to have been interminable.

The campaign for the nomination was waged against overwhelming odds. For some twenty months after the 1968 Democratic convention that nomination was little more than an idea carried around in the mind of one man, George McGovern. Then, for the twenty-four months following the spring of 1970, he shared that idea with a meager staff and relatively few supporters around the country. Contrary to some of the latter-day prophets who emerged in June, 1972, claiming to have had the vision all along, McGovern had been scoffed at as the Democratic nominee for almost four years.

Now, particularly in light of the defeat in the 1972 election, our campaign's accomplishments leading up to the Democratic convention seem relatively inconsequential. This has led the second-guessers and post-election authorities to wonder why, earlier in 1972, prior to the convention, this move wasn't made or that step wasn't taken in preparation for the fall campaign. One fact, however, remains: for those inside the campaign, the contest for the nomination was a consuming, exhausting, uphill struggle whose outcome—because of the last-ditch, kamikaze efforts of a die-hard element in the party—remained in question until the opening night of the convention itself. There was, in fact, not time in which the security of having won the nomination prior to the convention permitted unencumbered preparation for the general election campaign.

In spite of the pressures of preparing for the convention, its politics, and its massive logistics, plans were made for the general election campaign, and fairly elaborate plans they were. We were very aware of, and properly awed by, the incredible task that lay ahead in the fall. But the very process of making the plans had its price in terms of preparation for the convention and the immediate responsibilities of the nomination. In circumstances of limited political manpower, every investment of energy involved energy not spent somewhere else. All this is simply to say that, although this description and analysis of the events leading up to the nomination will give the impression of an all-consuming venture— and rightly so, we were always aware, dimly or clearly, of the greater task that lay beyond if we were successful in obtaining the nomination.

FEBRUARY, 1971

The next major visit to a vital primary state, following the late January journey through California, was the first formal campaign swing through

New Hampshire. Earlier, in December 1970, I had made my third reconnaissance trip into the state and had spent time talking to a number
of leading Democrats. I consulted at length with Joe Grandmaison, largely
on the recommendation of State Chairman Harry Makris who had earlier
assured me that Grandmaison would be far and away the best young
political organizer we could find in New Hampshire. We wanted to find
a regional coordinator for New England; someone who could undertake
in New England the arduous task then being performed by Gene Pokorny
in the Midwest, of traveling throughout the region recruiting supporters
and beginning to set up statewide campaign organizations. Despite a
widespread reputation for volatility and impatience with human frailty
(i.e., stupidity), Grandmaison fit all the other requirements perfectly,
particularly with respect to his knowledge of New Hampshire politics
and people. In our discussions in December, I raised this possibility somewhat indirectly and Grandmaison did not dismiss it out of hand. Within
a matter of weeks, the Muskie people apparently had similar ideas and
approached Grandmaison with a variation of the same proposal. Although
he had not determined by February which candidate to support, when I
contacted him after the first of the year he was willing to arrange a four-
day visit by McGovern in New Hampshire and Massachusetts.

And, typical of many later Grandmaison trips, he knew how to make a
candidate work. Accompanied by a dozen members of the national press
corps whose leads, I imagine, were written before leaving Washington
("Believe it or not, the 1972 campaign is already underway. Senator
George McGovern today brought his longshot candidacy into the earliest
primary state; one year ahead of schedule," etc.), the Senator had a New
Hampshire schedule that went as follows:

Wednesday, February 24, 1971

9:00 P.M.	Lv. National Airport
10:00	Ar. Logan Airport, Boston
	Drive to Sheraton Wayfarer Inn, Bedford, N.H.

Thursday, February 25, 1971

8:00–8:45 A.M.	Private breakfast, Wayfarer
8:45–9:15	Drive from Bedford to Concord
9:30–10:00	Press conf., State House, Concord
10:00–11:00	Brunch with Democratic members
11:00–11:15	Introduction to N.H. General Court (Assembly)
11:25–12:00	Rest, Concord
12:00– 1:15 P.M.	Luncheon with Concord area Democratic leaders

1:30– 2:00	Drive from Concord to Antrim
2:05– 2:20	Reception with Nathaniel Hawthorne College officials
2:30– 3:30	Seminar at Nathaniel Hawthorne College
3:40– 4:45	Drive from Antrim to Durham (On the way across the state, the Senator did some ad hoc handshaking and self-introductions in one small town and had spectacular success; one man recognized him.)
5:00– 5:45	Interview at Channel 11–Durham
6:00– 6:25	Rest, Durham
6:30– 8:00	Dinner at New England Center–Univ. of N.H.
8:15–10:00	Reception at Bob Craig's home
10:00–11:00	Drive from Durham to Bedford (During which McGovern made a semi-serious monologue about the fundamental weakness of his staff: "Not one of these guys has a sense of humor; I can't get one funny line out of any of them to use in my speeches. I don't know why they can't come up with just one joke or funny comment, but they sure are at a loss." I was doubled up in the front seat.)

Friday, February 26, 1971

7:30– 8:00 A.M.	Drive from Bedford to Nashua
8:00– 9:00	Breakfast with Nashua Democratic leaders
9:00– 9:30	Drive from Nashua to Bedford
9:30–10:30	Meeting with McGovern supporters in state (Most of the ten or so people there indicated their willingness to commit to a McGovern candidacy if they received assurances that we were serious about the effort and would allocate substantial amounts of money and the candidate's time. This group became the nucleus of the McGovern campaign in New Hampshire.)
10:45–11:45	Handshaking tour of Elm Street, Manchester
12:00– 1:15 P.M.	Luncheon at Sheraton-Carpenter hotel
1:30– 4:00	Telephoning political leaders from state hdqt.
4:00– 4:45	Interview at WMUR Channel 9, Manchester
5:00– 5:30	Rest
5:30– 5:45	Drive from Manchester to Bedford
5:45– 7:15	Dinner at Lamplighter with potential supporters
7:30– 9:30	Seminar at St. Anselm's College, Goffston (Over 800 in attendance, as opposed to fewer than 100 for

McCarthy a few weeks before the 1968 primary;
good omen.)

9:45–10:30   Reception at Lamplighter for Democrats
10:30–10:45   Drive to Wayfarer

Saturday, February 27, 1971

8:30– 9:00 A.M.   Drive from Bedford to Salem, Mass.
9:00–10:00   Breakfast with Salem Democratic leaders
10:00–11:00   Drive from Salem to Framingham, Mass.

I talked to the Senator about recruiting Grandmaison as a full-time
staff member and, worn-out but pleased with his efficiency and wide
contacts in the New Hampshire party, the Senator agreed we should get
him if we could. On the drive from Salem to Framingham, the Senator
asked Grandmaison to join us, and he did so willingly. Thereafter he operated as McGovern's man in New England. As with Gene Pokorny, and
eventually the other regional coordinators, the design was for him to
focus his attention more and more on his key primary state—New Hampshire—toward the end of 1971 and take over day-to-day operations of the
New Hampshire campaign after the first of the year.

The New Hampshire trip was the first in which we had significant
traveling press coverage and it led me to wonder what political reporters
do between campaigns. As the reporters boarded the plane, there was
grousing and grumbling all around about what American politics was
coming to when people started running for the Presidency more than
a year before they should, forcing them, solid home-loving citizens, to
tromp around the countryside, particularly in such God-awful places as
New Hampshire, when all they really wanted to do was stay in Washington where things were calm and life was easy. Aboard the plane, coats
off, ties loose, drinks served, card games underway, it was a transforma-
tion—reluctant Sunday School pupils released, spring training at a football camp, an American Legion convention, the seasonal convocation of
a ripened circus troop. Stewardesses were importuned: "C'mon, Linda,
just gimme your Boston phone number!"; previous adventures were recalled: "Hey, Julie, remember the time we came up here with Goldwater
and his car got stuck?"; old bets were resurrected; "When are you going
to pay me the twenty you owe me on the Goldberg race?" A number of
the good ones came along: the reserved Broder, the ebullient Germond;
the droll Witcover; the crafty but bloodless Biosatt, huddled (as he
would be regardless of temperature) under undetermined layers of sweat-
ers, mufflers, and overcoats. All, it turned out despite the grumbled pro-

tests, clearly were relieved that someone had finally invented the perpetual campaign.

MARCH, 1971

During March, McGovern made major trips to Wisconsin and Michigan. The evolution of the campaign in the crucial state of Wisconsin, like those in the other key states, was a remarkable triumph of sacrifice, persistence, commitment, and quiet heroism. Gene Pokorny first started working seriously in December, 1970 contacting the few names he had and learning the political landscape in Wisconsin. One of his first contacts was a young attorney in Milwaukee, Bill Dixon, who had, on his own, begun some months earlier to make tentative steps to create a McGovern organization in the state. Dixon had written our headquarters in the fall offering to help and we had given his name to Gene. When they met, Dixon told Gene: "I would do anything to help McGovern because I have been following him on the war for two years or so and found him to always have been out front on the war and think he is the only one honest and courageous enough to really end it." Dixon and Gene, it turned out, had more in common than their mutual goal of electing McGovern—they shared common sense, anonymity, pragmatism, and commitment. Dixon again: "*Everything*—personal interests, egos, money, family—was secondary to electing George McGovern—a decent, courageous, honest man—President." When Gene established his Midwest regional base in Wisconsin in February, 1971, Dixon invited him to live in his home, to save the campaign money, which Gene did for more than a year until after the Wisconsin primary. "When Gene left in April, 1972, my kids couldn't figure it out. He was like a second father to them," Dixon says.

Dixon was an archetype of the McGovern volunteer. There were dozens, if not hundreds, of Bill Dixons, men and women, around the country. Tens of thousands of others worked under their leadership. Dixon's professional life, his status in his law firm, and undoubtedly his personal and social life, suffered greatly from his involvement in the campaign. In a variety of ways, that involvement cost him money. And most of all, that investment of time and personal resources occurred over an unprecedented length of time—in Dixon's case, as well as for many others, a year and a half on the Wisconsin primary alone. Many other people have given of their energies for several months in previous Presidential campaigns. But rarely in American political history have so many given so much for so long with so little interim reward. These elements of patience, endurance, persistence, and conviction distinguished the McGovern citizen leaders across the country. They are qualities which characterized the

McGovern campaign and which will have a profound impact on national politics in the future.

People like Bill Dixon were so valuable to the McGovern campaign because they worked cooperatively with and under the direction of the staff level leadership of the campaign, the regional and later state coordinators; because they were sane and sensible, refusing to fall prey to the traditional ideologue's diseases of perpetual dialectic and debate and blood-testing of the candidate to ensure his ideological purity; because they were not above honest, but unglamorous, work—raising money, getting out mailings, drafting press releases, raising rally crowds, getting leaflets distributed, patiently and with good humor indoctrinating endless numbers of volunteers; because they were not particularly concerned about personal reward or publicity, being satisfied to remain anonymous but effective; and because, finally, they did not automatically assume, on the basis of unfortunate past experience, that those of us in Washington were incompetent or their enemies or both.

Eventually there came to be many Dixons, but meantime the structure was thin. With Gene driving, the Senator in his usual spot in the front seat and Dixon and Pat Donovan, the Senator's secretary in the back, the one-car McGovern campaign caravan set out across Wisconsin on March 5, 1971. The Senator held an airport press conference upon arriving at Milwaukee's Mitchell Field, spoke at the Marquette University student union, flew to Madison for a later afternoon press conference and dinner with uncommitted Governor Pat Lucey, addressed over 4,000 whooping, cheering students at the annual Wisconsin Student Association symposium in Madison, and attended a reception sponsored by the Dane County Democratic Party. The next day the Senator flew to Waussau for another press conference and a lunch with Marathon County Democrats, then to Waukesha to speak to the annual Waukesha County Democratic dinner that night. On Sunday, the Senator had a morning meeting with area labor leaders back in the Milwaukee area, attended a luncheon in Racine, then went back to Milwaukee for a meeting with black leaders and a public reception. He wound up the trip at a dinner with members of the Milwaukee County Democratic executive committee.

Gene's scheduling of events on this trip is a perfect example of our long-range campaign attitude and formula: at every opportunity, particularly early in the campaign, meet with party regulars at the state and local levels to assure them that the McGovern candidacy is in the mainstream of Democratic Party traditions and not a radical fringe operation. These meetings took place in each state time and time again. Such meetings and contacts, both by the candidate and the field staff, are one of a number of proofs that, contrary to later mythology, the McGovern campaign, both in the nomination and general election races, was not anti-Democratic Party and, in fact, made extraordinary efforts not to alienate the party regulars. Typically, the national staff sent out over 1,000 letters in advance of the trip inviting members of various Democratic groups to meet with the Senator and discuss his candidacy.

Of the Senator's campaign style, a *Milwaukee Journal* reporter wrote: "In Wisconsin, he showed himself to be an able person-to-person campaigner, shaking hands at a comfortable pace and taking time to chat with individual questioners—time he can afford at this stage of the campaign." The *Chicago Tribune* reported that McGovern was beginning to broaden his political base from merely an anti-war constituency to one which included labor, through his treatment of economic issues, taxes, inflation, and unemployment, and farmers, by attention to agricultural issues. The Senator was encouraged, as he was by almost every visit to Wisconsin, by the enthusiastic reception and the possibility of an upset victory.

In mid-March the Senator delivered an address at the Central Baptist Church in Atlanta, a rousing, emotional, evangelical appeal for racial harmony and social justice. The Senator's advisor on preparation of this speech/sermon was the Rev. Walter Fauntroy (soon to become the first non-voting Congressman from the District of Columbia) and it left little question in the minds of those who heard it that McGovern could speak with passion when it was called for. The speech was heavily responsive in style. It called for the Senator to chant a theme—"Come Home America" —and the crowd to answer with some similar refrain. Yancey Martin positioned himself near the most vocal elders and, at the proper moments, bellowed "Come Home America" in response to McGovern. The congregation quickly picked it up and the closing portions of the speech sounded like a revival meeting.

MAY, 1971

The May schedule included a trip to Ohio, then back to Washington for a speech to the Women's National Democratic Club, to California for speeches on the Berkeley campus and at the Constitutional Rights Foundation, then across the country to New York for the Westchester County Democratic Dinner. On May 11th the Senator campaigned in the northern New Hampshire town of Berlin and delivered a speech that night in Nashua. The following day he addressed a joint session of the Massachusetts legislature and spoke to the World Affairs Council in Boston. On the 15th he flew to Chicago for an Amalgamated Clothing Workers dinner, then went on to Milwaukee for the Wisconsin State Democratic Party dinner. The next day was spent campaigning in Groton, Connecticut, with the local Boilermakers Union, and in New Haven with a major address sponsored by the Yale Political Union. Later in the month, the Senator made one more appearance in Chicago and spent three days among his constituents in South Dakota.

At the Wisconsin dinner, our state organization pulled off something of a coup. The dinner, which attracted well over 1,000 leading Wisconsin Democrats as well as McGovern, Muskie, Bayh, and Hughes, was being awarded meticulous scrutiny by the state press corps to determine which of the candidates and potential candidates evoked the most party enthusiasm. To guarantee equal treatment for all, Governor Lucey instructed his dinner chairman to bring them all into the dinner together through a side door near the dais, thus preventing any singular demonstration. McGovern would unavoidably be delayed, and special arrangements were made for our staff to deliver him to the rear door where he would be met by the dinner chairman and brought without fanfare to his place on the dais. Pokorny, Dixon & Co. had other ideas in mind. Dixon describes what happened:

We had all our McGovern supporters at the dinner take aisle seats so if we could get him in the front door they could stand up and applaud and shake hands with him as he went by thus slowing him down. Next, I gave the band leader a $50 bill and told him that when I gave him a signal he was to start playing "Happy Days are Here Again" NO MATTER WHAT THE HELL WAS HAPPENING AT THE HEAD TABLE. When McGovern arrived in Gene's car with Gene and me, we parked quite a ways away so I could go up first. Gene and the Senator were to follow me in 30 seconds. I went up to the front door where the dinner chairman was pacing back and forth to head off McGovern and spirit him in a back door. I gave a signal to Walter Kelly whose job it was to distract the chairman and get him out of there. He did it great. Then I went inside and gave some of our people a signal. In seconds McGovern came in the front door. Muskie was in the middle of a speech on how he would end the Vietnam war; he had been talking for about five minutes. All of a sudden, in mid-sentence, the damn band cuts him off playing "Happy Days"—McGovern walks in—our people jump up applauding and shaking McGovern's hand. Lucey was FURIOUS—at the band, at his dinner chairman—but not at McGovern. He really thought McGovern's people had pulled off a coup. We turned a non-candidate, $100-a-plate dinner with 1,000 leading Democrats one year before the primary, into a McGovern rally—at Lucey's expense. As a politician for 25 years, he secretly admired what we had done. From that time on Democrats in Wisconsin knew we were not really the amateurs they thought we were.

And neither apparently did Governor Lucey who became, after the Wisconsin primary, one of the Senator's most effective supporters among elected officials and who picked Dixon as his legal counsel after the election.

We moved from our original headquarters on Maryland Avenue to much larger space at 410 First Street, S.E., in Washington. The move was necessitated by additional staff, primarily for our growing direct-mail operation and the evolution of our regional desk system. We remained at the First Street location through the convention in July, 1972.

The selection of the First Street headquarters space, a windowless, airless, Alamo-like bunker on the socially marginal fringe of Capitol Hill, between a liquor store and a carry-out sandwich shop, was significant for one reason. It represented, perhaps symbolized, our continuing awareness that our campaign was unconventional and non-traditional; that to take headquarters in the commercial/professional heart of Washington, as most Presidential campaigns did, would somehow jeopardize its mood of class-lessness, democracy, and insurgency, its spirit of parity and egalitarianism, its élan. The McGovern campaign headquarters was once compared by Gordon Weil to an Israeli ministry—spartan, lacking in grace and style, but also lacking in neckties, indicia of rank, and pretension.

In his *History of the American People,* Samuel Eliot Morison describes the concessions made by the Continental Congress to democratic social conditions in raising the first Continental army to fight the British. Differences in pay and privileges between officers and enlisted men were substantially narrowed, and fraternization, particularly among the New England line regiments and the hardy frontier units, was common. Morison notes that one result of this was to render officer recruitment difficult. In perhaps the same kind of way, some party regulars—used to strict command and control traditions in politics—felt uneasy toward our "people's" campaign. In the First Street headquarters, the campaign leadership was readily accessible to whoever might wish to discuss an idea, a grievance, a conflict. The atmosphere lent itself to a sense of participation and openness. These virtues were later to be mistaken by veterans of more traditional campaigns and a few reporters insensitive to the changing structure of American politics as chaos, confusion, or disorganization. They mistook lack of neatness for lack of efficiency.

JUNE, 1971

The completion of the intense spring travel schedule brought another of the campaign's cycles to a close and permitted a period of self-evaluation. It was now five months since McGovern announced his candidacy and a full year since our maiden trip to New Hampshire. The Senator had thought about a Presidential campaign for two years. Then, having set it in motion, he had appeared in almost two dozen states in the fall of 1970 for other Democratic candidates and had traveled into almost that many states in the winter and spring of 1971 on his own behalf. What was his attitude now?

McGovern was never a man for concentrated philosophizing or introspection concerning his own campaign. After Joe Dolan and others had shut down the valve of the campaign as an educational process and worthy social endeavor in and of itself, there was little articulated, comprehensive analysis of the "meaning" of our efforts. It was too early to decide whether we were winning or losing, though there were precious few signs we were winning.

George McGovern, is, if anything, a man who is not easily discouraged. His single strongest characteristic is his belief in himself. Throughout this long, trying, troublesome year, he gave no reason to believe that he wished he had not decided to run or, moreover, that he doubted his ability to triumph. I am sure both thoughts must have occurred to him, perhaps over and over. But, to my knowledge, he confessed them to no one. His determination came, morally, from his extreme opposition to the war and, politically, from ambition—that special desire to lead and govern without which no man can endure the hardships of a Presidential campaign. The two impulses managed to get him through many long nights and saw him through countless homogeneous receptions, inane conversations, unenlightening interviews, dreary advice and harangues, unproductive appearances. He exhibited tenacious goodwill, patience, endurance, and stubbornness.

Occasionally, his down-to-earth quality encouraged more loquacious, demonstrative, and extroverted types to impose themselves upon him to his own detriment. He suffered fools too gladly. He often listened to people who wasted his time by their own ignorance or by telling him something he already knew. He found it very difficult to shut people off. By his own admission, he considered rudeness the cardinal sin. This made tolerance and patience cardinal virtues. Many people, particularly friends, escaped unprosecuted for the theft or murder of his time.

Although the McGovern campaign never flourished on meetings, too many of those meetings which were held consumed too much time, and too many voices at them expressed too many bad ideas or repeated ideas already expressed. I suspect those meetings also involved the candidate in too much therapy for too many people. McGovern spent much of his time bolstering, fathering, brothering, encouraging, and consoling his own friends, supporters, contributors, and staff. Often he seemed to resemble a circus owner who, besides being ringmaster, also served as confessor to the clowns, counselor to the acrobats, money-lender to the roustabouts, currier of the horses, groomer of the bears, waterer of the elephants, and tamer of the cats.

He is a man about whom it was uniformly said: he is good, he is kind, he is decent—above all else, decent. After a while it seemed that "decent" was his first name or at least an earned title, like Reverend: Decent George McGovern. And, in its usual, most positive definition, he was all of that—kind, obliging, generous. But decent has a passive, almost negative meaning as well; one which, ironically enough, applies almost more to his opponent Richard Nixon. Decent means: "conforming to recognized standards of propriety." Thus, a one-dimensional conformist more concerned with manners, with conventional, acceptable behavior, than with change or invention. Rigid. Richard Nixon most assuredly. George McGovern never. After all, which candidate told a heckler to kiss his ass?

Strike "decent." McGovern always resented the public image that he was a plodding, colorless, conventional, predictable, introverted, humorless, cautious milquetoast. Who wouldn't? It was an approximate description of his archfoe, the incumbent President. In the early days, Pete McCloskey was described as the tough, jut-jawed Marine officer who opposed the war. It galled McGovern. "Why doesn't anybody ever say," he asked, "'tough George McGovern, former World War II bomber pilot?'" George McGovern is a complex man concealed behind the veneer of a simple man. Like most complex men, he chooses not to display those characteristics that make him so. He thought his toughness was demonstrated amply in his acceptance and survival of campaign vicissitudes. He was often puzzled, and distressed, that reporters didn't adequately perceive and relay his humor. He is a proud man, and he is independent. That pride and independence, combined with an essential shyness and reservation, set him apart, perhaps estranged him, from many of his colleagues. So much so that only after he had received the nomination did one or two of his earlier Democratic opponents, particularly Senator Muskie, really get to know him.

Like most men of any stature whatsoever, McGovern had weaknesses. He suffered from an occasional bout of Churchillian laziness. Not sloth— for his mind was always working—but a desire for physical immobility, particularly when it came to keeping up the backbreaking, unrelenting schedule. He also hated telephones, particularly when there was another politician on the other end. His reluctance traced to a combination of reservation and discomfort with small talk. Or, as someone said: "George McGovern reads the morning papers for information; Ted Kennedy reads it to see who he should call that day."

But the most difficult characteristic was the Senator's approach to problems of people—friends, staff, supporters. His tendency was to resolve such a problem by telling the supplicant what he or she wanted to hear or, since many of these problems had to do with authority, responsibility, title, or position, by constructing an organizational solution that was inevitably and inherently unworkable. It was a way out of difficult, annoying, irksome personality problems. It was a sad case of an unfortunate trait being reinforced by unfortunate experience. The Senator found it next to impossible to refuse to listen to someone who worked for him or supported him. But this tendency was a weakness only on a personal level, because McGovern was not averse to telling the Senate, an electorate, or an entire nation what it did not want to hear.

In addition, he had, in effect, been his own campaign manager in five statewide campaigns in South Dakota; he was not accustomed to delegating absolute authority, even in the area of internal organization. How much grief he could have saved himself simply by saying: "I'm sorry. You will have to talk to Gary (or X) about it. He handles those things." Heartless? Perhaps. But it is the only way to run an organization, particularly a campaign. It was next to impossible to make a decision stick so long as almost everyone—staff member, contributor, or media consultant—knew that there was an automatic appeal on almost every question to the candidate himself. The more widespread this knowledge became, the more appeals were taken to the Senator. Rarely did an appellant inform the candidate that the campaign manager had already ruled on the matter. And often the candidate didn't bother to ask. Thus, on many occasions I had the extremely uncomfortable experience of learning that I had been over-ruled on a particular question before I knew it was even under debate.

This was the source of much of what the press perceived as disorganization, especially during the general election campaign. What was thought to be the noise of confusion was really the sound of a well-conceived, organized campaign being subverted by the rush to get the candidate's ear for approval of this idea or that project or some other scheme. I take my share of the responsibility for this problem. That blame must result, at least in part, from my failure to instill enough confidence in the candidate to break down the conditioned ways of doing things, the tendency for the candidate to make organizational and personnel decisions. Had that kind of confidence existed (and I am not yet sure it could have with anyone) decision-making would have been simpler and the impression of internal confusion much less.

But even as minor personality crises came and went, things had improved—for a change—on the financial front. Much of the pressure created in the pre-announcement period of the campaign had been alleviated by the unqualified success of the announcement-letter fund appeal. This was unquestionably the first financial turning point of our campaign. I cannot imagine surviving politically through 1971 under the financial restrictions of 1970. Without additional financing we undoubtedly would have faced the same starvation conditions encountered by the Hughes and Harris campaigns as they set out, like wagon trains on the desert, for the promised land.

By the standards under which we were then operating, the returns from the more than 250,000 letters sent were nothing less than spectacular. In the first three weeks of February we received $305,000. This money financed the campaign through the middle of 1971. It was crucial for two reasons: it permitted us to expand our staff capabilities to a level necessary for a respectable pre-primary Presidential campaign, and it demonstrated that a national McGovern constituency did exist whose convictions were strong enough to lend financial as well as political support. Other mailings went out, our list of contributors continued to grow, and the facts behind this fund-raising effort were reported as we released them. But the political implications—that there were a lot of people out there who believed in McGovern strongly enough to send him money—were never adequately explored by the press.

Unlike struggling prospectors who strike it rich, we didn't rush out and buy many of the things we had wanted for so long. The money was stored and carefully budgeted. We did, however, begin to make much-needed staff additions. In the three months after the announcement we spent $79,000. By July, 1971, our monthly budget had risen to $75,000, and for the period from the announcement through the end of July we spent $262,000, of which $63,000 went into the direct-mail fund-raising effort.

We discovered very early that the rules of campaign financing were going to be much different in 1972 than in any previous Presidential year. In other years candidates had been able to run up immense debts with airlines, telephone companies, hotel chains, printers, and car-rental companies. Because these debts became so large in 1968 and were not paid off, these traditional campaign creditors resolved that they would refuse to carry the 1972 candidates, regardless of who they were. No more dice rolling on a potential friend in the White House. Cash in advance or c.o.d. became the rule. The creditors were very tough. The telephone company was particularly heartless. It required awesome deposits, far in excess of any bill we could accumulate—at one point our deposit amounted to more than $40,000.

Through 1971, operating costs continued to rise, cash was demanded, and we were constantly strained, despite the success of the direct mail effort. By September, we were spending $158,000 a month, of which $53,000 was going into direct-mail expenses. An analysis of the budget from February 1st, 1971, through September 30th, 1971 reveals the following allocations: national operations—$172,308 (staff, travel, overhead); field operations—$85,419 (staff, travel, headquarters); special group operations—$31,643 (staff, travel); candidate activities—$29,787 (scheduling and advance staff, staff and candidate travel); political intelligence and research—$13,175 (staff); advertising and promotion—$44,637 (materials, design); fund-raising activities—$4,934; direct mail—$162,021 (production and computer costs).

One of the many unsung heroes of the campaign was John W. "Bill"

Branner, a Washington accountant who single-handedly assumed the monumental task of keeping the books and records from 1970 through much of the nomination race. Bill Branner made no demands, did not possess an ego which required massaging and never sought to counsel the candidate; he went quietly and efficiently about his work, trying to bring meaning out of chaos, and performed all his invaluable services without charge—an incredible contribution.

Throughout the spring of 1971, additional staff members were brought on board. Jeff Gralnick, a C.B.S. television producer, became the campaign press secretary through that year. Marian Pearlman, a Washington lawyer with a healthy sense of irony born of previous campaigns, became first the director of the national citizens organizations and then, throughout the winter of 1971 and all of 1972, the campaign treasurer—a loathsome and unrewarding job which she managed with skill and tolerance. Steven Robbins brought to the job of campaign scheduler the kind of demonic fury and marginal hysteria often necessary to survive that experience, and made of the scheduling and advance operations a minor Faulknerian kingdom within a kingdom. Ed O'Donnell, a Harvard Divinity School dropout who managed to amalgamate political pragmatism with an existence along the margin of the counterculture, joined the campaign early and became director of student operations during the long period when idealistic students thought McGovern was too conventional and pragmatic students thought he couldn't win. Amanda Smith, who initially relieved me of scheduling responsibilities and then organized the women's division of the campaign, graduated ultimately to the role of full-time field organizer. Three additional regional coordinators were added in the field: Joel Swerdlow, a New Yorker and doctoral candidate from Cornell, joined us in the summer as the principal organizer in the industrial states—New Jersey, Pennsylvania, Ohio, Michigan, Indiana, and Illinois; Ron Field, like Swerdlow a graduate student and political activist, became the regional coordinator in the Northwest, organizing the campaign effort in Washington, Oregon, Idaho, and eastern Montana. Natividad "Nat" Chavira, an unassuming but highly industrious and effective Southern California educator, became our key organizer and contact with the Spanish-speaking communities in the Southwest—California, Arizona, New Mexico, Texas, and Colorado.

By mid-1971, we had developed a "desk" system under Rick Stearns' immediate direction. This consisted at first of five and then six people who were responsible for day-to-day communications and contact with the campaign in the several states in their respective areas. Their specific duties included negotiating the Senator's schedule of appearances, providing campaign materials when available, responding to routine mail and calls from the various states, discussing political problems in the state with our field organizers and state committees, and, most important, gathering every bit of political information and intelligence that could conceivably help the campaign.

Of particular importance was information concerning each state's delegate selection process: critical caucus and convention dates; the way the system worked and what its results were in 1968; who the 1968 convention delegates were, their political philosophies and attachments, and the likelihood of their running again; who controlled whom, what alliances or feuds existed, who wanted what, and which levers turned people off or on; who we wanted to attract or avoid. Names and more names—with as much data as possible on each—were indispensable for our organizational activities. They also formed the basis for the "trip books" prepared by the desk officers. These books, which accompanied the Senator on every trip, contained his schedule, political background on the areas to be visited and information on the key people he would meet. This is the kind of intelligence every candidate must have to be knowledgeable and personable with local political figures. The candidate must seem as naturally familiar with the local scene and personalities as possible without revealing that he has been boning up between stops.

The desk system proved superb. Our first desk officer was Judy Harrington, a bright, meticulously detailed Nebraskan, who vacuumed up political information in the Midwest and ultimately became Gene Pokorny's alter ego in Washington. She knew intuitively what her responsibilities were, and set a sort of pattern for the others who came along: Ted Pulliam for the South, Barbara MacKenzie for the Rocky Mountain and West coast states, Laura Mizel for the industrial states under Joel Swerdlow's direction, Alan Kriegel for New York and New England, and Scott Lilly for the border and central states. Each desk officer formed a jealous attachment to his or her region, arguing forcefully for more of the candidate's time, for more money, for more materials, for more attention. Legitimate efforts were made to convince us that primary states we considered impossible were indeed winable, that certain field staffers were incompetent and should be fired or were spectacular and should be promoted, or that particular supporters were certifiably insane and should be avoided like the plague.

The desk officers bore much of the brunt of complaints from the field staff and our state committees, the endless requests for money and for the poor, indivisible candidate. But most important, they amassed the political information which led to victories in the primaries and the selection of many delegates in the non-primary states.

By mid-1971 several refinements had been evolved in the tactics to carry out the basic left-centrist strategy developed a year before at Cedar Point. First, the essential development of a superior grassroots citizen-

McGovern, with Yancey Martin, on the campaign trail.

oriented, volunteer campaign organization around the country was underway. Enormous numbers of people had to be motivated to carry out the extensive direct voter contact program—through canvassing, phoning, and mailings—necessary to carry the important primary states and influence the delegate selection process in non-primary states. These vast numbers of volunteers would probably be new recruits to political activity. However, we were also trying to recruit experienced leadership from the 1968 Kennedy and McCarthy campaigns as well as from the regular party where possible, to direct these citizen efforts in the states.

Second, we were constructing a McGovern coalition of the Kennedy-McCarthy activists, the young, minority groups, anti-war organizations, women and others whose commitments to the principles of the Democratic Party generally outweighed the voice they had exerted in its affairs. This was a movement already in progress, seeking leadership after assassinations and rejections, and looking for someone with the kind of vision and courage necessary to question entrenched institutional assumptions. To a surprising degree, the disillusionment among this constituency was mirrored in the brooding anti-establishmentarianism of the so-called Wallace voters. This led us to believe, to a large degree rightly, that substantial elements of this blue-collar constituency could be added to the McGovern coalition.

Third, bridges were being built to the regular Democratic Party organization at all levels. But to the degree that we could not obtain regular party support, we were developing an insurgency campaign outside the regular structure to capture the nomination with this separate McGovern organization. Our example was the 1960 John Kennedy nomination race, but there was a major difference. In 1960 the Democratic Party contained a number of important power-brokers, without whose support neither Kennedy nor anyone else could have been nominated. These men—largely mayors, governors, and state party bosses—controlled substantial numbers of "uncommitted" delegates, i.e., delegates whom they could lever and direct. In 1960 Kennedy had to bargain with these brokers prior to the convention to get the nomination; in 1972 the reform rules permitted us to get a majority of the delegates in an open process without making any deals.

Fourth, we adopted the tactic of creating a steering committee in each state. This committee consisted of the early 1971 supporters who realized, in almost all cases, that as the campaign succeeded in 1972, new leaders, of sufficient stature to require recognition, would emerge. Therefore we decided to delay the formation of the official McGovern-for-President committees in most states.

Fifth, the system of regional organizers based in the field rather than Washington had already been developed. This was a crucial tactical, organizational move. It drastically reduced national-state conflicts and yet permitted us to control the course of the campaign in almost every state. It was also a vital element in our overall strategy of decentralization, of keeping the Washington operation small and flexible and placing the maximum manpower resources in the field, where they were needed.

JULY, 1971

The campaign turned a major corner with the addition of Frank Mankiewicz and Ted Van Dyk. Ted had extensive contacts throughout the Democratic Party from his days as an assistant to then Vice President Humphrey and as a key Humphrey campaign aide in 1964 and 1968. At the time he joined the campaign as a full-time advisor on a volunteer basis, Ted was managing his own consulting and congressional liaison firm in Washington. Frank had received recognition in 1968 as the Robert Kennedy campaign press secretary; to him had fallen the brutal assignment of briefing the press corps on the assassination.

Frank had helped McGovern during the brief 1968 Presidential campaign and the Senator valued his advice and counsel. In 1971, Frank was a partner with Tom Braden in a syndicated political newspaper column and was involved in a heavy lecture schedule around the country. The Senator's effort to get Frank to join the campaign succeeded in mid-1971. More than anyone else to that date, Frank gave the campaign's credibility a much-needed boost. It was a signal to many people that the campaign had to be taken seriously if a well-known, established political figure with close Kennedy identification would abandon a successful journalistic career to join the McGovern effort. It was taken as a sign by some, not nearly enough, that there might be more to the campaign than had previously met the eye, that perhaps Frank had perceived something that others had missed.

More political reporters began to spend time at the campaign headquarters. Some, affiliated with major national publications, had never before acknowledged the existence of the year-long campaign effort. Having been a journalist, Frank understood how to create the shadow of a doubt necessary to pique a reporter's imagination, to create a possibility which hadn't previously existed in the reporter's mind. And, of course, he introduced a much-needed feature into the public face of our campaign—an irrepressible, iconoclastic, inexhaustible sense of humor.

Frank's responsibilities included being official campaign "spokesman," advising the candidate on new ideas for speeches and appearances, supervising the press operation and providing political judgment and expertise in the preparation of issue papers and position statements. In short, he was to focus and sharpen the issues side of the campaign and make the campaign believable to the press and public at large.

Ted's role encompassed supervision of the scheduling and advance operation (now becoming fairly complex), developing coherent promotional materials, planning for our primary state media campaign, supervising the special divisions (minorities, youth, women), and assisting in financing and fund-raising projects. I continued in the capacity of overall campaign director, occupying the desk where the buck ultimately stopped. With some of the other operating areas now covered by Frank and Ted, I concentrated even more time on the state organizations.

By the summer of 1971 the campaign was beginning to need additional management capabilities to supervise day-to-day operations. Not only was I not resistant to sharing this load, but by this time fatigue was becoming so great that the appearance of highly qualified, seasoned campaign veterans like Frank and Ted was extremely welcome. I had known from the start that the day would come, and should come if we were successful, when older, more experienced leaders would arrive to help. Indeed, we needed all the help we could get. What was most surprising to me throughout the campaign was the scarcity of experienced talent available to McGovern, the limited number of people like Frank and Ted willing to make personal and professional sacrifices to help this extraordinary man become President. The heroes of the Kennedy and McCarthy campaigns were, except for people like John Douglas and Blair Clark, not available to us. If McGovern built an organization with unknown leaders such as Hart, Stearns, and Martin, it was not because he sought to by-pass established party pros; it was, rather, because, in large part, he had no choice—no one else believed in him strongly enough to make the commitment of time and effort.

Inevitably struggles over authority and chain of command arose, but the first contest occurred somewhat sooner than I expected.

Throughout the long previous year, the limitations on money had caused me to adopt a style of dealing with financial demands, particularly from the field, which combined imminent promise with cheerleading, exhortation, patience, and understanding of the plight of the local workers. I had spent too many months plugging up leaks and bailing out the boat, pleading and listening, to be blunt, abrupt, or demanding of people who labored continually near exhaustion. Somehow this style of operation led Ted and Frank to conclude that decisions were not being made. In late August they apparently approached the Senator with the plea that I be moved aside or down to save the campaign. The argument seemed to be that a tougher, more experienced campaign manager was needed. Sensing some agreement from McGovern, they made plans to accomplish the transition during a trip I was making with the Senator to my home state of Colorado.

I was already in Colorado advancing the trip when the Senator arrived. Gordon Weil, accompanying the Senator, had learned of calls between

Washington and the Senator to the effect that the coup was afoot. He took me aside to advise me to look to my flanks. Several calls to staff members in Washington confirmed that something was indeed going on. I promptly called both Ted and Frank and told them I would fight any efforts to upset the existing management arrangement and would do so directly with the Senator. After he completed a morning session at the World Methodist Convention being held in Denver, I met him at his suite in the Brooks Towers hotel and asked what was going on. He said that Ted and Frank questioned the procedures being used to manage the campaign and had suggested an arrangement whereby most policy decisions would be made by them and I would be relegated to carrying them out in the field.

We discussed at length the personalities involved and the implications of such a move for other staff members and the direction of the campaign. I repeated the position I had always taken, that I would willingly relinquish the responsibilities of campaign manager to anyone obviously better qualified. But I argued that both Ted and Frank had demonstrated approaches to campaigning and personalities that, in spite of their other attributes, were sure to guarantee at least as many problems for them as I faced; that the selection of one or both of them for the position I then held would not necessarily solve the problems the campaign faced—almost all of which involved money. The Senator then told me to continue as campaign manager and, frustrated with the complexities of the problem, told me to return to Washington as quickly as possible and "work it out with the others."

I cut short my Colorado trip, called Ted and told him to cancel a staff meeting scheduled in my absence, to announce the shift in leadership and arranged to meet with him and Frank to "work it out," as the Senator suggested. Upon arriving in Washington, I told them of the Senator's decision, and suggested that in the future such matters be discussed with all the principals present since McGovern, like most reasonable men, was subject to counter-arguments once they could be presented. I also strongly asserted that major shifts in leadership were best accomplished with all the people affected present and participating. In short, no behind-the-back maneuvering. That seemed to be that—at least for another two or three months.

SEPTEMBER, 1971

Senator McGovern determined that his efforts to lead the opposition to Nixon's Southeast Asian policies could best be served by a trip to that area with a stop in Paris to meet with representatives of the North Vietnamese. Hurried arrangements were made by Gordon Weil and John

Holum and they, together with Frank Mankiewicz, Pat Donovan, and a long-time McGovern friend, Joe Floyd, a South Dakota television executive, accompanied the Senator on the eleven-day trip.

The party left Washington on September 9th, arriving in Paris the following day. The Senator met with the North Vietnamese representatives to discuss primarily their terms for the release of United States prisoners of war. Arrangements for these discussions had been made by Pierre Salinger, who had been living in France for several years. The talks proved inconclusive, except to confirm the Senator's judgment that no prisoners would be released so long as the war continued and that, they would be released within a specified number of days only following an unconditional cease-fire instituted by the United States and South Vietnam.

On September 12th the party flew to Saigon. The Senator had been invited to meet with a group of political opponents to the Thieu regime in a Saigon church. Shortly after the Senator and his staff got there, the church came under attack from a hostile, rock-throwing crowd outside which threatened to set the place on fire and kill its occupants. The Senator and staff trapped inside were convinced that there was a good chance they would be seriously injured, and perhaps killed. A call to the Saigon police had no effect—according to one theory they were already present and re-enforcing the violent crowd. Finally, a desperation call to the United States embassy produced sufficient police to disperse the crowd and rescue the beleaguered group inside the church. While under seige, the Senator had picked up one of the larger rocks thrown through the church window, thinking to defend himself with it in the final crunch. Then, pondering the ridiculousness of a United States Senator and Presidential candidate standing in a Saigon church with a rock in his hand, he put the rock aside because, as he later said, "all I would do is break my damn hand with it."

Later that night a bomb exploded in a building adjoining the Senator's hotel; the staff was convinced that it was merely part of the pattern of harassment. The following day, McGovern met with General Thieu, and prior to discussing the issue of prisoner releases and cease-fires, accused Thieu of condoning the attack on the church the previous night. Thieu's defense was essentially that the Senator deserved what he got for conspiring with political dissidents and that he, Thieu, could not be responsible for McGovern's well-being in Saigon if he chose to mingle with opponents of the government. Needless to say, the discussion did not prove fruitful or productive.

On September 23rd, back in the United States, the Senator addressed the Washington Press Club on his Asian trip. The theme of his address was taken from an observation made by André Malraux, with whom the Senator had met in Paris. Malraux had remarked that the United States was attempting the impossible, to be a great power without a consistent foreign policy. After documenting our inconsistent policies toward China, Japan, Pakistan, and our European economic allies, the Senator returned to the theme that most, if not all, of our problems at home and abroad could be traced to Vietnam. Acknowledging the political risks to his own campaign in continuing to stress the war, he nevertheless concluded that it was responsible for many national ills and would not go away:

If it is a single-issue campaign it is becacuse the poor and the working man and those who live in our cities have been short-changed and made to pay for the immense distortion of our economy caused by war and defense, and are now being forced to pay for the remedy. ° ° °

Is credibility an issue in this campaign? Is it a matter of concern that Americans no longer trust their public officials? If it is . . . then it is because American administrations have fought a war and built up a defense establishment which they knew the people would not support if they knew the truth. ° ° °

Will the reordering of national priorities be an issue in the campaign? . . . If we are to pay for the things we must pay for and if we are to repair our society and play the role of a great power, then the priorities which must change are those which commit our assets and our resources to death and destruction. . . . The research and development which might have produced domestic items—or for that matter a decent rapid transit system—has been drained else-where. ° ° °

And so I have concluded that it is impossible to discuss any issue in this campaign without an awareness that it is part of that larger issue of which I spoke. What kind of people are we and how do we use what we have? And in the answer to that question lies the possibility that we might truly change America's course and finally bring her home.

Earlier in the summer, after months of accusations that he was a "one-issue candidate" and hours of advice that he had to demonstrate competence on other subjects and problems such as the state of the domestic economy, the Senator had summoned a half dozen reporters specializing in economic affairs into his office to announce that he intended to spend more time and attention on problems such as inflation, unemployment, wage and price spirals, and job safety. Did this mean he was abandoning the war as his major issue, he was asked. No, he replied, he merely intended to prove he was as well-rounded a candidate as any in the field, and that he knew something about a large number of Presidential topics. Predictably, the headlines read: "McGovern moves away from war theme: looks to economic issues to broaden support."

Predictably also, this produced uneasiness among those who had joined the McGovern ranks on the war issue. I think the Senator undertook the Vietnam trip, with the publicity it was sure to generate, as a means of quieting these apprehensions and demonstrating his continued commitment to leadership on ending the war. The net result, however, was to return his political posture to its starting point and eliminate the benefits received from the signals two months earlier that he was going to broaden his base.

The entire episode is significant because it highlights a persistent problem for the campaign. McGovern had risen to national prominence as an oponent of our involvement in Vietnam. It was the source of his image as a forthright, courageous, outspoken, "non-political" leader. Yet it was also the source of criticism that he was narrow and limited, a "one-issue candidate." Almost every move he made to broaden his field of interest was interpreted as an abandonment of his constituency and a purely political gesture to enhance his chances for the nomination and eventual election. He was unquestionably and endlessly trapped by the "one-issue candidacy" charge, on the one hand, and the charge of political motivation when he discussed other topics, on the other hand.

It proved what I began to understand about the public and press treatment of George McGovern—he was always held to a higher standard than other politicians. Like a minister's son, which he is, he was closely scrutinized for deviation, for the faintest hint of transgression or error. His every move was dissected, and it was assumed that he should be above the human motivations and the calculation that have marked the moves of other politicians. Like Billy Budd, he was judged too near perfection, and the Claggart in us all seeks to make of every stutter, every fault, the reason for perfection's ruin. Certainly a part of McGovern's stutter, his fatal flaw, was the tendency to reveal flatly and publicly his intentions, making them quite often seem more political than indeed they were and leaving him no room for later reversal. When he did reverse, as he seemed to with the Saigon trip and subsequent speech, it was perceived by the casual observer to be shifting, waffling, mind-changing, directionlessness. And this was the pattern which would prove so costly in 1972.

On his return from Vietnam, the Senator set off on yet another crowded series of campaign stops to key primary and non-primary states. These included extended tours through California, Florida, Nebraska, Wisconsin, Massachusetts, New Hampshire, Oregon, New York, and New Jersey. A number of these states were visited several times between late September and early December.

On the way to join the Senator at a Milwaukee appearance, I stopped on September 30th to meet with two Illinois supporters, Barbara Howarth from Chicago and Jim Hall, a downstate farmer from the Champaign-

Urbana area. After prolonged discussion, it was tentatively agreed that we would adopt a strategy of concentrating our organizational efforts on six Chicago-area suburban congressional districts and six downstate districts where we would run full or partial slates of committed McGovern delegates. They estimated that running this kind of limited primary effort would cost about $50,000, some of which could be raised in the state. I encouraged them to raise as much as possible in Illinois, since we planned to commit the limited money available to New Hampshire and Wisconsin and could not see a clear-cut victory in Illinois as the situation looked then. The Illinois political climate was always beclouded by the omnipresent Mayor of Chicago, who remained Sphinx-like throughout this period. A further complication was the bitter Democratic gubernatorial primary shaping up between Lt. Gov. Paul Simon and Dan Walker, a fight guaranteed to split McGovern supporters in the state. March 21st was still the day set for the Illinois primary, but there was consideration being given in the state's legislature to a date in April or May. We favored such a move to enable us to collect some initial political successes and, we hoped, gather enough money to run a respectable primary, something we were not equipped to do on a date earlier in March. I also discouraged the Senator from entering the preferential ballot, which had no binding effect and which would require an all-out media campaign—an expense sure to come from out of our New Hampshire-Wisconsin funds. That was a difficult position to argue, since the Senator always felt that Illinois was a favorable state for him. The debate on Illinois was to continue for several months inside the campaign.

After making contact with the traveling party in Milwaukee, I picked up Warren Beatty at the airport. Warren had met the Senator several times in Los Angeles, had offered to help and was asked to appear at several rallies in the Midwest. The first, on the night of September 30th at the University of Wisconsin—Milwaukee campus, turned out to be a circus. About 2,000 students jammed into the student union auditorium to be entertained by Floyd Westerman, Indian folk singer, and a raucous rock band called Sam Lay's Blues Revival. Electricity and madness mingled in the air as Warren tried to direct the crowd's thoughts to politics and to introduce the Senator. Fatigued by a flight from England and numbed by two hours in a New York dentist's chair, Warren was unable to cope with a belligerent claque, at the foot of the makeshift platform, stoned into anarchistic hostility toward the system and all its representatives—including politicians and actors. They set up a cacaphony that never gave Warren a chance. Finally introducing McGovern, and contemplating revenge at the following night's concert, Warren clambered down from the stage muttering, "wait'll I get my hands on those _____ _____ tomorrow night."

McGovern thanked all the entertainers, then laced into the hecklers for their treatment of his friend, whom he described as one of the finest young actors in America. He had written himself a note in early 1970 saying: "Identify with young people, but lead them—as Bobby did—don't capitulate to them as Gene did." Since rudeness angered him as much as ignorance in foreign policy, he was not about to capitulate under these circumstances. When the heckling continued, he challenged the ringleader to come up on the stage or shut up. The direct confrontation and distinct edge in McGovern's voice convinced the rabble-rousers that this man meant business, and they retreated.

Later, in a car heading back to the Sheraton-Schroeder Hotel, Milwaukee's monument to Willie Lohman, Matty Troy consoled Warren: that crowd, he said, was one of the toughest he had ever encountered. Troy, the Democratic leader of New York's borough of Queens, was a certified veteran of tough crowds. He was one of the earliest of a very small collection of major urban party regulars to endorse McGovern and had recently gone on the speaking circuit for the Senator. A day or two before, he had run into a hostile reception in an American Legion hall in Omaha where a member of the audience suggested that McGovern and probably everyone who supported him, including Troy, were communists. Troy, who looks and sounds like one of the guys who used to stand right behind James Cagney, reminded the Omaha heckler that McGovern flew 33 combat missions in World War II, crash-landed twice, and received the Silver Star; Troy also strongly suggested the man himself was probably a phony veteran. Assured that the man had served in an air-support capacity in the Mediterranean area in World War II, Troy shouted: "You probably serviced McGovern's plane and that's why it crashed!"

Walking around downtown later that night, Warren and I discovered a place called McCabe's Bar, distinguished by its possession of the oldest continuous liquor license in Milwaukee. Warren, intrigued by the name of the place (his latest movie was "McCabe and Mrs. Miller") was informed by the bartender that Mr. McCabe still lived, some 81 years old. Accustomed as I thought I was by then to life's incongruities, I still found it incongruous that there sat Warren Beatty, "McCabe," in McCabe's Bar, unrecognized at midnight in Milwaukee.

We conducted a single sample poll, the bartender. He thought McGovern would run against Agnew in 1972, and Agnew would win. I asked if he had seen "McCabe and Mrs. Miller." He hadn't seen it but remembered its stars to be Ernest Borgnine and Bette Davis. Choke strangled laugh. About 1 A.M. we were joined by two late-partying couples. One man, a doctor, bought us a drink and immediately agreed with the bartender that Warren looked familiar; after some consideration, "like that guy, what's his name, Warren Beatty!" Warren said he'd been told that before.

Friendships warming, we now included the doctor in our poll. He thought a darkhorse would probably be President. Who? Well, (mumble) from North Carolina or "Turbot" from Indiana. Choke again strangled laugh. With that, we bade Mr. McCabe's venerable establishment good-night.

The next morning, October 1st, I flew to New York where Frank and I interviewed two candidates for key staff jobs in our New York campaign. We then met with Dick Aurelio and Ronnie Eldridge, both close advisors and aides of Mayor Lindsay. The subject was Lindsay's political intentions and a possible detente with the McGovern campaign. Polite fencing. Finally, I summarized our situation: McGovern was a serious candidate who intended to stay in the race until the end; we have demonstrated broadbased support by our mailings and have been setting up a national political organization. Aurelio said that the Mayor was thinking and that he, Aurelio, "honestly doesn't know" what Lindsay will do; December will be the decision month for them. That will be necessary to meet filing deadlines in early primary states. The Mayor was primarily interested in having the issues he was concerned about thoroughly discussed in the election. I had heard that before; it was political shorthand for, "I want to be President."

After much gossip and story-swapping, interruptions and phone-calls, we agreed that the principals would get together after the New York Liberal Party dinner on October 6th and that we would keep informal lines of communication open at the staff level. Aurelio said he wanted to make an analysis of the respective political bases; he didn't want to accept my assumption that McGovern and Lindsay would naturally appeal to the same constituencies or that the two candidates would mutually co-opt each other.

I left the meeting convinced that we could seriously undermine Lindsay's desire to run by strengthening our organization in Florida by early December (Aurelio had indicated that would probably be their first state), and that by focusing on urban issues we could deprive Lindsay of his major rationale for entering—that McGovern didn't know anything about cities. Further, we had to continue our efforts to gain widespread support among students and minority groups to deny Lindsay those bases of strength. Finally, McGovern had to convince Lindsay that the Mayor would tarnish his image in the Democratic Party if he damaged an existing serious liberal campaign, and that he could, in fact, enhance that image by supporting McGovern.

The spring and summer of 1971 had been used to broaden the liberal base of support and pre-empt it from other liberal candidates. The pattern here was Nixon's successful maneuver of the same sort in 1967 in the

Republican Party. In the meantime, we calculated that our activities on the left would tempt Muskie to move our way to counter the beachhead we had established, which he did in the early spring. This prompted both Humphrey and Jackson to emerge on the right, sensing Muskie's failure to nail down that wing of the party. Predictably again, in the late summer, Muskie moved back to the right, particularly during a trip to Texas, to counter the Humphrey/Jackson threat. This effort to romance the conservative elements in the party had two results: it sealed off liberal support for Muskie for good, and it confirmed an image in the minds of the press and party pros of a vacillating candidate. We felt then—and we were proved right—that this inevitably would lead to a confrontation between McGovern and Humphrey representing the two ideological wings of the Democratic Party.

Since decisions to run for the Presidency are never made simply on logical grounds, we could never by sheer organizational effort force other candidates out. Hughes had already dropped out; for the rest, the best we could do was enlist as many supporters as possible while they were making up their minds. If others, such as Lindsay or McCarthy or Harris, entered they would find workers scarce and would be forced to adopt an expensive media-oriented campaign to counter the McGovern army. Since money was indeed scarce for that kind of campaign and no one around seemed to have the personal wealth of a Kennedy, such a media-related campaign would be doomed to fail. And, as Lindsay later proved, it did.

OCTOBER, 1971

On October 6th, we held one of the first of our major fund-raising efforts in New York, a luncheon sponsored by the Business Men and Women for McGovern; it drew about 1,350 people who heard the Senator give a rousing, fighting speech. This event plus several developments provided a real sense of momentum in the fall of 1971. Wherever the Senator went the crowds seemed to be larger, supporters more enthusiastic and press treatment of his candidacy more consistently serious.

Out of our national campaign budget we were now funding headquarters in Manchester, Boston, New York, Miami, Chicago, Milwaukee, Omaha, San Francisco, and Los Angeles. The campaign policy was to have all money raised around the country sent to Washington to be allocated according to a national budget among the various campaign priorities. As in all national campaigns, this policy was a continuing source of friction and resentment, particularly in New York and California, where substantial amounts could be raised. Our staff and steering committees in those states generally wanted to keep money raised for the inevitably expensive campaigns in those states. In both cases, the most telling argument for sending the money to the Washington headquarters was that without respectable showings or victories in the early primaries, such as New Hampshire and Wisconsin, there would be no campaigns in California and New York.

On October 12th, Bayh announced his withdrawal from the race. Three days earlier it was discovered that his wife, Marvella, had a serious malignancy, and Bayh said this situation absolutely precluded his continuation. Bayh, like McGovern, had started his efforts early in 1970, traveling into 35 states that year. He was proceeding on a schedule almost that frenetic in 1971 as well and had recruited a large, capable staff of 30 to 40 people in Washington and 20 more around the country under the direction of his administrative assistant, Bob Keefe. Rumors persisted that Bayh's campaign operation had grown too large and costly by mid-1971 and that he was out of money. However, at the time of his withdrawal, Keefe maintained that the campaign had been refinanced and that sufficient funds were available to go into the primaries.

On that same day, October 12th, deliberations over the chairmanship of the temporary rules committee for the convention precipitated the first real intra-party scrap of the season. Party Chairman Larry O'Brien, his treasurer (and future successor) Bob Strauss, and the Democratic National Committee staff lined up strongly behind Patricia Harris, black attorney from Washington who had served in other party posts. Her credentials and alliances were considered to be mostly with the non-reform elements of the party and her selection by O'Brien was taken as a signal to many reformers that key convention posts would fall into the hands of those who had controlled the bloody 1968 convention and that important decisions and rulings would once again go against the reform elements—possibly precipitating a party split.

Eli Segal, who had helped manage the Hughes Presidential campaign staff and who had worked with the Reform Commission and in the reform effort for several years, felt even more strongly about this than most of us. He convinced Senator Hughes to seek the rules committee chairmanship as a representative of the reform movement. We lined up strongly behind Hughes. At this time it seemed that the party officials had seriously underestimated the political strength of the reform movement around the country, as demonstrated by the recruitment of people such as Jean Westwood, Democratic National committeewoman from Utah, to an active role in the McGovern campaign, and the number of "new politics" advocates who had assumed local party leadership roles in many states.

I was afraid that a bloody, divisive fight would develop leading into the convention.

Great attention was directed toward the role that Muskie as a "centrist" candidate would play in this squabble. It seemed to be a curious one. Two key Muskie staff members, Jack English and Mark Shields, after some delay, made calls to a number of National Committee members on Hughes' behalf. Other reports were that Muskie himself either did nothing, let people off easy on the question of voting for Hughes, or subtly encouraged votes for Harris. The confusion was compounded by Eli Segal's reporting a lack of Muskie cooperation when both Dave Broder and the columnists Evans and Novak were reporting a firm Muskie-Hughes alliance.

The news stories suggested that the price for Muskie support would be the Hughes national mailing lists and state contact lists, as well as later assistance in the Iowa caucuses in January. Since we had made an all-out effort for Hughes, I called Ed Campbell of Hughes' office to check the accuracy of these reports: "It's a damn lie," he assured me. About two months later, in one of the bitterest blows of the campaign, Hughes endorsed Muskie's candidacy.

Both Frank and Rick Stearns argued strongly for outright war upon the Democratic National Committee based upon the Harris appointment. I demurred on several grounds: first, we couldn't be sure that O'Brien had not merely made a mistake of judgment; second, a divisive assault would wreck our left-centrist strategy and probably make the nomination worthless if we won it; third, such a fight would be premature and we would lose it. As it turned out, Patricia Harris won the chairmanship and generally carried out her duties fairly and evenly.

On October 17th I went to Florida with Rick Brown who had assumed responsibility, on a volunteer basis, for supervising our Florida organizational effort. We attended a meeting of the statewide McGovern steering committee in Orlando where overall primary strategy, financing, publicity, and organizational activities were discussed. By this time we had developed an excellent leadership cadre in the state. One supporter cornered me on my arrival with the proposal that the Senator be brought into and receive credit for an incredibly intricate business deal then underway for the sale of 100 Boeing 707's to the Republic of China. I could just imagine the reaction of the prototypical middle American to an announcement that McGovern had been instrumental in delivering an entire potential jet air force to Red China!

On October 31st I traveled to Wisconsin Dells for the second meeting of the Wisconsin McGovern steering committee. Like the Florida meeting, this session was to review progress on the state campaign to date, to lay plans for the next two or three months, and to report on the national campaign. There were many anxious questions about the progress of other candidates, the prospects for heading off a Muskie bandwagon and the meaning of the national polls, which never seemed to move. After explaining why the nomination was still a wide-open race and attention should not be paid to the polls or prognosticators, I stated that we could and would win the Wisconsin primary with 35 percent to 37 percent of the vote, and that that would be the boost we would need to successfully continue the race. I also stated that the key would be financing, and that it would take $250,000 to $500,000 for the next five months of the campaign in Wisconsin. As in Florida, the spirit was high and the level of competence among our supporters was excellent.

My travels had by now convinced me that what the country really needed and wanted was another Andrew Jackson, but that in recent years the closest we had come to that was Harry Truman. Those who were then dabbling with "populism" seemed to many people to be merely plastic replicas of Jackson or, worse yet, plastic Trumans.

NOVEMBER, 1971

I visited New Hampshire again. As usual, Grandmaison had scheduled two strenuous days, during which we met with Merv Weston, who had agreed to commit his promotional and advertising agency to the campaign. It was one of the best things that happened to us, although our first discussion turned out to be a prolonged, ridiculous debate about whether to put the first name "George" on our materials. Merv had already begun to commit us to various advertising projects. Sitting poker-faced throughout the meeting, I kept thinking to myself: "He's going to want money soon. Where is it coming from?"

Later, Pat Caddell arrived in the Manchester headquarters to observe the Yankees first hand. He was a 21-year-old Harvard senior and a Floridian who had begun conducting political surveys as a high school student for a class project. He turned out to have a natural affinity for sampling public opinion and voter attitudes. In college, he formed a small company with two other students and conducted polls in statewide campaigns in Florida, Ohio, and a number of other states. When I met Pat on an organizational trip to Florida in the fall of 1971 he was certain that, with the right kind of campaign, McGovern could win. Although Pat soon convinced me that he could provide valuable services for us in the early primary states, we had absolutely no money to pay him and, therefore, could not encourage him to work for us in New Hampshire. He came up anyway and eventually carried out some invaluable surveys for us

for almost no money. I was particularly interested in having him sub-
stantiate our theory about a potential McGovern vote in the southeast
part of the state.

Stopping in Boston briefly on the way back to Washington on November 10th, I met with members of our Massachusetts committee to discuss
the possibility of participating in an effort to coalesce liberal and anti-war
groups in the state to create a unified endorsement of a single candidate
for the April primary. I suggested we hold off cooperation for the time
being since the principal organizers of the effort were long-time McCarthy
supporters and the proposed two-thirds vote required to secure the endorsement seemed then to be unrealistic. Afterwards, I talked to John
Ruether, our Massachusetts coordinator, about the need to expand our
base in Massachusetts to include not only anti-war activists, of whom
there were many, but also more regular party Kennedy types, of whom
there were few for McGovern. Dave Harrison, former state party chairman and by then our McGovern chairman in the state, later proved to
be valuable in bridging that gap.

I returned to Washington to confront an internal struggle which had
long been brewing and had finally crystalized. It involved, once again,
the conflict between two schools of thought: one, that the judgment
of field staff and local supporters should generally be heeded, the
other, that political tradition and professionalism dictated that most
major decisions should be made in Washington. Gene Pokorny and Joe
Grandmaison represented the former point of view and Ted Van Dyk
the latter. The narrower issue was the role the local media and public
relations firms would play in the total campaign planning effort in the
respective primary states.

Ted, generally responsible for the media and promotional planning,
was accustomed to campaigns which relied heavily on a centralized media
package, usually prepared in New York, which the national campaign
then imposed upon the state organizations. The field organizers wanted
to develop grassroots media and promotional efforts which were more
tailored to particular states and which relied upon the wisdom and expertise of local firms. The argument escalated rapidly, since both sides
sensed it represented a fundamental policy decision with far-reaching
implications for the campaign. The younger organizers felt Ted was being
high-handed and arbitrary and was challenging their authority to coordinate the campaigns in their respective states. Ted felt they were
wrongfully questioning his judgment and experience and were challenging his authority to develop a media program. There was much shouting,
table-banging, and accusing.

The battle raged and swirled across the hall into Mankiewicz's office. Frank essentially sided with Ted and chastised me for not presenting a united front among the three of us to the rest of the staff. I countered that the campaign would be won or lost not in Washington, but in the states, and that the reason the regional coordinators had been hired was to make judgments of this sort. I was essentially for them, and I said, "I don't like the suggestion that this Hart-Mankiewicz-Van Dyk troika is a damn fraternity which requires its members to pledge unswerving mutual agreement on matters of policy." Tempers cooled, but the fundamental issue would not be resolved for several days.

Meanwhile, word of the conflict filtered throughout the office and gossip, rumors, and speculation mounted about some high-level internal dispute. Too much time and energy was being spent in discussions of who had what authority and who was "really" in charge of the campaign. This kind of speculation didn't particularly disturb me until it clearly began to affect the progress of the campaign or confuse state committees or field staff about where to look for final answers. For two or three weeks I was reminded almost hourly that such a state of confusion did exist and that most campaign people were pressing for some resolution of the leadership struggle.

On Sunday, November 20th, the Senator and I flew to Chicago for a fund-raising reception. On the flight back to Washington that evening I talked to the Senator about the confusion of authority at headquarters and the conflict between Ted and the field staff. The Senator agreed that roles had to be clarified and that only he could do it. On the 29th, after a Thanksgiving week trip to Utah and New Mexico, the Senator called most of the staff into his office and announced that he wanted Frank to concentrate on new issues and ideas, press matters, speeches, and contacts with political "heavies." Ted was to direct his attention to fund-raising activities and to act as an advisor. George Cunningham, the Senate administrative assistant, would come to the headquarters as budget watchdog and supercomptroller. Once again, I was to remain in charge over-all. After this meeting, the Senator went to the headquarters to announce the assignments and reassignments to a campaign staff still unsure what it all meant. Thus ended, for the time being, the second in a cycle of byzantine leadership skirmishes occurring now at regular four-month intervals.

November saw further fluctuations in the Presidential stock market. Senator Harris, who had announced his candidacy less than two months before on a generally populistic, specifically tax-reform-related, platform, folded his efforts for lack of financial support. For reasons unclear to almost everyone, Los Angeles Mayor Sam Yorty announced his candidacy and his intention to enter the New Hampshire primary. And in November Senator Jackson joined the list of Presidential contenders, believing, apparently, that he represented a point of view on Vietnam, law-and-order, and defense spending not then present in the race. The effect of this was to bracket Muskie between McGovern and Jackson and put the "centrist" theory to a classic test.

DECEMBER, 1971

We entered a period of heavy despondency which was to last almost to the eve of the New Hampshire primary in March. The principal cause was lack of money. Nothing had changed politically which altered my deeply rooted conviction that we could get the nomination. In fact, everything seemed to be going pretty much according to schedule. The difficulty was that the campaign was entering a new phase which would require substantially greater amounts of money for heavy media promotion and organizational activities in the early primary states, and we did not have the money. I was beginning to come under tremendous pressure from these states, particularly New Hampshire and Wisconsin, but also to some degree from Florida and Illinois. There was an increasing sense that the campaign was beginning to grind to a halt for lack of fuel. Organizers could not rent the desperately needed storefront offices, or add the phones, or print the literature; state coordinators were unable to commit the organization to the purchase of the most advantageous television and radio time, or prepare mailings or add needed staff. Morale was dipping to a new low.

For the first time, the campaign began to head into heavy debt. We resorted to deficit financing. Creditors, previously paid promptly, began to accumulate and grow restless and strained. The immense burden of holding them off fell largely on our treasurer, Marian Pearlman, and on Jeff Smith, who dealt with the direct-mail suppliers and printers. Jeff prepared more mailings but, for the time being, the well had run dry. The polls were not moving. We were heading into the election year after a year and a half of campaigning, one year with a public candidacy, and George McGovern had still not moved even one point in the public opinion polls, that all-important thermometer for campaign contributors. Henry Kimelman, practically the only person in the campaign making an effort to solicit large contributions, day after day ran into a stone wall. More candidates entered the race. Other campaigns seemed to flourish. Money seemed to appear on the very doorsteps of other headquarters.

Sensing for many weeks the advent of this harshest, coldest, bitterest period, I had warned the state coordinators and organizers to hunker down and ride out this storm. Help was on the way. The money would come in. Someone somewhere would appear to relieve this embattled garrison. Wait a little longer. Next week, always next week. Meantime, don't give up—keep organizing, keep doing the few things that don't require dollars. Hold meetings, encourage each other. Above all, don't let pessimism and gloom settle in. We *are* going to win!

Still the pressure from the field continued—send us money, we can't win without money; dire warnings of disaster from Pokorny, outraged screams and cries from Grandmaison. Rick Stearns has begun to gear up organizations in the early caucus states. We needed an office and supplies in Des Moines. Nothing was moving in Arizona for lack of money. We needed to send an organizer to Seattle. We might pick up some delegates in Georgia if we could just pay one person $50 a week.

Frank repeatedly compared our prolonged debates over money to the scene from *Catch 22* where two atheists discuss the nature of the God they don't believe in. One prefers not to believe in a New Testament God, forgiving and understanding; the other likes not to believe in an Old Testament God, full of wrath and righteousness. That's what the money meetings were like.

Mayor Lindsay announced his candidacy in December. We were now bracketed between Muskie's pragmatic liberals on one side and Lindsay's charismatic liberals on the other. The New York rumor mill (which operates around the clock every day of the year, and occasionally produces a shred of truth) had Lindsay trying to show in Florida, place in Wisconsin, and win in Massachusetts, then pick up Oregon and California to ice it. None of the Lindsay people were able to explain how he expected to handle the primary in New York, where he had demonstrated less than charismatic appeal and where he had occasionally been forced to operate City Hall practically under siege. Someone suggested that Lindsay's chances to get delegates were in direct proportion to the distance the delegates lived from New York. I proposed, only half jokingly, that we could eliminate Lindsay from the race by flying all the 1968 Democratic delegates to New York and taking them on a three-day tour of Gotham.

In mid-December I flew to Oklahoma for meetings with our steering committee. We agreed on a two-prong strategy in the state. One thrust would be a highly visible "citizens" effort aimed at mustering as much public support for McGovern as possible, an effort which our citizen chairman Tom Boyd and others would direct; the other would be a low-visibility "political" effort, led by Jim Barrett and other seasoned in state politics, aimed at electing uncommitted but liberal delegates who could later be converted to McGovern before the convention.

I also visited Iowa twice in December. We had decided to make an all-out effort to get delegates from the local caucuses, both to demonstrate McGovern strength and to prevent a Muskie sweep which would suggest his invincibility or the inevitability of his nomination. The Iowa caucuses grew in significance with the increase in rumors that Muskie intended to wrap the state up. Such reports from an early caucus state prior to the first primary would seriously damage morale and further hinder latent fund-raising possibilities. During the second trip, on the 20th, we officially opened the state McGovern headquarters in a corner of the decrepit Jefferson Hotel in Des Moines and I gave a number of speeches in Davenport, Moline, and elsewhere.

On the return trip to Washington I stopped in Detroit and Pittsburgh to discuss the situation with our Michigan and western Pennsylvania organizers and coordinators. On the morning of the 31st I traveled to Phoenix to discuss our plans for the January caucuses in that state with our supporters there. At a press conference in the Phoenix Press Club in the waning hours of 1971, I confidently predicted Senator McGovern's nomination and eventual election.

We were still at 3 percent in the polls.

1 9 7 2

The year of the Democratic Convention. The year of the general election. In ten months the country would elect a President.

On the 6th of January I went back into New Hampshire to plan for the primary with Grandmaison and Merv Weston. I wanted to talk about our organizational efforts, and Grandmaison wanted to talk about money and the Senator's schedule, which was the second-worst topic of conversation. The New Hampshirites were jealous of the candidate's time spent out of the state and were particularly resentful of time spent in Florida or Illinois.

Grandmaison was full of threats, dire predictions of catastrophe, and gloom. He hammered away at me as if all his problems were my fault. Finally, after two days of constant assault, I let go—Joe Grandmaison was the only person in the entire McGovern organization who could provoke me to acrid, sulfurous rage—and we had a table-pounding, arm-waving shouting match which reverberated throughout the Manchester headquarters. Volunteers in the outer office quaked, anticipating blood. None flowed. Finally, exhausted, Grandmaison agreed to continue the New Hampshire campaign at least one day more.

On the night of January 5th, on the way to New Hampshire, I stopped in New York with Rick Stearns to attend the second in a short series of seances held in the penthouse apartment of Stewart Mott, an engaging philanthropist, who had managed to create a noteworthy reputation both for giving money away to liberal political causes and for riding a bicycle and growing a vegetable garden outside his elegant Fifth Avenue penthouse apartment. Stewart had conceived these sessions to seek avenues of cooperation and reduction of hostilities among the various liberal Democratic candidates. Thus, besides Rick and me, he had invited Ronnie Eldridge, representing Mayor Lindsay; Sarah Kovner and John Boyles, representing Gene McCarthy (who was, during this period, fanning the ardor of the remaining disciples and piquing the ire of his former colleagues with suggestions of resurrecting Quixote); and a man named Gore, representing Congresswoman Shirley Chisholm, who was soon to announce her candidacy. Stewart was there with his assistant, Kathy Eigner, and his cat. After a health-food dinner, there was a lengthy discussion concerning the possibility of mutual cooperation in the non-primary states. It was clear that the other campaigns, including Lindsay's, had done little constructive thinking about the impending first-level caucuses. The McCarthyites made an asinine proposal about leaving South Dakota and Iowa to us if we would give McCarthy a free ride in Minnesota and Massachusetts. We laughed. Rick delivered a short lecture on how to organize a non-primary state, particularly the systems used in Iowa and Arizona, the first two caucus states. He then made what I considered a too-convincing argument that Lindsay should get into the delegate scramble in Arizona. His rationale was that Lindsay would pick up delegates we could not get because of lack of money, and after Lindsay's inevitable departure from the race, those delegates would come to us. In any case, his arguments to the Lindsay people were so convincing that they soon invested a great deal of time and money in Arizona and got more delegates than we did.

For several weeks leading up to the Lindsay announcement a number of New York McGovern supporters had been hammering away at Lindsay in the press, led in almost every case by the irrepressible Matty Troy, who was believed by many to be candidate for the Mayor's job. The leaders of the Lindsay campaign, convinced that the direction of this assault came from Washington, were not particularly happy with those of us from the McGovern headquarters. Midway through the Stewart Mott evening, Ronnie contacted Aurelio on the phone and suggested that he come reinforce the team. Before Aurelio arrived, the others at the meeting opened up on me for our unseemly treatment of the Mayor. Upon Aurelio's arrival Ronnie pleaded with him to explain the importance of calling off our critics. Aurelio, all moustache, blank glasses, and scowls, sounded ominous: "All I can say is that in about six months some important decisions will be made by all of us and we will remember what happened along the way." Mott's luxuriant indoor flora seemed to grow and hover nearer, threatening to reclaim Gotham in the name of nature (starting in Stewart's penthouse) as man, this petty political animal, locked with himself in mortal combat. Heavy stuff.

On January 9th, a gray, rainy Sunday afternoon in Washington, the financial siege was temporarily lifted. In an emergency finance session at the Senator's house, twenty faithful or potential financial supporters were summoned to hear a report on the campaign, our strategy and our chances for success. Gene spoke, Charles Guggenheim talked about the media program, I talked about how we were going to win, and Frank asked for money. $405,000 was pledged. Twenty days later we had received less than $50,000, but it was enough to save the campaign and get us into the New Hampshire primary. The cavalry had arrived in the nick of time to save the fort and rescue the pioneers.

On the 12th I went to Wisconsin to meet with Gene and to try to recruit additional support. Like Grandmaison, but with much more restraint, Gene wanted to talk only of money. Later I met with Ray Majeris, principal United Auto Workers political representative in the state. His support would have been immensely helpful, but he had crushing news. It looked, he said, as if the UAW board and the entire union were going to Muskie. Majeris said that meant about 300 full-time staff members committed to the Muskie campaign. Disastrous.

I received a call from the Senator that afternoon in the Wisconsin headquarters. Get to Chicago, he said. He had flown in that day to file his slates of delegates in a dozen and a half districts and had found the slates contained a substantial imbalance of males. Since he had taken the lead in espousing women's rights and equality, this was a political calamity.

We had six days in which to file amended delegate slates. I got to the Chicago headquarters that evening and began the tedious process of urging, arguing, cajoling, pleading, beating, and oiling necessary to get our local committees to rearrange their slates. It meant, in many cases, dropping people who had worked hard for the Senator and replacing them with others who may not have been that active. Although these people supported McGovern, it did not necessarily mean they would automatically do what we asked them to do. The arguments continued into the next day with only two or three districts balking at our instructions. Once these problems seemed settled we began the unhappy task of getting supporters out on the street corners over the weekend to gather the necessary number of signatures on petitions so the new slates could be filed. Most of the state was locked in a blizzard; the wind-chill factor in the Chicago area during that period was −45°. But the staff and supporters rallied admirably and on January 19th filed our amended slates containing 106 delegates—almost 45 percent of them women—in 17 districts.

From Chicago, I flew to Miami to solve an equally serious campaign problem. The Florida campaign was broke. I met with Sandy D'Alemberte, the state chairman, and Yancey Martin, who was spending all his time in that state, to discuss the budget. I said there was no money in the national treasury; they said there was no money in the state. They argued strenuously the importance of preventing a Wallace sweep in the state. They also pointed out the number of congressional districts, and thus the number of delegates, we could win. I was skeptical, particularly since the money requested would have to come from the hard-pressed New Hampshire and Wisconsin campaigns. But I finally agreed to send $10,000 and to send Rick Brown into the state as a full-time state coordinator.

This discussion took place at a Miami restaurant which gained some prominence from the fact that President Nixon dined there often enough while at Key Biscayne to have the Secret Service bullet-proof the window near his table. Ironically, the management seated us at the President's table (what if he had known what we were up to?). We debated whether we could legally be made to move if the President came in.

On January 18th, the anniversary of the Senator's announcement of candidacy, Frank and I held a press conference at the headquarters to summarize the year's progress: we had a viable campaign organization in almost every state in the union; the Senator had visited approximately two dozen states during the year, a number of them several times; and while other candidates had come and gone, we were still in the race. I suggested that it was the first Presidential campaign in American political history to have annual Christmas parties.

Beneath our accomplishments lay the continuing, plaguing, nagging worry about money. The long winter of our discontent was coming to an end, but we still had many difficult weeks ahead before any sunlight could be seen. We were, in fact, at the very depths of despair, the Valley Forge of the McGovern campaign. It was true we still supported the best candidate. The Senator never gave any indication of backing off the issues or giving up the race, even in the face of overwhelming adversity. And we had the most dedicated, loyal, effective workers any campaign could hope for. They were just as determined and persistent as their candidate. Yet every day, almost every hour, during this time there clung to me like an evil demon the consuming question: What if we run out of money? What if we cannot pay staff salaries, or buy the media time, or print literature to hand out on New Hampshire street corners?

At this most difficult and desperate period of the campaign it was never certain from one day to the next whether the campaign could go on.

PART III

General Kutuzov and the Grassroots Army

(January, 1972, to July 15, 1972)

In the minds of some, the historic hero of Tolstoy's epic *War and Peace* is General Kutuzov, the aged, afflicted commander of the Russian army who delivered his homeland from Napoleon's legions. Considered by Moscow society and much of his own officer corps to be an incompetent visionary, Kutuzov nevertheless kept his own counsel, preferring to endure the skepticism of those around him rather than try to justify his view of history. According to that view, which Kutuzov shared with his literary creator, men do not control events—events control men. Plans may be made, strategies may be conceived, the enemy may be studied, diagrams and charts may be prepared, but in the end there is a tide in the affairs of men which may either be taken or not taken—but can never be artificially created. Kutuzov's genius was in perceiving the tide when it ran and knowing how to take it. Those about him, not sharing his insight, panicked under pressure, sought action as an escape from crisis, and damned Kutuzov's forbearance and watchfulness, mistaking them for languor. But for the shrill and critical Russian court, Kutuzov had an answer: "Everything comes in time to him who knows how to wait." And to the chafing, captious "advisors" who demanded action he said: "It is not difficult to capture a fortress but it is difficult to win a campaign. For that, not storming and attacking but *patience and time* are wanted . . . there is nothing stronger than those two: *patience and time*, they will do it all."

In those distressful weeks in January, February, and March of 1972, one could sympathize, and occasionally identify, with General Kutuzov. It seemed the closer we came to the actual combat—the opening of the primary races—the more uneasy even our most committed supporters became. It was almost as if all our theories about the Senator's strengths and our opponents' weaknesses began to be doubted the nearer we came to the actual test. I found myself constantly reassuring staff, contributors, and supporters that nothing had changed and that political circumstances still favored McGovern; the polls, the columnists, and the network and newsmagazine projections of delegate strength were all speculation, erroneous and ill-informed.

In late January and early February, both *Newsweek* and CBS presented calculations concerning the number of convention delegates each candidate could reasonably expect. Both gave Muskie approximately 1,000 first-ballot convention votes. Both made the mistake of basing their predictions on the opinions of party officials in each state and on 1968 delegate results. These kinds of projections had a devastating impact on morale in our campaign, which relied so heavily on the support of political amateurs—those people most likely to believe that networks and news magazines had special political knowledge. But the impact was temporary; the same amateurs, both workers and contributors, were also less deeply establishmentarian in their thinking and could be shown why the so-called experts were mistaken much more readily than the more inbred members of Washington's political society, who relied exclusively on the conventional political wisdom they created for themselves. Nevertheless, there it was, night after night and week after week, the constant prediction that Muskie was only a step away from the nomination, that step being only one or two easy, early primary victories.

JANUARY, 1972

Besides McGovern, the race now included, after the jockeying, announcements and withdrawals of 1971, the following: Senator Edmund Muskie, who had announced his candidacy on January 4th on nationwide television (the Muskie announcement, for us, was like a visit to the dentist; we knew it was going to happen, but that didn't make it hurt any less); Senator Hubert Humphrey, who had announced his third try for the Presidency on January 19th; Mayor John Lindsay; Senator Henry Jackson; Governor George Wallace, who announced his candidacy on January 13th; Congresswoman Shirley Chisholm, who came in on January 25th; and Senator Vance Hartke, who entered on January 3rd. This list was to be increased in the coming weeks by Congressman Wilbur Mills, former Governor Terry Sanford, and Congresswoman Patsy Mink, all of whom announced in early March.

Approximately 2,000 of the 3,016 delegate votes to be cast at the 1972 Democratic National Convention would be selected from 22 primary states and the District of Columbia, and approximately 1,000 would be selected in 28 non-primary states. Throughout the delegate selection process our goal in the primary states was twofold: first, to win or make a strong showing in half of them to show political strength, momentum, and popularity; second, to obtain as many delegates as possible from the organization and campaign investment. Some primary states, like California, Oregon, and South Dakota, were "winner-take-all," binding all their delegates for one or more ballots to the winner of the popular vote. Other states, like Ohio and Massachusetts, elected delegates by popular vote at the Congressional District level, with an at-large slate of delegates going to the winner of the statewide contest. Other primary states, like New Hampshire, elected delegates only by congressional districts, and some states, like Illinois, added a non-binding Presidential preference poll to the ballot.

In almost all primary states, the individual delegates themselves were selected through a caucus, convention, and slate-making process which resulted, in most cases, from elaborate attempts to harmonize state law with state party rules and with reform guidelines recommended by the National Committee and adapted by the state party to its particular circumstances. In most states, this process went very smoothly, with a maximum of public participation and a minimum of contention. In other states, however, confusion was rife and resulted in bitter parliamentary disputes.

In the case of every state and voting jurisdiction, whether primary or non-primary, it was absolutely imperative to maintain constant watch on the political calendar to insure awareness of filing deadlines, caucus dates, and the steps necessary to prepare for each step of the delegate selection process. In this respect, the work done by our regional desk officers in Washington and our procedural specialists in every state, under Rick Stearns' direction, gave a tremendous advantage over all the other campaigns, none of which ever seemed to be familiar with the rules of the game or the procedures to be followed in the various states.

Contrary to later accusations, the McGovern campaign did not benefit from any inside information resulting from the Senator's chairmanship of the reform commission. Rather, any superiority we possessed in terms of rules and procedures resulted almost entirely from hard work and diligence, using information available at the same time and in equal measure to all the other candidates. Unquestionabley, we benefited from Rick's academic background in state laws and procedures, as well as his—and later Eli Segal's—experience on the staff of the reform commission. But the greatest impact of this experience was to sharpen their awareness of the importance of learning each state's rules and watching the all-important calendar.

In those 28 states not relying on some variation of the Presidential primary, procedures were established for selecting delegates from a pyramiding system of caucuses and conventions. A typical example of such a system was the one in my home state of Colorado. There, caucuses, or informal, neighborhood meetings of registered Democrats, were held at the precinct level in April. Four delegates were selected to the conventions held in each of the state's five Congressional Districts in May. The McGovern campaign leadership in the state, as in all other non-primary states, had organized for months to insure a large turn-out of committed McGovern supporters at these precinct caucuses so that as many McGovern delegates as possible would be elected to the intermediate conventions at the county and district levels. At these intermediate conventions, delegates were selected to the state convention, 27 delegates to the National Convention were selected at the district conventions and the remaining nine of the state's 36 delegates were selected at the state convention in mid-June. Because of the pyramiding nature of the caucus-convention system—delegates selected at one level selecting delegates to the next level—it was crucial in all of the non-primary states to elect as many McGovern delegates as possible at the base-line caucus level.

The techniques for doing this are very simple and depend primarily on hard work. What T. H. Huxley said of science can be said of politics: "It is nothing but trained and organized common sense." The only sophistication required was in the selection of areas of the state where the McGovern campaign stood the best political chance of electing delegates, and thus where it would make its greatest effort. In many states like Colorado we made a statewide effort to elect delegates to subsequent caucuses or conventions. In others, particularly the southern and some midwestern states, we concentrated our efforts in counties or legislative districts which naturally had large McGovern constituencies, such as campus communities, or which had a history of heavy support for liberal candidates.

Once these areas of concentration were selected, the system, as implemented by Rick Stearns, Eli Segal, Gene Pokorny, our desk officers and other staff organizers, simply involved opening a headquarters, equipping it with phones manned by volunteers, acquiring lists of names of people active in 1968 Kennedy or McCarthy efforts or other recent, ideologically compatible campaigns, and calling those on the list to locate volunteer organizers in each precinct. As precinct coordinators were identified, they were instructed to obtain lists of registered Democrats in their precinct from local registration or party officials. Then these names were called by the precinct coordinator to identify McGovern supporters or convert "undecideds," all of whom were asked to attend the coming precinct caucus and vote for McGovern delegates to the county, district, and state conventions.

It was tedious but rewarding work. In Colorado, the structure of a state organization was established in September, 1971. The actual precinct organizational work began in January, 1972, and continued for the next five months. Lists of contact names already possessed by McGovern supporters were supplemented by every Democratic name that could be found. The work done by the volunteers in Colorado, as in every other

non-primary state, was uniformly superb. A Humphrey organizer sent
into the state two weeks before the caucuses later testified that the ballgame was all over by that time, that the McGovern organization had
sewn up great areas of Colorado. The precinct and county caucuses held
on May 15 produced over 60 percent McGovern delegates. By the
completion of the county, district, and state conventions in mid-June,
McGovern had 24 of Colorado's 36 National Convention delegates. This
pattern was repeated in state after state across the nation.

A serious strategy struggle had developed inside the campaign regarding the significance to be given to Florida and Illinois primaries, in terms
of the amount of the candidate's time, money and staff attention to be
provided. The disagreement had arisen in the late fall and winter of
1971 and continued into early 1972. Although there was brave talk about
money becoming available, as the initial primaries approached, I remained skeptical, choosing never to believe money was actually available
until it was in hand. If we decided to make an all-out effort in each of
the first primary states, we would run out of money regardless of the
rightness of our cause.

This was a view not necessarily shared by Frank and Ted, and led to
some continuing disputes. Ted spent time inspecting the Florida political
scene and our campaign there and presented forceful arguments to the
Senator that we not only should make a stronger effort there, but probably had no choice. He argued that New Hampshire would be treated
as an easy Muskie win against limited opposition and that the press would
look upon Florida as the first large-scale competition involving a full field
of candidates, that Florida was considered a fair cross-section of the
national voters, that it was open to a liberal candidate since the upset
victory of Governor Reuben Askew in 1970, and that the relatively power-
less Democratic Party in the state could not materially assist more regular candidates like Humphrey or Jackson. Ted contended that the press
would roast us if we didn't jump in with both feet.

Frank seemed to share these convictions during some of this period.
He also believed we should make a strong investment in the Illinois
primary. He had made a trip into the state in the winter of 1971 and had
announced that we intended to run slates of delegates in almost every
Congressional District, including Chicago districts, and had suggested
we were seriously considering entering the non-binding preferential primary ballot as a test of strength against Muskie. These efforts would
clearly require a substantial investment of our campaign resources, the
candidate's time, money for media, and staff, since Illinois was a large
state with one of the three largest media markets. Because there was a
severe limit on all these resources, they would have to be drawn from

New Hampshire and Wisconsin, states selected over a year and a half earlier as high-priority, key primary states in our long-range strategy.

Clearly what was involved in both cases, Florida and Illinois, was a major decision related to the strategy and conduct of the campaign.

In all cases, state organizations involved provided strong arguments to support the point of view most in their interests. I was supported by the New Hampshire and Wisconsin coordinators, Joe Grandmaison and Gene Pokorny. My position throughout was that both the Florida and Illinois campaigns had to be almost totally self-sufficient financially; that we could send money only if it would not jeopardize our long-range goals of running a respectable second to Muskie in New Hampshire and running first or second in Wisconsin. We did provide coordination and leadership from the national staff in both Florida and Illinois and agreed, of course, to make radio and television spots available if money could be found to buy time.

Strategically, New Hampshire continued to be crucial for the reasons that had influenced our original decision to run there. It was historically the first primary and therefore would merit national attention. It was a chance to confront Muskie in his own territory and dent his image of invincibility and for McGovern to demonstrate his courage in tackling a difficult political situation. And it provided the earliest opportunity to distinguish the Senator in the public mind from other candidates, particularly those who might seem ideologically similar. Besides, we had already made a substantial investment in the state—well over half a dozen trips by the candidate, heavy organizational effort for months and constant attention by the national campaign leadership.

All of these considerations applied with equal force to Wisconsin. In addition, Wisconsin was a ballot designation state, where the candidates were placed on the ballot automatically by the secretary of state. Although the same was true of Florida, Florida was not, like Wisconsin, a mid-Western, agrarian state with a long primary tradition where McGovern would be expected to do well. We had the makings of a superb grassroots organization in Wisconsin, beginning at the most local level, as a result of months of effort by Gene Pokorny and our state committee.

Above all, if we spread our limited resources so thinly that we did poorly or made only a mediocre showing in the first four states, it would so discourage our political and financial supporters that we would be forced out of the race. Wallace's entry into the race in mid-January confirmed my conviction that the Florida primary would be a wash-out at best and a Wallace sweep at worst. Also, Lindsay had clearly thrown down the gauntlet by making his first major stand in Florida. Inevitably, our performance there would be compared to his. We could either try to match his massive media expenditure, and bankrupt the campaign, or shrug off the challenge and make the confrontation meaningless. After several weeks of wrestling with the Florida problem while the rest of us were concentrating on New Hampshire, Ted altered his original view, concluding in February that the national investment in Florida should be limited.

The Illinois problem was somewhat different. Although a substantial media expenditure would be necessary in Chicago and its suburbs, the Illinois situation was complicated further by the presence of Mayor Daley and at least the semblance of a Democratic organization in the state. If we, in fact, entered slates of delegates in the Chicago Congressional Districts, would this be considered a challenge to the Mayor, who up to this point had claimed to be neutral or uncommitted in the Presidential race? If, on the other hand, we launched a considerable, visible effort elsewhere in the state, but obviously neglected the Mayor's districts, wouldn't many of the people who remembered 1968, and were still deciding which liberal candidate to support, interpret this as a weak-kneed concession to the last political boss, the symbol of anti-reform? It was a clear and real dilemma. Frank, who at that point was in a fierce anti-establishment, anti-"old politics" phase, felt strongly that we should tackle the Mayor head-on as a signal that McGovern was the symbol of reform and was not afraid of any boss or party figurehead. I continued to argue that it was an academic discussion since we didn't have the money anyway, without backing off New Hampshire, and that we should simply sidestep the confrontation—as we would in Florida—by making an organizational effort in a few of our strongest districts and discount the importance of the statewide totals. Further, I tried to refurbish our left-centrist strategy, reminding the others that we were committed to a policy of not alienating the party regulars such as Mayor Daley needlessly, on the theory that we would need their support after we won the nomination.

As in the case of most major controversies inside the campaign, there was no specific point at which it was resolved. Rather, the decision had been made many months earlier to emphasize New Hampshire and Wisconsin. It would have taken a concrete decision on the candidate's part to turn it around. To my knowledge he never reconsidered the matter.

The schedule allocating the Senator's time from the first of the year through the April 4th, Wisconsin primary called for 22 days in New Hampshire, 21 days in Wisconsin, 19 days in Florida, 14 to 15 days in Illinois, and brief appearances in the early caucus states of Iowa, Minnesota, and Arizona. In each of the early primary states, except Illinois, the entire week prior to the primary was to be spent campaigning in that state.

The draft schedule was produced by Steve Robbins, who kept in constant contact with our state coordinators, compiling their insatiable requests for the Senator's time and doing his best to harmonize these demands with the actual time available and the Senator's physical endurance. As it was, after more than a year and a half of heavy campaign travel, the Senator was entering a five-month period of uninterrupted campaigning, from early in the morning to late at night seven days a week, with no more than a day or two a month for rest. Once Robbins had prepared and negotiated a "block" schedule, allocating specific days to specific states, for a one-month or two-month period, it was given to Frank and me for political review and approval. There followed further negotiations with the state coordinators, each of whom could make a legitimate case that success in his state was almost totally dependent on getting McGovern in there more often. After we amended the proposed schedule, it was sent to the Senator for review and approval. Occasionally, the Senator felt the schedule provided too little rest time and was surely designed by heartless Marine drill instructors who merely wanted to test the limits of his endurance. Usually, however, he did have constructive suggestions concerning reallocation of his time among the the various states.

On an average of once every month or two, a lengthy meeting would be held in the Senate office or a hotel suite on the road in which the Senator, Frank, Steve, Gordon Weil, whoever was the current press secretary, myself, and other staff members would review the block schedule for the coming months and revise it according to the prevailing political circumstances. During these sessions, occasional policy or strategy disagreements would emerge, related in most instances to differences of opinion about the effort to be made in Florida or Illinois or some other primary state. Although these disagreements were seldom resolved in the scheduling discussion, the candidate's thinking was usually apparent by the amount of time he finally agreed to spend in a particular state.

The schedule was the source of constant difficulty, occupying more of the candidate's time and energy than almost any other aspect of the campaign. It was, after all, his time and energy we were parceling out, in his judgment rather callously at times. He spent more time reviewing and revising the schedule, both in its extended and in its daily form, than he did on problems relating to the media, finance, and organization combined. But wouldn't we all, if a schedule became the bible which ruled, directed, and controlled our lives—telling us when to eat, when (and how long) to sleep, how much time to spend in a car, how many speeches and public appearances to make in a day, and with whom to spend our time?

One remarkable thing did occur: the closer we came to crucial contests the less time McGovern spent fussing with the schedule. The greater the pressure and heat became, the more willing he seemed to be worked, ruled, and guided. There were even a few times in the heat of the nomination race when he seemed eager to take on more appearances, to shake more hands, to convert more voters. When we seemed to have the inside track on the nomination, the red pencil came out again.

Lest anyone doubt the role that physical stamina plays in becoming President, let him or her accompany a candidate in a contested campaign. Campaigns are merely devices conceived to ensure the survival of the fittest. In a certain way it makes sense. If the Presidency is an office where pressure resides and where strain disorders the fainthearted, then best to weed out frailty and instability before it is placed to a test which might endanger us all. McGovern, after two years of backbreaking campaigning, was physically strong enough to be President. For, during January and February, 1972, as in later months, he traveled from New Hampshire to Florida, from Illinois to Wisconsin, back to New Hampshire and around again, starting each day at 6 or 7 in the morning and ending it well past midnight. And on he went, over and over again.

On January 23rd, the Gallup poll showed Muskie leading Kennedy as the favorite of most Democrats for the nomination. A September Gallup had shown Kennedy leading as the favorite of registered Democrats; a November poll had shown Muskie in the lead among announced or presumed candidates. But the January poll was the first showing him in the lead with Kennedy also in the race.

We were forced to confront and respond to the polls before audience after audience for almost two years. I consistently took the position that the polls were essentially name-identification devices which automatically elicit the names of the best-known figures; that they do not measure the support which a new figure, a little-known leader, can develop in a very short time with a political organization and national media exposure. I argued time and again that in 1972 the polls would reflect, not predict, our political successes; that as McGovern began to win and gain increasing exposure he would rise in the poll standings. The Senator himself was even more burdened by this problem, and grew weary of repeating that the only poll that counted was the one taken on election day.

The Iowa caucuses on January 24th represented the first test of political strength. The only two campaigns making statewide organizational efforts were ours and Muskie's. Although there were isolated pockets of support for other candidates, particularly Humphrey, the third organized force in the state was a coalition of party leaders, labor officials, and other hoping eventually for a Kennedy candidacy; this third force urged delegates elected in the local caucuses to remain "uncommitted" until the political picture clarified itself.

Our effort in the state began early in 1971 when Gene Pokorny made the first reconnaissance and recruitment trip there. He found limited but committed early support among some 1968 McCarthy backers and anti-war activists. Calls were made to as many leaders of both groups as possible, and contacts were made with leading Kennedy supporters. The Kennedy people were not moving, preferring to wait well into 1972, or even up to the convention, in hopes of a Kennedy candidacy. The handful of McGovern supporters identified during this initial trip were cultivated and encouraged by subsequent visits by Pokorny and calls from the Washington headquarters. They soon formed a statewide committee.

In the fall and winter of 1971 several elements crystalized. Almost simultaneously with a Muskie determination to make a strong effort in the state, we decided to make an all-out raid on the Iowa caucuses. Statements were made to the press by Muskie campaign officials that the Iowa and Arizona caucuses would demonstrate broadbased Muskie support in early pre-primary states and set the stage for a Muskie bandwagon in the initial primaries, all leading to the conclusive wrapping-up of the nomination by April or May. Although we maintained a low profile and continued to be extremely modest in projecting our goals, citing particularly the Senator's 3 percent standing in the polls, it soon became apparent to the national reporters, drawn to the scene by the Muskie claims, that some kind of early confrontation was shaping up.

In the meantime, we increased our organizational effort. Our state committee was expanded, we dispatched Lou Lamberty, our Nebraska organizer, into Iowa in the last few weeks to coordinate the effort on a full-time basis, and we added Washington staff support. I worked with one of the Washington people, Carl Wagner, whose background was in labor organization, to crack the unions for support, especially the UAW, but to little avail. Whatever chance we had in this regard, as well as any chance to pull off a tremendous upset, was crushed in early January by the surprise announcement by Hughes that he supported Muskie and urged all his fellow Iowa Democrats to do likewise.

The Hughes endorsement was stunning. If two leading Democrats had more common interests—the war, party reform, progressive legislation, bold and outspoken concern for what was right—than Harold Hughes and George McGovern, it was difficult to see. If there is any conviction left in politics, if there are any islands in the sea of political cynicism, if there are indeed men left who believe what they purport to believe, then of all men in the Democratic Party, Hughes should have supported McGovern, and he should have done so early. Someday men will follow their convictions or admit they have none; someday men will consistently support their beliefs or admit they are false; someday men will do what is right. But this was not the day and Harold Hughes was not the man.

The Hughes endorsement merely capped a trend, highlighted a parade. For Hughes followed, or was soon joined by, an honor roll of "liberals." Frank Church of Idaho (a close McGovern friend), Tom Eagleton of Missouri, Philip Hart of Michigan, Tom McIntyre of New Hampshire, Frank Moss of Utah, Claiborne Pell of Rhode Island, Adlai Stevenson of Illinois, Stuart Symington of Missouri, John Tunney of California, Harrison Williams of New Jersey. A few other Senators, who had remained uncommitted, endorsed McGovern—after the voters in their states had clearly shown his popularity. To his credit, Senator William Proxmire of Wisconsin announced his intention to vote for McGovern before the primary in his state.

In Iowa we could not gauge the impact of the Hughes endorsement. Nor could we calculate the effect of an effort organized by the Catholic Church to elect caucus delegates who would attend district and state conventions as opponents of pro-abortion legislation. Three days before the caucuses we visited the woman in charge of political action for the Des Moines diocese. We made an effort to assess the scope and direction of their effort, which seemed to be considerable, and managed to assure ourselves that it was not a Muskie organizational front, as had been rumored.

We spent caucus day checking the disposition of the troops, making sure all the precincts and counties were being covered. It was a bitterly cold day with a wind-chill factor of −56°. In mid-afternoon a severe blizzard struck the northwest corner of the state, causing state party chairman Cliff Larson to cancel the caucuses in the 20 hardest-hit counties across the north. I urged Larson to keep the caucuses on. Our theory was a conventional one: committed supporters turn out under adverse conditions, and we had the committed supporters. Larson held fast and postponed the caucuses. Although some of our people argued that we should challenge Larson's decision, the storm was so severe that we might be asking people literally to risk their lives in the rural counties, and the idea was abandoned.

A number of reporters drifted in during the day seeking predictions. I contended that it was a contest of Muskie versus the field, essentially McGovern plus the uncommitteds. My argument was based upon the fact that Muskie had almost unanimous support among elected and party officials, many of whom had fallen in line after the Hughes endorsement, and strong labor and regular party support. Indeed, Iowa became the first test of two classic political strategies. Muskie was relying heavily upon endorsements and the ability of party and labor leaders to "deliver," to produce workers and supporters in the precincts. The McGovern campaign, as it was to do in every state, relied on a grassroots campaign, starting from the ground up, locating workers in every precinct and county, the leadership coming from citizens, relatively anonymous and unknown, turning out thousands of people on caucus day.

By 10 P.M. on January 24th early caucus returns began to come into the state Democratic headquarters where representatives of the campaigns and the press corps, some 30 to 40 reporters, had gathered. With slightly over 5 percent of the precincts reporting, Muskie had 40 percent, McGovern 20 percent and the uncommitteds 35 percent. I was not pleased. By 11:20 P.M., with 14 percent of the precincts in, Muskie had 38 percent, McGovern 22 percent and the uncommitted 36 percent. Some movement our way, but not enough. At midnight, 25 percent of the precincts had reported, Muskie slipping to 36 percent, McGovern moving steadily up to 24 percent, the uncommitteds steady at 36 percent.

Editors were waiting and new leads had to be filed. R. W. "Johnnie" Apple, Jr., of *The New York Times* opened his story with the lead that Muskie would get most of the delegates, as expected, but that McGovern was making a "surprisingly strong showing." Most other reporters followed that lead. No Muskie bandwagon. We had "won." I circulated quietly around the room, suggesting that we would hold a 10:30 A.M. press conference to assess the results. I muttered to the other staff members to look as happy as possible, and it worked. The jollier the McGovern people began to look, the more solemn the Muskie staffers appeared. It helped the entire impression we were creating when, by 2:30 A.M., 30 percent of the precincts showed Muskie at 35 percent, McGovern up to 25 percent and the uncommitted delegates with 35 percent.

I was up at 7:30 A.M., after several hours of celebrating and two hours of sleep, to relay the results to the Senator. Inexplicably, he seemed disappointed. For reasons still unclear to me, he always seemed to think we would defeat Muskie in the first one or two primary and nonprimary states. I had always believed that it would be a process which would not clearly succeed until at least mid-way through the primaries, sometime in April or May, and that we should be elated to halt the bandwagon psychology in the early states. At the height of my elation at this minor miracle, the Senator wondered whether we couldn't increase our radio spots in the northern counties to get more delegates when the postponed caucuses were held. I explained that the Iowa story was being written that minute, that we had accomplished our goal, and that whatever happened thereafter would attract no national attention. He still seemed unhappy that we had not won a majority of the delegates.

Groggily, I made my way down to the headquarters for the press conference. I claimed an unqualified moral victory for McGovern, stating that we had far surpassed our expected turnout, that we had drawn within 10 percent of Muskie with all his political weight and advantages, and that, together with the uncommitteds, there were an overwhelming majority of Iowa Democrats who preferred some other candidate to Senator Muskie. In the middle of the press conference, I was handed a note that showed, with 49 percent of the precincts in, Muskie, 34 percent, Mc-Govern, 28 percent, uncommitteds, 36 percent. There was a great flurry among the press. I suggested we might win yet.

With that I hot-footed it out of the state as the confusion over statistics continued, to Muskie's detriment. That night, the late correspondent Bill Lawrence summed it up on the ABC evening news: "The Muskie bandwagon slid off an icy road in Iowa last night." We sweated blood for that one sentence.

As we were to do in most states, we later increased our percentage of delegate support from Iowa as the convention process continued. Starting with 26–28 percent of the delegate votes to the county level conventions, we ended up with well over 40 percent of the 46-member Iowa delegation to the national convention. This resulted from the conversion of uncommitted delegates and some maneuvering at state conventions.

Muskie's campaign was clearly and explicitly based on a plan to create the image of a "winner," an unstoppable frontrunner, and to bolster that image by assiduously seeking the support of elected officials and party officials whose endorsements would make the nomination appear inevitable and who would be able to produce voters at the polls. Throughout the fall of 1971 and the winter of 1971–72, those endorsements were announced in what seemed like battalion strength. One after another the big guns were fired. The political assumption was that each name represented a large number of votes and supporters.

We did not believe this strategy would work, partly because we had no choice and partly because we thought we had entered a political period when the people at large were not about to be told by their political leaders whom to support or for whom to vote, particularly where the Presidency was involved. The endorsements, like the public opinion polls, hurt us in two ways, both serious but both temporary. They had at least a momentary effect on campaign morale and they further hindered the already difficult task of fund-raising.

As it turned out, all the endorsements meant very little. They did in fact prove that the people will not follow the leader when it comes to deciding on a President. For the Muskie campaign, they may have been a net liability. They lulled his campaign into believing he had broadbased support when he didn't. This took much of the pressure off them to organize at the local level, pressure we constantly felt because that was the only thing we could do. Accumulating those endorsements must also have occupied a great deal of the candidate's and the campaign leadership's time, which could have been spent more profitably on other things.

For us, the absence of political support was something of a disguised blessing during the nomination race. It made McGovern appear to be above or apart from politics, perhaps that long-awaited figure, the honest man. His being essentially his own man, the lonely campaigner, not surrounded on every platform by "politicians," was undoubtedly attractive to large numbers of voters.

But that asset became a liability later, when it came time for voters to consider the depth and warmth of commitment he could inspire in fellow Democratic leaders when the race focused on Richard Nixon. Then there would be the recollection of the candidate virtually without leadership support in the party, even from his friends. It had to make some voters uneasy, and it had to raise some questions. The failure of McGovern's more liberal colleagues to stand with him as a matter of principle, if nothing else, had an impact on the outcome of the Presidential race. It appeared to the average voter not only that the regular and more conservative elements of the party were against him, but that he could not even get the support of those who agreed with him ideologically. It raised a question as to why more people didn't like him, especially those who should have. Surely it couldn't be because of his stands on the issues, because they voted with him and agreed with him. A number of these Senators had more liberal voting records than McGovern and were not ashamed to be identified with liberals or liberalism. Many voters must have reasoned that there was something wrong with McGovern the man.

Arizona, the second state to begin the delegate selection process and the first to complete it, was a textbook case of the impact of party reform. In 1968 five Democratic leaders in the state selected all 32 national convention delegates, none of whom was under 30 and only six of whom were women. On January 29th, 1972, thanks to an open caucus system instituted under the leadership of state party chairman Herb Ely, 35,000 Democrats across Arizona voted in caucuses selecting approximately 500 delegates to the state convention, which in turn selected all 25 Arizona national delegates. Almost half the 1972 delegates were under 30, one third were women and another third were blacks or Chicanos.

Our campaign in Arizona followed the pattern laid down in Iowa, with Rick providing day-to-day coordination of our organization during the last ten days. We relied heavily on volunteer phone banks and leafleting, as well as on limited radio spots. Our effort was of low visibility compared with the campaign waged by Lindsay. Apparently intrigued by

Rick's penthouse-meeting argument, Lindsay's people entered the Arizona contest with a vengeance, spending nearly $75,000 for a high-visibility, media-oriented campaign. We spent between $2,500 and $5,000. The contest between the McGovern and Lindsay campaigns became heated when it became clear we were competing for many of the same voters. When the dust settled, however, Muskie, with strong party and labor support under Congressman Morris Udall's direction, had captured enough support to gain 9 national delegates, Lindsay had 6, and we had 5. We were to increase our number to at least eight by convention time in mid-February.

JANUARY 28-29. I spent two days at the site of the National Convention to begin the tedious task of making arrangements for our participation in July. I also met with our Florida supporters preparing for the primary in March.

In spite of a successful direct-mail program and various fund-raising activities wherever the Senator went, we could never raise enough money to stay ahead of the creditors and run more than a meager campaign. As '72 began, we instituted almost daily finance meetings, usually in Frank's office, and involving me, Frank, Henry Kimelman, national finance chairman Marian Pearlman, our treasurer Jeff Smith, and occasionally one or two others. These sessions were a constant reminder that we were spending more than we were taking in and that the prospects of reversing the situation were dim. Marian and Jeff reported on the rising level of the debt and the creditors who were becoming most insistent. Henry would discuss plans for additional fund-raising and the need to cut down on expenditures. Frank and I analyzed the amounts that had to be sent to each of the state organizations that week.

An informal process evolved for sorting out immediate needs from tomorrow's needs, desperate needs from immediate needs, frantic needs from desperate needs. Priorities were agreed upon for meeting these needs. We would then call the state coordinators to let them know whether they could expect any immediate relief and, if so, how much. Inevitably, it was never enough and a new round of negotiations would begin, interspersed, in Joe Grandmaison's case, with threats and table-pounding and, in Gene Pokorny's, with moans and dire predictions. Somehow, we managed to keep the campaign afloat during those wintery weeks. In our desperate struggle to do so, we made at least one fruitful discovery—that it usually took several days for checks to our creditors to return to our bank. Since we were guaranteed a fairly steady stream of revenue from the direct-mail effort, we often raced to the bank to make sure checks already sent to creditors would be covered. When the total amount of the checks due to come in on a given day exceeded the amount available for deposit, frantic calls were made to our meager list of large contributors to seek additional contributions, or at least loans, to tide us over the crisis. During some periods, every day was a crisis. Every morning, as I walked into the headquarters, it was like stepping into a giant pressure-cooker. Money, money, where was the money? It never let up.

The direct-mail program, conceived by Morris Dees a year earlier, was a story unto itself.

The first mailing, accompanying the announcement in early 1971, produced over $300,000 and a letter which intrigued Morris' fertile imagination. A farm woman sent in $7.50, describing it as her "egg money" and promising to send in a like amount each month if she could. "This," Morris said, "was the key to an idea that became the backbone of our pre-primary and then pre-convention financing. The McGovern for President Club was formed." I thought, when Morris first outlined the idea, that it sounded like a gimmick, that political contributors generally considered themselves too sophisticated to join a club. But Morris was, if anything, persuasive. On March 1, 1971, a letter went out over my signature to the 22,000 contributors who had responded to the announce-ment letter asking them to contribute $10 a month through 1971. A coupon book with a payment slip for each month was enclosed. Over 20 percent of those first donors joined the original McGovern for Presi-dent Club, and new contributors thereafter were given a chance to join. Each club member received an "insider's" newsletter on the progress of the campaign and a reminder of the next month's "dues."

By January, 1972, the club's membership, which started at about 4,000, had risen to almost 10,000. Morris decided to continue billing the members through July, 1972. The monthly income from the club, approaching $100,000 by early 1972, kept the campaign alive.

The commitment of the club members bordered on the incredible. One elderly lady from Santa Monica wrote asking "permission" to send her "dues" every other month because of the long walk to the post office where she purchased money orders. And a 97-year-old man joined with the understanding that he might not be able to complete his commitment because of his uncertain tenure on this mortal coil. Over 90 percent of the members paid each month and the dropouts were few, even in one disastrous period when McGovern slipped from 3 percent to 2 percent in the polls.

"The club idea itself proves," Morris said, "that Alexis de Tocqueville was right when he observed almost 150 years ago that America was a nation of joiners."

When the announcement letter was prepared in January, 1971, the New York direct-mail experts Tom Collins and Stan Rapp joined Morris and Jeff Smith to form our small contribution team. In an effort to increase the pool of contributor names, test mailings of 5,000 or 10,000 each were made to 20 or so lists rented from organizations or publications whose members or subscribers were felt to have McGovern-supporter characteristics. The test letter paralleled the announcement letter except that it requested a donation—"even though you haven't selected a candidate"—so that McGovern "will have a chance to get his message across." If the test proved successful in direct-mail terms—pulling from 2 percent to 5 percent with an average donation near $15—the entire list was mailed. By this process, the total contributor pool was increased to 110,000 during the pre-convention period.

As the campaign entered the primary phase, special appeals were made to all donors prior to each important primary. Night letters went to all donors who had given more than $50. The Wisconsin primary letter described how important winning that state was to the overall prospects of the campaign. Just before the Ohio primary, donors were urged to "add up all they had given and double it as a contribution" if they could; if not, they were urged "to consider it a loan that I (McGovern) will personally see is repaid." Over $400,000 came in from this appeal, with only $26,000 designated as loans. Morris noted that many people responded with the observation that if a man felt so confident of his chances that he offered to repay a political loan, he deserved all the help he could get. The special appeal on the eve of the California primary indicated that Stewart Mott, who was heir to a General Motors fortune, had offered to match all donations for the McGovern California primary effort dollar for dollar. That appeal brought in over $400,000. Dees: "Poor Stewart."

The entire direct-mail program during the race for the nomination brought in $4,850,000. After subtracting costs of approximately $650,000, the net amount made available to the campaign was $4.2 million. This is a tribute not only to the Dees-Collins-Rapp-Smith fund-raising genius, but also to McGovern's ability to inspire tens of thousands of people to invest in the political process, often at great individual sacrifice. Unquestionably, McGovern could not have become the nominee without these small individual contributions. It was a revolutionary event in American politics whose impact has not begun to be fully appreciated.

THE PRIMARY CALENDAR. February brought almost constant attention to New Hampshire. But out beyond it were 22 other primaries, in all of which some organizational effort would be made and in 15 of which additional campaigning would take place. In February, 1972, the entire course seemed like a combination maze, marathon, and steeple-chase. The calendar of primaries:

March 7	New Hampshire	
March 14	Florida	
March 21	Illinois	
April 4	Wisconsin	
April 25	Massachusetts	
	Pennsylvania	
May 2	Ohio	Alabama
	Indiana	District of Columbia
May 4	Tennessee	
May 6	North Carolina	
May 9	Nebraska	
	West Virginia	
May 16	Michigan	
	Maryland	
May 23	Oregon	
	Rhode Island	
June 6	California	South Dakota
	New Jersey	New Mexico
June 20	New York	

New Hampshire impressions: Very young McGovern staff. Operates out of abandoned auto club building. David Sugarman 19–20. "Sugar." Chief press officer in the state. Earnest, proficient. Drives releases to Concord at 2 A.M. to make the papers' deadlines. Dave Aylward, 22, Dartmouth. First campaign. Ironic, uncertain. Lance Lalor, 24. Harvard Law. With Aylward, Congressional District coordinator. Sardonic, driven, emotionless, taut. John McKean, 23. Humorous, mature, detached, patrician. Administrator. Still motivated by the memory of RFK. Jim Keller, scheduler until Robbins arrived, then chief advance man. Robbins, sleeping on a cold linoleum kitchen floor covered only by a sheet during bitter winter weeks. Awakened throughout the night by the light inside refrigerator constantly being opened. Polly Hackett, Jean Thulemeyer. Round-the-clock advance women. Sleep standing up, or on a floor somewhere. Jacque Joseph Grandmaison. Garrulous, gargantuan. Vesuvian temper. Combination junior high basketball coach, priest, spoiled child, shrewd French trapper. Father to the staff ("For Chris-sake, don't crack up that car, it costs money!") Acid, sarcastic. Understands New Hampshire voters. Largely responsible for developing strategy emphasizing house parties and local receptions for the candidate, local campaign leadership, emphasis on New Hampshire issues—taxes, jobs, etc., reliance on local media experience.

F E B R U A R Y ,   1 9 7 2

The Senator's campaigning in New Hampshire had evolved a routine. Stopping in four, or as many as six, towns in a day, he mixed local radio appearances with handshaking tours of main streets and shopping centers, house parties, speeches at schools and on campuses, receptions and press conferences. Most important were his visits to plants and factories. Many of the state's voting Democrats work in factories—shoes, textiles, electronics. So it was out early—5:30, 6, 6:30 A.M.—to the plant gate to shake hands with the morning shift. Cold, freezing, dark. "Hello, I'm George McGovern. I'm running for President and I'd like your help." Later, if the advance people had been persuasive enough with the management, a tour of another factory, shaking hands bench by bench, the press corps trailing: "Who are you going to vote for? What do you think of this guy? What do you think of Muskie?" Sometimes, late in the afternoon, another shift change, another factory, another town. "Hello, I'm George McGovern. . . . " Somehow he had to get to "the people," the workers, the blue-collars. Muskie would get the regular Democrats, McGovern would get the liberals and "peace people"; in between was this vast multitude, this turned-off majority, over-taxed, distrustful of politics and politicians, worried constantly about layoffs, knowing that bankruptcy was one operation, one hospital-visit away. They would nominate a Democrat; they would elect a President.

McGovern began more and more to talk about taxes. Taxes paid to the federal government for costly, wasteful, inefficient, unnecessary weapons systems and bombs. Taxes paid, in increasing amounts, just to keep school systems alive. Taxes on everything you buy. He talked about jobs. The personal devastation caused by unemployment. The need for more government concern about the job market. Jobs totally dependent on a wartime economy and the massive unemployment which a shift away from war would cause. McGovern promised an administration which would commit itself to a job for every man and woman who needed and could take one.

McGovern talked about inflation. Rising food prices. Rising costs just to maintain a home to keep kids in school, to pay the bills. He criticized Phase I *and* Phase II. He stated over and over that wages were being controlled, but prices were not. That the economic policies and the control boards created to implement them were tilted toward big business, the haven of Nixons, Connellys, Mitchells, Stanses—and what did they care about the little man?

And even as McGovern talked, leaflets were being distributed: Mc-
Govern cares about jobs; McGovern wants to cut your taxes; McGovern
will reduce needless defense spending. Leaflets distributed at the plants,
leaflets handed out on street corners, leaflets given out door to door.
Literature moved first in lots of a dozen, then hundreds, then thousands,
and eventually millions. It was simply written, plain, straightforward—
the McGovern position in print. It was something people could take into
their homes and think about. And many did.

We had scheduled a media event or press conference every week for
six or eight weeks for the Senator in Boston on his way to campaign in
New Hampshire. During each stop, he made a major statement on a
problem of concern to New England voters. Each statement received
wide coverage on Boston television and radio. The highly populated
areas of southern New Hampshire are dominated by the Boston media
market. We received tens of thousands of dollars' worth of free media
exposure in New Hampshire in this way.

Senator Muskie, who chartered his own plane, didn't stop in Boston,
and didn't receive the extensive Boston media coverage.

It was there in New Hampshire that the McGovern army was born.
The purpose of a political organization is to contact voters. The more
voters you want to contact, the larger the organization must be. It is
possible to get elected without an organization; if a candidate is widely
known or can afford expensive media, occasionally he can wage a successful campaign without a widespread organizational effort. But Mc-
Govern was practically unknown and had no money.

From the very beginning, the Senator and I both assumed we would
have to develop the best political organization in the field in 1972.
Having very little money to pay people for their work, we had to rely
almost totally on volunteers. Although a volunteer-based effort is the
least expensive, it is also one of the most time-consuming and difficult
kinds of campaigns. Great discipline is required to run an effective campaign organization, and volunteers, being unpaid, are not as easily disciplined as paid staff members. Also, volunteers in general cannot contribute unlimited amounts of time. Their time, a precious commodity,
must be used as effectively as possible.

The steering committees were set up in each state in 1971. As state
coordinators were selected and assigned in late '71 and early '72, they,
in turn, identified local leaders, and those local leaders were responsible
for organizing their town or county. Establishing this structure was the
first step in winning a state. Step two was actually carrying out the voter

contact work—canvassing, phoning, leafleting, and mailing. Each of these programs requires people, lots of people, and that is where the volunteers came in. By February, 1972, in New Hampshire, the leadership structure, the officer corps, was set. But to win the war the army needed soldiers.

We had planned massive canvassing drives throughout the state for the last four or five weekends before the primary. The one great pool of manpower for such drives are the campuses, but we had already tapped the New Hampshire campuses, which do not have a long tradition of political activism, of all available help. In January we opened up recruitment drives on New England campuses, particularly among the quarter of a million Boston-area students. Student leaders organized door-to-door recruitment drives in the dormitories; special ads were placed in college and underground newspapers; appeals were made on local student and rock radio stations. Although some staff members had romantic recollections of the 1968 McCarthy New Hampshire campaign with thousands of students flocking to the cause, initially there was great lethargy on the campuses. The war no longer represented the personal threat that it had four years earlier and Ed Muskie was not Lyndon Johnson. In addition, every Friday afternoon, with clockwork regularity, the storm clouds rolled in over Vermont and Canada and great layers of snow fell until Sunday.

Nevertheless, the last three weekends of canvassing proved to be spectacular. A viable campaign, like most complex organisms, has its own internal clock, its own sense of timing and appropriateness. By the weekend of the 19th and 20th, all the efforts began to pay off. Between 700 and 800 canvassers came in and were assigned to various areas of the state to work under the direction of our staff and local organizers. The following weekend, over 1,000 people came into the state, and on the first weekend in March, two days before the primary, almost 2,000 McGovern workers came into New Hampshire to knock on doors and hand out leaflets. Although most were students, there were a considerable number of working men and women, professional people, housewives, and supporters of all kinds. Some came from New York and Philadelphia, some from as far away as eastern Pennsylvania and North Carolina; staff people came up from Washington.

One of the most gratifying moments of the campaign came on the Saturday night before the primary. I visited a Manchester area student dormitory where over 800 people, mostly students, were housed, sleeping on the floor in sleeping bags. After 22 months of lonely, frustrating work on a campaign with little if any visible results, with no apparent success, given practically no chance of winning, now to see the results of those efforts on the eve of the first big test, now to be surrounded by friends,

THE NEW YORK TIMES

New Hampshire coordinator, Joe Grandmaison, right, instructs the officer corps of the McGovern army.

was indeed a moving experience. Furthermore, it was proof that we had passed our first organizational trial even before the New Hampshire primary.

If we had been unable to raise that volunteer army, if those workers had not been moved by McGovern's courage and admonished by our organizers, the campaign would have come to naught. They were absolutely crucial to our success. The McGovern message had to be carried person to person. Thousands of voters in over a dozen primaries would be moved by the simple fact that they had been personally contacted by a McGovern worker. The army that was born and grew to hundreds in New Hampshire would swell to thousands in Wisconsin and to tens of thousands in Ohio and California. Many would follow the campaign across the country through three, four, or five primaries, from January to July and into the fall. They were on the front lines dealing hourly with the voters. They were the last, and most crucial link in the chain connecting McGovern with the people at large; they were the grassroots upon which he relied so heavily. And they were in New Hampshire when we needed them.

From the very beginning and throughout 1972, all our television and radio production, with few exceptions, was carried out by Charles Guggenheim and his associates in Washington. Charles is a slight, soft-spoken, self-assured, occasionally impatient and mercurial, film artist. Winner of many film-making awards, he was a media consultant to McGovern when he was Director of Food for Peace in the early 1960s and then was responsible for the media program in McGovern's two South Dakota Senate races. He knew McGovern well, and their personalities, styles, and outlook on politics meshed precisely.

Essentially, for the New Hampshire and later primaries, Charles did what he does best. He showed the candidate in informal situations talking and relating to small groups of citizens about particular problems they faced. Those problems might be taxes, health-care, the war, unresponsive government, agriculture, or one of many others, but the format was essentially the same: several people briefly stating their concerns, McGovern listening, then McGovern simply and clearly stating what should be done to solve the problem, what he would do as President. Very honest, very straightforward. No gimmicks. McGovern listening, always listening—uniquely, the leader who listens. And the faces of the people. Archetypal. Charles' associates have a genius for finding the most common, the most representative, yet the most absorbing, faces imaginable. Your neighbor, your friend, your co-worker. You know each one instantly. In the best sense of the word, very effective political media.

We also relied heavily in New Hampshire on Merv Weston and his associates, a firm specializing in advertising and public relations. Merv and his people prepared our literature, designed, produced, and placed all of our newspaper advertising, produced some local radio spots and placed all our television and radio spots. Over the course of the campaign, Merv became personally involved in our effort, treating it not as a client but as a cause. In the closing days, he permitted his offices to be disrupted by phone banks and supplementary staff, and hosted many campaign leadership meetings, a few of which became heated and tense. Through it all, he and his staff cooperated in every way possible to produce materials which reached the New Hampshire voters.

I spent most of February in New Hampshire lending leadership and decision-making support to Joe Grandmaison. Between us, we carried most of the campaign around in our heads and on little scraps of paper. However, in the last two weeks of the campaign we were joined, on an advisory basis, by an extremely wealthy and successful, and at that time somewhat mysterious, industrialist, Miles Rubin. Later to become greatly involved in our California primary effort and a principal fund-raiser in the fall, Miles came into New Hampshire asking a thousand questions and convinced that we were headed for disaster. With questioning, vaguely mocking eyes, and a sad, almost reproachful smile, he probed and poked, testing the campaign design, its plan, its direction.

At that time Miles' understanding of politics was limited to the quantifiable—pure numbers. His keen, systematic mind constantly demanded answers. How many phones? How many cars? How many canvassers? How many votes? If you don't know, how can you plan? He made it apparent that he thought the campaign was amateurish, chaotic, illdirected, and failing. It was a constant problem to explain to Miles that our shortcomings were largely a product of poverty rather than ignorance. We knew what to do, we just didn't have the money to do it. Over and over: "Why don't you do . . . ?" "Because we don't have the money." Miles soon got the picture and, from the seemingly bottomless pockets of his inconspicuous blue ski parka, helped fund a number of important projects, particularly additional phone banks which we could not previously afford, as well as radio and newspaper appeals for workers.

I had steadfastly argued, with some conviction, to the press during most of 1971 that we would be pleased with 10 percent of the vote in New Hampshire. As the field of potential major candidates narrowed in early 1972 to Muskie and McGovern, and as the minor candidates—Mills, Hartke, and Yorty (the latter two came to be lumped by the reporters into "Yortke")—seemed not to be making serious inroads, our official expectations rose to 15 percent and then, on the eve of the primary, to

between 20 percent and 25 percent. However, three events occurred in
late February which substantially increased our private expectations and
unquestionably affected the outcome of the primary.

First, during a routine tour of the J. F. McElwayne Shoe Company
factory in Manchester on the morning of the 18th, for the first time in
more than a year of campaigning, workers got up from their seats all
over the plant when they saw McGovern or heard he was there. They
wanted to shake his hand, to offer their support, to see him or have
their picture taken with him. His message was getting through, he was
reaching the voters, the people were beginning to find out who he was
and what he stood for, he was beginning to capture the imagination of
the workingman. From that day forward no serious reporter used the
word "charisma" to describe why McGovern couldn't win. Momentum
was with us. The phrase "McGovern surge" entered the political vocabu-
lary. Robert Healey, *The Boston Globe*'s political editor, wrote in the
closing days:

> When they talk about the surge here, they're talking about McGovern. It's
> the only game in town here in this primary week and at least it is making a con-
> test out of what appeared to be no contest. * * * There is no question that [Mc-
> Govern] has aroused enthusiasm for his campaign. * * * When he first came
> into this state a year ago his own people were saying he should not talk about
> getting more than 10 percent of the vote. And they were dead serious. Now, he
> talks about the brass ring. . . . What happened? 'My position on domestic is-
> sues has finally started to come through. People come to me on the street and
> say they like the way I answer questions,' says McGovern. * * * That's what the
> surge appears to be all about.

The second major event was the controversial appearance by Muskie
on the steps of the Manchester *Union Leader* on Saturday, the 26th.
During that appearance, Muskie defended himself against a *Union
Leader* report that he had called New Hampshire's citizens of French
extraction "Canucks," an ethnic slur, and he defended his wife against
allegations made in a separate article. It was widely reported that he
became so emotional that he cried and/or broke down. Analyses at the
time were unclear as to the overall impact of this event on the course of
the primary, but national stories began to be written shortly thereafter
showing the Muskie campaign in some difficulty. Under a headline in
The Washington Post, "Support for Muskie Wavers in New Hampshire,"
David Broder wrote on the 28th: "Sen. Edmund S. Muskie appears to be
in trouble in New Hampshire. Voter interviews . . . in the past four days
indicate an erosion in the presumed front-runner's strength that could
leave the Maine senator with an embarrassingly low percentage of the
vote in the March 7 Democratic primary contest he has counted on to
send his presidential campaign off on a flying start." The sub-headline

read: "Vagueness, Lackadaisical Drive Cited." There was no question
that, in the closing days, the Senator's own determined campaigning,
Charles' television and Merv's literature, our saturation phone banks, and,
most of all, the persistent and committed effort of the hundreds of door-
to-door canvassers, were beginning to have their effect. On March 1,
under a headline, "For Muskie, Mild Support; for McGovern, Intensity,"
The New York Times' "Johnny" Apple wrote: "The New Hampshire
Presidential primary next Tuesday may not be the walkover for Senator
Edmund S. Muskie that many people expect. * * * McGovern has
emerged, in New Hampshire at least, as something more than a frivolous
left-wing candidate."

The third turning point occurred on the 28th. On that Monday, in
Washington, we voluntarily disclosed the entire list of campaign contributors—a move unprecedented in American political history—and challenged all other candidates to do likewise. The list contained 42,472
names. The average contribution was $29.36. The total contributions since
January 18,1971, exceeded $1.2 million. The list contained the names
of 88 people who had given more than $1,000, gifts approximately only
one-fourth of the total contributions. The other Democratic candidates
took refuge in the fact that no law at the time required disclosure, completely missing the political impact and importance of what we had done.
For the first time a candidate for the Presidency of the United States had
voluntarily opened his financial records for the people to see. It not
only showed that McGovern was not the captive of any special interests,
but it further dramatized that he was the candidate of tens of thousands
of people, that this was the first popularly funded campaign in the
nation's history. Earlier, on a "Meet the Press" interview, Muskie had
stated that to disclose his contributors would mean the end of his campaign. He was merely emphasizing a fact of political life, except that it
served to confirm a popular feeling that politics is dirty, and that there
must have been some strings on his contributions. The disclosure, opposed
for a time by some of our financial people on the ground that it would
depress large contributions, was as important as anything we did in setting
the tone of the campaign.

MARCH 7, 1972. Primary day. All the headquarters across the
state emptied out except for the local coordinator and those manning the
phones. Every worker had an asignment; drive a car taking voters to
the polls, baby-sit with voters' children, knock on the doors of, or call,
every person in the state who has indicated support for McGovern during
our foot and phone canvass, watch the polls to check off our voters as
they came in, run the poll lists to the phone banks throughout the day,
hand out leaflets, take coffee to the poll workers, pull, pull, pull, . . . pull

every McGovern voter in the state. Experts in political technique say that an organization which can pull 60 percent of its supporters on election day is extraordinary. I believe we pulled 90 percent to 95 percent of the McGovern vote in New Hampshire. All the tensions and pressures which had been mounting through the previous weeks reached a peak during that primary day. The strain on nerves and energies was perceptible. Raw vitality crackled almost audibly in the air. And each McGovern vote cast that day represented a tribute to the teeth-gritting determination of the candidate and his followers.

The final result: Muskie, 46 percent; McGovern, 37 percent; Yorty, 6 percent; Mills, 4 percent; Hartke, 2 percent.

Nine points. Nine percentage points between McGovern and Muskie. McGovern—3 percent in the polls, from South Dakota, unknown no "charisma," little regular party support, a one-issue candidate, starting with no money, no chance. Muskie—leading the polls, solid financial backing, many-issue candidate, the endorsements of most of the Democratic Party leadership, expert staff, the neighbor from Maine.

In February, 1971, on his first campaign trip into New Hampshire, the Senator had placed courtesy, introductory phone calls to a list of leading Democrats drawn up by Joe Grandmaison. He called Dr. David Underwood of Concord. "Hello. This is Senator George McGovern. Is Dr. Underwood there?" Puzzled receptionist: "I'm sorry. Who did you say you were?" McGovern: "Senator McGovern. Capital M . . . c . . . capital G . . . o . . . v . . . e . . . r . . . n."

Election night footnotes. The Senator was irritated and disappointed. On the night of the first big breakthrough of his two year up-hill quest for the Presidency, he was upset because he not lived up to his own somewhat unrealistic expectation of winning, of beating Muskie in New Hampshire. His mood, which I was to see only one time after that, brought the young New Hampshire staff, already on the brink of physical collapse, to tears. Their jubilation was almost crushed.

Shortly before 4 A.M., the wife of a network employee in the Howard Johnson's motel with us in Manchester awoke Shirley MacLaine, who in turn woke me. The woman, frenzied to the point of incoherence, claimed she had received a call from someone threatening to blow up the motel and kill the Senator. I awoke the Senator in the next suite and moved him and Eleanor down to a first-floor room next to the press room. Through the walls could be heard the sounds of celebration—another New Hampshire primary survived. Warriors who had lived through another fire ritual.

A search by a thoroughly befuddled Manchester fire department failed to reveal any bomb. It did manage to arouse an adled Mankiewicz, who allowed as how the bomb could go off for all he cared, he needed the sleep. It also managed to arouse one of our contributors who was in for the primary. He had made considerable money in off-shore securities and, hearing the heavy-handed pounding in the middle of the night, groggily thought some irate investors had finally found him.

After a while, the Senator, calm as always, said to the diminutive Eleanor, now sleeping huddled on the floor next to the uproarious party, "Come on, Eleanor, let's go back up, I don't think there is any bomb in here." And off they went, climbing up the interior fire escape in their bathrobes.

MARCH 10, 1972. Miami. Thursday. 4 P.M. Three days after the New Hampshire primary, I knew McGovern would get the nomination. I had arrived in Florida the previous day and had spent most of the day on the phone around the state and conferring with Rick Brown, our state coordinator. After some investigation, both with our staff in Florida and with members of the press corps, two highly significant facts became apparent: the Muskie campaign was failing and the Lindsay campaign was in serious trouble. Muskie needed to do well in Florida after his setback in New Hampshire. If he ran worse than second it would signal the continuing weakness of his national effort, would begin to dry up much-needed financing, and would further demoralize a staff beginning to be riddled with rumors of internal conflict. On that Thursday, I judged that he would run out of the money in the Florida primary.

Lindsay was making a very big play in Florida. He spent a great deal of time in February and early March campaigning there. The press estimated his media expenditures at $350,000. We estimated his total expenditures in Florida in excess of $500,000, perhaps as high as $700,000. A great deal of that money went to hire organizers. On the theory that the Lindsay campaign command was too intelligent to pay people unnecessarily, this alone meant that the campaign had abundant difficulties, that sufficient workers were not available who would volunteer their services. With such an investment so readily apparent to the press, a campaign is judged severely, and it must produce. All signs on the 10th were that Lindsay's would not.

These two situations taken together meant that McGovern would soon emerge as the candidate of one great force in the Democratic Party, with no Lindsay to challenge him, and Humphrey would soon assume representation of the more traditional elements of the party upon the final demise of the faltering Muskie campaign. There was no doubt in my mind that McGovern, the new face, the standard-bearer of change and progress, would defeat Humphrey in the conclusive later primaries. As I sat pondering all this in a sunlit parking lot behind the converted paint store we used for our Florida headquarters, I saw a triumphant Mc-Govern, victor in the decisive California primary, returning to Miami four months later and finally returning to Washington as President.

In the meantime, after the initial debate inside our own campaign, we had resolved to reduce our effort in Florida. Our total cash expenditure in the state amounted to approximately $50,000, of which over half went for media. We had no more than six paid staff members and relied almost totally on the organization work of our state committee and local supporters. In his attempts to create a genuine McGovern grassroots organization throughout Florida, Rick Brown encountered the phenomenon I had perceived in my earlier trips into the state. Florida is a little California without the western state's tradition of political activism. Both states rely heavily on media in political campaigns and neither maintans statewide political organizations which can be mobilized by out-of-state candidates. It was practically impossible to mount the kind of intensive canvassing drives which worked so well in smaller or more politically structured states.

Unlike McGovern, and like Lindsay, other candidates made major efforts in Florida. Muskie, Jackson, and Humphrey all launched intensive media campaigns. Humphrey also invested in an elaborate professional phoning services to contact voters in various parts of the state. Humphrey particularly felt that he had a base of support in Florida upon which resurrection could be established.

George Wallace also campaigned in Florida.

MARCH 14, 1972. Primary day. Governor Wallace won a smashing victory with almost 42 percent of the vote. Humphrey was closest to him with only 18 percent; Jackson had 13 percent; Muskie was fourth with just under 9 percent; Lindsay and McGovern both had 6 percent, with Lindsay a fraction of a percentage point ahead.

Wallace was obviously the big winner. He would now be a factor for the Democrats to reckon with in nominating a Presidential candidate. From the immediate McGovern campaign point of view, he would not take votes from the Senator. But if Wallace ran up sizable votes in other states, somewhere along the line McGovern, like the other contenders, would have to demonstrate an ability to attract and appeal to the Wallace voter.

Television reception at the Everglades Hotel in Miami, our election-night headquarters, was miserable, so I accepted an earlier invitation from David Brinkley to watch the early returns at the NBC facilities across the street from the hotel. As the Wallace vote mounted I was taken back to the fall of 1968 and I saw history beginning to repeat itself.

Wallace, with his slogan of "Send Them a Message!" would now emerge as the popular anti-establishment messenger of the millions of discontented voters. His Florida campaign signalled a broadening of his base; his appeal was not simply racist, but extended to taxes, governmental waste, "pointy-headed bureaucrats," welfare give-aways, and special treatment for the rich. But through it all there continued to emerge the theme of "busin' li'l chilern." So much so that "busin' li'l chilern" became a motto for all those other ills. The same people who bused little children gave money away to welfare chiselers, took too much in taxes, wanted to duck out of a fight with the communists, were "pointy-headed bureaucrats who didn't have enough sense to park a bicycle straight." Send THEM a Message! Wallace, surely subconsciously harking back to a previous era, once stated in a speech: 'We *own* those li'l chilern. THEY can't tell us what to do with our own li'l chilern. THEY got no business busin' those li'l chilern. We *own* those li'l chilern."

Did Wallace's showing in Florida signal a replay of the 1968 election? Or, perhaps, might he not stay in the Democratic Party this time and bring a sizable portion of that 10 percent to 15 percent of the popular vote over to the Democratic nominee? It was too early to say, but those were our thoughts on the night of March 14th, 1972.

And so, apparently, were they the thoughts of George McGovern. After the trend seemed obvious, I went back across the street to the Senator's room in the Everglades. He had discarded the text of a statement prepared that afternoon and was completing a new draft which addressed itself particularly to the Wallace showing. He read portions of it to me, to Frank, and to Ted Van Dyk, asking our advice on its content. After we had each made minor suggestions regarding the language and tone, he went downstairs, to speak to several hundred supporters. His statement essentially attributed the Wallace vote to widespread citizen discontent with governmental performance and to disenchantment with politics and politicians. In sharp contrast to the statement we had watched Muskie deliver a few minutes earlier, McGovern did not suggest that those who had voted for Wallace were necessarily bigots or racists. The Senator, rather, suggested that the Florida Democrats had indeed sent a message and that he had received and properly interpreted the significant part of it.

MARCH 16, 1972. Milwaukee. The previous day on the flight back to Washington from Miami, Frank told me the Senator wanted us to meet with him and a few other staff members in Milwaukee to review plans for the Wisconsin primary. We met at 10 A.M. in a suite at the Red Carpet Inn near Mitchell Field, the Milwaukee airport. The morning meeting consisted essentially of a discussion of scheduling strategy. Senator Gaylord Nelson of Wisconsin had proposed to McGovern that he rely heavily on local radio and television appearances, getting into as many local media markets as possible each day by participating on talk shows and public-service programs. Nelson also urged hitting hard on the entire tax structure, particularly property taxes, which he felt were a cutting issue in Wisconsin. We discussed at some length the detailed implementation of the scheduling proposal and then broke for a brief lunch. Afterward, McGovern asked Frank and me to remain for a discussion of campaign assignments.

My internal political clock told me, on the way to Milwaukee that morning, that we were in for another of those profitless and corrosive leadership struggles. Gordon Weil, Yancey Martin, and Kirby Jones, the press secretary, joined the meeting. After some preliminary discussion, the Senator suggested that I assume responsibility for the non-primary states only and that all the other aspects of the campaign, including responsibility for the remaining primary states, be placed under Frank's direction. Someone, it seems, had convinced him that the non-primary operation was not working and that courting and cultivating the uncommitted delegates, another job he suggested I do, was in fact a real political task.

If there was unhappiness in the field with the way the primary state campaigns were being conducted, it had to come from the states which suffered by my refusal to overextend and bankrupt the national campaign, particularly Illinois. It was very easy for a state coordinator or anyone in Washington who didn't share that view to convince himself, and try to convince the Senator, that I was not providing the help they needed. When I refused to approve more funds for a state, or a greater media allocation, or more staff, the person with the responsibility for organizing in the state could conclude that he was right and I was wrong. If the Senator made a mistake, it was to listen to and believe too many of these complaints.

The arguments made to him in this instance were wrong on several counts, and so I attempted to convince him during the meeting. The organizational effort in the non-primary states was proceeding as smoothly as possible with extremely limited resources, under Rick Stearns' and Eli Segal's direction, and what it needed was more field organizers and more money, not additional day-to-day leadership. It had enough chiefs. Further, very few states were selecting large numbers of uncommitted delegates and it would be a waste of my time to be given that assignment. Finally, since the campaign was unfolding exactly as had been planned months earlier and we were approaching the threshold of success, it made no particular sense to tamper with the leadership structure. Nothing was going wrong that additional money couldn't cure. The only reason could be to satisfy discontented egos.

I was angered that someone had gone behind my back to the Senator with spurious arguments and, further, that he had accepted those arguments without giving me an opportunity, except in the presence of other staff members, to present what I considered to be the true situation. The conclusion of the meeting was that I would give the plan some thought and respond shortly, but the Senator made it clear that he strongly favored the idea.

My impression at the time, as it was in previous instances of this sort, was that the Senator had not really sorted out the merits of the arguments, but was merely trying to settle a somewhat sticky personality problem. Although arguments presented to the Senator were cast in terms of responsibility and roles, behind these struggles was the primary motivation of power. Those who wanted me moved down sought the authority to run the campaign. I fought to stay on because I thought I could do a better job. But, as in all political campaigns, power was the source of the few controversies we had.

Before leaving, I talked to the Senator privately in his room, expressing my dismay that these situations had to arise. We agreed that the matter would be resolved before the Wisconsin primary. I then left for meetings with Gene Pokorny, and the Senator went into Illinois to campaign.

MARCH 17, 1972. Milwaukee. St. Patrick's day. I gave serious thought to resigning from the campaign after the Wisconsin primary. These recurring leadership struggles were personally exhausting and, in my judgment, were debilitating to campaign morale. One way or another, most staff members found out what was going on (sometimes before I did) and most of them found it enervating and distasteful. To me, all this pulling and hauling made no sense.

When I began to commute to Washington in June of 1970, and later joined the campaign full-time, my understanding with the Senator was that I would step down as campaign manager when the time seemed right. There was now an overwhelming and unrelenting sense of fatigue. Almost two years had passed since I first met the Senator and had begun some kind of involvement on his behalf, and occasionally a combination of pressure and exhaustion reduced me to a robot. Perhaps the time was now right.

That night, Friday, I received a call in the Milwaukee headquarters from the Senator in Chicago. He asked, with a note of urgency, whether I had made up my mind to accept the proposal put forward only the previous morning. I reminded him that he had agreed that it need be resolved only before the Wisconsin primary which was still more than two weeks away. With some vexation, he said that it had to be settled that weekend, that the campaign could not drift along with the leadership question uncertain. I said that most of the staff in the field and in Washington didn't particularly think there was a leadership question and, that to the degree it existed at all, it existed in the minds of a few reporters who seemed to relish those things. Nevertheless, the Senator said, he had to resolve it—he was under great pressure from a "couple of people" to do so. Who were the people, I asked, did I have a right to know who was pressing him? He said he couldn't tell me. I was appalled and angered that he was being harassed concerning this matter and that I was being pressured indirectly by people who wouldn't confront me with these differences so they could be resolved without troubling the candidate. I merely repeated the arguments I had made the previous morning regarding the capabilities of the principals involved in this matter, and the conversation ended inconclusively.

MARCH 18, 1972. After a brief discussion with Gene Pokorny and Joe Grandmaison, both of whom were aware of the struggle, I returned to Washington. I told them both that I was torn between loyalty to the Senator and a feeling that I had had enough of this nonsense, that the Senator would now go on to win with the machinery that had been established over the past two years regardless of who possessed what title, and that life was too short to live through these wrenching personality conflicts.

The trip had been worthwhile in spite of the hassle. I spent time with Gene reviewng our most troublesome problem, the Wisconsin campaign budget, as well as media and promotion plans, our organization in each Congressional District, and staff assignments.

MARCH 19, 1972. Late that afternoon I received a call from the Senator whose manner and tone had turned 180° from our previous conversation on Friday night. He said he had had an opportunity to talk to a number of people in the past two days and had received a completely different picture of the campaign's progress than had recently been presented to him. He was complimentary toward the work I had done and sincerely hoped that I would stay on as campaign manager with full responsibility for the entire campaign. He suggested he had been misled by one or two people (still nameless) and was grateful that several other people in the campaign had accurately informed him subsequently. So he wanted the entire controversy to be written off. He would so inform the others involved and wanted us to iron out any disagreements among ourselves. I said I would be more than happy to try.

Thus ended the third or fourth leadership skirmish in a campaign on the verge of becoming byzantine. This one played itself out, went through an entire oscillation, a complete pendulum swing, in less than four days—but it seemed like four weeks.

MARCH 21, 1972. The Illinois primary. There were two contests, one for the popular vote, and one for the convention delegates from the respective Congressional Districts. After a bizarre series of events in January we made a last-minute decision not to enter the non-binding preferential primary, the so-called beauty contest. Only Muskie and McCarthy had indicated an intention to enter this side of the primary. To engage in a three-way race in which one of the candidates was not a serious contender who might, nevertheless, divide the potential McGovern vote, did not seem wise. In addition, a great deal of money for media would be needed to counter the well-financed Muskie campaign in Illinois and get the still little-known McGovern better known almost overnight. This money was badly needed for Wisconsin.

However, we could not be sure that a number of other major contenders might not enter at the last minute and leave us out in the cold. As a precaution, our staff and supporters in Illinois had collected the necessary signatures on petitions. Therefore, on the day for filing entry petitions, we instructed Bill Rosendahl, our state coordinator, to fly to Springfield and stand by, prepared to file by 5 P.M. if others entered. A serious difficulty arose because an affidavit, signed by the candidate, was delayed in Washington and arrived in Chicago too late for Rosendahl to catch a plane for Springfield. He then chartered a helicopter, which was forced down in a cornfield 40 miles from Springfield at 4 that afternoon.

Rosendahl to us: "I'm in a phone booth next to a Phillips 66 gas station outside McLean, Illinois; the helicopter had to land because of a blizzard and I'm trying to thumb a ride from this phone booth. What do you think I ought to do?"

Meanwhile we had our Springfield scout on another phone from a hotel room opposite the state capitol watching to see if recognizable representatives of other candidates went in to file.

"Get down to Springfield anyway you can, Bill, just in case."

The helicopter took off but had to land again only a few miles closer to Springfield. The exhausted, but indefatigable, Rosendahl struggled into the capitol a few minutes after 5, needlessly as it turned out, because only Muskie and McCarthy had filed and we didn't want to be in that race. Unfortunately a Chicago staff member, overwhelmed by the sheer excitement of it all and mistaking comic opera for serious drama, informed the press of Rosendahl's epic journey. The reporters were on it like dogs on a bone. Thereafter, we spent days trying to explain that, in spite of the helicopter, spies with binoculars, and other machinations, we had never intended to file anyway. Few believed us.

We did, however, file slates of five, six, or seven delegates in 17 of Illinois' 24 Congressional Districts. As in Iowa, the contest for delegates was among McGovern, Muskie, and uncommitted (the uncommitted being essentially pro-Mayor Daley or pro-Humphrey). Our campaign in the state was very uneven, with some districts having well-planned efforts and well-disciplined workers, and others extremely unorganized and divided. We sent in a substantial number of our best organizers (some, like Bill Lockyer, from as far away as California) in the closing weeks to help with the organizational activities, but often they clashed with local supporters more concerned about their own power and prerogatives than electing McGovern delegates. Because money was not available from the national campaign to send to Illinois, Bill Rosendahl had to spend a disproportionate amount of his time with fund-raising and campaign-financing.

An extreme example of the kind of conflict which occasionally arose between local supporters and outside organizers, more often it seemed in Illinois than anywhere else, occurred in the Tenth Congressional District where the locals rose up en masse and drove out staff member Harold Himmelman. Himmelman: "I learned the painful lesson that for some people McGovern was just a vehicle for their own assertion of power . . . it was far more important that they control things and control them their way than that McGovern win." Later, on election night, after Bill Lockyer had replaced Harold, Bill fell into an argument with one of our local supporters in the district over control of several boxes of three-by-five cards containing the names of McGovern voters (she wanted to keep them and Lockyer wanted to take them to Chicago, where they belonged) and she bit him on the hand. Difficult as things were to become, few were called upon to make such a vivid and immediate sacrifice. We considered giving Lockyer a variation of the Purple Heart. Maybe a Purple Hand.

The primary results. In the preferential primary poll: Muskie, 63 percent; McCarthy, 36 percent. Delegate count: Muskie, 59; McGovern, 13; uncommitted, 88. In terms strictly of the investment made, this was the worst showing of our campaign. It was also the high-water mark of the Muskie campaign, rehabilitating Muskie at least long enough to see him into Wisconsin. And thus the stage was set for what we hoped would be our first big breakthrough, the Wisconsin primary.

LATE MARCH, 1972. Wisconsin had become an important primary state for a number of reasons. It marked the end of the first series of primaries and would be a watershed for several candidates, determining in part which ones would continue and which would be forced to drop out due to poor showings. It was a ballot designation state, candidates' names being automatically placed on the ballot if the Secretary of State deemed them serious contenders. Thus the field would include—besides McGovern—Muskie, Humphrey, Jackson, Wallace, Lindsay, McCarthy, and five other "also-ran" Democrats. There was historic justification for considering Wisconsin important. It had given John Kennedy a slight edge over Hubert Humphrey in 1960, thus proving Kennedy's vote-getting ability in a Midwestern, agrarian state.

McGovern would be expected to do relatively better here than in New Hampshire. The reporters knew that we had been making an extensive, widespread organizational drive. And this was a state much more similar to South Dakota. We had factored all this in with the Senator's own judgment that he could do well here and had made a determination—which was never seriously challenged inside the campaign—that we should go all-out in Wisconsin. Throughout 1971 and early 1972, the Senator literally spent weeks there. We assigned a number of our best staff organizers there. And our total campaign budget, from late 1970 through the primary, was $440,000.

But it had not always been so. Bill Dixon, our Milwaukee coordinator, tells the story of our second staff member in Wisconsin, Gordon "Harvey" Werner, who had never been involved in politics in his life but who was hired at the magnificent sum of $15 per week to work around headquarters. Because we were short of trained advance men in 1971, Harvey was sent up to the Fox River Valley to advance one of the Senator's stops. Aside from fundamental instructions, he was told to read Jerry Bruno's book, *The Advance Man,* to find out what to do. The Senator was scheduled to drive through Neenah, a little town on Lake Winnebago, at 5 P.M. on Friday, stop and do a 10-minute event. Harvey got into town Thursday night and dutifully (that's what the book said to do) asked the Police Chief where most of the people in the town were at 5 P.M. on Fridays. The Chief gave him the name of a restaurant and said that was where half the town's population was at that time every Friday. Dixon: "Harvey was elated at how easy it was to advance a trip and he called Gene and me and we put the stop on the schedule. Later, Harvey went to check out the restaurant and on the door was painted a big sign 'If nudity offends you—do not enter!' Sure enough, we quickly canceled the stop. That's how it was in the early days here."

In addition to the pinched, undernourished nature of our own resources in the early days, our organizational efforts were hindered by the obscured intentions of Wisconsin's senior Senator, William Proxmire, to seek the Presidency himself. Extremely popular with his constituents and with a national following resulting particularly from his efforts to reduce wasteful defense spending, Senator Proxmire had, like a number of others, gone so far as to spend several weekends in 1971 shaking hands in some New Hampshire villages.

Since the Proxmire rumors caused many of the best local political leaders in Wisconsin to await his decision before involving themselves in the primary for any other candidate, our supporters approached them on the basis that they should help McGovern in the meantime; then, if Proxmire definitely decided to run, they would be released from their commitment to McGovern with all good wishes. This proved highly successful, according to Dixon, allowing us to receive unshakable commitments from many of the best local organizers even before Proxmire withdrew on November 6, 1971.

Gene had devised an ingenious organizational plan for the final few weeks before the primary. After 15 months of intensive organizing around Wisconsin, first developing Congressional District McGovern organizations, then county organizations, then local "grassroots" organizations, he had built up a card file of tens of thousands of names of McGovern supporters, some in the Milwaukee headquarters, some out in local offices. This master list was supplemented in February with a newspaper insert in the Sunday edition of major Wisconsin newspapers describing McGovern, his background and record, and containing a response envelope for contributions and offers of support. This insert went into 75 percent of the homes in Wisconsin, and the returns were substantial. These names were added to the existing names of supporters and a mailing was prepared to the total list, now numbering more than 10,000 McGovern supporters. Each was asked to donate to the campaign two hours a week for the last four primary weeks. The first week, raise one dollar from each of ten friends and send the ten dollars to the state headquarters; the second, put McGovern bumper strips on the cars of ten friends; the third, find ten new McGovern voters in their neighborhood; the final, primary week, get those ten new McGovern voters to the polls. Thus, every McGovern supporter in the state was given meaningful assignments for the crucial last four weeks.

Underneath this mass citizen effort continued the traditional canvassing, leafleting, and phoning—the direct voter contact work being carried out by the hundreds of local McGovern organizations throughout Wisconsin. This effort continued relentlessly night after night, day after day, out at the plant gates and on the street corners. Squads of canvassers systematically approached every door, every household, neighborhood by neighborhood, area by area, city by city, county by county. Special mailing went to farmers, labor groups, and peace groups, and registration drives were held on campuses and other areas of greatest strength. Radio and television spots were used, most intensively in Milwaukee and the other major media markets. And, of course, newspaper ads.

But most of all the candidate. The Senator went into almost every community in the state, into some towns and cities six times, carrying his message: Let's make the tax structure fair for a change. If we reduce waste in the Pentagon and close tax loopholes favoring the rich and the powerful then money will be available from the federal government to help the states with the costs of education, and your property taxes can be reduced. Let's make sure there are jobs for every man and woman who needs one. Let's do more as a nation to care for the sick and elderly—our treatment of older people is barbaric. Above all, let's end the war.

During the primary season, the candidate's wife was campaigning with great vigor. Eleanor McGovern is an extraordinary woman. Some obvious things can be and have been said about her. She is extremely attractive, possessing a mature beauty which seems to have that rare quality of increasing with time. She is also very small—"petite" is the standard description—not five feet tall and barely 100 pounds. Eleanor McGovern is political in the best and most fundamental sense of the word, exercising an exceptionally keen insight into human nature and the motivations of the average voter. The Senator does, in truth and not just for magazine copy, pay close attention to her judgment on many things. She plays a much greater role in his political life than that of simply companion and social display object.

From New Hampshire on, Eleaner McGovern showed no reluctance to campaign on her own, preferring in many cases to give her own speeches for a time, and then accompanying the Senator for a few days to re-educate herself on any new themes, ideas, or illustrations he might be using. Nor did she confine herself merely to women's groups or domestic forums. She plunged into plants and factories, public facilities and rowdy rallies, standing on tip-toe to deliver vigorous, partisan campaign speeches into microphones often aimed over her head. Dauntless; intimidated only, in my experience, by huge crowds pressing close to her from all sides. She would confess to occasional moments of panic that, because of her diminutive size, she might literally be crushed.

Although she spent much of 1971 in Washington remaining with the two teenage children, of the family total of five, Eleanor began to campaign vigorously in New Hampshire as well as in Wisconsin and the later important primary states. Operational or structural aspects of the campaign were often not clear to her. She had special difficulty on occasion with our scheduling policies and the strategy behind them, preferring, as did the Senator, to recommend other trips that might be taken or other stops that might be made. But, in both cases, they were the people being moved around and called upon to respond, and I always considered they had a right to participate in the ordering of their own lives. Politicians' wives are too often described as "assets," a term that reduces them to objects or chattel; but Eleanor McGovern was indeed and in fact an asset, converting voters and supporters to her husband's cause everywhere she went. In a Presidential campaign, one cannot help but imagine the candidate's wife in the role of First Lady. Eleanor Mc-Govern would have been right at home in the White House.

EASTER SUNDAY. APRIL 2, 1972. A sense of calmness and detachment settled over the campaign on the eve of the Wisconsin primary. It seemed strange to me to be away from home on Easter, to be shuttling instead between the Milwaukee headquarters and the University Inn where the Senator and staff were staying. Two weeks before, Pat Caddell collected survey data showing McGovern trailing Humphrey by five or more points but leading Muskie by a substantial margin. Then, a week before, the same sense of surge, of momentum, that had developed in New Hampshire began to be felt, and a poll conducted by the state AFL-CIO and showing McGovern leading Humphrey by seven or eight points leaked to the press. Senator Proxmire's office in Washington issued a statement several days before saying that Proxmire had cast an absentee ballot for McGovern and had given very persuasive reasons for doing so. Although the statement specifically denied being a formal endorsement, we reproduced it overnight and moved approximately 150,000 copies of it around the state. Finally, that weekend, Bill Dougherty, Lieutenant Governor of South Dakota, a wiry, fiery, blunt McGovern ally, brought his friend, Wisconsin's Governor Lucey, out to the airport to greet the Senator during a stop in Madison, knowing that reporters would press the Governor for a prediction at least. And although he remained scrupulously uncommitted during the primary, Governor Lucey did admit to the persistent journalists that he thought McGovern would win the primary. We moved that story around a lot, too.

There was a quiet sense of confidence on that Easter Sunday that we might win the Wisconsin primary. An overwhelmingly comprehensive effort had been made for more than fifteen long months. The total man-hours invested in Wisconsin for McGovern, including his own, were practically incalculable. So the final hours had to be given to testing, probing, and retesting the get-out-the-vote apparatus in each district, making sure that all the procedures were clear and all the machinery set. Mark Segal and Marty Munn, specialists in these procedures, had come in from New York to work with the local organizers and field staff to make sure all the McGovern votes got to the polls.

STUART BRATESMAN

Watching the early primary returns: (left to right) Liz Stevens, Roger Saunders, Frank Mankiewicz, Senator McGovern, Jean Westwood, Dick Dougherty.

Convention delegates were elected by Congressional District. Thus we had to carry as many districts as possible to increase the number of McGovern delegates from Wisconsin. We were particularly concerned about Muskie and Humphrey strength in Milwaukee and Humphrey strength in the agricultural districts bordering Minnesota. Milwaukee was the stronghold of the regular party, labor, ethnic groups, and blacks, all elements that we were supposed to be weak with. And Humphrey had campaigned hard all across the state, but particularly in the areas closest to Minnesota and under the influence of the Minneapolis-St. Paul media, as the "third Senator from Wisconsin," the old friend and neighbor. He had, in rough measure, the same advantage in that regard as Senator Muskie had in New Hampshire.

Governor Wallace spent approximately a week campaigning in Wisconsin after the Florida primary and then, inexplicably, disappeared. Senator Jackson seemed not to pose a serious threat; by our calculations, whatever votes he got would be taken from Humphrey or Muskie. Lindsay, trying desperately to recoup after the disastrous Florida showing, campaigned in fits and starts, resorting to gimmickry—staying overnight with a laborer and his family, sleeping on the couch—and never really convincing Wisconsinites that he was anything more than a refugee from New York City. (In the heat of the campaign, Brooklyn Democratic leader Meade Esposito, considered by many to be a Lindsay ally, issued a public appeal to the Mayor. "Little Sheba, come home" and run New York, he said.)

Clearly now, the McGovern strategy of taking the lead, of forcing the issues, was paying off. Humphrey listed his campaign contributors on March 14th, Muskie listed his on the 28th, and Wallace followed suit on the 29th. Also during March, Muskie followed the lead on two principal McGovern proposals—major tax reforms and substantial cuts in the defense budget. The tide was beginning to run.

APRIL 4, 1972. The Wisconsin primary. The Senator spent most of the day quietly with his family. I was tense. That night we moved our election headquarters to the Pfister Hotel across the street from our Milwaukee campaign headquarters. In an upstairs command post (the "situation room") we monitored precincts carefully selected by Pat Caddell days in advance to give us the earliest possible indication of the trends. Individuals assigned to these precincts called special phone numbers in the situation room to report the count the minute it was available.

The polls closed at 8 P.M. and key precinct reports began to come in within minutes. By 8:15 it appeared that we would win by a substantial margin. At 8:30 Oliver Quayle walked into the suite to offer his congratulation just as NBC, the network which used the data Quayle had provided, called McGovern the winner.

Frank shouted and hugged Pierre Salinger and they pounded each other on the back. Pierre danced with a cigar in his mouth. Drinks were poured. The telephones continued to ring with more precinct reports. The veterans of previous political wars filled the room with merriment and noise. Gene and I shook hands.

From the sample precincts reporting, it soon became clear that Mc-Govern was running strongly in almost every area of the state and among almost all voting groups. We swept eight of Wisconsin's ten Congressional Districts, narrowly losing the remaining two. We carried the First District, Kenosha-Racine, south of Milwaukee, heavily labor, blue-collar; the Second District, Madison, the University of Wisconsin; the Third District, the southeast part of the state bordering Iowa and Minnesota, rural, agricultural; the Fourth District, south Milwaukee, urban, ethnic, Catholic, blue-collar, the biggest surprise and the most important politically, the "Archie Bunker" vote; the Sixth District, north of Milwaukee, Sheboygan, combined suburban, labor, and rural; the Eighth District, east-central, Green Bay, Appleton, Manitowoc, combined small towns and agricultural; the Ninth District, Waukesha, suburban Milwaukee, another supposedly marginal McGovern vote; and the Tenth District, the northwest, rural-agricultural, Humphreyland on the Minnesota border. We narrowly lost the Seventh, the central part of the state, and the Fifth, north Milwaukee—both districts going to Humphrey. The loss of the Fifth District was attributed to wide Humphrey margins in several heavily black wards, and our failure to turn out a McGovern vote in those wards.

As the returns continued to pour in, the dimensions of the astonishing McGovern victory began to appear. The popular vote: McGovern, 30 percent; Wallace, 22 percent; Humphrey, 21 percent; Muskie, 10 percent; Jackson, 8 percent; Lindsay, under 7 percent; and a fraction of a number of others. The delegate totals: McGovern, 54; Humphrey 13.

Much of the press corps evidenced shock at the breadth of the McGovern sweep, expecting a more divided and confused primary. These results undeniably thrust McGovern right to the front of the pack with the emerging Humphrey. The shape of the 1972 Democratic nomination race was now beginning to appear. In previous weeks, the popular encrustations we had been forced to live with for almost two years had begun to disappear—one-issue candidate from a nowhere state, no party support, lack of charisma, no financial support, no political base. All those were gone now, and Wisconsin eliminated one of the last—that McGovern can't win. But McGovern could win and did. It was a whole new ballgame.

And it was apparent that night in Milwaukee. The Senator arrived at the Pfister Hotel and came up to the suite about 9 P.M. There was restrained jubilation, much congratulating. Eleanor, still somewhat skeptical, couldn't quite believe we had done it: "Are you sure?" she asked me. "Should we really be celebrating yet? Are there enough votes in to really tell?" I tried to assure her that it was true. The Pfister was now beginning to rock and heave with the mass of McGovern supporters surging in from all over Wisconsin. The Senator made his way down to the main ballroom about 10 P.M. to thank the 3,000 workers and to do network interviews. In the ballroom he singled out Gene for his masterful organizational effort over many months and our state chairman, Frank Nikolay, and the other key McGovern Wisconsinites who had performed so well.

Footnote: Shortly after we learned that we would win the Wisconsin primary, Pierre Salinger made an observation which puzzled me for some time. He said he didn't think our campaign was psychologically prepared for victory. Although I am still uncertain what he meant, I suspect he was struck on primary night by the absence of more excitement or demonstrative behavior by some of the younger staff members, such as Gene and myself, who had been working for what seemed like years for that night. The McGovern staff happened to be composed of rather undemonstrative people. Perhaps they took their cue from their candidate. Perhaps it is merely a characteristic of a new political generation.

We did not evidence such outward elation—little singing, dancing, shouting—for several reasons. Rather than being psychologically unprepared for victory, I think it was quite the opposite. The entire campaign was unfolding in an almost uncanny manner according to the script laid out more than a year and a half before at Cedar Point. I was to say to a reporter later in June that, "I honestly don't think there has been a major surprise in the last two years." And I meant it without arrogance or boastfulness. It had happened as we had planned. On the other hand, Gene was refusing to predict a Wisconsin victory days before the primary because, as he said, he suffered from innate pessimism, "a congenital disease of the spirit." For someone as ebullient by nature as Pierre, that is a personality characteristic difficult to understand—and a characteristic I happened to share with Gene. Those who have it work for the best and are not surprised by the worst.

Additionally, I felt throughout the campaign that it was the best publicity to underestimate our chances somewhat, for the same reason a football coach likes to be an underdog. Our workers would try harder, our opponents might let up slightly and everyone would be surprised when we did better than expected. (This was a view not always shared by the

Senator, who believed that people worked harder if they thought they were winning, causing him to predict some sort of victory almost everywhere.)

Finally, I am a planner, not a savorer. Planners rarely savor interim victories. Premature savoring can cause let-ups. The only thing to be savored is the ultimate victory. That night in the Pfister Hotel I was thinking four to six weeks down the road, to the tough middle primaries, to Michigan and Ohio and Pennsylvania, to the two big primaries at the end, California and New York, and I was thinking of all the non-primary states which needed help. More immediately, I was thinking of the disposition of several hundred organizers and workers—to which states should they be sent and in what proportions. Such is the lot of a planner. We were psychologically prepared for victory alright—it was just a long way off.

*　　*　　*

With such intensive concentration on the earliest primary states, a number of the later primary states and many of the non-primary states felt they were being neglected. Despite constant contact by the regional desk person in Washington and frequent contact from Frank or me on the road, the focusing of national attention on an upcoming primary made supporters in other states feel lonely and left out.

On March 26, I had gone to New York to meet with Dick Wade, then our chairman there. He felt there was little attention being paid to our campaign there, and I agreed that either Frank or myself would spend more time communicating with him about New York political problems. He reported that the organizational effort in the state was going well and that by the deadline for filing delegate slates in May we would have full slates in 37 of the 39 Congressional Districts. But before we arrived at the late primaries, including New York, we had some major hurdles.

The three big industrial states, Pennsylvania, Ohio, and Michigan, stood astride the primary passage. We had set out, in 1971, to organize each of these states, assigning highly skilled young state coordinators in each case and developing state and local committees. But crucial decisions concerning the amount of time the candidate should spend in each state, the amount of national campaign money to provide and the commitment of major media resources were delayed pending the outcome of the early primaries through Wisconsin. Earlier decisions on these big states could not be made because we couldn't predict our own strength, the field of candidates that would be left in late April and early May and the issues which might begin to take hold in each state.

In mid-summer of 1971 John Douglas had helped us assemble some two dozen Washington attorneys who were interested in volunteering time to the campaign effort. From this group, Harold Himmelman took most seriously my admonition that those who wanted to help should just jump in and not wait to be begged. Initially assigned to southern Ohio, by the end of the year Harold had assumed organizational responsibility for the entire state. In January, he went to work with our state chairman, Bob McAllister, a Columbus attorney, in putting together and filing delegate slates in each of Ohio's 24 Congressional Districts. Our organization in that state was still a struggling one, with some districts having practically no McGovern presence. Harold, by now a full-time campaign organizer, then went to Illinois to work in the primary. I asked him to go back to Ohio between the Illinois and the Wisconsin primaries to prepare a detailed report on the condition of the Ohio effort, with recommendations on what should be done.

Several days before the Wisconsin primary he came up to Milwaukee with three alternatives for Ohio: (1) depend almost exclusively on local effort, commit little candidate time, send in no organizers, raise and spend $25,000 to $30,000 in the state; estimated results—11-15 McGovern delegates; (2) have the candidate campaign five days, spend $100,000, half of it from the national campaign, and send in six staff organizers plus support; results—33-36 delegates; (3) have the candidate campaign 10 days, spend $200,000 to $250,000, three-fourths from national, and send in 12 top organizers and many second-level people; results—67 delegates, minimum. "Option 3," Himmelman said, "really involves a decision to try to win the state outright." Most discouragingly, he reported very little meaningful organizational activity at the local level in late March.

The Pennsylvania primary, involving 182 delegates, was April 25, the same day as Massachusetts'. Ohio's primary, for 153 delegates, would be March 2nd. Michigan, with its 132 delegates, would have its primary May 16, the same day as Maryland. There were in those three big industrial, traditionally Democratic, states, 467 delegates. Their primaries came within the space of three weeks. The situation in Michigan and Pennsylvania roughly paralleled Ohio's, as reported by Himmelman, with the same three options generally applicable. It was clear we couldn't exercise the "all-out" option in all three states; we didn't have enough money. Indeed, at the time Harold delivered his report on Ohio we didn't have a quarter of a million dollars for a full-scale assault on any one of the states. Further, the Senator clearly could not spend ten to fifteen days in each of the three states, and we didn't have enough experienced organizers to go around, particularly with Massachusetts coming up on the 25th and Nebraska on May 9th. On the other hand, the Senator could not seek the Presidential nomination of the Democratic Party and duck out of all three of those Democratic primaries. Some decision had to be made, and soon.

APRIL 5-8, 1972. California. This Ohio-Pennsylvania-Michigan problem lurked in the back of my mind during the next three days of meetings with our steering committee and finance group in California. Our California committee arranged two highly successful fund-raising dinners, April 5th in San Francisco and April 6th in Los Angeles, and Frank and I went out with the Senator to meet with our key supporters and make final plans for the crucial June primary. For almost four hours on April 7th we met with our California steering committee in Los Angeles, reviewing media plans, organization, scheduling policy, staff assignments, financing, and budgets—always budgets. Media expenses are astronomical in California and California is a media state. In discussing the budget, it was clear we would not win California cheaply. Pinch and trim as we might, there would be no way to erect *that* pyramid by sheer brute force —on the bodies of the workers—the way we had in the earliest states.

There was always the additional problem in California, shared only by New York, of determining a proper allocation of funds raised in each state between the state and national campaign efforts. Since so much Democratic money comes from both states, much of it going traditionally to liberal candidates, it is always natural to look to New York and California to supply much-needed funds for a national Presidential effort. However, to run full-fledged campaigns in each of those states takes a great deal of money. Thus, contact negotiations were maintained between the state committees in both states and the national political and financial offices regarding the disposition of money raised in special fund-raising events in both places. No fixed rules or formulas would ever work, but both states were understanding of the very pragmatic fact that the national campaign had to continue and succeed for the individual state efforts to have any meaning at all. This was particularly true since California and New York were the last two primaries. However, the truce hammered out on the question of sharing money was always an uneasy one.

APRIL 8, 1972. The Ohio decision. Frank and I had arranged to fly to Washington together from the West coast to assess the status of the campaign. I had reached a conclusion on the big-state problem since the Wisconsin primary and wanted to check Frank's thinking.

Pennsylvania would be especially difficult because it came first—it was only two weeks away—and on the same day as Massachusetts, April 25. We were deeply committed by now to the Massachusetts race, our chances there substantially increased by our strong showing in Wisconsin and New Hampshire and by Muskie's tailspin. Our organization in Pennsylvania was uneven, being stronger in the Philadelphia suburbs and certain western portions in and around Pittsburgh. We had made little headway in a concerted effort to crack the regular party organization/labor/big-city blocs, most of those traditional elements being somewhere between Muskie and Humphrey. Earlier in the year, at the peak of his strength, Muskie had signed up Governor Milton Shapp and much of the progressive/regular elements of the state party, as well as the Philadelphia Democratic chairman, State Senator Peter Camiel. The Pennsylvania Humphrey forces were led by former Governor George Leader and former Philadelphia Mayor James Tate, both powers in state and national Democratic politics in the 1950s and early 1960s. Humphrey also had strong support from old-line labor interests, represented by Steelworker President I. W. Abel, and the more conservative elements of the black community. Between Shapp, elected essentially as a reformer, and Mayor Peter Flaherty in Pittsburgh, a maverick, the Democratic machine in the state was crumbling, and when Shapp took his forces to Muskie, the traditional old-line elements went with Humphrey.

All this left us little room to maneuver in the party. Our base of support was essentially among the 1968 McCarthy supporters and anti-war elements. Although a number of these people were generous financially, it was not nearly enough to match the resources available to Humphrey.

Michigan was another story. The state party had delayed reforming traditional procedures for selecting convention delegates, clearly unacceptable under the new delegate selection guidelines, until early 1972. In the meantime, much of the party leadership, Senator Philip Hart among the first, had committed to the Muskie candidacy. The leadership of the United Auto Workers (traditionally a dominant force in Michigan politics), including President Leonard Woodcock, almost uniformly supported Muskie. Our persistent and effective regional coordinator, Joel Swerdlow, had labored to erect a McGovern organization and his team had done its utmost to build bridges to the regular party organization. Nevertheless, in Michigan as in Pennsylvania, the regular/labor/black elements were breaking somewhere between Humphrey and Muskie. We had solid strength on the campuses and in the suburbs, but it was difficult to see a McGovern statewide groundswell developing in early April. Furthermore, as in Pennsylvania, and to a lesser degree Ohio, sufficient money was not available to finance an all-out primary drive. If we decided to do it, the money would come from the national treasury and from Massachusetts, Nebraska, Oregon, and the later states. Finally, and perhaps most importantly, busing had become a prairie fire in Michigan, hottest in areas like Pontiac and Flint, but fanned statewide by continuing litigation in the federal courts. Wallace was on the Michigan ballot and there was every indication he would make Michigan his northern Florida. He was not tied down as we were in a number of other primary and non-primary states and could devote much of his energies to a demonstration of strength in a northern, Democratic, labor state.

That left Ohio. The problems were obvious: spotty, uneven organization; insufficient funds in the state; party regulars for Humphrey or Muskie; only three weeks until the primary, May 2nd. But Ohio did have some advantages over Pennsylvania and Michigan. Wallace had not filed delegate slates and therefore would not be on the ballot. We would have a clear confrontation with Humphrey, presuming Muskie were out by early May. Humphrey was committed to a race in the Indiana primary against Wallace on May 2nd, and thus would have to divide his time. Ohio had a broader agricultural base than the two others and a greater potential for McGovern financing. The state party organization, led by Gov. John Gilligan, was committed to Muskie and, if Muskie were out, would effectively be neutralized. Although much work needed to be done, the base had been laid for a statewide organization which might be activated with immense work, in three weeks. Finally, if Massachusetts began to look as good as we thought it might by mid-April, we could begin to divert key staff organizers, led by Harold Himmelman, into Ohio's Congressional Districts early and get some jump. Geography was also important. Several divisions of the McGovern army, moved back to Massachusetts and Pennsylvania from Wisconsin, could be airlifted into Ohio for the last seven days on the way to Nebraska (May 9th) and Oregon (May 23rd).

Shortly after Frank and I settled into our Denver-Washington flight, we discussed the assets and liabilities of each of the three states. Frank had gone through much the same process of elimination that I had, and it was soon obvious that we agreed on an Ohio blitz. There were three conditions that had to be met: first, the candidate had to agree; second, an agreement had to be reached with our Ohio finance committee for the commitment of a substantial portion of the estimated $250,000 from within the state; third, Caddell's survey results had to support our intuitive judgments about our chances in the state. We agreed on a meeting of staff and advisors for the following day and divided the names to call that night.

APRIL 9TH. McGovern's office. Present were: Henry Kimelman, Marian Pearlman, Rick Stearns, Jeff Smith, John Douglas, Frank, and myself. We were later joined by Charles Guggenheim and Pat Caddell. Since we had not had a general campaign assessment for some time, the earlier part of the meeting involved a report by Rick on progress in the non-primary states (he concluded, after a region-by-region analysis, that

we would meet our goal of 300 non-primary delegates, if we could continue to finance the operation), a report by Henry and Marian on finance
(despite the success of the direct-mail effort, we were still running a
substantial, revolving debt), the current status of the primary state organizations was analyzed (good to excellent), and Charles described
plans to supplement our media library with additional filming in late
April.

Then the discussion turned to the major topic, what to do about the
major middle primaries. As a hedge against future circumstances, we
had asked Pat to survey Ohio and he had done almost 500 samples on
March 8th and 9th. Pat summarized his findings: Humphrey was strong,
with about 33 percent support; Muskie was at 21 percent; McGovern at
15 percent, and a substantial 23 percent were undecided. Humphrey,
however, was near the ceiling of his support, with little indication that
the undecideds or a large portion of the Muskie vote were enthusiastic
about him as a second choice; 35 percent of those surveyed were unable
to express an opinion about McGovern and over half of those describing
themselves as undecided knew nothing about him. Pat also had discovered strong evidence of a phenomenon noticed in many other areas of
the country, the so-called "alienated voter," who had great distrust of
politics and known political leaders and who looked for a new face, an
honest leader. In conclusion, Pat wrote: "The situation in Ohio is definitely fluid enough to permit a McGovern victory, if sufficient time and
resources can be devoted to the Ohio campaign." His report also identified the critical source of later problems: "In order to win the [primary]
election, some way must be found to cut some of Humphrey's margin
with the blacks."

Frank and I both summarized our conclusions concerning the Pennsyl-
vania-Ohio-Michigan problem. I urged that, if a decision were made to
go in Ohio, it be done quietly with no indication to the press of our intentions until after Massachusetts. By then, any McGovern media program then in progress would have tipped off the Humphrey people to
some McGovern move, but we might have the advantage of two weeks
to lay an organizational base with Humphrey lulled into a false sense of
confidence while off campaigning in Pennsylvania and Indiana. Charles
indicated that we could be on the air in Ohio by the middle of the week,
about April 12th, and that for $125,000 to $150,000 we could get good
media coverage for almost three weeks in the state's five principal media
markets.

By now we had been in session four or five hours and the Senator
arrived from the airport after a full day of campaigning and travel. I
summarized the general feeling of the group, which by now was strongly
directly toward an Ohio race, and indicated that the remaining elements

were his concurrence and a guarantee of $100,000 to be raised in Ohio. He asked a few questions, and Pat once again stated his findings. Then, extremely fatigued (he was as tired as I had ever seen him), the Senator said that he would let us know his opinion the following morning. Before he left, we tried to call Howard Metzenbaum, Cleveland businessman and former Senate candidate, to determine if he would take the lead in raising the Ohio portion of the needed funds. He was not in, the Senator went home, and the meeting disbanded.

APRIL 10, 1972. Washington. The Senator called from his home. Metzenbaum had been contacted, the commitment had been made and the Senator thought we should try to take Ohio. The decision was final. Sensing that he would make this decision, I had previously contacted Harold Himmelman in Massachusetts, where he had just arrived with his family, and told him to turn around and get himself to Ohio as fast as possible and get an organization set up. We were going to try to win it.

MID-APRIL, 1972. McGovern spent eight solid campaign days in Massachusetts concentrating on the urban areas in the East, with one swing into the western part of the state. Most public appearances were scheduled into the pockets of heavy industry and communities of blue-collar working men and women—Lowell, Fall River, Springfield, and South Boston. We knew we would have the academic and student vote, but we wanted to undercut the very base of the state political leadership which had almost universally supported Muskie back in the halycon days of January and February. Oliver Wendell Holmes had spoken of the Boston State House as the hub of the universe, and many politicians in Massachusetts still believed it. But, if Massachusetts voters were anything like voters in other states, they were not going to be led to the polls by elected officials, so we went after those elected officials' own constituents.

I could not help but recall those days in 1971 when I went to the Boston State House in search of support and found only legislators who were bound to end up with the neighbor from Maine because "he looked like a winner" or who saw the shadow of Edward Moore Kennedy behind every pillar of that august, historical hall. (I was amazed at the combination of awe, respect, fear, and apprehension in which the senior Senator from Massachusetts is held by politicians in his state.)

The Muskie campaign had been more successful with the leadership of the Massachusetts Democratic organization, making that state a classic test of its endorsement strategy. Massachusetts would elect 80 delegates from its 12 Congressional Districts and 20 delegates at large—that is, the candidate obtaining the most votes statewide would control the 20 as well as the delegates from the districts he carried. The Muskie at-large slate was a who's who of Massachusetts politics; Boston Mayor Kevin White, Senate President Kevin Harrington, House Speaker David Bartley, State Treasurer Robert Crane, Attorney General Robert Quinn, Secretary of State John Davoren, U.S. Representative Thomas P. "Tip" O'Neill. District slates contained equally prominent local politicians.

During this period of campaigning in Massachusetts, the Senator took time out to travel into Pennsylvania, concentrating only four days of effort in the Philadelphia and Pittsburgh areas. Joel Swerdlow was coordinating our campaign there and doing superb work against overwhelming odds, with very little outside help. He had only those four campaign days, almost no media money, and few resources for printing literature and keeping offices open. As the results would later show, he managed to concentrate those resources wisely in 10 to 15 of our strongest state senatorial districts, the jurisdictions from which convention delegates would be selected.

APRIL 15, 1972. In the heat of the Massachusetts-Pennsylvania campaigns, the Senator took a day out for two major events: the Michigan Jefferson-Jackson Day dinner in Detroit on the 15th and, later that evening, a fund-raising concert in Los Angeles. The dinner seemed to be a must. Humphrey and Muskie would be there, as would the state and local party leadership from all over Michigan, 4,000 to 5,000 strong. Don Tucker, our state coordinator, and our key supporters argued strongly that McGovern's absence would be construed as an abandonment of the Michigan primary and its delegation. On the other hand, Warren Beatty, who almost single-handedly had put the Los Angeles concert together, had scrupulously avoided a public commitment that the candidate himself would attend. The concert, in the Los Angeles Forum, was a sell-out, with more than 18,000 people expected, and it promised to raise over a quarter of a million dollars. If McGovern could show up, it was thought it would be a great morale booster for the California McGovern effort. After considerable negotiations between myself and Warren, with the Senator receiving contradictory advice from various sides, it was decided we would charter a small jet and fly from the Detroit dinner to Los Angeles in time for the concert's conclusion.

A few days before the Michigan dinner, a prominent Washington columnist wrote of the country's need to return to the "establishment center." His thesis seemed to be that candidates such as McGovern were some sort of political aberration and that talk of change, progress, and reform of our social institutions threatened an established way of doing things by people used to doing those things in the way they felt was best for the country. Those not in the "establishment" could obviously not be in the "center." The Senator took the occasion in Detroit to blow the "establishment center" right out of the water, and it turned out to be one of the best speeches of his campaign. He was greatly angered by "the conventional view of men who write and read each other's syndicated columns," as well as the view of pollsters and public opinion analysts, "that the American people wanted not a hard-fought battle over the great issues, but quiet coronation of the status quo." Instead of glorifying the establishment center, the Senator asserted that most Americans see the establishment center "as an empty, decaying void that commands neither their confidence nor their love."

It is the establishment center that has led us into the stupidest and cruelest war in all history. * * * The establishment center has persisted in seeing the planet as engaged in a gigantic struggle to the death between the free world and the Communist world. The facts are that much of the so-called free world is not free . . . and most of the Communist nations are far more obsessed with their own internal divisions than they are with Washington, London, Bonn or Saigon. * * *

It is the establishment center that has erected an unjust tax burden on the backs of American workers, while 40 percent of the corporations paid no federal income taxes at all last year. * * *

It is the establishment center that tells us we can afford an ABM, but we can't afford good health care for the American people. * * *

It is the establishment center that says we can afford a $250 million guaranteed loan to Lockheed, but we can't afford a decent retirement income for our senior citizens. * * *

It is the establishment center that says it's okay to tell the American people one thing in public, while plotting a different course in secret. * * *

The people of this country are not left or right or centrist. Rather, they seek a way out of the wilderness. And if we who seek their trust, trust them enough to speak the plain truth, the people will find their own way.

Down the long and often troubled history of this great Republic the people have never been found lacking in imagination, resourcefulness, courage, and generosity. They will, given a leadership responsive to the best in their nature and equal to the demands of their essential goodness, work their way through to a just, compassionate and well-ordered society. To say this, for me, is to state a simple faith in the unique quality of the American people.

What is needed is a revitalization of the American center based on the enduring ideals of the Republic. The present center has drifted so far from our founding ideals that it bears little resemblance to the dependable values of the Declaration of Independence and the Constitution. I want America to come home from the alien world of power politics, militarism, deception, racism, and special privilege to the blunt truth that "all men are created equal—that they are endowed by their creator with certain inalienable rights and among those are life, liberty, and the pursuit of happiness." * * *

The speech galvanized the Michigan Democrats with the combined ruggedness of its assault on political élitism and its compassion for human need. Some of the reporters particularly liked this vision of the quiet preacher's son taking the gloves off against those most threatened by his candidacy, a candidacy obviously threatening the established way of doing things, the "old boy" network. The crowd voiced its enthusiasm throughout. (Elsewhere in Detroit that same night, George Wallace, excluded by the Democratic leadership from the guest list after much debate, was addressing his own enthusiastic rally of almost 10,000 people.)

Immediately after the Senator's speech, we bolted across Detroit, boarded the small jet and headed for Los Angeles. En route, I discussed briefly with the Senator the need to increase our efforts to win over regular party leadership in as many states as possible, including contacts he himself should make and steps that could be taken by others in the campaign. We were both aware of the national attention that would continue to be brought to bear by a combined Massachusetts victory and Muskie withdrawal and wanted more than ever for our campaign not to appear a strange hybrid to Democrats around the country.

We were met in Los Angeles by Dick Dougherty, press advisor and speech writer (and later, press secretary). An Irishman who could truly make a word ring, Dougherty came to the campaign in early 1972 from his post as *Los Angeles Times* New York bureau chief, having before that been a journalist here and there, a novelist, and a Deputy Police Commissioner of New York. Dougherty had the dismaying news that, only minutes before, Nixon had announced American bombing assaults on Haiphong harbor and certain areas around Hanoi. Arriving at the Los Angeles Forum, the Senator immediately held an impromptu news conference. He denounced the military escalation as a tragic and dangerous mistake which would not advance the termination of the hostilities or the return of our prisoners of war by a single day, but rather would prolong the fighting and increase the killing of civilians.

As the Senator ended his remarks, I entered the arena area behind the stage and couldn't believe my eyes. I had never seen so many people at a political event in my life—over 18,000 had gathered to hear James Taylor, Carole King, and Barbra Streisand. After months of candidate appearances before groups of 20 or 30 or 40, this was overwhelming. Warren had labored for weeks to schedule the performers, arrange for the Forum, and, with Miles Rubin and other California fund-raisers, promote the concert and sell the tickets. It was an immense success, not only because it added many desperately needed dollars to the campaign treasury, but also because it dramatically demonstrated broad public support for the McGovern candidacy in southern California.

At the end of Barbra Streisand's performance the stage lights dimmed and the Senator and Eleanor joined the performers as they went back up on the stage and the lights came up. The immense crowd, not suspecting McGovern to be within several thousand miles, went wild. Afterward, a mad scene ensued in what turned out to be the Los Angeles Lakers dressing room in the Forum, with the candidate caught in a crush of performers, managers, several dozen movie celebrities who had acted as ostensible ushers (Gene Hackman, Gregory Peck, Burt Lancaster, Dustin Hoffman, et al.), cameramen and reporters, politicians, contributors, well-wishers, and what seemed like the rest of the population of southern California. It was a fitting conclusion to an incredible day.

LATE APRIL, 1972. Following the New Hampshire primary, we had moved several of our best staff organizers into Massachusetts to provide full-time support for a host of volunteers. John Ruether, our original coordinator in the state, had assembled the nucleus of an organization and had then been assigned to develop key labor contacts in the industrial states. In his place we sent in John McKean, one of the original New Hampshire veterans, as state coordinator of the McGovern campaign. After Wisconsin, additional staff was sent in to join the growing battalions of workers. The organizational clincher came when Dave Harrison, our state chairman, recruited a group of tough young political in-fighters, headed by Billie Nickerson, who worked as a unit and who became known to the rest of the staff as the "Boston mafia." Their initial assignment naturally was their home turf, the roughest wards in Boston, and they did a masterful job of moving literature, canvassing, and delivering the vote. They later saw action in relatively docile political neighborhoods like Bayonne, New Jersey, and Brooklyn. The Boston mafia survived armed threats and gang challenges and were alleged to have deposited more than one box of literature belonging to particularly unfair opponents in New York's East River.

McKean, the ringmaster for the Massachusetts circus, managed, with aplomb and good humor, to stay on top of this unlikely mixture of Nickerson's mafia, young New Hampshire veterans, fervent peace activists, Cambridge intellectuals, Boston pols, quarrelling and bickering local factions, Nobel Prize winners, Father Robert Drinan (a delightful Jesuit who became the second Roman Catholic priest—the first was in 1822—to be elected to Congress), Kennedy followers and Kennedy haters, and an assortment of supporters committed to a variety of other causes besides George McGovern. Somehow all this came together in Massachusetts to produce an overpowering political operation.

The candidate himself was mounting a crest. He campaigned vigorously, enthusiastically and effectively in Massachusetts. He reached the

THE NEW YORK TIMES

McGovern reaching the people.

people. From South Boston shipyards to Cambridge to Holyoke to Fall River to Springfield to Pittsfield the people heard him and believed him —believed that he was honest, that he was strong and that he wanted change. They believed that he understood their dissatisfaction and discontent with the process and with the status quo. They believed that this man from somewhere out on the prairie, this man the politicians didn't seem quite comfortable with, might just be able to bring America back where it belonged, to make it a place to believe in again. McGovern created a primal faith among the voters of Massachusetts, created the kind of mystical, unshakable conviction that had elected men like Harry Truman.

In the closing days of the primary race I went with the Senator to the Lithuanian-American Club in South Boston. The place was jammed with 400 to 500 of the most Democratic, white, Catholic, blue-collar, ethnic-American people ever assembled, and as they cheered this plainsman supposedly so unlike them I went downstairs to the bar and casually polled the half-dozen Boston policemen escorting our caravan.

"Who do you think will win Tuesday?" . . . "This guy upstairs."
"What do you think of him?" . . . "I kinda like him. He knows what he thinks and he says what he thinks. And he's got the kids listenin' to him for a change. That's good."
"What about Muskie? Wasn't he supposed to win?" . . . "Nah! He changes around too much. Doesn't seem to know what he believes."
"Who will you vote for?" . . . "This guy upstairs. This guy McGovern."

After that, I quit worrying about Massachusetts.

But other worries continued. Harold Himmelman calling from Ohio: The money promised by the Ohio supporters hadn't been raised yet, the money was slow in coming from Washington, and if literature didn't get printed in the next 48 hours and phone banks installed, forget about an upset in Ohio. Poor Harold. I was beginning to wish I had recorded a money plea to give to each state coordinator so that it could be played to me every other day from the next state on the circuit and the beleaguered coordinator could be doing something else. The words, except for details, were the same whether they came from Grandmaison or Pokorny, Swerdlow or Brown, Rosendahl, McKean, or Himmelman: "You don't know how tough it is here. There isn't a dime in the bank account, in fact I'm $5,000 overdrawn. The phone company takes out every phone in the state tomorrow unless I give them another $7,500 and the printer won't give me the literature until I pay him the $8,900 for the last job. The kids haven't been paid for over three weeks. The stations won't take any more spots unless we pay for next week in advance. Humphrey is spending money all over the state." Desperation! Frustration! Despair!

I called Morris and told him the Ohio campaign was about to go under.

I told him we had cut back Massachusetts media because things were going so well there and had sent to Ohio every penny we could save from Massachusetts. I outlined the reasoning behind our sudden effort there and how potentially important Ohio could be to a nomination victory. Morris said if it was really that significant he would see that Harold received the needed money the next day. He then called Harold, verified the need and sent $100,000. That contribution was as important as any we received throughout the campaign.

APRIL 25, 1972. Primary day in Massachusetts and Pennsylvania. Believing that we would definitely carry the statewide vote in Massachusetts (*The Boston Globe* poll on April 23rd, the Sunday before the primary, gave McGovern a 2–1 lead over Muskie, 43 percent to 19 percent), we concentrated our attentions election night from the "situation room" in Boston's Statler Hilton on the individual Congressional Districts themselves, hoping to carry as many as possible, and on the returns from Pennsylvania. It became apparent mid-way through the evening that the *Globe* poll was essentially accurate and the big margin would hold up. The final percentages in the total vote were: McGovern, 51 percent; Muskie, 21 percent; Humphrey, 8 percent; Wallace, 8 percent; Chisholm, 4 percent. Of the 102 total delegates, 84 individual McGovern delegates were elected, including the entire slate of at-large delegates. Under state law all 102 delegates would be bound to vote for McGovern at the convention since he won the statewide vote and, amazingly, swept all twelve Congressional Districts. It was reported that many of those on the Muskie slates were incredulous over their defeat, Congressman O'Neill asking plaintively, "Did I really get licked five to one in Cambridge?" Mayor Kevin White failed to carry his home precinct. (He later said with regard to his chances of seeing Miami Beach: "I didn't even take my bathing suit out of mothballs.") The McGovern margin was almost as large in blue-collar wards as it was near campuses. We carried the city of Holyoke, described by one election official as "probably the most Catholic city in the nation."

The news from Pennsylvania was almost as gratifying and, in some sense, more gratifying. With less than four days of campaigning and little expenditure, McGovern finished second to Humphrey in the delegate race and in a tie with Wallace and Muskie for the popular vote. The vote tallies were: Humphrey, 35 percent; McGovern, 21 percent; Wallace, 21 percent; Muskie, 20 percent. The delegate count: Humphrey, 57; McGovern, 37; Muskie, 29; Wallace, 2; uncommitted, 12. (In one of a number of tactical oversights, the Wallace campaign had failed to file statewide delegate slates.) The 137 Pennsylvania delegates elected from state senatorial districts later chose 27 more delegates at large, in rough proportions to the relative strength of the candidates, and 18 more at-large delegates would be selected by the state Democratic committee in early June.

McGovern ran much better than expected in inner-city areas of both Philadelphia and Pittsburgh, demonstrating once again his appeal to working men and women. It was later reported that his showing in Pennsylvania materially affected our decision to run in Ohio, but this is incorrect since that decision had been made more than two weeks before.

At about 10:30 on election night the Senator came down to the ball-room of the Statler Hilton to speak to 3,000 to 4,000 frenzied supporters. They had been inflamed for almost two hours by an incredibly loud rock band. Strange sensations occur on these occasions. I was struck by the heat from the human masses in the dead of winter in Boston and thought that if we held a victory celebration in the Arctic Circle it would be just as hot. A law of politics might arise: the heat in a room of victorious politicians is in direct proportion to the size of the victory.

After doing an election analysis for Sander Vanocur and Robin McNeal on the Public Broadcasting Network, I went back to the hotel and fell into bed. It was about 1 A.M. I had spent part of the day fending off reporters from the national news magazines who had suddenly, after almost two years, discovered the McGovern campaign.

That night proved typical of many to follow. Three calls came in during the night, one at about 3:30 A.M. from the Rev. Jesse Jackson, progressive young black leader from Chicago, who was calling from California to say that he agreed with remarks made on the television interview earlier. Questioned by Vanocur concerning McGovern support from the black community, I had stated that the older, more conservative black leaders would undoubtedly stay with their old friend Humphrey, but that the vast majority of blacks, led by younger, more progressive leaders like Julian Bond, Jesse Jackson, Mayor Richard Hatcher, and others, would soon come to support McGovern as the candidate most likely to under-stand the current problems of the black community and as the rightful representative of the still potent Kennedy legacy. Jackson seemed to sup-port this distinction wholeheartedly in an eliptical, 45-minute conversation brilliantly punctuated (or so it seemed in the middle of the night) with metaphors and similes and an occasional "hear where I'm coming from" to make sure I was following the analysis.

Jackson, Bond, and a number of other leaders did join our cause, cam-paigning particularly intensively in California.

APRIL 26, 1972. The combined Massachusetts and Pennsylvania primaries of the previous day crystalized the 1972 nomination race tre-mendously. After one day of assessment, Muskie bowed to the inevitable, suspending his campaign on April 27th but refusing to withdraw as a candidate. If one should major in political irony, then the Muskie campaign must be looked to as a classic study. Post-Chappaquidick, he was the odds-on favorite for the Democratic nomination for more than two and a half years. For months, his nomination, and possible election, had been accepted by many of the media and political wise men as practically foregone. Networks and newsmagazines, watched, read, and respected by millions, had only weeks before projected his convention delegate total in excess of 1,000 delegates. And yet, dating from the first real test of popular strength, the actual life of his campaign could be placed at only 50 days.

Muskie's similarities to McGovern were striking. Both were from small states. Both were relative loners in the Senate. Both were reserved, private men who had risen to national prominence without personal wealth or inherited status. Both had successfully marketed Democratic philosophies and principles in Republican environments. Both were relatively religious and family-oriented.

But the differences far outweighed the similarities—differences of style and manner which may in part account for the divergent courses of their campaigns. Muskie careful, pondering, deliberate to a fault, seeking some hidden wisdom, some signpost to certainty. Seeking the center, the middle, that political equator, perfectly dividing the voting hemispheres, which no political explorer has ever found. Searching, like Diogenes, for the lost consensus, that mythical coalition wired, taped, and glued together by the canny old foreman, Lyndon Johnson, lasting just enough months for the nation to recover from Lee Harvey Oswald's bullets and then disintegrating during a foreign holiday called Tet.

McGovern, in sharp contrast to his Maine colleague, outspoken, almost imperturbably blunt and audacious. As almost no other of his peers could do, he alleged, in his methodical tones, during the McGovern-Hatfield amendment debate that the United States Senate, that hallowed chamber, "reeked of blood." Throughout the nomination race he had few to advise and fewer still to heed; like a sea-captain born to his craft, he carried his most trustworthy compass and sextant in his head, trusting neither polls nor sage outdated advice, never canvassing the crew to determine which way to sail, but reading the mood of the political ocean by the roll of the deck under him.

The parson's facade concealed the guts of a safe-cracker. With Muskie out of the race, however, the safe-cracker now confronted the canny old bank guard, Humphrey. And Humphrey's mood—coming out of the first major primary victory in his long political career and having inherited the more traditional elements of the Muskie support—was very much to protect and defend. To protect the party from those radicals so anxious to change outmoded institutions and to defend its symbols of power from that safe-cracker with the tools of reform. Humphrey and his friends would not let *that* bank be taken without a fight.

As if to mock this classic confrontation, there now began to emerge the Governor of Alabama, after a Florida victory and a respectable showing in Pennsylvania, with Indiana, Michigan, Maryland, North Carolina, and Tennessee ahead of him. Why not grab those jewels himself while the other two fought it out and, when the case came to court, claim that many of the gems had belonged to him all along.

After almost two years of work, more than a year of campaigning and only fifty days of hand-to-hand combat, McGovern had become the man to beat. *The Boston Globe* led its edition this day: "Sen. George McGovern (D-S.D.) today became the frontrunner in the race for the most delegates to the Democratic National Convention this July." Many found it hard to believe.
.

M A Y   1 ,   1 9 7 2 . McGovern had closed his Massachusetts campaign with two highly symbolic gestures. The Saturday before the primary he met secretly with Boston Mayor Kevin White in the Mayor's office. I had arranged the meeting to permit the two of them to get better acquainted (I had met White on two previous occasions and had been impressed with him personally) and to implement further the campaign policy of building bridges to political figures who had prominently supported other candidates and who occupied party leadership positions. The meeting was secret only to protect White, who was leading the Muskie Massachusetts delegate slate; we did not want to submit him to the incorrect impression of having conspired with the "enemy." The meeting was cordial and friendly, leading to White's later whole-hearted support in the fall election. Other contacts were made or attempted with Democratic leaders, including the venerable former House Speaker, John McCormack. Some were reluctant to talk to McGovern, either out of pique for the rout they were due to suffer at his hands or out of embarrassment for what was now at best a theoretical commitment to defeat him.

As if to illustrate the dual course his campaign was destined to pursue, after his election night appearance at the Statler Hilton McGovern went out to Boston's Logan Airport to thank, and bid bon voyage to, 90 of his top organizers who were boarding a charter flight to Columbus, Ohio. They would arrive there in the early morning hours and be assigned to various pressure points around the state. Within hours after delivering the last vote in Massachusetts, they would be canvassing on the streets of Ohio. The Ohio campaign blended the best and worst of what was swiftly becoming a McGovern campaign style.

The New Hampshire and Wisconsin technique had been to use hand-made political bricks, methodically cut and shaped to fit, and to build with them a solid, undramatic, workmanlike factory that would turn out votes like hubcaps. But not Ohio. Ohio was highly condensed; the campaign was now on a roller coaster, events flashing by like the Twentieth-Century Limited run amok. Ohio was the Keystone Cops building the Taj Mahal. A circus! A riot! Chaos! Dave Aylward, who helped Himmelman direct field operations, described the state headquarters in Columbus 20 days before the primary: "Three tiny offices upstairs, a separate closet for press and audio, and a slightly larger cave downstairs for operations and scheduling. The lights downstairs never worked (we brought in a strange collection of standing lamps) and the fuses blew every time the mimeograph and the Xerox were operated at the same time. It was an omen of what was to come."

The first meeting of field organizers was extremely discouraging. Morale was low and the organizers were young, inexperienced (even by McGovern standards) people from the Columbus area. Only the 22nd Congressional District (Cleveland) under the wily Dick Sklar had a systematic canvassing program; fewer than half a dozen out of the total of 24 districts had so much as an uneven canvassing drive. There were no phones and practically no literature.

But within 48 hours three things began to turn the Ohio campaign around to demonstrate what a McGovern-style campaign could do at its best. Additional experienced organizers came in; Guggenheim's media hit full stride; and money came from the national campaign. Carl Wagner came in to assist Sklar and Dennis Townley in Cleveland's four difficult districts (20–23); Tom Southwick took Canton (where, as Aylward reports, "in a rare display of affection for national staff, he was met at the Canton bus station by a large greeting committee and some local press."); Jeanne Nathan organized Dayton; Bill Gigerich came from Indiana to help in Cincinnati; Ed Graham, a North Carolina native, took the tough 18th district, the home of belligerent Congressman Wayne Hays; Mike Levitt and others arrived in advance of the Massachusetts troops. Jim Keller and Polly Hackett arrived, sick and exhausted, toward the end of April to schedule the Senator's final seven-day campaign blitz and promptly fell asleep during the first night's dinner. (The Ohio campaign staff was disappointed that the legendary scheduler Steve Robbins—the man who snacked on carpet tacks and spat brimstone—did not come out.)

The television and radio spots, running every day for 20 days, coming during a moving tide of McGovern interest in Ohio and around the country, made a tremendous impact, telling hundreds of thousands of Ohio voters who McGovern was and what he stood for. As financing came in from the national headquarters, literature was printed for canvassing, offices were opened all around the state, and telephones—more than 400 all across Ohio in less than 10 days—were installed. Aylward and the district coordinators had to convince the local volunteers to use the phones for voter contact, since we didn't have time to implement the massive personal contact approach used so effectively in earlier states. Through all this, Himmelman, working with Bob McAlister and the Ohio McGovern committee, was the link with the national campaign, the press and the separate black organizational effort in Cleveland.

In the final analysis, the McGovern successes were based upon the incredible energies and commitment of the local McGovern supporters, as Harold Himmelman recognized in his summary of the Ohio experience:

> What happened in Ohio during the three weeks before the vote was phenomenal. It was as though an explosion had taken place. From next to nothing that state was humming in a matter of days. Our organizers had access to some damn good locals in key districts and were able to fan them out into their communities with a vengeance those last three weeks. We got several million pieces of literature out in that time. Also, the opposition did nothing. So we monopolized the shopping centers, factories and neighborhoods. All of this combined with the national McGovern phenomenon. He was becoming a winner. He was new and exciting.

MAY 2, 1972. Ohio primary day. Within minutes after the polls opened, the phones at the state headquarters in Columbus started ringing off the wall. Reports from all over of various kinds of voting irregularities. No machines at certified polling places. Polling places locked and unmanned. Keys to voting machines unavailable where polls were open. Long lines of voters with no movement. People being denied access to the polls—or being turned away. From the volume and intensity of the screams of outrage and fury all over the state the Ohio primary was shaping up as one of the most fraudulent or one of the worst-managed in history. The shock waves seemed to be emanating from Cuyahoga County (Cleveland), with the epicenter somewhere near the 21st District, the predominantly black part of the city.

After a number of calls back and forth to Dick Sklar and Carl Wagner in Cleveland to verify the rumors of irregularities, we learned from them that Humphrey was then entering a meeting of the Cleveland election board from which our representative was barred. Our lawyers in Cleveland and Columbus rolled into action, scouring the election code for remedies, while a press release strongly denouncing the apparent irregularities was drafted by Pierre Salinger and issued in his name and mine. (Later, Pierre made a statement to a radio station which questioned the propriety of Humphrey's conference with an election board on primary day. He was roundly blasted by Humphrey on national television that night.) Early that afternoon we brought actions in the State Supreme Court in Columbus and the federal district court in Cleveland. Between them they caused the election board to hold well over 100 polling places open until midnight—a move which, in retrospect, may have hurt more than it helped us.

The mood of the day was complete confusion and uproar. Governor John Gilligan was so appalled by the potential disrepute into which the pandemonium threatened to draw the State of Ohio that he suggested the removal of the election board chairman on grounds of incompetence. Late in the afternoon, reports came in from a number of campus communities, obvious McGovern strongholds, that polling places had run out of ballots and young voters were being sent home. McGovern, happily, was out of the state most of the day, coming in late in the afternoon to greet this election-day bedlam.

That day highlighted a feeling I was to experience more than once during the remainder of the campaign. The campaign and the political process of which it was a major part had now become so massive, so unwieldy, so gargantuan that any individual or small group of individuals, whatever authority they bore, was almost incapable of knowing what was going on at all points at once. There was an overwhelmingly frustrating sense of powerlessness, of inability to either know or control. How was it possible for public servants and bureaucrats whom one had never met and never would meet, to so thoroughly frustrate the efforts of so many people, such an investment over such a period of time? The stakes were too high, the odds too great, the chance too near to have it all blown away at the end by administrative incompetence or—worse yet— political venality. I could not help but wonder if that same sense of helplessness must not afflict every general on the day of any great battle as, with all the planning done and fate now the judge, he waits and hopes, trying to make sense out of confusing, contradictory, uncertain reports.

That night the returns came in slowly and, as in the other states, not particularly favorably in the early hours. The worst time was over, how-ever—the late afternoon and early evening hours of every election day. An infinite limbo between exertion and exhilaration, when the bones grow leaden, the eyes dark-circled, the leg muscles turn to hot wires, and the brain to oatmeal. By midnight, the Humphrey lead had narrowed to a point or two and was wavering. We were going to carry Cuyahoga's 20th, 22nd, and 23rd Districts, but still nothing from the 21st. We had clearly broken the back of Humphrey's labor-regular coalition all across the state, running strongly in almost every labor district in Ohio. The rural vote was good. We were getting our share of the major urban areas. On the strength of key precincts studied by election analyst Oliver Quayle, NBC gave Ohio to McGovern about 1 A.M. just before going off the air. The upset seemed at hand, and the demise of the Humphrey candidacy just as near. But it was not to be so. In the middle of the night the 21st, where the election would now be decided, began to report in-

THE NEW YORK TIMES

Ohio Primary Night: Victory went down the drain when the plug was pulled in the 21st.

credible Humphrey margins—110 to 2, 98 to 1, 116 to 4. As cries of theft and fraud rang up and down the halls of the Neil House in Columbus, our election-night headquarters, the Ohio upset slipped into obscurity with the rising of the sun.

Final tally: Humphrey, 41 percent (of the vote cast for statewide delegate slates—the candidates were not on the ballot); McGovern, 40 percent. With more than 900,000 votes cast in the Ohio primary, we lost by only a few thousand. Delegate count: Humphrey, 79; McGovern, 61. Since Humphrey's total included the statewide delegates, McGovern actually carried more Congressional Districts than his opponent.

That same day Humphrey had also successfully stood off a Wallace challenge in the Indiana primary, winning 48 percent of the vote to Wallace's 42 percent, but not keeping the Wallace vote down nearly as much as he should have with unanimous Democratic Party, labor, and minority support throughout the state.

Following a disappointing 8 percent showing in Ohio, Senator Jackson became the next campaign casualty, announcing his retirement from the race.

MAY 3, 1972. Goodby, Columbus. We held our customary post-primary press conference, now widely known as the "Frank and Gary Show," with the Ohio campaign leadership. A large collection of reporters heard us claim victory (which we somehow managed to do under whatever circumstances), citing the disputes still raging all across Ohio and particularly in the 21st District. We placed the outcome in its proper context of a 20-day campaign against an extremely well-known party leader who had widespread party and labor support and who should have, all things considered, done much better "Were we prepared to officially allege vote fraud?" "No." I said, remembering McGovern's oft-repeated admonition that, once victorious, we would have to pick up the pieces and run with the party we had defeated, "not at the present time." Then the questions turned to our involvement in the Michigan primary. "Did we intend to take Wallace on head-to-head on the busing issue?" "Didn't we have a responsibility to do so?" We took the position that we would supplement our excellent state organization with additional staff organizers, and would do our best to make a financial outlay for media, but Nebraska was coming up in a week and the Michigan primary on May 16 was the same day as Maryland's. Therefore it was unclear exactly how much time the Senator would himself commit to campaigning in Michigan. Six different, garbled, versions of the McGovern Michigan strategy were filed later that day.

*   *   *

During March and April, when public attention was focused on New Hampshire, Florida, Wisconsin, Massachusetts, Pennsylvania, and Ohio, the intricate delegate selection process had begun in a number of non-primary states. From Minnesota's precinct caucuses, held toward the end of February, McGovern and a coalition of liberal forces carried into the county conventions on March 18 over 50 percent of the delegate strength as against a combined Humphrey-Muskie total of about one-third of the delegates, with the bulk of the remainder uncommitted. In the Iowa Congressional District conventions on March 25th, we had consolidated our precinct and county convention gains until we stood to control at least a third of the Iowa delegation. We stormed the Virginia caucuses on April 8th, and won almost 40 percent of the delegate strength in a state not originally thought to have any appreciable McGovern support. The same day, in Kansas, another highly unlikely McGovern state, and in spite of a Democratic Governor who strove mightily to lead an uncommitted delegation, a quietly efficient McGovern organization rounded up the troops and took a third of the state's caucus delegates. The next day, April 9th, the Vermont town caucuses began and the smoothly functioning McGovern team completely surprised the party regulars—almost totally for Muskie—by capturing nine of the state's 12 national delegates. In Louisiana, where Southern staff organizer Bebe Smith helped local McGovern forces concentrate their energies on our strongest districts and where there was little organizational attention from the other campaigns, more than one-fourth of the 44-person delegation was for McGovern. The Idaho delegate selection process began on April 17th and we captured almost half of the state's delegation. The Missouri caucuses opened on April 18th. There we ran into concerted party organizational opposition led by Governor Warren Hearnes which prevented us from pyramiding our caucus strength, thus limiting our ultimate delegate contingency to about one-sixth of the Missouri delegation. Similarly, in Kentucky in late April, the party regulars and elected officials, headed by Governor Wendell Ford, ran uncommitted slates or Muskie slates in every district against the McGovern delegates and limited us to about one-fifth of the delegates selected for the state convention.

Of this organizational effort, the *Wall Street Journal*'s Norman "Mike" Miller wrote: "No other Democratic presidential contender is even approaching [McGovern's] effectiveness in organizing." Miller was reporting in late April not only our "brilliant successes over the party's old pros in the complex preconvention political maneuvering," but also our persistent efforts simultaneously to put out "peace feelers to party regulars in the hope of eventually swinging some of them to Sen. McGovern."

We knew from the outset that our ability to organize and get delegates from the non-primary states was in almost direct proportion to our success in the primaries. From the momentum developed in New Hampshire, Wisconsin, and Massachusetts came the motivation to turn out supporters in neighborhood caucuses all across the country. But even momentum cannot completely account for it. The technical skills and competence must also be there, as it was not in all campaigns. Nor was the depth of conviction and commitment, necessary to perform the countless hours of thankless work, present in any other campaign. Great credit must be given to Rick Stearns and Eli Segal, the state coordinators, desk officers, and organizers, as well as to the hundreds of volunteers who maintained this persistent, complex non-primary delegate operation well outside the public limelight while the primaries ground on.

MAY 5, 1972. Washington. The Senator had gone directly to Nebraska, after a day's rest, to start the last campaign push for that primary coming up on May 9th. I received a call from him saying that we had some serious political problems in Nebraska. Humphrey supporters had begun a concerted campaign, largely through brochures and newspaper ads, to misrepresent McGovern's views on the so-called "three a's"—abortion, amnesty, and acid (drugs generally). In all, he was portrayed as a radical on these deeply felt social issues and, by implication, a radical on practically everything else. Additionally, the White House had taken note of our emergence. Senator Hugh Scott, Republican Minority Leader, had taken the floor of the Senate that week to denounce McGovern in vitriolic terms for his positions on the "three a's," a phrase Scott and the White House coined. Scott's misrepresentations matched those of the Humphrey supporters.

McGovern definitely felt, four days before the vote, that he was being hurt by these attacks. For the first time, our campaign was forced on the defensive. The Senator was spending a great deal of his time responding to these erroneous allegations instead of concentrating aggressively, as he had done in every other state, on the vital issues of the war, tax reform, cuts in defense spending, and re-ordering of national priorities.

Pat Caddell, who customarily preceded the campaign into each state to test voter attitudes, had warned us some weeks earlier that the attacks begun by Jackson in Ohio and perpetuated by Humphrey's Nebraska supporters were beginning to hurt. More and more Democrats in conservative states like Nebraska were showing some concern about McGovern due to information they were receiving that he was "some kind of a radical." Some of them were beginning to think that the change he was trying to bring about had more to do with personal or social values than with national institutions and directions.

I discussed a number of alternatives with the Senator, and among those selected were a special television presentation with the highly respected

former Governor of the State, Frank Morrison, who was also the Mc-
Govern Nebraska chairman. We decided as our basic campaign strategy
that these charges would be tackled head on. During the first couple of
days of campaigning the Senator had dismissed these charges, trying at
every point to redirect public attention to the real issues. Thereafter, he
brought the charges out in the open and refuted them. Three days before
the primary he did so on statewide television, with Governor Morrison
saying: "Now Senator McGovern, you are an old and trusted friend of
mine from right next door in South Dakota and there are some folks out
here who are saying you're a radical and want unlimited abortions and
free drugs. Now I certainly wouldn't support a radical and my good
friends here in Nebraska know me well enough to know that. So why
don't you just go ahead and set the record straight." Morrison pitching,
McGovern batting, and ball after ball sailed out of the park. In addition,
adjustments were made in scheduling to put the Senator into areas where
the damage was potentially the worst—Catholic areas, farm areas, conservative strongholds. Strong ads were taken out accusing the opposition of distorting the McGovern record and confusing the true distinctions
between the two principal candidates—McGovern for change to benefit
the average citizen, Humphrey for the status quo.

All these efforts, particularly the television broadcast, began to have
their effect in the final 72 hours of the primary campaign. The momentum
could be felt shifting from Humphrey to McGovern. When I had spoken
to the Senator on Friday morning, he evidenced for the first time in his
campaign a real concern about the favorable outcome in this crucial
stepping-stone state. He was genuinely doubtful about ultimately carrying Nebraska and had been particularly jolted by the possibility that, for
all our hard work, we might not be permitted to win this nomination
purely on the merits of our case. This was the birth of the anti-Mc-
Govern resistance in the party, a movement consisting largely of elements
threatened by Senator McGovern's emergence and the possible trans-
formation of the Democratic power structure. It was to build from early
May to a crest in Miami Beach in July. Meanwhile, on the day before
the Nebraska primary, it looked as if we had beaten it at least to a stand-
still.

MAY 6, 1972. Miami Beach. On the way to Omaha for the close
of the primary effort I spent about 36 hours at the site of the convention
reviewing with Rick Stearns the layout and logistics, particularly communications arrangements. We met with telephone company officials to
review the communications systems designed and ordered months earlier.
Some modifications were made to account for our increased facilities. As
candidates dropped from the race and as the tide of political battle ebbed

and flowed, the Democratic National Committee (DNC) had adjusted the initial allocation of rooms on January 24th, giving Muskie, for example, 550 rooms and McGovern only 62. Obviously, recent events had to affect these arrangements.

Rick and I walked over the convention floor with the telephone people, laid out the floor plans for our trailer command centers outside the convention hall and the phone requirements for our hotel command posts on the penthouse floor of the Doral Hotel on the Beach. We hoped that the elaborate system, now almost perfected, would enable us to speed communications anywhere throughout what now appeared would be a far-flung McGovern network at the convention. It was a vital operation and one that could not be put off to the last minute; it required more than six months of planning, planning which would hopefully reap its reward in July.

MAY 8, 1972. On primary eve the Senator and his press entourage motored to Lincoln, the state capital, from Omaha to appear at another fund-raising concert. Late in the afternoon it had been announced that Nixon would appear on national television at 8 P.M. with an important announcement concerning Southeast Asia. As we watched in a small room in the Lincoln arena, Nixon announced the mining of Haiphong and other North Vietnamese harbors and the bombing of northern supply routes. This new escalatory announcement, the second in three weeks, had an ominous, foreboding quality about it. It could legitimately be considered a direct challenge to the Russians and the Chinese and its possible consequences could include major power confrontations.

The Senator made notes throughout the announcement and drafted a brief statement immediately afterward for distribution to the press. He then went into a larger room nearby to read his response to the President's announcement and answer questions from the press. He maintained, essentially, that these increased military actions could not help but elevate the hostilities, prolong the war, delay the return of our prisoners, and broaden the scope of the war. It was, the Senator said, a perfect illustration of the failure of the Nixon "Vietnamization" policy and proved that, even though ground troops might be withdrawn, we would replace them with increased air and sea activity. Vietnamization was merely a term, he concluded, for an alteration of our strategy and tactics. The press conference ended with a few questions raised concerning the outcome of the Nebraska primary.

Following the Lincoln concert, on the return to Omaha, the Senator and I discussed what he should do the following day, in light of the Vietnam situation. The press bus soon informed us on the Secret Service communication system that Humphrey had announced his plans to terminate campaigning in Nebraska and return to Washington the following day. We immediately decided to do the same on the grounds that it would seem crass to continue to seek votes in a time of quasi-emergency and that the Senator could make his voice most effectively heard on the floor of the Senate.

MAY 9, 1972. Nebraska primary day. Most of the day was spent, with the Senator gone, in making sure that the standard efforts were being made to get out the McGovern vote and in discussing future staff assignments for what were now hundreds of campaign organizers. The logistics of moving people from state to state with a different primary going every week had become enormous. Part of the process was the constant evaluation of personal capabilities to determine which person could perform which tasks.

The early returns coming into our situation room on the top floor of the Omaha Hilton were not encouraging. Throughout the first few hours of the evening, Humphrey maintained a four- to five-point lead which refused to shrink. Then, toward midnight, our totals began to move and the gap slowly closed. A point or a fraction of a point at a time, we inched our way up until, by 11:45 P.M., we began to take the lead. By the time the results began to look firm shortly after midnight, we had widened the lead to almost eight points. The final figures: McGovern, 42 percent; Humphrey, 35 percent; Wallace, 12 percent. Delegates: McGovern, 15; Humphrey, 7.

In the West Virginia primary held that same day, Humphrey triumphed over Wallace, 67 percent to 33 percent. But Wallace had abandoned his campaign in the state, preferring to concentrate his energies on the Tennessee primary May 4th, which he won without opposition, the North Carolina primary May 6th, which he carried over favorite son Terry Sanford, 50 percent to 37 percent, and the Michigan and Maryland primaries coming up on May 16th.

As a minor irony, if Wallace had campaigned in West Virginia, keeping Humphrey at least partially occupied there, we would have won the Nebraska primary handily. When Wallace pulled out of West Virginia, it permitted Humphrey to campaign all-out in Nebraska.

The Nebraska victory was important to the ultimate McGovern success for a number of reasons: it was one of the primaries we had originally selected in our 1970 game plan; we had made it clear to the press that we thought we could win Nebraska; it was a neighboring state to South Dakota and a farm state, and therefore McGovern would be expected to do well there. Also, after Ohio, we had to prevent a Humphrey victory streak and to prove that the Ohio results had been essentially a standoff. If Humphrey had defeated us in Nebraska it might have been a rallying point for a stop-McGovern effort and placed Humphrey in a commanding position to lead that movement. Finally, Nebraska proved that the strategy of misrepresenting McGovern as a radical could be defeated by open campaigning.

MAY 15, 1972. The several days after the Nebraska primary had been spent in Washington planning for the remaining eight primaries, including the difficult Michigan contest with Governor Wallace and the absolutely crucial California showdown coming up on June 6th. Typically, the problems involved finances and scheduling. The Senator was dividing his time between Maryland and Michigan, both of which would hold primaries the following Tuesday. He would then head for the West Coast after a brief rest, spending a few days in Oregon before its May 23rd primary, and then campaign almost non-stop in California for two solid weeks. There were, however, three other primaries on June 6th—in South Dakota, New Mexico, and New Jersey—and staff and supporters in those states wanted some appearances by the Senator very badly. Urgent requests continued to be made for just half a day of the Senator's time in Maryland, New Mexico, or New Jersey, with the same argument in each case—we can carry this state, but we need McGovern; he hasn't been here for weeks, and he has to make just one more stop here before the primary. So the schedule was juggled and reworked, but with little expectation of satisfying all the demands.

Also, as in all the states that had come before, the harassed state coordinators always needed more money. More phones had to be installed, more literature printed, rent and salaries had to be paid, and radio and television time purchased. California, particularly, was becoming a very expensive operation. Although our California fund-raisers labored mightily, the funds required to meet the heavy demands in California were no longer available in the other primary states equally hard-pressed. Additionally, we had entered the most intensive 60-day period of district and state conventions in the non-primary states, necessitating the expenditure of money for staff and travel into more than a dozen and a half states. In terms of the number of separate state political operations, primary and non-primary, being conducted simultaneously, we were in the peak period of the campaign. And it cost money.

The circus atmosphere which had permeated the Washington headquarters from the beginning was intensifying. It now seemed as if thousands of people were jammed into fewer than 4,000 square feet of space, reducing the quality of the limited air supply below that of a high school locker room. Communication traffic by now had completely overloaded the modest switchboard, and more sophisticated equipment soon had to be installed. Offices were crowded beyond their limits, with groups of people arriving for and departing from meetings overlapping each other and surging out into the hallway. Finally, most major decisions came to be made in the narrow passageway through which all movement in the building had to pass. In desperation, the regional desks and delegate-information operations were moved next door, above a seedy liquor store, leaving the front third of the headquarters for political management and financial operations and the back two-thirds for volunteers and mail.

On this Monday, we resumed a practice tentatively started a few weeks earlier of issuing periodic summaries of delegate strength prepared by Rick Stearns and the regional desk officers. The delegate chart dated May 15th showed the results of primaries actually held or non-primary delegate selection processes already begun in 33 states. Eleven of these state results were based upon projections of ultimate delegate allocation from caucus commitments already made in non-primary states.

The totals showed McGovern with 516½ delegates, Humphrey with 309½, Wallace with 227, Muskie with 141½, Jackson with 36, Chisholm with 21, 44½ delegates scattered among other candidates, and 386 delegates uncommitted. I analyzed these numbers like a doctor inspecting an electrocardiogram, an engineer his drawings, or an investor a prospectus. With the proper understanding of the politics of these 33 states these numbers were just as meaningful—the condition of the Democratic Party's heart, the soundness of the structure we were erecting, the chances of our enterprise's success.

These numbers told us that we would win the nomination unless one of two adverse circumstances occurred, such as losing California and one or two other late primaries, or being blocked by a solid stop-McGovern coalition of Humphrey, Muskie, and uncommitted delegates.

We believed strongly that we would win the California primary, as well as South Dakota and Oregon, since we had no serious opposition in either, and would do respectably well in New Jersey and New Mexico. We also felt that we could win at least 175 to 200 of New York's 278 delegates on June 20th. This string of primary successes would seriously undermine any effort to stop McGovern before the convention, particularly among the pragmatic politicians who would want to be with the winner in Miami. The breakdown of uncommitted delegates revealed an interesting pattern of old politics surviving. Eighty-eight uncommitteds from Illinois belonged to Mayor Daley. Five governors controlled 135 more: Carter (Ga.,), 36; Burns (Ha.), 17; Docking (Kan.), 12; Ford (Ky.), 38; and West (S.C.), 32. Additionally, approximately 40 Texas uncommitted delegates would follow gubernatorial nominee Dolph Briscoe, and 25 to 30 uncommitteds in Virginia belonged to the remnants of the Byrd machine. All told, this represented over three-quarters of the uncommitteds. The majority of the Muskie strength, another vital element in any stop-McGovern convention scheme, would come from the 59 Muskie Illinois delegates, led by Senator Adlai Stevenson, and 29 Pennsylvania delegates led by Governor Milton Shapp. Since these leaders and the delegates were considered nominally liberal at least, it was doubtful they could be brought en masse into an anti-McGovern coalition. Therefore, we had to win the remaining primaries as solidly as possible and take the steam out of a negative, rear-guard effort. Besides, if Humphrey were defeated, there would be no viable candidate to bring forward at the last minute.

Even as these thoughts went through my mind during a mid-afternoon meeting in my office with Owen Donley and Rick Stearns concerning convention arrangements, a wild-eyed, bearded face—Joe Daly's from the mailroom—thrust itself abruptly through my door: "Wallace has been shot! He was just shot five times by a guy over in a Maryland shopping center. I just heard it on the radio!"

I felt sick—a physical and mental nausea. I remember pounding my fist on the desk, saying dammit, dammit, dammit! I dashed for the wire-service ticker in the storeroom and watched bits and pieces emerge from its automatic keys, thinking will it ever stop, thinking Dallas, Los Angeles, Memphis, thinking no one is safe anymore. I assumed immediately that the crazed man now in the Montgomery County jail had acted in protest against Governor Wallace's policies and that he must, therefore, have some sort of left-wing identity. Could he have had any contact with our campaign? Could he possibly have been involved in or identified with our effort at any level? If so, then the Senator's life might be endangered by some irrational retaliation; if so, then none of our workers anywhere in the country would be safe.

Within minutes the name Arthur Bremer was broadcast and the home-town of Milwaukee identified. By late afternoon the suggestion arose that he may have had some involvement in our Wisconsin campaign or elsewhere. One or two press inquiries were made to our headquarters. I told one reporter that we had no information whatsoever that Bremer had worked in our campaign and requested that while we checked it out, he please not report the speculation since it would place tens of thousands of workers in jeopardy around the country. By mid-evening we notified the press that Arthur Bremer had never been involved with the McGovern campaign in any way.

Meanwhile, the Senator, campaigning in Michigan on the day before the primary, cancelled his remaining appearances immediately and returned to Washington. He also notified me through one of the traveling staff that he had publicly instructed the McGovern campaign organization in Michigan to suspend election day activities. By that time I was getting frantic calls from Don Tucker, our Michigan coordinator, for clarification of this order. Did it mean our people couldn't get out the vote, couldn't knock on doors, make phone calls, distribute literature? Since the statement had been made in Michigan, our Maryland organization, faced with a primary also within twelve hours, wanted to know if the instructions applied to them as well.

Upon his arrival in Washington, I discussed the problem with the Senator and he made it very clear that the kind of massive door-to-door voter turn-out effort we had mounted in other states would be considered unseemly and heartless less than a day after Governor Wallace had been attacked and while he still lay in serious condition in the hospital. For my part, I was still concerned about possible irrational reprisals against our workers.

MAY 16, 1972. In the Senator's absence, I went to Michigan as the campaign spokesman, as well as to assist Don Tucker with any primary day problems. Our campaign workers in Michigan and Maryland were extremely discouraged at having their hands tied after working for many months for this day; they felt, in both cases, that they could have made suprisingly strong showings in states where we had not made a major effort. Everyone now realized that there would undoubtedly be a sympathy vote of some major proportions in both Michigan and Maryland for Wallace which would skew the results out of any meaningful proportions. Oliver Quayle told me that he had done a survey for NBC on Sunday, May 14th, showing McGovern leading Wallace by two or three points in Michigan, with Humphrey running a poor third. Immediately after the shooting, Quayle re-surveyed and found a nine-point Wallace lead. Had we been able to defeat Wallace in Michigan, it would have challenged Wallace's purported appeal to northern "middle-American," or blue-collar voters, and would have further established McGovern's claim to these disaffected Democrats. But the assassination attempt eliminated any chance of making this crucial breakthrough.

A number of students of modern American politics believe that any chance a Democrat had to defeat Richard Nixon was lost on May 15th. That theory is based on the presumption that the votes Wallace received in 1968, and might have received in 1972, were votes that otherwise would have gone to Nixon. In my judgment, if Wallace had not been in the general election race in 1968 Humphrey would have been defeated by a much wider margin than he actually was—that, in other words, the bulk of the Wallace votes would have gone to Nixon. We also believed that Wallace would decide not to run in 1972 and could have been persuaded to support the Democratic candidate, as it turned out, Senator

McGovern. But the assassination attempt—sheer mindless destruction in itself—threw that strategy awry.

At a press conference following the Michigan primary I suggested that the meaningful race was between McGovern and Humphrey and that there we had triumphed. The final results were: Wallace, 51 percent; McGovern, 27 percent; Humphrey, 16 percent. This would translate into the following number of delegate votes: Wallace, 65; McGovern, 34; Humphrey, 19. In Maryland, where we had made almost no investment of national campaign resources, Wallace received 39 percent of the vote and 41 delegates, Humphrey 27 percent and 6 delegates, and McGovern 22 percent of the vote and 6 delegates. In the McGovern-Humphrey contest, then, this had been a profitable day for us. We had run a solid second in Michigan and a close third in Maryland in the popular vote, and had won a total of 40 delegates to Humphrey's 25, in the two states. And the name of the game, after all, was delegates.

MAY 18, 1972. Only the Oregon primary now preceded the decisive confrontation in California, and, since Oregon looked like a sure winner, every attention could be—and had to be—turned to the Golden State.

By this date, mid-May, campaign management roles had been assigned. Two of our best organizers, Eli Segal and Don O'Brien, had been assigned to help coordinate the California effort. As campaign policy, we had assigned outside staff members to manage each of our state organizations. (This policy would continue in the fall.) The reason was best stated by Dr. Samuel Johnson, according to whom "every man has a lurking wish to appear considerable in his native place." Segal had been working with the California McGovern committee, and specifically Miles Rubin, to establish the organization in the field and gear up the media program. While Segal concentrated his efforts on the grassroots organization, Rubin was developing the sophisticated, computer-based voter contact program. Don O'Brien had arrived to coordinate organizational activities in the south. Bill Lockyer, Democratic chairman of Alameda County was his counterpart in the north.

Eighteen days before the primary our operation in the state was anything but tidy. But California has never worshipped neatness. If New York politics is gothic, California politics is baroque—lavish, ornate, extravagant, improvident. Our practices, the McGovern style campaign, were as foreign to California traditions as bows and arrows in the nuclear age, our army of canvassers as out of place as the Viet Cong in a Cecil B. DeMille version of the Battle of Waterloo. For California had perfected and grown accustomed to the long bomb, the big splash, the sudden score, the lightning-like thrust—MEDIA. Vivid, stunning television spots (go-go chick in silver lamé bikini: "Put a McGovern in your tank. He's a gas!"; fast-talking Ralph Williams-type car saleman: "Friends, drive on out the Santa Anna Freeway and get your new McGovern—63 models to choose from!"), catchy billboards, rocking, thunderous radio, punchy newspaper ads, riotous parades.

But we marched into Lotus-land with the Prairie Statesman at the front of a rag-tag army of guerrilla warriors, political green berets out of a dozen different battle trenches. Nobody had ever heard of such a thing, and some knowledgeable California politicians said it would never work. California couldn't be organized. But Segal, with the help of much of our best political talent, was trying to do it. Storefronts, literature, canvassing, card files. And overlaying this grassroots operation was the sophisticated, computerized voter identification and voter-contact program designed by Rubin. Printouts, mailings, phone banks, lists. We not only tried to organize California—we tried to do it two ways at once.

MAY 19, 1972. Humphrey publicly called for debates between himself and McGovern. There were minor skirmishes in the press. We issued a statement pointing out that McGovern, in a letter to Party Chairman Larry O'Brien in July, 1971, had been the first candidate to seek debates among Democratic contenders. At that time, none of the other Democratic hopefuls, then far in front in the polls, seemed too interested. Now Humphrey, obviously in some trouble, with the momentum running against him, treated the idea like a shiny dime on the sidewalk. Prior to the opening of formal negotiations, we used the press like a Swedish peace-keeping team, shuttling moves and counter-moves from one side to the other. What about equal-time problems? We didn't want to get into a re-run of the comically ridiculous New Hampshire "debate" where the show was stolen by poverty-worker, quasi-Presidential candidate Edward "Ned" Coll waving a large rubber rat. The networks, eager for the blood the two principal gladiators might spill, thought they had a way around that problem. Humphrey, desperately low on media funds, wanted as many debates as possible, sure that he could outpoint his more deliberate, heavyweight-slugger opponent with his dazzling verbal footwork (Mohammed Ali vs. Joe Frazier?).

I talked about it to the Senator, who was then in Oregon for the last weekend before that primary. Although he recognized it was an idea more to Humphrey's advantage than ours under the circumstances, he thought we had no choice but to accept the challenge, particularly since it was our challenge in the first place and he would look weak avoiding Humphrey now. He seemed very confident that he could at least hold his own in a one-to-one confrontation. I took this as a sign of his own increasing self-assurance where Humphrey was concerned; he had told me many months before that he hated to share a platform with his old friend and neighbor Hubert Humphrey, whose voluble virtuosity, that sheer ability to produce a Niagara of words, left the more methodical McGovern feeling virtually tongue-tied and speechless.

With the candidate's agreement then, Eli Segal, Miles Rubin, and I set out, like the Earp brothers and Doc Holliday headed for the O-K Corral, for a luncheon negotiating session with the Humphrey representatives at Perino's restaurant on Los Angeles' Wilshire Boulevard. But the O-K Corral, Perino's is not. The elegance of the Louis Quinze upper room—its mirrors, linens, and white-tie waiters—made it the kind of place in which Henry Kissinger might conduct negotiations. I immediately began to plot how we could escape and leave the Humphrey campaign with the check. The Humphrey representatives included John Morrison, deputy campaign manager; Joe Cerrell, dour veteran of many California political wars and Humphrey's California campaign chairman; and D. J. Leary, national media director. We interrupted our polite fencing to order lunch, which was followed by more minor skirmishing. Then I asked for the proposal.

The Humphreys wanted a head-to-head confrontation on each of the major networks. The McGoverns suggested voter boredom. Besides, there was great conflict among the networks as to which one asked first. We had earlier voiced no objection to opening the negotiating session to reporters, but the Humphreys voted that down. We let them take the heat for chasing the reporters out. Then we had to call Sam Donaldson of ABC back in to confirm that his network didn't want in on the deal unless it could be first. More discussion on network priorities.

The finely honed tension was interrupted by a soft "pop." Leary had placed a large briefcase on the linen and, even as the filet of sole in white wine sauce was being served, had reached inside to extract and open a can of diet root beer. The briefcase went back on the ornate bar behind his seat. The captain and I stared transfixedly at the root beer can sitting now like a hand-grenade on the linen. I could not have been more awe-struck if Leary had produced a live cobra. And so the elegant waiters treated it. Back and forth, in and out, they dipped and swirled, always with an eye on that awful can, praying that it wouldn't suddenly lash out and sink two metal fangs in a careless wrist or finger. Would the gentleman care to have a glass? No thanks, said Leary, I'll just drink out of the can. And so he did, can after can. By mid-afternoon, with the negotiations completed, we arose to go, hand-shaking our way out the door and leaving behind six empty diet root beer cans and three stunned waiters.

We had agreed that the two principal candidates would appear on face-to-face confrontation programs on each of the major networks if asked. We understood that the format had to be consistent with the traditional interview programs—Meet the Press, Face the Nation, Issues and Answers—to avoid equal-time problems, and that this would preclude an actual debate. We further agreed, upon my insistence, that candidates' answers had to be monitored and timed to prevent Humphrey from monopolizing the available time. We would try to get in-state newsmen on the interviewing panels to insure that California issues were raised. The details of the agreement were to be worked out in Washington among representatives of each candidate and the respective networks.

MAY 23, 1972. Primary day in Oregon and Rhode Island. The Senator had campaigned no more than three or four days in Oregon and not at all in Rhode Island. Oregon was a ballot-designation state, the Secretary of State had endorsed the names of eleven Democratic candidates on the ballot. In the closing weeks before the primary, interest in the state had fallen off, with both Humphrey and Wallace relying on their local supporters to construct a vote for them.

Our day-to-day activities in Oregon were being supervised by Jean Westwood from Utah. Like John Douglas in Washington, Jean's efforts on the Senator's behalf had gone largely unnoticed and unsung through the nomination race, but both had given substantial amounts of their personal time and energies to the campaign in various states. John was most effective in advising the candidate and his managers concerning new issues and strategies; he also traveled into several states to encourage our workers and spent a great deal of time on the phone to various state coordinators boosting morale during the many dark days. For her part, Jean Westwood was on the road throughout much of 1971 and the early months of 1972, traveling from state to state in the Western region. She specialized in advising our local supporters and state committees on organizational matters, referring them constantly to the nuts and bolts of everyday politics and insisting that the groundwork needed to win campaigns be carried out during the months when many saw little purpose. Furthermore, since Jean had extensive experience in Democratic Party affairs, she was able to contact, and in many cases convert, party officers and regular leaders who respected her background and credentials. She was a qualified regular herself and someone we could point to as proof that the campaign was not just a fringe operation. During the nomination race, Jean never once hesitated to carry out any assignment she was given. She was instrumental in helping structure a political organization designed to turn out an impressive Oregon primary vote for relatively little expenditure.

The Oregon results, even though somewhat anti-climactic with McGovern running against his expectations, continued the victory momen-

tum begun in Wisconsin: McGovern, 50 percent; Wallace (something of
a surprise second against Humphrey in this "liberal" state), 20 percent;
Humphrey, 13 percent. We picked up 34 delegate votes as a result of
the victory.

The Rhode Island results were surprising. There we had organized
the state with almost no help from the national headquarters, save that
attention given by regional desk officer Alan Kriegel. The Senator hadn't
been in the state for months, and we spent practically nothing on media.
The entire party establishment, from the Governor and the two United
States Senators on down, had gone for Muskie early and big. And in any
other year that would have been the ballgame. But we organized, largely
under Dave Evans' leadership, with the supporters available, trying at
every point possible in a party-dominated state to avoid alienating the
party and falling completely into the hands of the fierce anti-party faction. It was a middle-ground policy almost impossible to carry out in
the hostile environment then prevailing. But the results were a tribute to
our workers, who merely did what party leaders have been trying to get
workers to do since political organizations first breathed life in the caves
—go rap with the folks in the other caves and, when you find some
friendly ones, get them to join you. Rhode Island results: McGovern,
41 percent, Muskie, 21 percent (which proves the party is worth one-
fifth even after the candidate fails to register on the thermometer);
Humphrey, 20 percent, Wallace, 15 percent. McGovern picked up all 22
of the state's delegates.

And so the stage was set for California. Twenty-two months before,
we had felt it would be the deciding battle, the last great showdown.
George McGovern against Ed Muskie or Hubert Humphrey, but probably Hubert Humphrey. And I had always felt that California would
decide more than just the party's 1972 Presidential nominee. It would
decide control of the Democratic Party for the future. California was
Armageddon.

THE INVASION OF CALIFORNIA. MAY, 1972. They started
coming all the way from Massachusetts and Pennsylvania in late April.
Traveling all the way across the country. Then after Ohio, the stream became almost a steady one. Some stopped over for a week of campaigning
in Nebraska and then headed west. More continued out of the east after
Michigan and Maryland. Driving, flying, busing, hiking. And, after
Oregon, down from the north. More came in every day. Carloads from
every state in the west.

The campaign that had begun with a few now numbered in the
thousands. The army that had started with a handful was now 50,000
strong in California. The officer corps, the paid staff, numbered some

250, with more than three times that number organizing on a full-time basis without salary. They operated out of 230 offices around California. Hundreds of phones operated throughout every day from 34 phone banks across the state. These full-time phones were supplemented on the eve of the primary with hundreds of others in law offices and empty hotel rooms.

The army moved more than five and a half million pieces of McGovern literature, most of which was printed in our campaign print shop, which operated 24 hours a day every day. Local offices covered the whole range of style, from a boutique storefront in the plush Beverly Wilshire Hotel to seasonally out-of-use H & R Block tax offices. The army was everywhere.

MAY 20, 1972. The day after our preliminary agreement with the Humphrey representatives, I flew to Oakland to travel with the Senator and brief him on the terms for the debates and obtain his comments before completing the negotiations. He generally agreed with the position we were taking and seemed eager for a chance to counter Humphrey's increasingly strong and inaccurate charges face to face.

During the stop in Fresno, where he was headquartered, I talked to Gene Pokorny. Speaking for the grassroots people, Gene said he was upset by the way in which decisions were made and resources allocated in California. He had been in touch with other area coordinators and all had the same complaint: the state headquarters in Los Angeles was trying to run the entire canvass operation, sending out computerized voter-contact lists and requesting that canvass results (the system of ranking each voter contacted on a 1-to-5 scale) be sent back to Los Angeles so a personalized computer letter could be sent out from the main headquarters.

This system was diametrically opposed to any previous McGovern primary campaign, where all voter contact was locally oriented. Earlier, neighborhood storefront offices had been used as headquarters for local canvassing; card files on each voter contacted (the ranking system which was the nerve center of our entire campaign) had been maintained locally and used to get out the vote. The citizen-volunteers who carried the bulk of the load under an experienced staff organizer had felt a great sense of direct control and, therefore, responsibility for organizing their neighborhoods for McGovern. They prided themselves on their efficiency and dedication and felt that centralization and control from a state headquarters was a sign of lack of trust and confidence in them by the campaign leadership. And this struggle, going on in the last two weeks of the California primary, was at the very heart of the McGovern campaign.

Other campaigns, John Kennedy in 1960, McCarthy in 1968, Robert Kennedy in 1968, had relied heavily on the classic insurgency technique of rousing the countryside—the volunteers—to beat the entrenched powers. Like most political techniques, this one is based on military principles; it is New England citizens with pitchforks and muskets against George III's troops. Though the citizens need direction and leadership, it may be laid down as an unswerving law of politics that a campaign dependent upon citizen volunteers will succeed to the degree that it is able to motivate and use those citizens and will fail to the degree that it ceases to rely upon them and their judgment.

The McGovern campaign's unique contribution to insurgency politics was its grassroots character—its decentralization. The role of the national campaign leadership was to allocate resources—staff, money, the candidate's time, and media—and to select and assign the most qualified political organizers available to the states. The role of these organizers, the state coordinators, was to recruit and motivate the most talented citizens in the state to positions of local leadership and responsibility and to further allocate the resources granted from the national campaign in the most judicious manner possible. The role of the citizen leadership was to continue the recruitment process throughout the state until every block in every neighborhood in every community had a responsible McGovern supporter who would identify and deliver every McGovern vote on election day. The image is that of a pyramid with the peak as small as possible, the base as broad as possible, and the entire structure as short as possible. Reduce the number of layers of leadership. Keep the leaders at the very top in close touch with the people at the bottom. (I found out more about the overall condition and health of the McGovern campaign in a half-hour visit to a local headquarters than in a dozen lengthy, ponderous meetings in the national headquarters with all the other campaign leaders. It is symptomatic of later difficulties that, as the campaign became larger and more successful, I had fewer and fewer opportunities to visit local headquarters.)

These were the things Gene and I discussed on a sunny sidewalk in Fresno as the Senator addressed an enthusiastic rally crowd in the city square. He was getting expensive and sophisticated computer lists but no money for stamps to send out local mailings on local issues. Carl Wagner, in very conservative southwest Los Angeles (Carl wanted to sell "McGovern for President" gunracks for pickup trucks), was burning candles for light in his shabby storefront offices because he didn't have money for the light bills. Priorities were becoming warped.

After talking to Gene and confirming trends which already seemed apparent, I returned to Los Angeles to discuss the problem with Eli Segal and Miles Rubin. Eli was particularly aware of the problem, having been in touch with each of the area coordinators daily. Miles, the father of the computer operation, assured me that the initial expenditures for the computer had been made and, thereafter, more money would be going directly to the local offices. The procedural problems, concerning contact of voters by the machine from Los Angeles or by local supporters, were not resolved and continued to be a policy disagreement throughout the primary.

MAY 24, 1972. Less than two weeks before the California primary we updated our delegate chart. It showed 44 states in which the delegate selection process had begun or was completed. The figures from eight of the states were somewhat conservative projections from early caucus commitments. In nineteen of the states primaries had already been held; the remaining 25 states or jurisdictions had caucus-convention systems. The count: McGovern, 671½; Wallace, 368; Humphrey, 350½; Muskie, 162½; Jackson, 44; assorted other candidates, 57½; uncommitted delegates, 445. The magic number to achieve the nomination was 1,509. Day by day, we were moving up.

Negotiations went forward in Washington with myself, D. J. Leary, and press secretary Dan Hackel for Humphrey and each of the networks. Generally, the candidates' representatives wanted something approaching a debate format—candidates standing behind lecterns, opening and closing statements of some length, and the opportunity to respond to each other's answers. The networks, on the other hand, had been advised by their attorneys that significant deviation from their regular interview format would subject them to equal-time challenges and they would end up having every Presidential contender on television. Finally, after lengthy discussion, the details were arranged.

MAY 26, 1972. A week after my discussion with Gene Pokorny, organizational problems had smoothed over temporarily. The logjam created by the inability of the computer to get voter lists out to the local areas had been broken. A little more money was available for local operations, but substantial amounts were still being spent—for the first time in the McGovern campaign—for professional services. More people were being paid to do things which had previously been done for nothing by volunteers.

But the motivation of those among the California leadership who favored major expenditures and professionalism was honorable. We all realized that California was the nomination watershed. Humphrey was stepping up his attacks and promised to intensify the battle until the final hours. The California poll, just released, showed Humphrey slightly ahead. This was for the big apple, all the marbles. Better to throw in every resource, fire every gun, than to take a chance. California is an unpredictable political jurisdiction; anything can happen there, and probably will. As Steve Roberts, a California-based reporter for *The New York Times*, wrote hours before the vote; "Senator Humphrey's basic tactic here has been to try to scare people. If Senator McGovern wins, he has warned, poor blacks and Chicanos will get less welfare, middle-class homeowners will pay more taxes, factory workers will lose their jobs, Israel will lose military aid, and the United States will become a 'second-rate power.' And in this chaotic and unpredictable state, fear is a proven political weapon. Loyalties can collapse as quickly as a tract house in an earthquake."

With the stakes running as high as they were, and in this chimerical political climate, we had no choice but to try everything. But the results were to sow the seeds of paranoia among our dedicated grassroots workers, to create the impression that the campaign was losing its soul— if it hadn't already—and to cause the citizen-volunteers to wonder if they were any longer needed. They had waited so long for that inevitable and dreaded moment when the "pros" arrived to take over. Since 8:20 P.M. on April 4th, when NBC gave the Wisconsin primary to McGovern, they had seen the nameless, faceless "pros" flitting silently from pillar to pillar, in and out of the campaign plane, ever seeking the candidate's ear, ever grasping for power and responsibility in the campaign. And now it looked to many of them as if the worst had come true. Their champion surely must be selling them out. It was a fearsome mood and it would follow us across the country to Miami's Doral Hotel and into the fall.

M A Y 2 7 , 1 9 7 2 . In 1968, Robert Kennedy had taken a train down the San Joaquin Valley, stopping to give speeches in eight or ten towns along the mainline. It was not a particularly novel idea in California politics, but it was a relatively simple, yet visible, means of reaching into those agrarian, fairly conservative, communities of 10,000 to 20,000 each —Modesto, Merced, Madera, Fresno, Tulare, Delano, Bakersfield. Now, after months of airplanes, a train for us was sort of a novelty. Like other aspects of the 1972 McGovern California primary campaign it was also a sentimental journey.

We started about 10 A.M. in Modesto, almost an hour behind schedule, with a departure rally at the train station. The Senator spoke from the back of the train to a crowd of 1,500-2,000. The whistle blew and we headed south down the Atchison, Topeka, and Santa Fe mainline. Between stops, the Senator entertained local politicians who had driven up the line to meet us and then introduce or be introduced by McGovern to their local constituents at the next stop. By mid-morning the valley

San Joaquin Valley: The people's train, the people's state, the people's country.

began to heat up in the late spring sun and, in spite of the air conditioning, the bodies of staff, celebrities, politicians, reporters, cameramen, and
well-wishers surging up and down the narrow passageway brought coats
off and caused ties to be loosened. The two carloads of newsmen bought
roll after roll of the purple theatre tickets which could be traded for
strong drink.

Every 45 to 60 minutes the next stop would be called; the train would
ease to a halt; the second and third cars from the end would disgorge
sweating cameramen and increasingly mellow reporters; John Gage, the
soundman, would mount the portable sound system; and the candidate,
accompanied by Eleanor, Shirley MacLaine, and the local political leaders,
would crowd out onto the rear platform. The crowds, most of which
waited for more than an hour as the roadshow struggled to catch up on
the late start, would drift out from the shade of the train depot roof and
collect around the back platform.

At each stop, the Senator spoke briefly of reordering priorities, returning the country to its former values and direction ("come home America")
and replacing war and armaments with peace and jobs. The response was
uniformly vigorous, but more rapt than unrestrained. One reporter drew
the inevitable comparison with Robert Kennedy in California, noting that
McGovern probably couldn't give his cuff-links away, but also suggesting
that McGovern did not suffer from the backlash of fear that the Kennedy
frenzy had generated in many voters.

Before the day grew long and tedious, and those on the train became
sticky and tired, there arose a warm, relaxed, almost tender and peaceful
mood. There we were on our very own train gliding through some of the
most fertile farmland man had ever wrested from the desert, through the
land of milk and honey, the Golden State, the dust bowl emigrants' Promised Land. Hubert Humphrey and the few McGovern-hating labor bosses
were far away. McGovern was not campaigning *against* anyone; he was
campaigning *for* something—for America's heart and soul; he was seeking
to lead America home again. The only opponent was Richard Nixon, and
who could gainsay the rightness of that cause. The confusion of Ohio, the
tedious months of Wisconsin, the bitterness of Nebraska, the loneliness
of New Hamsphire, the boredom and exhaustion of 1971 and the ridiculous impossibility of 1970 were long ago and far away. This was the
people's train, and the people's valley, and the people's state, and soon it
would be the people's country. And the train swayed and glided south
down the Santa Fe mainline through the peaceful valley.

MAY 28, 1972. On the ninth floor of the Wilshire Hyatt House in
Los Angeles, the California campaign's residential headquarters, the campaign leadership gathered in my room to prepare for the first debate with

Humphrey. Our purpose was to analyze the issues thoroughly, anticipate the direction Humphrey might take, determine the points the Senator should make most accurately to reflect his position throughout the state, and then advise the Senator of our conclusions. Although we were vitally concerned with the outcome of the California primary, the *sine qua non* of the nomination, even more importantly we realized these debates would be the first searching national exposure the Senator would have. In a real sense, they were looked upon as the opening round of the race against Nixon. The background discussion went on for almost two hours.

Several of us had produced our own memoranda for the Senator, giving personal points of view. It was hoped that half a dozen to a dozen consensus points of view could be achieved to supplement the memos done by Pierre Salinger, John Holum, myself and others. In my memo, I had urged him to present short, simple answers wherever possible and to be calm, deliberate, and thoughtful to counter what would surely be a voluble, verbose opponent. I also tried to emphasize the importance of humor and almost total lack of relief in what had been a very sober campaign. If the occasion arose, I strongly suggested, he shouldn't be afraid to counter and disarm the highstrung, straining Humphrey with a gentle, "Come on now, Hubert, you know better than that."

It was fairly clear what Humphrey would land on. Day in and day out he had been claiming up and down the state that McGovern's proposed 55-billion-dollar defense budget would decimate California's economy, causing the loss of tens of thousands of defense-oriented jobs, that his plan to replace the confused welfare system with an income redistribution plan would drastically increase middle-income tax rates and confiscate wealth at the upper income level, that McGovern's resistance to foreign military involvements jeopardized the survival of Israel, and that somehow—even though their positions were essentially the same—McGovern was a radical on problems such as abortion and marijuana. Of all this, the Senator was by now well aware.

The background session breaking off, Frank, John Holum, and I went up to the Senator's suite where we summarized initiatives which should be taken and answers which might be given to counter anticipated Humphrey charges. Since, in circumstances such as this, I always felt McGovern already knew most of the things his advisors were telling him, I tried to relay in summary form the observation of the field organizers: people wanted to make sure that he was not like other politicians, that, on the other hand, he was really not a radical; they wanted to get a personal sense of the man they hoped might restore faith and confidence in government again.

3 P.M. CBS studios. Moderator, George Herman. Panelists David Schumacher of CBS and David Broder of *The Washington Post*. Humphrey's

Armageddon: The old order passeth away.

opening was shrill, hoarse, and intemperate. He looked fatigued and angry. Watching from the control booth, I leaned forward, scarcely believing my eyes and ears. This was Nixon in 1960. After the first ten minutes, I turned to Charles Guggenheim, smiled, and breathed a deep sigh of relief. The pent-up tension created by the fear of a Humphrey coup—a composed, concise, astute senior statesman—disappeared. Confident that McGovern could handle himself, I now believed we had won this and the two coming debates.

"Senator McGovern has concocted a fantastic welfare scheme which will give everybody, even Nelson Rockefeller, $1,000 and it will cost the taxpayers 60 or 70 billion dollars, mostly middle-income taxpayers," ranted Humphrey. Picking it up, one of the panel asked, "how much will your plan cost, Senator?" McGovern: "I don't know." Then McGovern went ahead to explain that much of the cost would be covered by savings in administrative expenses, closing of loopholes, and reduced military expenditures.

Afterward, in the network dressing room, I told him he had definitely won the debate, that most voters would be judging demeanor quite heavily, and that Humphrey had seriously hurt himself with the harsh, divisive, bitter tactics. But, I suggested, we had lost some points on the welfare program and some figure for the total cost of the program would have been better than none, even if the economists couldn't agree on the specific figure. "I wish," said Senator McGovern, "that I had never heard of the goddamn idea."

MAY 29, 1972. The Senator went back on the road, shuttling between south and north, with an occasional shot down to San Diego. The scheduling theory was an early morning "media" event in either the Los Angeles or San Fransico area media markets, then off by mid-morning to the other end of the state for a full day's campaigning, including a late morning "media" event, then overnight, an early morning "media" event, then off to the other end of the state, where the cycle was continued. In this way, the candidate was on the evening news every evening in both major media markets of the state. The Senator was to maintain this pace for many of the fourteen days between the Oregon primary and the California primary, with the exception of the three debate days, when, understandably, he dropped off the campaign trail to rest and prepare.

Like most other aspects of the California campaign, the scheduling and advance operation was fraught with hassles. The hyperthyroidal Steve Robbins, after a year of Presidential campaign scheduling (unprecedented, brutal punishment), now found himself supervising two separate candidate scheduling operations, north and south, as well as an elaborate secondary scheduling bureaucracy designed to assist Mrs. McGovern and a bewildering variety of actors, performers, politicians, celebrities, speakers, and other significant personages including, but not limited to Mrs. Martin Luther King, Senator Frank Church, former Interior Secretary Stewart Udall, the Rev. Jesse Jackson, Leonard Nimoy, Rep. Julian Bond, Senator Fred Harris, Dennis Weaver, Senator Abraham Ribicoff, Shirley MacLaine, and Pierre Salinger.

Poor Robbins. He came to me several days before the primary and pleaded for another assignment in the fall campaign. A burned-out volcano, a mere shadow of a man. In this primary he was particularly harassed because his advance people had been struggling unsuccessfully for days to get copies of the computer print-outs for crowd-raising purposes. The struggle raged back and forth between the scheduling and advance people and Max Factor, Carl D'Agostino, and the others controlling the computer operation. But Robbins' advance people, by now veterans of every battle since New Hampshire, performed masterfully, under the increasingly critical eye of the expanding national press corps, managing to avoid catastrophes lurking at every turn.

MAY 30, 1972. We followed the same procedures that we had the previous Sunday in preparing for the second debate. Essentially the same group of people collected in Miles Rubin's suite. The assessment of the previous debate was that the Senator had handled himself very well but that he definitely needed back-up support on his economic proposals, specifically figures on tax reform and income redistribution. Once again, the group's consensus judgments were taken to the Senator and that was followed by an economic briefing and a briefing on defense budget cuts by John Holum.

The second debate, taped in the late afternoon at NBC's cavernous Burbank studios, saw a subdued Humphrey, a Humphrey now convinced that his initial tactic of bristling attack had seriously backfired. He rather abjectly apologized for suggesting in the first debate that the Senator was a "fool," a remark our canvassing data revealed stuck in many people's minds to Humphrey's detriment. The Senator scored with specific information on the military armaments his budget would provide. But, in the main, it was a fairly mild affair. The reporters covering these matches seemed to be getting bored. Not a lot of news was being generated. The ratings showed the second debate trailing its competition on the two other networks badly.

End of May, 1972. About this time there arrived in our whirling, turbulent, macaronic state headquarters the noted journalist Joseph Alsop. I was struck immediately by his resemblance to the British actor Trevor Howard, particularly where Howard plays an Englishman stranded for several decades on some tropical colonial possession, sitting in his panama suit at a wicker table under a slowly revolving fan, calmly, somewhat wearily, discussing the crumbling of the empire. Mr. Alsop was extremely philanthropic in his assessment of our organizational efforts, suggesting, as I recall, that what he considered to be our spectacular successes were the product of several parts 1964 Goldwater with a substantial amount of Chairman Mao and a dash of Fidel Castro. I tried to explain that we had relied upon none of these as a pattern, but Mr. Alsop had clearly made up his mind that the Senator had somehow created or fallen prey to monolithic, politically sinister legions unsurpassed in order and drill since the erection of the Great Pyramid. All in all, the twenty-minute interview was enjoyable, particularly Mr. Alsop's fascinating fifteen-minute account of how we actually had brought off this political miracle.

J U N E 2 , 1 9 7 2 . The Field poll, the most noteworthy political opinion poll in the state, announced its most recent findings. Astoundingly, McGovern was shown to be leading Humphrey 46 percent to 26 percent, with 10–12 percent undecided and the remainder for other candidates. Shortly before, Pat Caddell produced private figures from his almost round-the-clock sampling efforts showing McGovern ahead with a margin of 40 percent to 26 percent, and 14 percent undecided. Immediately, the Field poll results became the subject of heated debate and speculation, both within our own campaign and among the press corps. Did we really believe we were 20 points ahead? No; more like 10 to 12. Was there any chance the lead might increase? No. There were too many undecideds and our figures showed they were probable Humphrey votes. What did I think the final margin would be? About 8 points. And in California that's a landslide; no major primary had ever been won by 5 points or more.

But late in the last week before the primary and through the weekend, we began to see the impact of the Humphrey attacks in our canvassing and phoning results. The tabulations were showing an erosion of the undecideds moving to Humphrey. More and more often our workers were hearing that McGovern was too radical, or that he wanted to change things too fast, or that (in the Jewish areas around Los Angeles) he wasn't strong enough on Israel, or that he would increase taxes and put everyone on welfare. We were holding our own, particularly in the north, but our support had leveled off and the margin was narrowing each day as Humphrey picked up previously undecided voters in the Los Angeles area.

Humphrey went East, to New Jersey and New York on June 1st and 2nd, which many interpreted as a serious tactical mistake. But, besides bolstering his faltering New Jersey operation, he did seem to pick up some desperately needed dollars somewhere. Over the weekend, the 3rd and 4th, he stepped up his media purchases in the Los Angeles market dramatically. Besides blitzing the airways, he himself seemed to be all over the state in the closing hours—Humphrey here, Humphrey there, here a Humphrey, there a Humphrey, everywhere a Hubert Humphrey. He was either triplets or had superhuman glands.

McGovern, meanwhile, was not sitting still. We were in the closing hours of the closing fight. He maintained a steady pace up through Saturday night, but steadfastly resisted the temptation to mimic Humphrey's frantic gyrations, choosing not to appear panicked.

J U N E 4, 1 9 7 2. The day of the third and last debate, we went through the ritual of the first two. Morning meeting at the Hyatt House. Summary briefing of McGovern. McGovern making notes. Questions to anticipate. Proposed answers to deliver. All followed by yet another economic briefing in the Senator's suite.

During the initial debate, the Humphrey challenge and McGovern response to the guaranteed-income plan had stirred up a minor hurricane of controversy. Gordon Weil summoned from Washington a member of the campaign economic advisory board which had developed the plan. The economist's arrival was a comic mix-up. He was scheduled to fly to San Francisco, meet the traveling party and talk with the Senator and Gordon on a flight down to Los Angeles. He arrived on the wrong plane, missed the Senator, and ended up getting into Los Angeles in the middle of the night. The next morning he was brought before a press conference heavily weighted with economic specialists to background them on the specifics of income redistribution. It was an unmitigated tragedy (it would have been a farce except the stakes were so high). Having learned about the press conference almost accidentally, I sauntered into the press room Saturday to see if I couldn't educate myself on this subject further. The economist had clearly made a big mistake—he showed up. The reporters, after several minutes of elaborate economic theory, were hopelessly lost and, rather than being led out of the statistical wilderness, were being led more deeply in. What was wanting were simple facts and simple figures, straightforwardly delivered by someone with a sophisticated judgment of their political consequences. What was instead presented was an incredibly complex mass of numbers, a maze of statistics, a morass of theory, with no political appreciation for their consequences whatsoever.

Recovering slowly from the shock, I sent someone for Frank, who had been supervising issue development, and considered calling the conference to an early halt. The idea was rejected as impractical; it would merely underscore our own disarray. The only other alternative seemed to be tears—or laughter. The whole thing was swiftly becoming so preposterous that it created the fleeting hope that the reporters would take it as a great hoax, an elaborate put-on, and treat it accordingly. After what seemed like hours—Frank had arrived, initially disoriented, but then managed to interject a few clarifying remarks ("don't you really mean that the net cost of the program will be . . .")—the travesty thankfully ended. It was, in many respects, the political low-point and the comedy high-point of the entire nomination race.

Later that day, the ABC debate was taped for prime-time viewing, and, as anticipated, it was generally a lackluster draw. This debate's only distinctive feature was the participation of General Hardin, representing Wallace, and—by split-screen from the east—Congresswoman Shirley Chisholm. A court ordered that they had to be included. No blood spilled, few points scored. As before, McGovern won on demeanor with Humphrey repeating his attacks on the McGovern program, presenting few clearcut alternatives of his own.

Shortly after the taping, I received a call from Governor Pat Lucey, who was attending the Democratic governors convention in Houston. Having begun to circulate among his colleagues, a number of whom were ideologically to the right of McGovern, Lucey had sensed a mood of serious unrest and unhappiness with what was suddenly appearing to be an inevitable McGovern nomination. Lucey wanted a few hours to circulate and consult with Gov. Richard Kneip of South Dakota—one of the few other strong pro-McGovern governors deputized to convert, or at least neutralize, their colleagues. If the situation did shape up to be a sticky one, Lucey wondered, was there any chance the Senator could come over to Houston to meet with the governors and put out the fires? I said that I doubted it, that the only way we could do it was on the way out of California, Wednesday morning, June 7th. Lucey said the conference would be over, it would be too late. We arranged to talk later that night.

Meanwhile, our staff and supporters in New Mexico had been pleading in vain for several days for a brief McGovern visit before Tuesday's primary in that state. They felt they were on the brink of a victory and one appearance could make the difference. We were getting up-beat reports from New Jersey also. Since the fourth primary on Tuesday, South Dakota, was uncontested, the possibility of a clean sweep of four primaries in one day was intriguing. It could nail the lid right on the nomination. We could spend the entire five weeks before the convention in uninterrupted planning for the fall campaign and healing the breaches in the party.

I talked to the Senator about Lucey's concern and offered the possibility of a fast Monday afternoon trip out of Los Angeles to Houston, with an airport stop in Albuquerque to boost the New Mexico campaign. We agreed that we would await Lucey's call that night to decide. The staff was about equally divided on the trip. Meanwhile, I alerted Robbins to keep Monday afternoon and evening tentative on the schedule and to explore the logistics of an L.A.-Albuquerque-Houston-L.A. trip.

Over the weekend, other things began to happen which also promised to crystalize the nomination contest very quickly.

Surprisingly, delicate peace feelers were extended by the Humphrey campaign within 48 hours of the crucial vote. If the Field poll was correct and if McGovern did win big, how would we feel about Humphrey closing up shop immediately afterwards and endorsing McGovern? We would feel very good about that. How good? Wait a minute; here it comes. You see, Hubert has run up quite a debt in this campaign, particularly in the last few days. And our supporters would sure feel a lot better about letting Hubert go with George if they thought they would get some of their loans paid back. How much? Some suggestion of an offer that couldn't be refused. Clearly, if the terms were right, Humphrey was prepared to deliver an election night endorsement.

Throughout Sunday and Monday, Ted Van Dyk was gently lobbing back the peace offers, testing the authority of the third-party intermediaries, trying to determine conditions and degrees of seriousness. His principal contact, long-time Humphrey friend Max Kampelman, indicated that the particular condition related to a quarter of a million dollars of Humphrey campaign debts. They wanted us to assume it. After months and months of ideological doubletalk about centrism, radicalism, and so forth, it was clear that issues and ideology would play a very minor role in this potentially sudden changing of the guard, this possibly abrupt transition of power in this oldest surviving political institution, the Democratic Party.

But the Southern governors hadn't gotten the word that their horses were about to ride out from under them. Down in Houston mutinous mutterings wafted up and down the hotel hallways, discontent rumbled from lip to closely bent ear. Stop-McGovern was the theme, anybody-but-McGovern was its wildest echo. Could the party possibly nominate a candidate its governors didn't want? It had happened so seldom as to tax the memories of living men. But in politics, as at the race track and the bank boardroom, only numbers count. And gathered in Houston, *inter alia*, were Gov. Warren Hearnes with 61 Missouri delegate votes, Gov. Jimmie Carter with 36 Georgia votes, Gov. Wendell Ford with 36 Kentucky votes, Gov. John West with 30 South Carolina votes, Gov. David Hall with 24 Oklahoma votes, Gov. Edwin Edwards with almost 30 Louisiana votes, and Gov. Robert Docking with 16 Kansas votes. Even presuming we could override an attempted nomination veto by the gov-

ernors, these were not men we would want to remain permanently unhappy in the fall. Gov. Lucey: "Tell the Senator things are in pretty bad
shape over here and Gov. Kneip and I think he better come."

JUNE 5, 1972. The Senator had gone to sleep before Lucey's
urgent message came through, so I conveyed it to him immediately upon
his awakening at 7:30 A.M. with my strong recommendation that putting
out the Houston fires combined with carrying New Mexico outweighed
possibly winning California by another point or two. He said he would
go to Houston. I called Robbins and told him to notify Albuquerque and
put the out-of-state trip on. Kirby Jones got the word to the press corps
just as they were boarding the buses for a day of routine campaigning.

The memories of 1968 lingered throughout the state of California like
a tragic love affair. But they were felt most deeply in the hearts of those
who had worked for Robert Kennedy—Frank most, Pierre, myself, and
many others. A number of our original California supporters—Max Pa-
levsky, Mary Green, John Anderson, Elizabeth Stevens, Bill Norris, Bill
Lockyer—had lived through that wrenching, crushing catastrophe, tasting
the bitterness of victory suddenly turned to ashes. And the closer the
primary came, the more the sense of history playing itself out again descended. Apprehension moved in like a thick San Francisco fog. Primary
night, June 6th, would be four years to the day from the slaying of Robert Kennedy. George McGovern would appear at the Los Angeles Palladium four years to the very hour.

Frank and Pierre decided very early that they would not go. Not out
of fear, but out of respect and honor for Robert Kennedy's memory. I
was afraid—afraid for George McGovern's life. He was Robert Kennedy's
friend. He had taken Kennedy's place in 1968. He was surrounded by
many of the same people. They represented many of the same political
goals and ideals. McGovern was going to win the California primary just
as Kennedy had. Recently, Arthur Bremer had reminded every crack-
brain in America how easily it could be done. If anyone had a grievance
against McGovern—and some did—if anyone wished historical notoriety
—and there seem to be those who do—if someone was waiting for the
occasion, then the night of the California primary had to be that time.
Paranoia mounted throughout the campaign as the hours ticked off.

JUNE 6, 1972. California primary day. The Democratic Party
would never be the same after this day.

The Senator returned from Houston, having successfully defused the
threatened governors' revolt. Shortly after his arrival in Houston he appeared before the governors' caucus in a coats-off, shirtsleeves-up session

in which he performed his specialty—convincing the suspicious and ill-informed that he was not a radical. He had had years of practice in South Dakota, and he had mastered the art. After that, he had hosted a reception into the early hours which provided an even more informal opportunity to get to know some individual governors whom he had never met and to further strengthen the impression that he was just as solid a Democrat as any man in the house. Although it is unclear how many committed converts he won, he performed an operation almost as important in politics. It's called pulling the fangs. He neutralized the opposition.

Political history may well question the decision to go to Houston the day before the California primary. But the record should show that it was the only time in the entire nomination race, and certainly during his period as the frontrunner, when the Senator had an opportunity to meet with virtually all the Democratic governors. It was a vitally important element in our strategy of uniting with the regular elements of the party, without which we could not hope to win in the fall.

Tuesday morning I checked at the state headquarters to make sure the get-out-the-vote operation was underway, as I knew it would be, made a round of calls to the other primary states, and then set out around noon with Don O'Brien and a Secret Service representative to inspect sites for an overflow rally. Because of strict crowd limitations clamped on by the Secret Service at the Palladium, hundreds of McGovern workers would not have an opportunity to see the Senator at the victory celebration. A mammoth hangar-like building had been found on a nearby movie lot, and the three of us spent well over an hour in the place discussing how the crowd of more than 5,000 could be fitted in while still insuring the Senator's protection. As it turned out, the plan failed in the late afternoon, and the Palladium parking lot was selected as the appropriate gathering place for the overflow crowd.

I then spent much of the rest of the afternoon at the Palladium, walking over its vast dance floor, up and down its corridors, poking around through the backstage dressing rooms, up into the management offices where in a few hours we would establish our "situation room." Looking for something or maybe trying to make sure something wasn't there. Uneasy, restless, pacing, nervous. Even now the place was beginning to swarm with security officers of all sorts, plainclothed and uniformed. Yet I was driven to walk and look and search.

The returns came in slowly that night. Throughout the middle hours of the evening they were not particularly encouraging, with McGovern unable to open a lead of more than one or two points. A great part of the difficulty arose from the breakdown of the state election board computers in San Francisco. We had always calculated that our margin would come from the northern part of the state, but that vote did not begin to come in until almost midnight.

In the meantime, results began to come in from the other primary states. The Senator carried his home state primary, South Dakota, without opposition, adding another 17 delegates to his total. Then a great surprise in New Jersey. As in almost all the other eastern industrial states, the party and labor leaders had divided between Muskie and Humphrey; but the party leaders had been trapped in the Muskie wreckage and the labor leaders had proved incapable of turning out a vote for Humphrey. We had publicly set our goal at 55 of New Jersey's 109 delegates. The voting tabulations showed that we would win 73 delegates to Humphrey's 9, and 27 uncommitted. It was an astounding upset, once again a credit to committed, efficient supporters.

Then, later that night, from New Mexico came the word that Mc-Govern would win that primary with 34 percent of the vote to Wallace's 30 percent and Humphrey's 26 percent. Delegates were apportioned according to state law between the top two finishers, with McGovern winning 10 and Wallace 8.

Now, late in the evening, we had only to carry California to sweep all four primaries and pick up 271 more delegates. From our situation room in the manager's office at the Palladium, the returns were monitored and analyzed as they came in. The lead began to increase an agonizing fraction at a time. Finally, Humphrey, who had to take a plane out of the state that night, appeared before his workers, saying without much conviction that it was still a close race and that he expected to win. He then left for the airport. We were still hoping the lead would dramatically expand before he left the state, causing him to deliver the hoped-for endorsement which would end the nomination race. We naturally feared that once he got out of the state he would be out from under the pressure of the race and the sense of inevitability of the McGovern nomination and would pull back from his intention to drop out. Through our long-range negotiations we had certainly left open the possibility of helping pay off the Humphrey debts if he were out of the race. Now, if his defeat could be established decisively before he got away, he still might wrap up the deal.

In the next few minutes there occurred one of those accidents of politics upon which the fate of empires hinge. The breakdown of the computers in the north had caused the initial returns from the San Francisco bay area to seem much closer than they would actually turn out to be. This accident in turn led the NBC vote analysts to conclude that the race was going to be a very close one, with Humphrey running more strongly than expected in the greater Los Angeles area. Just as Humphrey was arriving at the airport to board his plane, John Chancellor of NBC was telling people not to go to bed—the California contest was a real horserace and Humphrey might still win it. This news was immediately communicated to Humphrey by aides anxious to see him stay in the race and not capitulate. And even as he stood at the steps of the plane, Humphrey turned to the reporters covering his departure and waiting for some last word on his intentions (rumors had by now circulated all over Los Angeles about a possible withdrawal) and said: "I've just been told that this race is not over yet and we may still win it. I just want all of my supporters to know Hubert Humphrey isn't out of this contest and I intend to stay in and fight for the nomination all the way to Miami." With that torpedo into the ship of reconciliation, Humphrey mounted the steps and bade California good-bye. Minutes after his plane took off and headed eastward, John Chancellor was back on the air suggesting that recalculations showed McGovern would carry the state, perhaps by four or five points, and that it wouldn't be a close race after all.

McGovern arrived at the Palladium with his family under incredibly heavy guard—I am now convinced every third person in the riotous Palladium, including several dashiki-clad blacks, were detectives or Secret Service. He thanked his many workers and supporters, noting particularly the satisfaction of sweeping all four primaries ("I can't believe we won the whole thing!") and then summoned the spectre in everyone's mind with a tribute to Robert Kennedy, fatally wounded four years ago almost to the minute.

Suddenly, it was all over. The Battle of Armageddon had ended.

Amid the tumult and celebration, exactly two years after I had accompanied George McGovern on our first trip into New Hampshire and on the crest of the greatest political upset in the century, I felt uneasy and troubled. Earlier that day, one of our workers at the Palladium had stopped me and asked, "Gary, do you really think we will win?" I said I didn't see any way we could lose the primary. He said, "No, I mean the nomination. These guys don't want George McGovern. They will do anything to stop him."

J U N E 8 , 1 9 7 2 . From Washington we issued the next in our series of delegate tabulations. All 55 voting jurisdictions, the 50 states, the District of Columbia, Canal Zone, Puerto Rico, Virgin Islands and Guam, were included. In fourteen states our calculations represented projections based on earlier caucus commitments. In the final primary, New York's on June 20th, our key advisors thought we would elect at least 225 delegates. The totals were: McGovern, 1346½; Humphrey, 374½; Wallace, 370; Muskie holding at 179; Jackson, 44; Chisholm, 22; other candidates, 84½; and uncommitteds, 595½. Clearly now, even if all the Humphrey, Muskie, and uncommitted delegates banded together (an unlikely political occurrence), McGovern would still be 200 votes ahead. The chance of adding the Wallace votes to that coalition, the only way McGovern could be surpassed, was extremely unlikely.

Somehow we had to find 163 more delegates in 30 days to make up the 1,509 votes necessary to nominate. That was our agenda for June.

We had devised, weeks earlier, a sophisticated delegate information system which started at the state level, with our key state staff researching almost 30 pieces of information on each delegate selected. The data were then screened and refined by the regional desks in Washington and fed into a computer. The computer then could print out the lists of any one of a couple of dozen special-interest groups to whom mailings could be sent. Several general mailings were sent in May and June to all delegates, including letters from the Senator, copies of his biography, and helpful information on convention arrangements and procedures. Key members of the McGovern campaign staff were identified to all delegates, regardless of commitment, so that, when the time came to negotiate on the convention floor, they would know with whom they were dealing. This delegate information and contact system was probably the most sophisticated in American political history; in a contested convention, we had no choice but to be as precise as possible. One or two votes might make the difference.

Even though the negotiations leading toward a possible Humphrey endorsement and withdrawal had vanished somewhere in the wires of NBC's adding machines, hope was held out that Muskie would throw his support to McGovern. On this Thursday McGovern and Muskie met in Washington. Muskie, discussing a possible endorsement, indicated unhappiness with the McGovern welfare proposal. McGovern said he intended to revise it in any case. Regarding Muskie's other area of concern, defense, McGovern assured him their positions were not that adverse.

Late that afternoon, Frank was contacted by Berl Bernhard, formerly the Muskie campaign manager, who said that Muskie had decided to endorse McGovern and would publicly announce his support the following day in a speech scheduled at the National Press Club. Terms were discussed. Muskie had lingering campaign debts; it was agreed that we could help resolve an urgent debt of some $75,000 and then produce a like amount for other debts within a week or two.

Frank relayed to Muskie, through Bernhard, McGovern's invitation to join him on a trip that day from New York to Oklahoma for a campaign stop and a demonstration of unity and party solidarity. Muskie was agreeable and tickets were ordered for Muskie and Bernhard from Washington to join the Senator's traveling party in New York for the trip west. This would be it—the peace agreement which would end the Democratic wars of 1972, the official transition of power in the Democratic Party, the red carpet rolled all the way to a harmonious Miami. We would have to assume approximately $150,000 in Muskie debts, but a contested convention could cost us several times that amount financially and an incalculable amount politically. All that now could be avoided. Frank and I contemplated a bacchanalian revel that night.

But it was not to be. Bernhard was back on the phone late in the evening. Muskie was being strongly urged by "several people" to stay in the race. On what ground? On the ground that he had no right to "hand the nomination over to George McGovern." *Hand it over???* George McGovern has won eleven primaries and over 300 delegates from two dozen non-primary states, had amassed 1,350 firm delegate votes, all against overwhelming odds—and someone was talking about Muskie's endorsement as if it were an unexpected inheritance! In a year of incredible, bizarre, outlandish occurrences, this won the prize! Surely Muskie wasn't considering changing his mind again. McGovern had been told the announcement was on, the press was already calling our headquarters having sniffed the story out, arrangements had been made for Muskie to go to Oklahoma. Well, Senator Muskie would like to meet with his advisors tonight, sleep on it, and make his *final* decision tomorrow morning. *Final decision!* For God's sake, the speech was at *noon!*

By all accounts, Muskie—because of his ingrained tendency to listen to all sides of every argument to the point of exhaustion—once again became the knot in the rope of a vicious tug-of-war that night. Many of his more sensible supporters preferred that he remove himself from the race in a gracious and statesmanlike way. It would permit him to salvage considerable political reputation from the debacle and would free his delegates to cast a meaningful vote at the convention. Most of them would have gone with McGovern by inclination even if uninstructed. (Therefore, from our point of view, he could have withdrawn even without endorsing McGovern and could have thus have resolved his seeming dilemma.) Others—their true motives would not come out for several days—argued that McGovern would wreck the party, that he was the candidate of radical elements and that Muskie must hold firm and carry the fight to the convention.

J U N E 9 , 1 9 7 2 . Muskie awoke and announced to Bernhard, who relayed it to us, that he intended to tell the Press Club audience that he would not support McGovern. It was, like the calamitous Humphrey decision in California, a crucial turning-point in the extended Democratic campaign.

* * *

Starting shortly after the Massachusetts primary, we had begun to plan for the fall campaign. I was giving much of my attention throughout May and June to the July national convention and the fall effort which would begin almost immediately thereafter. In devising a general-election campaign plan we had to lay out an electoral strategy (determining in which states to make the most effort to obtain the most electoral votes) and decide what kind of campaign to conduct (which resources to use and in what measure to obtain the greatest number of votes). For example, should a greater effort be made in Minnesota or Maryland—both have ten electoral votes and Democratic voting traditions—and what kind of campaign would win the most votes—media, many hours of the candidate's time, grassroot canvassing, phoning, mailings? Five general steps were involved.

First, the states were ranked on a scale of one through five, with A, B, C, D, and E designations, using as criteria: (1) the number of electoral votes; (2) the tendency of the state to vote Democratic in the last three elections; (3) the condition of the McGovern campaign and the Democratic Party; (4) the quantity of resources, mostly money, needed to carry the state; (5) the degree to which McGovern/Democratic issues were affecting voters in the state. The groupings of the A through E states were falling together fairly neatly and would carry through the fall with occasional adjustments.

Second, I began making tentative staff assignments of state coordinators using as standards each person's experience, individual strengths, talents, and background in the state. More difficult was the assignment of second-level and third-level staff people, those several hundred experienced organizers who would become the key support staff to the state coordinator. An analysis would be made at the conclusion of the primaries of each person's capabilities before a final judgment could be made.

Third, the difficult task of preparing a campaign budget. I didn't think it especially profitable to work with pie-in-the-sky estimates of funds that might become available, preferring rather to assume that money would be almost as difficult to come by in the fall as it had always been; that we would have to win this general campaign with perhaps half the money the Republicans would have. A major factor was the limitation placed by the new campaign disclosure law on media expenditures, both electronic (television and radio) and print (newspapers, mailings). Accordingly, I estimated that we would spend approximately $7 to $7.5 million on electronic media, and approximately $2.5 to $3 million on print media, that it would take approximately $1 million to operate the national headquarters and staff, that approximately $1 million to $1.5 million would have to be spent on candidate activities (travel, staff, advance, etc.), and that approximately $10 million would be needed to run campaign operations in the 50 states, with the bulk of that amount being spent in the 15 to 20 highest-priority states. This brought the original general-election projected budget to $21.5 million to $23 million (it turned out to be strikingly accurate).

Fourth, considerable thought was given to the media programs. It was almost certain that we would continue to use Charles Guggenheim for almost all our radio and television production and perhaps placement as well, and that Tom Collins' agency in New York would play a major role in our developing print program. These arrangements would change only if a major restructuring of the campaign leadership occurred and new managers wanted to bring in new people. Obviously, in both cases new production would be required because the race would now be against Richard Nixon and not other Democratic opponents, although a substantial amount of the material Charles had produced for the primary races, particularly the 30-minute McGovern biography, would be readily usable.

Finally, the planning included preliminary thinking on the structure of a national campaign organization. Whatever system the McGovern campaign had developed for leadership and chain of command obviously had some merit, as reflected in our successes. However, no one questioned that some changes would have to be made for the fall campaign. Unlike the nomination race where we were running several non-primary states concurrently and a number of primary states serially, the fall campaign would be the equivalent of running 50 primary races simultaneously. In addition, we would not have many months of preparation in which mistakes could be made and recovered—the fall campaign would cover scarcely more than 90 days—we would be running against an incumbent, and there would be little, if any, room for mistakes or fumbling. Everything had to be planned in advance and it had to work. Although I would make recommendations to the Senator concerning the structuring of this campaign, the final decisions would be his. Meanwhile, before, during, and after the California primary, the planning went forward.

Even as the McGovern victory tide rose to inevitability in California, many of the more far-sighted reporters began to home in on the fall campaign. And what made particularly good copy was the nature of Mc-

Govern's general-election effort. Would a new style be introduced? Would the grassroots be abandoned? Who would be in charge? How, in short, will success affect George McGovern? This speculation led to intense concentration on the campaign leadership. Wouldn't the "pros" take over? Wouldn't the younger members of the staff be forced to step down? Wouldn't such changes be taken as symbolic either of McGovern's astuteness as a politician or his fickleness and calculation—depending on the point of view? All of this became, in the closing days of the California campaign, almost an obsession with some "observers."

To further confuse the matter, success brought to the surface previously latent struggles in the areas of finance and issue development. The slapstick handling of the welfare issue brought cries of grief and outrage from advisors and contributors, directed primarily at members of the staff with responsibility for issue development. The Senator was advised that, if he intended to run a serious race in the fall, this entire area of the campaign had to be substantially re-shuffled.

One of the few serious structural mistakes of the nomination campaign was the decision, initially made at Cedar Point in 1970, to separate issue development from the political-organizational backbone of the campaign structure, keeping the substantive research and writing apparatus in the Senate office, out of touch with day-to-day campaign operations and responsible directly to the candidate. This created few serious problems until late 1971, when, aside from his well-established position on Southeast Asia, the candidate was called upon to evolve the fundamental foreign-policy, economic-policy, and domestic programs upon which his candidacy would stand. When Frank Mankiewicz joined the campaign in mid-1971, he assumed responsibility, at the Senator's direction, for exercising critical political review over the position papers, programs, and speeches prepared by the Senate staff members. He was the link, which up to that time had been missing, between the main campaign and this somewhat autonomous issue operation.

And if this system had worked, as it was supposed to, things would have been fine. But three things began to go wrong. First, accustomed to dealing with the Senator, the issues people found it awkward to report first to Frank and let him add political content before proposals went to the Senator. The chain of command was never really established or respected. Second, Frank immediately became embroiled in many other aspects of the campaign—its organization, financing, and staff—and consequently had less time to spend on the issues, or substantive, side of the campaign as initially anticipated. Third, McGovern himself was accustomed, from five statewide races in South Dakota, not only to managing his own campaigns, but also to acting as his own best issues advisor, deciding pretty much on his own what his positions on crucial issues should be. This led him to consult with and listen to the advice of others but, inevitably to make up his own mind, in many cases, without extensive staff backup.

There were at least half a dozen times during the campaign when, sensing all this, I told Frank that we would win or lose not on the organization—it was there and it was superior—but on the issues; that sooner or later, the way the procedures were working, something was going to go out half-baked or wrong and it would do us irretrievable damage. I felt it as strongly as I felt from the beginning that McGovern could win. But I knew he *wouldn't* win unless his ideas for change and innovation were so carefully prepared, thought-out, and delivered as to make them both attractive and non-flammable. Often I pushed back the apprehensions, thinking that I had made the point strongly enough often enough, or that we would luck through (as we had for so long in the past), or that the control would finally be implemented. But it never was with any consistency. Occasionally, new proposals were sent over in time for political review, and they languished in the headquarters offices without comment. Sometimes, events would arise calling for a statement and it would be prepared and released without prior submission to the political side. About some issues, such as amnesty, McGovern himself felt so strongly that he merely announced his position without staff consultation. Sometimes issues would be researched, cleared, and presented to the Senator and he would adapt them, generally on the spur of the moment, to a form with which he felt more comfortable. The welfare proposal, perhaps our most troublesome single position, was really the product of all these processes. Nevertheless, for whatever reason, my worst premonitions proved correct. I believe we lost the election on the issues and not on the politics.

J U N E 1 2 , 1 9 7 2 . I went back to the Miami convention site for one last look before arriving for the convention. I reviewed room assignments with Owen Donley, the logistics majordomo, inspected hotel and trailer communications plans with the phone people once again, decided on trailer equipment and furnishings, and walked over the convention floor. Dick Murphy, the DNC convention manager, provided a helpful tour and lecture on the convention facilities and arrangements. After considering dozens of details and authorizing the efficient Donley to handle most of them, I headed back to Washington, with a brief stopover in Columbia, South Carolina, to meet with our supporters, several uncommitted delegates, and Governor West. Although West was remaining neutral toward Humphrey, I assured him the McGovern campaign was a responsible operation and we would look forward to his ultimate support.

JUNE 17, 1972. Well after midnight, five men were arrested in the Democratic National Committee's offices in the Watergate building. They were replacing previously installed electronic listening devices and photographing files. They were stealing. They were bugging. They were wire-tapping. They were spying. They had been hired by the Republicans. It was a conspicuous reminder that Richard Nixon had not lost his touch.

JUNE 20, 1972. New York politics is best represented in an observation Voltaire once made about England—that it is thought well there occasionally to kill an admiral to encourage the others. Political murder (not to say suicide) is carried out there every day in the interest of ideology or power. The power boys, it must be said on their behalf, are at least straightforward in their desires. You know what they want. The same cannot be said for the ideology people who often lie in wait in dark alleyways with a dagger here, a rapier there, usually out of some petty grievance, some ancient tribal wound, some slight, some trifling theoretical deviation, some blood feud.

Many months before, threading his way with a combination of political dexterity and professional obscurity, Professor Richard Wade had gone about the business of methodically organizing committees, holding delegate slating caucuses, rounding up support here and there, circulating delegate petitions, filing delegate slates—all according to the published rules. Like our other state chairmen, he had throughout 1971 and early 1972 the support of a hardy, seasoned band of 20- and 21-year-old veterans. Wade had also raised money, given speeches, held hands with contributors, and generally tip-toed through the thickets and minefields, managing to make only a reasonable number of enemies in the process.

Early in 1972, seeking to head off the Muskie juggernaut, he had made common cause with the Humphrey supporters in New York, educating them on the new procedures, encouraging them to file delegate slates, running a little double-agent operation, all on the theory that Humphrey would take support only from Muskie. With the Muskie collapse and resurrection of Humphrey, Wade had faced the possibility of his having played Frankenstein. But he proved not to have been a motivating teacher in this instance, for the Humphreyites dawdled and delayed until the deadline for filing slates had passed and McGovern sat, on the eve of the New York primary, with full delegate slates in 37 of the state's 39 Congressional Districts (slates in the two other districts were not filed for political purposes) and no serious political opposition. Thanks to Wade, the early McGovern committee members, and the accomplished young staff, McGovern could have been arrested for stealing. It was a piece of cake.

The results of the nation's last primary: of the 248 delegates selected

The Empire State was a piece of cake: 230 more delegates.

at the district level, McGovern won 231. Of the remaining 28 to be chosen at large by the elected delegates, we would get enough to bring our total to a minimum of 252 out of the total of 276. It was a nice way to wrap up the delegate selection process.

JUNE 26, 1972. Intensive negotiations over the weekend produced a Monday morning press conference announcement in Washington from a number of black leaders, headed by District of Columbia Congressman Walter Fauntroy, that they were lifting their previous neutrality and delivering their support to McGovern. Additionally, they stated that they had conducted extensive negotiations with blocs of black delegates and individual black delegates in a number of states and were prepared to commit over 160 delegate votes to the McGovern column. The Senator announced that these votes would give him a total of 1,510 delegates at the convention, one more than enough to nominate. Later that day, after our own desks had checked the commitments out, it was learned that some of them were less than firm, and a delegate chart was issued putting the McGovern total at 1,492¾.

JUNE 26–30, 1972. The rules, platform, and credentials committees convened in Washington to complete the preliminary work of the convention. McGovern supporters constituted a majority of each committee. The deliberations of rules and platform went smoothly. The platform evolved essentially as we had hoped, angering only the Wallace supporters by the pro-busing plank, militant women's rights advocates with a moderate abortion plank, and some welfare leaders with a moderate welfare plank.

Then, after a day of deliberations, all hell broke loose in the credentials committee. A motion was raised opposing California's winner-take-all primary and proposing that the 271-member delegation be divided according to the percentage of the vote each candidate had received in the primary. A quick headcount revealed that the vote would be close but that we could defeat the motion. But then the Chair ruled that none of the California members could vote on the question of the apportionment of their own delegation. Delegates on the credentials committee were apportioned according to the size of the state delgation. With California's ten committee members out, the picture changed. Instead of having a clear majority of five or six votes, we now were in the minority by four or five votes and faced with the prospect of losing 151 delegates.

We began to put the pieces together, and what emerged was a plan conceived sometime during the California primary by anti-McGovern forces to use the California challenge as a last-ditch stop-McGovern device. The theory was that the loss of more than half the California delegation would not only leave McGovern with just over 1,300 delegates, almost 200 short of a majority, but, more important, would halt his momentum. It would raise the possibility of a compromise candidate, perhaps one not even in the race at the time. Most significantly, it would prevent McGovern from taking control of the Democratic Party.

That was what the California challenge was all about. *Power.* It had nothing whatever to do with the merits or demerits of winner-take-all primaries. It was conceived and executed by a handful of men unwilling to share authority with new elements in the party, who resisted reform and despised its results, who couldn't conceive of a political process they couldn't control in a private suite, who—most of all—wanted to maintain political power unto themselves. Frank Mankiewicz used to quote an old movie line in connection with almost anyone who opposed us, but it fit with a vengeance here: "These are desperate men and they will stop at nothing." We had slain the dragon of old politics in California, but his tail continued to lash even in death.

We tried everything we could think of. Delegates undecided on the question were pleaded with. McGovern votes not present were rushed in. Those who couldn't come were replaced by those who could. Every last vote was wrung. But it was not enough. The motion carried by five votes and the majority report of the credentials committee would seat 120 California delegates for McGovern and 151 delegates for other candidates.

In postmortems both inside and outside the campaign it was suggested that this result could have been prevented by more careful attention to credentials committee appointees. I disagree. We permitted only one or two delegates onto the committee in states where we had the authority to decide and those were allowed on as a gesture of party unity and good will. My initial evaluation was that we had been stabbed in the back, that those most demanding conciliation by the McGovern campaign had taken advantage of our gestures toward party harmony and used those votes in an attempt to deny us the nomination. Later analysis showed that those one or two votes would not have made the difference, even though some duplicity and treachery might have been involved. What these forces—now clearly labeled the "stop-McGovern movement"— did was to form a solid coalition of Humphrey-Muskie-Jackson-Wallace-undecideds to come close to success. In addition, in large states where our delegates were in the minority—Pennsylvania, Ohio, and Illinois—the stop-McGovern operation shut us out of representation or reduced our proportionate representation on the credentials committee. Even they would have failed had the Chair allowed the California credentials committee members to vote. That was their gamble, which cost them nothing, and they won.

McGovern was furious. He immediately issued a statement describing the California challenge as a theft. In a *Life* interview given shortly thereafter, the Senator termed the California challenge a "negative, spiteful movement that subverts the democratic process" carried out by "a bunch of old established politicians" involved in "an illegitimate power play."

Following the California vote, McGovern representatives on the credentials committee could not be restrained. The challenge to Mayor Daley's 59 delegates came up the next day. That morning, the 28th, a key Humphrey aide called me to try to salvage the Daley delegates. I demanded our California delegates back and told him the stop-McGovern operation was responsible for whatever happened to Daley. Frank had made a courageous effort in the McGovern credentials caucus to promote compromise on Illinois, but almost lost his scalp for his efforts. The Illinois credentials committee representatives voted against us on California. With our California delegates voting and Illinois not voting on its own credentials, the reform (anti-Daley) delegates from Chicago were seated.

Thus the stage was set for the 1972 Democratic National Convention. We had less than two weeks to figure out how to get the California delegates back. If we failed, in all likelihood McGovern would not get the nomination. Over two years of bone-crushing work would be down the drain. And what could the so-called stop-McGovern movement do with the nomination anyway? Comparison might have been made to Oscar Wilde's description of an English gentleman chasing a fox: "the unspeakable in full pursuit of the uneatable."

THE CONVENTION

JULY 6, 1972. Like a smoothly functioning command post established on some foreign beach-head after the assault troops had moved inland, the mezzanine floor of our headquarters at the Doral Hotel was well dug-in by the first week in July. This task, carried out superbly by George Cunningham and Owen Donley, involved nothing less than moving our entire national headquarters from Washington to Miami. Switchboards were set up and operating, a well-stocked supply room was established, the car pool was organized and functioning, our research and writing unit was operating under John Holum's direction, Dick Dougherty, Pierre Salinger, and Gail Tirana were running a thorough and professional press room, with branches in every major hotel and a separate service for foreign press, volunteer and support staff offices

were established, Donley was busily juggling last-minute room assignments, and Larry Windsor was beamingly greeting each new dignitary
in the lobby. An ocean-view reception area had been set aside for enter-
taining individual delegates and delegations, the lobby was decorated
and, on the Doral facade, was a professionally lettered sign identifying
this as the McGovern for President headquarters.

Throughout the ornate-Baroque lobby and mezzanine floors there was
constant movement, endless motion, but it all seemed very efficient. There
was a distinct sense of order in the continuing flux. Nevertheless, in those
few days before the convention opened, there was a recurring feeling of
actors performing, of amateurs playing professional games, creating the
rules and procedures as they went along. How many subconscious re-
ferrals were there to Theodore White '60, '64, '68? "Let's see. How do
you suppose the Kennedy people did this in L.A.?"

McGovern delegates and general supporters were scattered throughout
floors 2 through 12. Above them were housed the key staff and financial
supporters. At the Senator's request, the South Dakota delegation was
housed on the 14th floor. The staff and financial and political supporters
were on the 15th and 16th floors. The Senator, his family, and the campaign management occupied the 17th, or penthouse, floor. Above us was
the Starlight Roof.

If the mind of the campaign was on the 17th floor, its nerve center
was in the 16th-floor "boiler-room." There, in the largest room on the
floor, desks were placed around the walls. At these desks sat ten people—
the six original regional desk officers plus four carefully selected, experienced campaign organizers—with one telephone each. Each of these ten
people had on his or her desk a card file containing data on each delegate
from approximately five delegations; each was responsible for an average
of 300 delegates, or about one-tenth of the 3,016 official convention delegates. Most of the desk officers had worked with members of their delegations over the previous months or had educated themselves in intimate
detail with the background of most of their 300 delegates.

The 55 delegations were housed in several dozen hotels in the greater
Miami area. At least one experienced McGovern staff organizer having,
in almost every case, some previous background with the state or delegation, was assigned to live with that delegation 24 hours a day. He or she
was to work on delegates not committed to McGovern, to monitor delegation caucuses where possible, to arrange for McGovern speakers at
those caucuses, to report on any shifts of sentiment within the delegation,
to provide to McGovern delegates information on anything relating to
the Senator's positions or the campaign, or to solve any problems which
might arise. Additionally, there were some McGovern supporters in all
but a few delegations. In the twenty delegations which we clearly con-

trolled, the delegation chairman was almost always the key McGovern contact inside the delegation as well as its leader. In the remaining delegations, a McGovern leader or caucus chairman was selected to speak for our delegates and to work with the staff member assigned to the delegation in converting new delegates and reporting on their attitudes. In delegations of a dozen or more, and this included over 40 delegations, whips were appointed on a ratio roughly of one for every eight delegates. The whips were the toughest, most committed McGovern delegates. They were responsible to their delegation or caucus chairman, the key McGovern contact in the delegation. The purpose of the whips was to communicate voting instructions to McGovern delegates on the floor of the convention. By the opening of the convention, some 250 floor whips would be selected.

The communication and intelligence system at the convention functioned as follows: the ten desk officers in the 16th-floor Doral boiler-room were in constant contact with a staff member and a delegation or caucus leader in each delegation. Each delegation or caucus leader had a system of whips, each of whom was responsible for approximately eight other delegates on the floor. The staff members, senior, experienced organizers, controlled the flow of information from campaign to delegation and from delegation to campaign. They particularly reported on the movement of uncommitted or wavering delegates.

As the delegates began to arrive in Miami on the 7th, 8th, and 9th, a constant conversion process was going on all over town, up and down Miami Beach, hotel rooms, lobbies, and bars. All information gathered was being constantly relayed by phone to the appropriate desk officer at the Doral boiler-room. The information was duly noted on the delegate card file and then relayed to Rick Stearns, who was supervising the process. Periodically, Rick met with the desk officers individually or collectively to make relevant adjustments in our delegate count. By now we were keeping two separate counts, one for votes on the nomination and the other for votes on the California challenge. The almost hourly adjustments, reflecting the movement of one or two delegates here or there, were relayed to me for purposes of calculating floor strength and strategy.

The McGovern convention operations were run out of a double room suite (Penthouse 17-19). This situation room or command post was divided between an office-like arrangement of desks on one side and a sitting room area on the other. Three color television sets, tuned in almost around the clock to the major networks, were in the sitting room area, as was the long bare table I used for a desk. There were ten white phones connected with our own switchboard, two black phones which were direct dial lines to the outside, and an automatic-ringing red hot-line

The Doral Hotel command post: Marcia Johnston fielding yet another frantic call.

phone connecting the Doral situation room with the command post trailer outside the convention hall.

This Doral situation room twenty yards down the hall from the Senator's suite was designed to be a sealed-off, secured area for Frank and me, our assistants, Marcia Johnston and Pat Broun, and few other people. Early in the convention week, that plan crumbled under the combined assault of family, friends, supporters, meetings, egos, confusion, and crisis. Several times throughout the week, this room designed for quiet, thoughtful but quick, deliberation and judgment, became an absolute zoo.

Roughly a mile and a half down the beach squatted the massive dun and pink convention hall heavily embroidered in chain-link fencing. In a drawing conducted by DNC officials months earlier, the McGovern campaign had won the top-priority trailer location. This placed our three trailers at the northwest corner of the vast hall, within yards of the only doorway on that side of the building, and protected by high, heavy-gauge fences. There was the command-post trailer for use by Frank, myself, Rick, and a team of floor communicators during convention sessions, a trailer for meetings and relaxation for the floor leaders, and a trailer for convention press. At one end of the command trailer was a small office which Frank, Marcia Johnston, and I used. Besides phones linked to our switchboard at the Doral (which in turn could be connected directly to our 15 phones strategically located on the convention floor or any of the dozens of DNC phones on the floor), there were two automatically ringing direct lines to the Doral situation room and the Senator's suite. When the convention was in session, direction of our floor operation moved to the command trailer.

On Wednesday, July 5th, 1972, we issued the last delegate count from our Washington headquarters. It showed McGovern with 1,154½ votes for the nomination. That included the full 271-member California delegation. If the "stop-McGovern movement" was successful in seating its 151 disputed delegates, we would have only 1,390½ votes, 119½ fewer than needed. So the struggle settled down to the question of the California challenge—the 151 disputed delegates. If we could win them back, we had the nomination. If we lost them, we would probably lose the nomination.

The United States Supreme Court eliminated any opportunity we had to recover our California delegates through the judicial process. On Monday, July 5th, Washington attorney Joe Rauh, assisted by California National Committeeman Stephen Reinhardt, sought an order in the Federal District Court in Washington enjoining the Democratic Party from

unseating our California delegates. The District Court judge dismissed
the action on the ground that it was a political matter over which the
courts had no jurisdiction. Hours later the decision was appealed to the
Washington Circuit Court of Appeals. Shortly after hearing the arguments and reviewing the pleadings, the Appellate Court, by a vote of
2 to 1, reversed the District Court and overturned the credentials committees action. The Court re-instated our full California delegation and
"set aside the arbitrary and unconstitutional action of the Democratic
Party." There was great rejoicing in the McGovern campaign; we had
been vindicated.

The case was immediately taken to the Supreme Court by the party's
attorneys. Although the high court was not in session, because of the
importance of the issue and the impending convention, Chief Justice
Berger polled the justices by telephone, scattered as they were around
the country. Two days after the Court of Appeals decision, the Supreme
Court summarily overturned that decision, characterizing the dispute as
"political" and one in which the courts should not involve themselves.
Frank compared the Supreme Court opinion to a Nixon speech, "full of
self congratulation."

J U L Y 8 , 1 9 7 2 . At 9 A.M. in the Executive Conference room at
the Doral, we had our first full-scale meeting of staff and advisors. I
announced the convention floor leaders. Most had personally been selected by the Senator during a lengthy meeting I had with him at his
home in Washington on July 1st. They were: Walter Fauntroy, Matty
Troy, Stewart Udall, Mayor Ken Gibson, Representatives Jim Abourezk
and Herman Badillo, Jean Westwood, Gov. Pat Lucey, John Burton,
Willie Brown, Pierre Salinger, Bill Dougherty, Senators Gaylord Nelson,
Abraham Ribicoff, and Frank Church, Don O'Brien, Doug Fraser, Delores
Huerta, Shirley MacLaine, and Anne Wexler.

After a brief review of our current delegate strength, the discussion
centered on the procedural and parliamentary questions surrounding
the California challenge. An informal subcommittee composed of Anne
Wexler and parliamentary experts Charles Ferris, director of the Senate
Democratic Policy Committee, and Bill Welch, key staff member of the
American Federation of State, County, and Municipal Employees, had
analyzed and researched the questions and conducted preliminary discussions with the DNC parliamentarian, Representative James O'Hara.
There were four principal parliamentary issues: first, can the unchallenged portion of a delegation (the 120 McGovern delegates from California) vote on the question of seating the challenged portion of the
delegation (the 151 challenged California delegates); second, what would
constitute a majority on the credentials challenge votes—an absolute ma-

jority, a constitutional majority (one more than half of those permitted to vote), or a majority of those present and voting; third, presuming the Chair would rule adversely on the question of what constituted a majority, at what point could that ruling be challenged and brought to a floor vote; fourth, what portions of the challenged delegations would be permitted to vote on the challenge to the ruling of the chair?

As we sorted our way through the pros and cons of these questions, discussing all the possible sets of circumstances that might arise, one thought stuck in my mind: Monday night was going to be a procedural nightmare which we could survive only with iron discipline and loyal, committed delegates willing to trust the campaign leaders. Clearly our floor strategy, the motions we intended to raise and the instructions to be given our delegates, could not be laid out until these questions were ruled upon. We had delayed a meeting with our floor leaders and delegation leaders and whips until most of the delegations arrived on Sunday. But now, two days before the convention opened, we had to press for rulings on these procedural questions so we would know where we stood, could plan our strategy and instruct our floor workers. Frank and I had been seeking a meeting for this purpose with Party Chairman Larry O'Brien and it had finally been arranged for later that Saturday morning.

The Californians, Brown, Huerta, and Burton, were adamant on the question of getting the California delegates back. They rejected any thought of deals or trades (such thoughts, involving Mayor Daley's Chicago delegates, had been floating up and down the Beach). Brown stated with great fervor: "People are either for us or against us. There can be no compromise. No trade-offs. The lines are drawn very hard." It was made clear to the Californians that the California challenge was absolutely equated in the minds of the campaign leaders with the nomination itself, that we considered this a fight to the death for control of the party, and the other side had left us no room to maneuver even if we wanted to. The meeting was adjourned, to reconvene that afternoon to hear a report on our visit with O'Brien.

A press release went out announcing our floor leaders. This was met by some press speculation that McGovern had abandoned the younger state coordinator types in favor of the older politicians. When I had met with the Senator a few days earlier to discuss our convention operations, he had specifically requested a number of his colleagues from the Senate and House to help in the floor operations. Normally calm and relaxed under the most adverse conditions, he was as agitated and upset over the California challenge as I was ever to see him. That fight troubled him immensely, and he told me: "I will feel a lot more comfortable having some experienced hands, some people with parliamentary skills, out on the floor on Monday night." Then he said: "Who will have overall responsibility for floor management?" I told him I was planning to take that responsibility. He didn't say anything. I had never been to a national convention in my life.

At 11 A.M. Frank and I showed up at the DNC headquarters at the Fontainebleau Hotel. We passed several checkpoints. O'Brien's office was heavily guarded. O'Brien seemed to be under heavy siege. Meeting with us were O'Brien, Congressman O'Hara, and Joe Napolitan, an advisor to O'Brien. From notes, I outlined the questions as we saw them and our recommended solutions. Unquestionably, the 120 McGovern delegates had to be able to vote. The entire delegation wasn't under challenge, just the 151 delegates. It further seemed to us that a constitutional, rather than an absolute, majority should decide each challenge, otherwise we would be there all night. (As it turned out, we were anyway.) O'Hara raised the question of the challenge to the ruling of the Chair. That was clearly troubling him. Our position on that question was murky, primarily because it would depend upon which way the Chair ruled. If the Chair didn't permit our 120 to vote, or required an absolute majority on the adoption of the minority report (seating the 151 McGovern Californians), then we intended to challenge the hell out of the Chair's rulings. Otherwise, we wanted to protect the Chair. I cited the precedents our experts had found in the interpretations of the rules of the House of Representatives—one of which went back to 1832. O'Hara seemed interested in whatever support we could offer for our arguments and we promised to submit a legal memorandum. The Congressman then dismissed himself. As we prepared to go, Frank said: "Larry, we'll do our best to keep our delegates on the track, but they're pretty upset about these people stealing our delegates. If we lose those 151 delegates, it's going to be awful tough to keep the lid on that convention." O'Brien nodding: "Well, I understand what you mean. It's pretty tough: we've been getting it from all sides here. Now I intend to follow the rules and I've told Jim [O'Hara] to give me his best judgment regardless of the politics. But I don't intend to have a donnybrook out there. I have to try to keep this party together."

That afternoon we reconvened with the key staff and floor leaders, reporting what we had said and what they had said. The California leaders, militant as always, wanted us to threaten publicly to burn the barn down unless we got our way. With the decisive issues still in the balance, I thought outright intimidation would drive public sentiment and Chairman O'Brien exactly in the opposite direction.

We, of course, could have no idea whether our arguments to the DNC officials had any effect. Later, Napolitan was to tell a reporter: "They were very impressive. It was almost like those police teams where Mankiewicz is the soft guy and Hart is the tough guy. I never met Hart before but in a very nice way he raised the theoretical questions and let us know the possibilities of what they could do on the floor. When O'Hara was there, Hart would talk law. When O'Hara left the room, Larry and Frank would talk politics. It was a very constructive meeting."

During the period between the credentials committee meeting and Monday night at the convention, we were in contact with both sides in the Chicago credentials dispute. Frank carried the brunt of the negotiations, but occasionally I got in. Our interests were very practical and very simple. We wanted to keep Mayor Daley *and* the reformers in the Convention, in the fall campaign and in the party. We worked very hard at compromise. Proposals were submitted and rejected, first by one side, then by the other. On Saturday night, in pursuit of this armistice, I called one of the Mayor's friends who was also a supporter of the Senator's, telling him: "I think we can sell a plan which would seat the Mayor's delegation and the full reform delegation with a half vote for each delegate—straight 50-50." Mystery man (he preferred to remain anonymous throughout): "I'll tell the Mayor, but I know he won't take it. He doesn't want to sit in the Illinois delegation with anyone who refused to support Democrats." (The reform leadership, Singer and Jackson, had endorsed local candidates running against Democrats.) "Try," I said. "Otherwise, the way things are going, the Mayor and the Democratic establishment of Chicago will not see Miami this year."

JULY 9, 1972. The convention would open the following day. Staff meeting at 9 A.M. The memorandum for O'Hara was nearly completed and would be submitted. Ted Van Dyk, who had immediate responsibility for selling the platform, reported, as expected, opposition on various planks—from women on abortion, from welfare rights people on the welfare plank, from tax reformers on the tax plank. Our positions, previously described as radical, were being challenged on every side as weak and compromising. There was further discussion of refinements on the procedural arguments people had come up with in their sleep or over strong drink.

Later that morning, McGovern, accompanied by Senator Ribicoff, visited Chairman O'Brien. The response seemed to be almost the same as that which Frank and I received. We had been trying to get a second audience with O'Brien ourselves, but the response came back—no dice.

At noon I responded to an invitation to meet with a group of Democratic governors to discuss possible pre-convention resolution of the numerous credentials challenges. I drove up the beach to the Kenilworth Hotel where the Maryland delegation was headquartered. We met in Gov. Marvin Mandel's heavily guarded suite. Present, besides Governor Mandel, were Gov. Frank Licht (Rhode Island), Governor Lucey, and Gov. John Gilligan (Ohio). Governor Mandel stated the governors' case. They wanted to mediate between both sides, McGovern and anti-McGovern, to compromise as many credentials challenges as possible and prevent bloodshed on the floor the following night and possibly a divided party in the fall. He singled out Mayor Daley, saying, in effect, that it was inconceivable that Daley might not be seated at a national Democratic convention, that Daley was a symbol to party regulars all around the country and that we were courting disaster in the fall if he were not let in.

I said: "I think it is unfortunate that attention is now being paid to these problems only twenty-four hours before the convention opens. This problem is not our fault. We have worked for two years, according to the rules, to win delegates in every state in the union. Over half our California delegates have been stolen and we want them back. There is not room to negotiate anything, including the Chicago delegation, until California is resolved, and resolved in our favor. The McGovern campaign and the candidate himself are outraged at this maneuver and will absolutely not listen to any talk of compromise until the full California delegation is restored. In addition, there are almost two dozen challenges, of which perhaps a dozen and a half could reach the floor. It is wrong to assume that the McGovern campaign brought each of those challenges or that we can resolve them. Many are brought by the women's caucus, minority groups, or young people. The McGovern campaign has officially endorsed only four challenges. Finally, once again, if you want Daley on the floor, if you want to prevent bloodshed, tell the other side to give us back our delegates."

Long silence. There was considerable amazement at my adamance on California. Governor Licht voiced the surprise of the others: "Are you sure you're not behind more of those challenges?" I assured him we were not and had no authority to compromise them. Governor Gilligan: "Well, it's clear California is the hinge, according to what Mr. Hart has said. What can be done to settle that?" "Tell the stop-McGovern people to give us back our delegates and then we'll talk about any other dispute, including Mayor Daley, that you want," I said. Governor Mandel: "Could we discuss giving you half the 151 California delegates and giving Mayor Daley half the disputed 59 Chicago seats?" "No," I said. "Presuming we helped get your California delegates back," asked Governor Gilligan, "what challenges are negotiable?" I opened the credentials committee report and went down the list of minority reports or challenges one by one. I pointed out seven or eight specific cases I thought we could resolve in return for four or five concessions on the other side and concluded that the entire list could be reduced to no more than half a dozen, and probably fewer.

"This morass of challenges can be reduced to a few symbolic cases," I said. "We will help work for a compromise on Chicago, but the roadblock is California. Nothing happens until we get our delegates back," Governor Mandel said he would call me after meeting with the stop-McGovern representatives. I thanked them and left.

About the time I left to meet with the governors, we received a call that O'Brien had reached a decision on the parliamentary rulings and that an announcement would be made at a 1:30 P.M. session at the Fontainebleau. Frank attended, returning, somewhat breathless, shortly after I did. The sacrosanct command center suite had by now succumbed to an onslaught of secondary activities. We met two doors down the hall in someone's unoccupied bedroom—Frank, Rick, Anne Wexler, Bill Welch, and myself. Frank laid out the rulings: First, the 120 McGovern California delegates would be permitted to vote on the seating of the remainder of the delegation. Good for us. Second, a majority would be defined as a constitutional majority, one more than half of those permitted to vote on each challenge. We would need 1,433 to carry California. Third, and most significant, O'Hara had stated that the ruling of the Chair on the nature of a majority could be raised, i.e., would be in order and recognized, only if there were an actual controversy. This meant the vote had to fall within a "window" between a constitutional majority with the unchallenged portion of a delegation voting (the 120 McGovern Californians) and an absolute majority. In the case of the California challenge, that "window" was a vote between 1,433 and 1,509. Thus, the stop-McGovern forces could seek to challenge the Chair's ruling permitting the 120 McGovernites to vote only if the vote on seating our total delegation fell into the zone where those votes made a difference. For us to win, we had to get more than 1,433 votes to re-seat our 151 delegates. Since we already had a firm 1,485 votes on California, that meant we would win our delegates back; then we would need to get fewer than 25 additional votes to defeat a procedural challenge.

But O'Hara had also ruled, over our protest, that the challenges would be taken in the order presented in the credentials committee report. California came after the South Carolina challenge. Trouble. The stop-McGoverns would try to throw that South Carolina vote in the "window," challenge the Chair's definition of a majority, carry that vote—since their 151 Californians could vote on that question—and replace it with a ruling that our 120 couldn't vote on the challenge. We would lose the California vote and lose the nomination.

Now all attention turned to South Carolina. That was a challenge brought by the women's caucus to the sexual imbalance of the delegation, only nine of the 32 being women. The entire male portion of the delegation was being challenged by the women in an effort to seat seven more women to make the delegation equally divided. The mathematics on South Carolina was as follows: Since all 23 male delegates were under challenge, none could vote. If 23 South Carolina delegates were prohibited from voting on the South Carolina challenge, a constitutional majority would be 1,497. Thus the "window" on South Carolina was between 1,497 and 1,509. If the vote on the first challenge fell in that range, the stop-McGovern movement went into action and we were in trouble. If we could keep the vote out of that "window," the Chair's ruling could not be challenged, we could raise the 1,433 votes necessary to win California, we would get our 151 delegates back, and we would win the nomination. It was a row of dominos. It just depended on which end was tapped first to determine which way they fell.

Late that afternoon we had another staff meeting. Frank outlined the rulings, their implications, and our analysis of them. The mathematics had to be repeated several times. I asked Rick if we had the votes to carry the South Carolina challenge. Our official policy, in support of the women's caucus, was to try to do so. As the delegates arrived in Miami, the desk and liaison staff had been doing a firm head-count and Rick had calculated their findings. He reported that we had 1,451 'til-hell-freezes-over votes on the California challenge. Additionally, through the intensive conversion process that had been going on around the country, we had picked up as many as 95 more votes, bringing the total to 1,546. But a quick round of calls that afternoon on the South Carolina challenge showed that we would have an extremely difficult time keeping enough of those 95 "soft" votes to win the South Carolina challenge. Nevertheless, our intentions at that time and up until the actual balloting took place were to win the South Carolina challenge, not only because it was a legitimate complaint based on the reform guidelines adopted by the party, but also because adopting a policy of purposely losing the vote would have alienated a considerable number of the 200 to 300 delegate members of the women's caucus.

There were several outcroppings of discontent over the weekend among the groups that had formed part of the campaign. Late Saturday night, first Frank, and then I, had been summoned to meet with black leaders who had become uneasy that they were not involved in something that even they could not define. Black leaders, Walter Fauntroy, Willie Brown, Ken Gibson, Jesse Jackson, and others, had consistently participated in campaign consultation and decision-making. But there still seemed to be growing restlessness and uneasiness throughout the campaign. It baffled me. Each special-interest group or caucus seemed to want to possess the campaign. There seemed to be an unwillingness to accept the fact that the McGovern campaign was an entity unto itself, that we solicited support (which was long withheld in crucial periods) from many quarters—blacks, Chicanos, women, youth—and made a supreme effort to seek involvement and participation in decision-making, but that we were not the creation or creature of any group. The single most important purpose of the campaign was to elect one specific Democrat, Senator George McGovern, to the Presidency, and to carry out the agenda of other, supporting groups only as they implemented that goal.

Frank and Eli Segal, our expert on the challenges, had attended a meeting with Congressman O'Hara and representatives of the other candidates late that evening. The conversation was brutal. The other side, having had most of the day to contemplate the implications of O'Brien's rulings, was seething like a boiling cauldron. Max Kampelman, for Humphrey, called the rulings "hostile," the result of "blackmail and intimidation" and O'Brien's playing politics. The Humphrey people threatened to blow the convention right out of the water: "We'll destroy the Democratic Party before we'll let McGovern have the nomination." "Scoop Jackson," said the Jackson man, "is triple-pissed!" The Wallace men, their candidate the recent victim of violence, seemed on the whole much less violence-prone. O'Hara listened quietly to the screams of outrage. As they failed to abate, Eli said, "You could see the blood rising up the back of Jimmie's neck." O'Hara, not accustomed to threats, dismissed himself with: "Gentlemen, you may do as you wish. The rulings stand. I don't have to listen to this further."

As Frank and Eli related the story, first to me, then to the Senator, I couldn't help but consider the ironic reversal of 1968. Then, those on the inside, looking out, deplored violence, even though many of them

were there through unfair, undemocratic procedures. Now, outside looking in, as the result of fair and open procedures, they were most willing
to rant and rave, threatening violence of their own.

Through the boiler-room communications system, I called a pre-
convention strategy meeting of all floor leaders, delegation or caucus
leaders, and delegation whips, for 10 P.M. in the Starlight East room at
the Doral. This meeting was crucial. If the information distributed there
wasn't clear or wasn't subsequently followed, we could very well blow
the entire nomination effort. After we had seated the 250 or 300 leaders
with their respective floor leaders as they would be arranged on the convention floor, I described for them the structure of our floor operation.
Our communications system, including the 15 floor phones, the trailers,
and the Doral switchboard, were outlined. (During the meeting the air
conditioning malfunctioned and the heat became intense. Through the
thin, temporary partition the dance band could be heard hammering
implacably away at the other end of the Starlight Roof)
I explained the three systems which would be used for voting instructions. One would be from the trailer to the floor leaders directly,
by phone, or from the trailer to the Doral boiler-room desks to the floor
whips by phone. One would be word-of-mouth communication from the
floor manager to the floor leaders to the delegation leaders to the whips
to the delegates. The third would be coded cards—one color held up
meant a yes vote, another color held up meant a no vote. The cards
were to be used only under emergency conditions where instantaneous
instructions were necessary or where the phone system failed or was
sabotaged. I said: "Unswerving, unquestioning discipline must be maintained. You must follow your floor leader's instructions. You must not
leave the floor under any circumstances unless a McGovern alternate is
in your place. The procedures tomorrow night will be extremely complicated. We will explain them tonight, but there will not be another
chance to explain them tomorrow night. You must explain them to each
of your delegates. When the signal is given, do not hesitate to vote as
you are told. Tomorrow night will determine the nomination of the next
President of the United States. It will be *very* close. The other side has
vowed to defeat us. Your votes tomorrow night will be one of the most
important actions of your life."
The previously restless crowd was now paying attention. Jean Westwood, who was coordinating the California challenge vote, then spoke
on procedures. She was followed by Frank, who laid out the intricate
details of the parliamentary questions, O'Brien's rulings, and the motions
likely to be presented Monday night. It was by now almost midnight and

hours of work lay ahead. The meeting was adjourned until 11 A.M., Monday.

Hopes for reconciliation, for compromise, faded in the evening hours with the chaotic meeting of campaign representatives with O'Hara and with the collapse of the governors' efforts. Governor Mandel had called me back with no particular offer, except the half-hearted suggestion to split the disputed California and Chicago delegates. I countered: "Governor, there are six or eight governors, including yourself, who control uncommitted delegates. You give us enough votes to win the California challenge and we'll do everything we can to resolve the other challenges, including a compromise to seat Mayor Daley." I listed the governors and the specific number of votes we would need from each. "Now if the governors are serious about avoiding bloodshed, this is the way they can do it. Just help us get our California delegates back."

Governor Mandel said he would give it a try, but he didn't sound too enthusiastic. We didn't hear from the governors again.

It was, in a way, like the frantic hours before Pearl Harbor: all efforts to prop up relations, to seek resolution, had failed. War was now unofficially declared.

J U L Y 10, 1972. Monday. 9 A.M. Regular morning staff meeting, primarily reconstructing the events of the past 18 hours, reviewing the procedures, and vote tabulations. Final plans were laid for the evening. Discussion of the speakers on the various challenges. Brown will speak for California.

11 A.M. Second meeting of the floor leaders, delegation leaders and whips. More exhortations about discipline. The order of the evening's events was reviewed. Overnight, many of the leaders had thought of questions, or introduced questions raised by their delegates. We did our best to answer.

1 P.M. The situation room had become a mad-house. The Senator and various speakers were being scheduled into key afternoon delegations in a last-minute attempt to convert undecided delegates. A great hassle developed over floor passes. The limited number available to our campaign had been quickly exhausted by the demands of supporters and contributors. There were not enough passes for our floor leaders. Throughout the afternoon hectic attempts were made to get extra alternate passes from various delegations. Phones rang incessantly. The television sets blared forth speculation about the evening events: "Will McGovern recover his California delegates?" Mid-afternoon canvassing of each dele-

gation. Who's moving? Which way? How many could we count on in Maryland, in Indiana, in Connecticut? The numbers came up from the boiler-room, a delegate at a time now.

5 P.M. Together with eight of our floor leaders, I went to the convention hall. To save time, we went on two fast outboard motor boats along the canal paralleling Collins Avenue. After passing through elaborate security check points, we went on the floor. Each floor leader familiarized himself or herself with the aisle area he would occupy and the seating arrangements of the delegations for which he would be responsible. McGovern floor phones were located. I walked over the floor area where, in three short hours, the final battle would take place. Two years of work would come down to one vote. All of the chips would be riding on that one dice-roll. The excitement and responsibility were intense. After going through the trailers, we returned to the Doral.

7 P.M. Larry O'Brien pounded the great gavel, and, with the Star-Spangled Banner, the convention got underway. Senator Lawton Chiles of Florida welcomed the delegates and O'Brien delivered the opening address. On the floor it was the opening minutes of a championship football game. Everyone seemed slightly startled that it had actually begun, that it was finally really happening, and that they were there. Delegates squirmed in their seats as if they were considering buying them. Then, tentatively, they looked around as though trying to decide if they might be arrested for walking in the aisle. Network floor reporters nervously adjusted their awkward, unaccustomed earmuff headsets, deciding whether to start their interviews. The ice still hadn't been broken.

More preliminaries. I walked the aisles, checking to see that the leaders were in the right aisle positions, trying to accustom myself to the look and feel of each delegation, real people, human faces now, not just paper plans. The football game again. Trying to develop the instinctive sense whether the players on your left are your blockers. Peripheral vision. Feeling the paths and the currents. The quickest way across the hall in an emergency. The nearest friendly phone for an urgent call to the trailer.

The time approached for the credentials report. I went out to the trailer for a quick conference with Frank. He was still on the floor. Rick and I re-stated the plan. We would try to win South Carolina. He told me he would know after 12 states had voted whether we were picking up enough votes to carry the challenge without falling into the dreaded "window." I looked at the roll call order. Kansas was eleventh. I said: "I'll talk to you at Kansas. We'll decide then." We had decided not to risk the nomination if it looked close. We would pull votes on later, friendly delegations to insure the vote did not fall within the parliamentary margin. We had forewarned the leaders of responsible, dependable McGovern delegations: Pat Lucey in Wisconsin, Arnold Alperstein in Colorado, Frank Morrison in Nebraska, Doug Fraser in Michigan, Dick Wade in New York. Back in the command trailer office, the red light on the hot line to the Senator's suite glowed as the phone rang. "Gary, this is George. How do things look down there?" "Fine, Senator, we're all ready to go. We vote on South Carolina before California and we will try to win it. But if it looks close we will have to let it go to avoid that parliamentary mess, so don't be worried if it seems we're losing South Carolina." "I understand," he said. "Do your best and let's get those California delegates back. That's what counts." I said, "Don't worry Senator, we will."

I went back on the floor, checked last-minute signals with Frank and, as the South Carolina vote was called, took up my post on the center aisle at the McGovern aisle phone eight rows back in the California delegation. I could look almost directly up twenty yards away into Larry O'Brien's glasses. "California." The roll call started. "South Carolina." "Ohio." "Canal Zone. . . ."

I had the phone up and Rick was evaluating each vote.

Rick: "Too short, too short! Not enough. We just dropped one there." "Kansas."

Rick: "It looks pretty bad."

Hart: "Can we do it?"

Rick: "I don't think so; it would be very close."

Hart: "O.K. then, let's let it go. Get the word around, but tell everyone not to make it look obvious."

I headed for Wisconsin and Pat Lucey. We dropped a few votes in Wisconsin, some in Nebraska, a few here and there, then California and New York changed votes the second time through. The leaders of the stop-McGovern movement seemed confused. I waited for their delegation to begin the vote shuffle to try to get the vote in the "window." It didn't happen. The final vote on the South Carolina was 1,555 to 1,429 against sustaining the challenge. Mrs. McGovern was in one of the front boxes. I went over and explained as briefly as possible what was going on so she wouldn't be concerned. As I turned, I was face to face with Mike Wallace and a live CBS microphone.

Wallace: "Mr. Hart, isn't this a serious defeat for the McGovern forces?" I said: "We did not look on the South Carolina challenge as a test vote on our floor strength." "Yes," Wallace said, "but you supported the women's challenge, and you were just beaten rather badly." Several nights earlier I had had dinner with Wallace and others and now I was having difficulty carrying the charade off. Wallace bore in: "If you have lost this test by dozens of votes, how can you expect to win California?" "We think we will have enough votes to regain our California delegates when the time comes," I said.

The fruitless dialogue finally tapered off and Wallace gave it back to Walter Cronkite with the observation that Hart certainly looked like a very troubled man. Across the floor, Frank dismissed the vote to another reporter with a shrug: "There must be more male chauvinists in some of those delegations than we realized." Cronkite reported to the watching millions that the McGovern campaign was in serious trouble. Elsewhere, leaders of the stop-McGovern operation, still unaware of what we had just done, were claiming success and ultimate victory in their efforts to deny us our California delegates.

Brown then took the podium to shake the hall with his cries: "Give me back my delegation!" Over and over, as the hundreds of McGovern people shouted and stamped. The vote was called. "California." "One hundred and twenty votes for the minority report." I went back to the phone and followed the vote on my sheet with Rick on the other end in the trailer. Now we were picking up additional votes in practically every delegation. Rick was making pleasant sounds on the other end. Two-thirds of the way through we knew we would win and three-quarters of the way through it looked as if we would have a clear, absolute majority. The Chair announced the totals: 1,618 votes for the minority report. We had an absolute majority—we controlled the floor. Norman Bie, Jr., Wallace delegate from Florida, challenged the Chair's parliamentary rulings. His motion was defeated by a vote of 1,689 to 1,162. The McGovern army had held. Willie Brown had his delegation back and George Mc-Govern had the 1972 Democratic Presidential nomination.

JULY 11, 1972. 3 A.M. Our work was not over after the California vote. Two major hurdles still lay ahead, the Chicago challenge and adoption of the credentials committee report as amended. Many of our delegates wanted to seat Daley. The reform delegates had, of course, voted solidly with us on the California challenge. Frank was talking throughout the evening with reform leaders Singer and Jackson. They were told we could not promise to deliver all our votes to keep them seated. They asked that we do our best. We told them we could deliver a majority for a straight compromise, a 50-50 division, half votes for both sides. They agreed to take it. The Daley people were approached. The Mayor still wouldn't take the compromise. Apparently, his advisors on the floor foolishly were convinced they had the votes to unseat the reformers. It was a poor risk. Although many of our more pragmatic delegates wanted Daley there, they still remembered that the six pro-Daley Illinois members of the credentials committee had voted to strip

McGovern of 151 California delegates before the Mayor's Chicago delegation was unseated in the fury of our supporters' backlash. They also had just seen the reform Chicago contingent vote solidly with us on reclaiming the California delegates. But the Mayor's people rejected the compromise even after the reformers had accepted it.

We decided, in a hurried series of meetings in the trailer and in front of the podium, to try to push through a compromise resolution anyway and let the Mayor publicly reject it if he chose to. The resolution was hastily drafted evenly dividing the Chicago contingent. Billy Dougherty rushed it onto the floor as the veteran Frank Morrison filibustered for time. Morrison interrupted his harangue and introduced the resolution. We worked the floor and the phones hard. We couldn't get the votes. A two-thirds majority was required to adopt the compromise resolution; it constituted a suspension of the rules. The compromise failed by a vote of 1,483 in favor, 1,411 opposed. The principal vote arose and Mayor Daley's effort to regain his seats was defeated, 1,486 to 1,372. Some saw it as a vindication of 1968. Politically, we were unhappy that the compromise attempt had failed; with even slight cooperation from the other side, it might have succeeded.

4 A.M. There was a frantic meeting under the podium. Chairman O'Brien was deciding whether to continue until the credentials were resolved. We huddled. An absolute majority was required to adopt the report as amended. If we kept the delegates there too long, they might tire and drift away. We might insure the necessary majority by putting it over until the following session; on the other hand, it would break our momentum. The stop-McGoverns would have an opportunity to regroup and plot more mischief. The tide might be turned by calculated maneuvering. Unpredictable things can happen at a political convention. We told O'Brien we wanted to forge on and would keep our delegates there. The word went out on the phones and across the floor: stay in your seats, don't leave—we are going to nail this down once and for all. Now intensive negotiations were taking place among Frank, Eli Segal, and representatives of the other side to settle as many credentials disputes as possible. Eli took papers around to various challenge leaders on the floor authorizing settlements. The other side did likewise. Finally, under the podium, frantic last-minute agreements were reached. Dawn was approaching and our delegates had been incredibly patient through the night. We wanted that final report adopted. The papers were taken up to O'Brien, who announced the settlements. The delegates shouted their approval to each. A motion was made and seconded calling for the adoption of the credentials committee report. O'Brien called for a voice vote. The convention roared its approval of the amended report. Our delegates had held once again. They were magnificent.

5 : 2 0 A.M. The convention's first session was adjourned after more than ten hours of backbreaking tension and pressure. Outside, after a hand-shaking, back-slapping celebration in the trailer, the sun was coming up over the Atlantic. I was breathing deeply and naturally for the first time in over two years.

J U L Y 11, 1 9 7 2. 10 A.M. Staff meeting. We discussed problems that would be confronted in the platform deliberations that night. Ted Van Dyk reported on the floor organization that would be used. Some additional staff members, familiar with the planks, would augment our group of floor readers. The atmosphere was decidedly more relaxed than it had been 24 hours earlier.

N O O N. Humphrey had earlier appeared before a press conference to withdraw from the race; now Muskie did the same. The luxury of having no opposition, no resistance, hoped for so strongly after the California primary, had finally arrived. We had only a day and a half in which to savor it.

A F T E R N O O N. Although the major political crisis had been surmounted, movement in and around the Doral situation room continued to swirl and flow. Throughout that week, at one time or another, an almost unbelievable number of things were going on: the regular staff meeting, morning and afternoon; floor organization planning; boiler-room communications; parliamentary and procedural discussions; California challenge strategy; compromise negotiations on Chicago; meetings with O'Brien and O'Hara; delegate counting; platform lobbying on a variety of issues, both by us and by special-interest groups; vice-presidential discussions and maneuvering; fall campaign planning; fund-raising and finance discussions; press interviews; fall staff assignments; discussions with the black leaders over their role in the campaign; similar discussions with the Chicanos; unrest among the grassroots workers and the women's caucus; negotiations with the governors; shifting of floor and trailer personnel each night; preparation of the Senator's acceptance speech; nominating and seconding speeches; continuing contacts with the Wallace people; confusion over floor passes; receptions for various groups and delegations; seminars for general election staff. It seemed throughout the week as if conflicts and crises leap-frogged each other.

7 : 3 0 P.M. C O N V E N T I O N F L O O R. After the ceremonies, Governor Reuben Askew delivered the keynote address. The rules committee report, put over from the previous night, was read. During much of this period the hall was darkened to reduce floor movement and focus attention on the speaker or presentation. The darkness merely increased the

confusion. Peopled bumped into each other. It was difficult to maneuver in the aisles. The radio and television reporters seemed to multiply in the dark. The atmosphere was that of a mammoth, crowded movie theater with no one watching the screen.

The only controversial aspect of the rules report, a provision concerning major revisions of the party's charter, caused brief flurries of activity. An internal revolt broke out in the New York delegation. Emotional fires flickered. Order was temporarily restored. Across the hall in every delegation, but particularly Massachusetts, Wisconsin, Oregon, New York, and Colorado, rumors erupted like geysers that McGovern had changed his position on Vietnam, only hours after nailing down the nomination.

That morning, Frank had appeared before a group of prisoner-of-war wives and read a statement prepared by John Holum and hastily approved by McGovern. The statement promised that while prisoners were still being held by the Viet Cong or North Vietnamese, McGovern, as President, would maintain a naval presence off Vietnam and would maintain our air bases in Thailand. The statement was not widely covered, but a reporter for the Knight chain, which includes the *Miami Herald*, picked the story up and it was read throughout Miami and the nation the following morning. In the meantime, word of mouth—that most unreliable form of communication—had begun to carry various confused versions of the statement around the Beach, and delegates, particularly from Massachusetts, began calling the Doral. The contact people in the boiler-room had not seen the statement, nor for that matter had I, presumably because neither Frank nor anyone else thought it that consequential. (It was a classic instance of one hand—political—not knowing what the other—issues—was doing.) So the fires began to rage unchecked. McGovern has sold out; McGovern is just another politician; McGovern can't be trusted. It was the first wave of a storm of political paranoia which swept Miami Beach throughout the remainder of the week. We spent the middle hours of the evening putting out the rumor. But by then the floor of the convention was transforming itself into a jungle. As the various minority reports were debated, lobbyists for particular proposals moved about the floor, trailed by lieutenants, hangers-on, reporters, and curious delegates. The platform was essentially a sane and reasonable statement of McGovern's basic positions, with a few minor concessions made here and there. But many of the groups that supported his candidacy, in some cases rather lukewarmly, preferred stronger, more radical and controversial measures and now began their drumbeats on the floor.

Unquestionably it is the nature of a democracy, and more specifically the Democratic Party, to permit and even encourage dissent. But what was palpable on the floor throughout Tuesday night was, rather an intemperance, a frustration, an intolerance with McGovern and his cam-

The Convention floor.

STUART BRATESMAN

paign because we would not support more extreme positions. It was not that we were discouraging dissent; it was that *we* were not permitted to dissent from some special-interest groups without being thought compromisers and sell-outs. Fanaticism of sorts waxed and waned throughout the night.

As the various special pleaders had their say, a mood of fractionization settled on the hall. This was no longer the cohesive army which had marched against monumental odds from New Hampshire to California to Miami. This was more a crowd of unhappy children, each anxious to get his own way, forgetting the purpose for which he or she had come. But even in the midst of it all the bulk of the McGovern delegates were loyal to their candidate and worked to give to him the platform he sought. And politics made strange bedfellows. On a number of votes we were joined by many of the people who had tried to beat us a day before. Resentments still lingered, however, and on some votes die-hard stop-McGovern people were voting with this radical fringe or that controversial cause in an effort to embarrass their party's prospective candidate.

The debates rambled on through the night until, finally, most of the thirteen minority reports had been argued and all had been voted upon. The platform report was adopted and once again we headed for the Doral. It was almost 7 A.M. and the sun this time was well up. It was the morning of July 12th, nomination day.

JULY 12, 1972. 9:30 A.M. I was awakened by one of our stairwell staff guards. "Mr. Hart, there are a lot of people upstairs who want to talk to you," he said apologetically. Half-asleep, I thought I had forgotten a previously scheduled speech. "How many people and who are they?" I asked. Voice wavering and face pale, he said: "There are about 800 people who say they are the grassroots workers." We had been planning sessions on Friday for re-indoctrination of general election workers. I concluded they were just eager to get going. "Tell them I'll talk to them this afternoon. I've only had four hours sleep in the last three days." Several minutes later the guard was back. "I think you better come now," he said. "They're pretty unhappy." His face was now very pale. I struggled upstairs. Sure enough, the ballroom, where happy couples had danced only hours before, now looked as if it had been occupied by the people's revolution. Five leaders were seated at a front table. One had a band around his head. They were passing resolutions. *Now* they were voting whether to let me speak. I pushed my way to the front and spoke for only a minute. I assured them that McGovern had not changed and that we intended to run a people's campaign in the fall in which they would all play a part if they chose. I didn't recognize many faces.

It turned out later that this group had begun to organize itself as a separatist wing of the campaign which intended to conduct a watchdog operation on the campaign's orthodoxy in the fall. Some of them had not played that great a role in the nomination race. But they had blanketed Miami with leaflets proclaiming the creation of a new "grassroots" organization. The campaign had spawned an institution.

Fear, apprehension and unrest gripped many of the people on the Beach that week. Victory was a novelty. Many, in one way or another, had been defeated or disappointed, by assassinations, by political process, by undependable leaders. The man they had worked for and supported now frightened them. What if he turned out to be like all the others? Maybe you can't trust anyone. Suspicion. Paranoia. Tuesday, Wednesday, Thursday, the unrest simmered.

The campaign leaders went from group to group in an effort to reassure, to calm, to soothe, to convey the message that nothing had changed. McGovern was the same. His campaign for the Presidency was the same.

Unable to sleep after the grassroots confrontation, I found the situation room across the hall the focus of the wrath of half of Miami Beach. The Vietnam statement had now created a forest fire. Reporters had laid seige to the press room downstairs with the appearance of the *Miami Herald* story. They demanded elaboration. Pierre came up. We discussed a clarification statement. It was drafted, approved by the Senator, and released. It said, essentially, that his position on Vietnam "has not altered one iota." After the cessation of bombing, the withdrawal of American ground forces, and the return of U.S. prisoners of war, he promised to "close U.S. bases in Thailand and remove all U.S. Naval forces from water adjacent to Southeast Asia."

But now the roaming bands of demonstrators, previously with little to protest, had a cause—George McGovern. Again, the ironic contrast to 1968 was overpowering. That afternoon they descended on the Doral and occupied the hotel lobby. There, amidst the palms and the filigree, the plaster-phony greco sculpture, the arabesque designs, the tawdry-gaudy finery, they camped. "Lean, hungry, savage, anti-everythings," in Holmes' terms. Scarcely one of them had spent one minute helping McGovern in his uphill struggle. Chanting, pleased to have a focus for their wrath, roused occasionally by flamboyant, irrelevant rhetoric, they called for the candidate's appearance, or his head.

Seventeen floors above, business continued. The candidate quietly asked for, and was given, separate pieces of paper upon which half a dozen campaign leaders gave their four recommendations for the Vice-Presidency, in order of desirability. Calls of conciliation had been made many hours before to Humphrey and Muskie. Other calls were made as the day went on to leaders from various states who had not opposed McGovern so vigorously and who, therefore, required less time for wound-healing. The Senator continued to work on his acceptance speech. A great deal of time was spent in the afternoon making final arrangements for the nomination that evening.

I met with Henry Kimelman, Morris Dees, Marjorie Benton, and other members of the finance committee to discuss the fall campaign budget and plans to raise the necessary $20 million. Occasionally, those who had been most helpful financially were taken in for a chat with the Senator. Once again, we had last-minute problems with floor passes. Inexplicably, the McGovern campaign was still having trouble on the eve of the nomination getting a modest number of its people on the convention floor.

Avoiding the lobby mob through the use of a service elevator now under Secret Service guard (the demonstrators had been threatening to storm the penthouse floor; the elevators and fire-escapes were sealed off), we headed for the convention hall and the nomination.

8 P.M. As the ceremonies opening the third session of the convention took place down the Beach, the Senator went down to the Doral lobby to talk to the demonstrators. Debate throughout the late afternoon and early evening on the top floor had ranged between such an appearance and forcible removal. The appearance was dangerous. The Secret Service and some staff members were concerned about the Senator's physical safety. Others were concerned about political dangers. Fighting might break out. The entire lobby, where network cameras were stationed, could turn into a battleground. On the other hand, it was clear the demonstrators had to leave sometime. The Miami police, at the request of the hotel management, were headed for the Doral in force to remove the demonstrators. Such a confrontation would undoubtedly lead to some sort of violence. We stood to lose under almost any set of circumstances. But the Senator, in blue sport shirt and slacks, went down to the lobby with a dozen Secret Service agents, the large ones in front. He spoke briefly and calmly. Several in the crowd, one girl in particular, responded rudely and profanely. He refused to be baited. The mass of the demonstrators, reacting as much to his demeanor as the content of his words, accepted his request to disperse. Consistently at his best in confrontation situations, he had defused the bomb and prevented what might have become a replay of the Chicago debacle of 1968.

11 P.M. "California proudly casts its 271 votes for the next President of the United States, Senator George McGovern!", co-chairmen Brown-Huerta-Burton chanted into the delegation's microphone immediately below the podium. The roll call was underway. Although neither Hum-

phrey nor Muskie was nominated, although the opposition at this point was token, for those committed to the McGovern nomination, the moment was electric. This was the hour for which so many had struggled for so long. This was the roll call to relish, remembering, as each state cast its votes, the investment in human time and talent required to hack those votes out of solid rock—the endless meetings, the pleas for support, the scratching for money, the seemingly monolithic opposition, the rejections, the disappointments, the scoffing of the politically savvy, the triumphs of the committed.

New York gave us 263 of its 278. State chairman Gordon St. Angelo then brought 26 of Indiana's votes over after Humphrey's demise. Seven out of seven in Puerto Rico. The running total was now 661 for McGovern. Pennsylvania gave us 81 votes, 25 more than we had projected in our last public count on July 5 and nine more than our private projection. Wisconsin, our first primary victory, cast 55 for McGovern. Illinois passed. Eleven votes from New Hampshire. I thought briefly of that 1970 jeep ride and laughed to myself. Twenty-one of Arizona's 25. Massachusetts, all 102. Nebraska's 21 brought the running total to 888. We picked up 89 of New Jersey's 109, 11 more than our July 5th projection. July 5th seemed like a year ago. We were now over the 1,000 mark.

I had the California delegation phone open to the trailer and was once again going through the count with Rick. We marked our ballot sheets and commented to each other on the new comrades who had just delivered a few extra votes or the s.o.b.'s who hadn't come through. Michigan passed. Enough big states had now passed to put the majority vote off until the second time through the roll call. Iowa, the first caucus state, 35 of 46. I remembered our precinct workers in the bitter cold. Colorado, 27 of 36. Thanks friends. Sixteen out of 17 in Montana. Thirty in Connecticut. John Bailey had given us a few. All of Oregon's 34. Oklahoma passed and the roll call was completed. Our running total was 1,279.

The question was now which state would put us over the top at 1,509. If we held our votes in Ohio and Texas, it would probably be the strife-ridden Illinois delegation where we had picked up the bulk of the Muskie votes to augment the reformers and our own delegates. On the second time through, Ohio gave us 77, exactly what we projected. The total was 1,356. The excitement was tangible. Most of the delegates were now standing. To see across to Illinois, I stood on Willie Brown's chair at the front corner of the California delegation. A great crowd began to surge and I had to hold the California standard to keep from falling off the chair. Immediately above us was the great gavel. Utah added 14 to bring the total to 1,370.

It would be Illinois. I looked across two aisles, the South Carolina, Ohio, Virginia, and Illinois delegations, the weaving, smoky, frozen motion on the floor, to the Illinois standard. There, beside Jim Wall, our delegation chairman, loomed the imperious, almost regal, black countenance of the dashiki-clad Jesse Jackson. The saucer-shaped Martin Luther King medallion around his neck stood out like a beacon. Jackson gazed over the heads of his brethren like a tribal king. I pointed at them in one of those gestures made futile by distance and noise, trying to send a communication by outstretched finger. Magically, they turned. And I gave a vigorous thumbs-up gesture, pointing at the Illinois standard and putting my thumb up. Texas had just given us 33 more votes. The total was 1,403. Illinois understood. They signalled. The Illinois vote was cast, minor numbers first. Then came 119 votes for George McGovern, and we had the nomination.

The California standard at the front and center of the hall became the eye of a hurricane celebration. Unable to climb down from my perch on Willie's chair, I alternately hugged Frank and California leaders who had climbed up beside us, or clung to the standard as if it was a mast in a storm, to keep from falling into the surging sea of humanity. The celebration continued to the cadence of the chairman's ineffectual gavel. Brown, Burton, and Huerta cavorted on their colleagues' shoulders in front of the podium. McGovern delegates streamed to the waving California standard from all across the hall. As the chant, "We want McGovern!" reverberated from rafter to eave, Shirley MacLaine raised a large hand-lettered sign: "Jimmie the Greek, where are you?"

The long march was over. The McGovern army had won. When I first met George McGovern at the Denver airport in March, 1970, he was a prophetic figure armed only with his cause. Now, 26 eventful months later, the more than 1,600 committed McGovern delegates on that Miami convention floor represented a fulltime staff of 200, state committees numbered in the hundreds, workers in the tens of thousands, and supporters in the millions. Not one of these delegate votes had come easily. Not one had been delivered by a political boss or been won by compromise or promise of reward. Not one had voted for McGovern out of duress or compulsion. Every McGovern vote on that floor represented the triumph of political reform, what the Senator himself had described as the most sweeping and successful reform of a political institution in recorded history.

The 1972 Democratic convention had just vindicated the faith of those who created this nation in the ability of people, citizens, individuals, to govern their own political affairs. A process that, for the first time, was open, democratic and available to all had been used by hundreds of thousands of committed Democrats to select the candidate who had most convincingly taken his case to them. Arms had not been bent, deals had

Another Eleanor: Hopefully on her way to the White House.

not been made, rewards had not been promised. The people had organized and made their choice, for the first time, in the broad daylight of
public scrutiny. The hold of the bosses had been broken, hopefully, for-
ever. The Democratic Party had trusted its people and they had responded by making it truly democratic.

The army recruited from the ranks of citizen volunteers in the best
American tradition, led by amateur generals and officers, drawn not from
political, but from civilian, ranks, had defeated, in honest, open combat,
the best of a tradition of trained, seasoned, tough, sophisticated professionals, the flower of a century of urban political domination, the best of
the "regulars."

Heading back up the Beach to the Doral in the Thursday morning dark
ness, I thought of General Kutuzov: "It is not difficult to capture a fortress
but it is difficult to win a campaign. For that, not storming and attacking
but patience and time was wanted. . . . There is nothing stronger than
those two; patience and time, they will do it all." And he was right.

General Kutuzov and the grassroots army.

EPILOGUE

JULY 13, 1972. This, the longest day in a long campaign, passed
in three segments; staff deliberations in the morning, consultation with
interest groups in the noon hours, decision-making with key staff members
in the mid-afternoon. The issue: the selection of a running mate.

9 A.M.–NOON. Executive conference room. The Senator asked
Frank the previous night to convene a loose collection of 20 staff mem-
bers, advisors and supporters to consider all possible recommendations
for the Vice-Presidency. Frank opened with an invitation to free-asssocia-
tion: "Let's bring up every name we can think of, including people in
the private sector." Names surfaced like popcorn kernels. Senators:
Ribicoff, Church, Nelson, Mondale, Kennedy, Tunney, Eagleton, Hart,
Hughes, Bayh, Stevenson, Harris, Hollings, Proxmire, Muskie, Humphrey,
Hatfield (a Republican, but this wasn't the time for narrow-mindedness).
Governors: Lucey, Askew, Mandel, Carter, Bumpers, Gilligan. Con-
gressmen: Mills, Udall, O'Hara. Mayors: White, Landrieu, Lindsay.
Prominent citizens, politicians, university presidents, labor leaders:
O'Brien, Shriver, Woodcock, Sanford, Hesburg, Gardner, Brewster,
Walter Cronkite.

For half an hour, the mood was light, relaxed to the point of frivolity.
Victory was being savored for the first time in the light of day. It was
like a group of fraternity boys who had spent most of the night successfully stealing the rival school's mascot. As names were raised, jokes were

born. Van Dyk, considering New Orleans Mayor Moon Landreau: "Never do. Never do. Can't you see the headlines, 'Moon over Miami!'" Comments were raucous, but the irony of the procedure was never lost. Eli Segal, red-eyed, slumped in his chair: "I can't get over this. Here we sit, unshaven, worn-out, knocking down United States Senators." Finally, after another round of coffee, people pulled up their mental socks and got to work.

From the complete list of 36 or 37, formal nominations were required with justification. The person responsible for raising each name was asked to support it or drop it. Twenty-two names were nominated. Justification arguments were made and countered. Action around the large circular table was quick, concise, blunt, but fair. Sides shifted. Some people thought of arguments in favor of nominees they had previously criticized. Original supporters became critics. Fairly obvious traditional standards were used; who would bring strength and balance to the ticket? Urban background, labor connections, ethnic or religious factors, ties to the party regulars, ties to the South; standing with minority groups. Despite the absence of real vetoing blocks in the modern party, who would be alienated by each choice? Personal characteristics: family, reputation, habits, business dealings, background, peer evaluation. But, most importantly, each potential candidate was thoroughly scrutinized regarding his ability to govern, to become President.

Slowly, names were eliminated. Sponsors agreed to withdraw their endorsements. The list narrowed. Rumors were sifted and, if the rumoree were still on the list, checked. Concerning Eagleton, Rick Stearns recalled a recent conversation with a national reporter who had mentioned problems of drinking and mental illness in the family, perhaps a parent in a mental institution. Although there is not general agreement on this crucial point, Rick remembers also mentioning the possibility of Eagleton's having a record of mental illness. "Who was the reporter?" I asked Rick. Since Eagleton was from Missouri, Rick thought it must have been Tom Ottenad of the *St. Louis Post-Dispatch*. (Chalk one up for fatigue. It was Loye Miller of the Knight newspaper chain.) Gordon Weil agreed to check it out. He dismissed himself and located Ottenad who, somewhat startled, said he had never heard the mental illness rumors. But he did confirm a lingering speculation centering around alcoholism, with no factual verification ever located. Gordon checked other sources and, after slightly more than half an hour, returned to say that he could find nothing to support the drinking or mental illness rumors.

Debate continued. One by one the names were dropped, in each case after serious, deliberate, often exhaustive scrutiny. Increasingly, I became dumbfounded at how few candidates fit the necessary qualifications and how many had some serious disqualifier or disability. Although the

Senator had called for about half a dozen names, names were kept on the list if at least one sponsor and a second felt strongly enough to insist. As it turned out, only seven names survived and one or two of those were kept on for symbolic or historic purposes. Deliberations finally completed, Frank, Pierre, Jean Westwood, and I conveyed the names to the Senator in his corner penthouse suite just before noon.

The list: Senator Walter Mondale, who was put on by popular consensus even though few thought he would take it because he was up for Senate re-election; Mayor Kevin White, of Boston, who was at that point the leading candidate; Governor Pat Lucey, the specific candidate of South Dakota Lt. Gov. Bill Dougherty; Senator Abraham Ribicoff, on the list particularly because it was known the Senator himself was considering Ribicoff; R. Sargent Shriver, the candidate of Pierre Salinger; Larry O'Brien, Rick Stearns' candidate; Senator Tom Eagleton, a last-minute entry put on primarily because he was Catholic, urban, and an unknown from a border state. John Holum also observed that Eagleton had a good staff, a persuasive argument to other staff members.

The names were presented to the Senator with supporting and critical arguments for each. I argued strongly for White, as his original sponsor. He was an urban, Catholic mayor, with administrative experience. He was from New England. He was known to be a vigorous, attractive campaigner who had learned to rely on some of the same methodical, grassroots campaign techniques that we had. He had impeccable personal and family credentials. All this was verified by Dick Dougherty who had covered him during his newspapering days. Most importantly, no one could think of anything materially wrong with him, a qualification met by almost none of the other candidates. Presuming that neither Kennedy nor Mondale (my first and second candidates respectively), were available, White was the consensus candidate of the group.

12 NOON–1:30 P.M. The Senator called various groups and individuals into his suite—the black leadership, leaders of the women's caucus, Chicano representatives, mayors. Calls of consultation were made around the Beach. When White's name was raised, it was greeted with surprise, particularly since it had not received much consideration in the press, but he passed the test with all groups.

As the groups came and went, the original staff group was augmented by Fred Dutton, Dick Dougherty, Bill Dougherty, John Douglas, and, later, Ted Van Dyk, Gordon Weil, and Kirby Jones. Liz Stevens and Polly Hackett were available to expedite urgent telephoning.

1:30 P.M.–4 P.M. The decision. After a brief concluding discussion, the phoning started. The Senator called Senator Mondale. A several-minute conversation ensued in which Mondale raised the problem of his own race. According to the Senator's account, Mondale rejected the suggestion that he join the ticket on the ground that it would cost him the Senate seat. McGovern then called Mayor White who, though somewhat shocked at the suggestion, readily agreed to join the ticket if formally asked. McGovern stated that he wanted to touch a few more bases routinely, and would call back in half an hour. It was just after 2 P.M.

Since it now appeared almost certain to be Kevin White, I walked down the hall to the situation room and contacted Rick Stearns, who had gone to bed after the morning meeting. (Most of us had gone virtually sleepless for almost a week.) I told Rick to gather the boiler-room staff and get them to start contacting the delegation leaders. Because of the rigid discipline exercised in the previous three sessions, some of the more independent, less committed McGovern delegates were discussing all kinds of Vice-Presidential possibilities and there had been the usual talk about throwing the decision open to the convention, a suggestion never taken seriously. Rick wanted to know who it would be. I said: "It isn't absolutely certain. Therefore, don't let the boiler-room people know. We don't want it around town until the official announcement is ready. But strictly for your information, it looks as if it will be White." I also asked how long it would take to prepare the nomination petitions, previously circulated in blank. Rick said only the candidate's name would have to be inserted and they would then have to be taken to the DNC offices at the Fontainebleau. I told him to get them ready. Although I didn't think we were absolutely bound, with the Senator now the party's nominee, by the 4 P.M. filing deadline, we still didn't want to invite an unnecessary procedural hassle over the question.

After talking to Rick and shaving for the first time that day, I went back to the Senator's suite. Incredibly, the tables had completely turned. The Senator had talked to Ted Kennedy, who was urging consideration of other candidates—Ribicoff, Eagleton, Wilbur Mills. We had tried our several possibilities with floor and delegation leaders earlier and had been assured that we would have a tremendous fight on our hands if we selected Mills and might not be able to carry the recommendation on the floor. But McGovern was deeply troubled. The fact that Kennedy had raised other names, plus whatever else Kennedy had to say, led McGovern to conclude that Kennedy was less than enthusiastic about the White nomination. In fact, whether by direct suggestion or implication, McGovern now believed Kennedy himself was reconsidering his own consistent decision to reject a position on the ticket. Turning from the phone after talking to Kennedy, McGovern said, with a degree of amazement, "Ted said he wanted to reconsider his decision." Regarding

White, McGovern did not believe he could take anyone about whom Kennedy was unenthusiastic. In any case, Kennedy had promised to call back in half an hour.

As this new set of circumstances was being pondered, two other events occurred which affected White's chances. Ken Galbraith called from the Massachusetts delegation claiming that the delegation would rise up en masse to oppose White; that he and Father Drinan thought it was a terrible choice. Second, Charles Guggenheim, overhearing the White talk now spilling out in the corridors, came in to tell the Senator that others, particularly Tom Eagleton, would be much more effective than White in projecting a new, non-political image. The case against White was mounting. But staff members and advisors now knotted about the suite in small murmuring clusters were fascinated by the possibility that Kennedy himself might come aboard. The super-ticket. A survey which we commissioned Pat Caddell to perform in June showed Kennedy making the most dramatic impact with McGovern in a race against Nixon-Agnew. The study, dated July 4, 1972, showed the McGovern-Kennedy ticket only two points behind the incumbent Republicans. The gradual demise of White, the consensus candidate after more than four hours' careful deliberation, seemed little noticed in the excitement about Kennedy.

Then Kennedy called back. No, he really wasn't interested, but he thought serious consideration should be given to those other names. It was just after 3 P.M. and we did not have a Vice-Presidential candidate. I had the sense we were starting all over again. The Senator called Abe Ribicoff. They talked generally. What did Ribicoff think about running? He wasn't enthusiastic. The offer was never forcefully made or forcefully refused. Frustrated, irritated, fatigued, preoccupied with the necessity of finishing his speech for the greatest audience of his career that night, the Senator turned to his closest Senatorial friend, Gaylord Nelson. Minutes passed as Nelson was located. The offer was made. Nelson declined. But like Ribicoff and Kennedy before him, Nelson was enthusiastic about Tom Eagleton. Eagleton wanted the nomination for sure and each respective friend of McGovern in his turn gave Eagleton the very highest recommendation. They had all served in the Senate with Eagleton for four years and respected his work. Besides, Guggenheim had worked with him on campaigns and gave him the highest praise as a campaigner. It was now almost 3:45 P.M.

I could scarcely believe what was happening. I recalled reading accounts of deliberations like this—particularly the confusion surrounding John Kennedy's selection of Lyndon Johnson—and thinking to myself: "if I ever get into a situation like that I am going to make sure the deliberations are careful, thoughtful, calm. That's no way to make such important decisions." But here it was happening and I was right in the middle of it. What had started as a happy day putting frosting on the cake was disintegrating into a nightmare.

The Senator now believes, in retrospect, that at this very point he should have called Larry O'Brien, explained the dilemma, and arranged to have the acceptance speech on prime time television that night and the convention put over another day for the selection of the Vice-President. Whether that could actually have been done, in theory or in practice, has never been determined. But Bill Dixon, who was deputized to take the nomination petitions to the DNC offices, told me subsequently that the three candidates whose petitions had already been filed were sitting in those offices to determine whether the McGovern selection conformed to the rules and procedures, particularly whether they were filed on time. If not, they were prepared to challenge the filing and carry the case to the floor of the convention. The party officials supervising the filings seemed inclined to support their technical case. That would have been a nice spectacle on prime time.

McGovern said: "I think I'll go with Tom." The call was placed. And the time-bomb destined to destroy the infant McGovern Presidential candidacy started ticking. After McGovern offered the Vice-Presidency and Eagleton eagerly accepted, Frank took the phone and a brief conversation ensued which will be analyzed as long as politicians breath. When, in the next few days, it became a seemingly critical issue, I distinctly remembered standing about six feet away from Frank as he concluded the brief instructions for the evening proceedings and said: "Now, Tom, is there anything in your background that we ought to know about, any problems, you know, like dames, a savings and loan that went bad that your law firm represented . . . ?" At that point I was distracted by a question about the petitions and walked from the room.

JULY 14, 1972. At 3 A.M. Gladys Knight and the Pips, together with a great rock band, had the delegates dancing in the aisles of Convention Hall. "This land is your land, this land is my land." The Democratic leadership had assembled in the traditional unity display on the podium. Hours of oratory and countless nominations—I suggested to one reporter that the Democrats planned to nominate the entire cast of "Aida"—had not deflated the delegates, now accustomed to all-night sessions. Although a speech by Senator Kennedy intoxicated the delegates on the floor, the candidate's appearance transported them to a plane above politics. The demonstration was a moving experience. Most vowed never to forget it. Following the Senator's eloquent middle-of-the-night

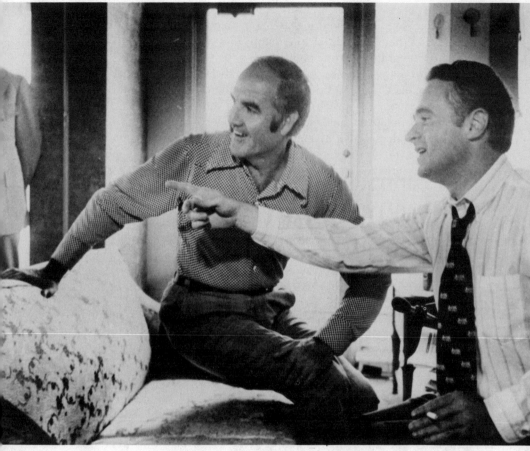

The candidate with his first running mate.

address, which incorporated most of the themes of both the nomination race just concluded and the general election race yet to begin, the great gavel fell.

To the degree that thoughts turned to the future and to politics that night, those who thought them were awed by the responsibility that had so recently descended, the responsibility for carrying out the dreams of millions of people, the responsibility for restoring hope and humanity and purpose to the country. But most of all, the responsibility for restoring the confidence of the people in their leaders and in their government. It seemed like a heavy task, but not an impossible one.

PART IV

Victory has a Thousand Fathers but Defeat is an Orphan

(July 15, 1972, to November 7, 1972)

A general election race is much different from a nomination race. First, it is a much briefer, more compact experience. The fall campaign took no more than 90 days, including the normally inactive month of August. Even though our plan was to rest and plan late in July, gradually build up steam through August, and hit full stride on Labor Day, events conspired to cause almost instant acceleration—like a child's racer which is wound up and placed on a track with its wheels spinning. Second, there was a much greater division between the visible portion of the campaign —the candidate and the traveling party out touring the country—and the organizational and support activities carried out by the national campaign structure headquartered in Washington. In the nomination race the campaign structure was simpler and much more cohesive, and it tended to focus itself upon each primary state in the series. The third difference is the sheer size of the undertaking. By the time of the California primary and the national convention, we had a very large operation. But it was nothing like the kind of organization and mammoth effort necessary to run a full-scale 90-day general election campaign for the Presidency. Fourth, a campaign by a candidate of a major party required immensely greater diplomatic energies. Whereas an insurgency nomination campaign owes little to established political institutions and can therefore move quickly and efficiently, like a guerrilla army, a general-election campaign requires constant attention to the established institutions of the party—its own permanent body and machinery, the Democratic National Committee, its elected officials in Congress and around the country, and its national party structure, the labor establishment, the political organizations and allegiances created by other candidates for the nomination, the party's procedures, traditions, codes and rituals. All this requires heavy machinery and an unwieldy apparatus, particularly when the campaign must perform healing, ministerial, and ambassadorial functions within the party itself while trying to win an election. A further difference is the requirement of running in every state simultaneously. Unlike the nomination race, which involved a series of a dozen or so primary races with side operations in an equally lengthy series of non-primary states, the general-election campaign was 50 primary races running at once. The swirl and flow of simultaneously occurring events may have created a circus-like atmosphere in the spring campaign, but the fall campaign multiplied that atmosphere by ten.

Finally, and perhaps most important, there were no sign posts or check points along the way. The series of primaries in the spring gave a sense of progress, of movement, of direction and success. There were no barometers in the fall except the public opinion polls—and we had conditioned ourselves to disbelieve them. Indeed, we had proved them inaccurate. So the fall campaign experience seemed more like the bitter days of December, 1971, and January-February, 1972, when all was dark, everything seemed to be favoring the other side and there were no tangible signs of progress.

In retrospect, the period between the national convention and the November 7th election seems like a long day, a Joycean experience part nightmare, part vivid recollection, a jumbled montage of absurd, painful, ridiculous, irrational, petty, bitter, tragic, and comic experiences. The only frame of reference is the passage of time—late July, August, September, October, early November. Therefore, since chronology is the only meaningful measure, one might adopt the figure of a day for the period of the fall campaign—a full twenty-four hour period in which late July will be the night hours (the tragic darkness of the Eagleton matter), August will be the dawn and morning hours (the beginning of the campaign), September will be the afternoon (the campaign in full stride), October will be the evening (the sun beginning to set), and the first week of November will be the hours before midnight (the end of the day). My apologies to James Joyce, and my respects to Leopold Bloom.

NIGHT

Henry Kimelman, our national finance chairman and one of the world's great hosts, opened his luxurious home in Charlotte Amalie, St. Thomas, Virgin Islands, to the Mankiewiczs, Harts, and Miles Rubin for post-convention recuperation and financial planning. Senator McGovern, for the next several weeks the second most important man in America, had heeded the sage political advice of Sander Vanocur to avoid a jet-set image, and had returned to South Dakota's Black Hills to retreat from the spotlight and re-establish the identification with his origins. Together with other staff members and advisors, we were to join him there in several days.

Between 4:00 and 4:30 A.M., Friday morning at the victory celebration following the acceptance speeches, Gordon Weil told Frank that he had learned from Doug Bennet, Senator Eagleton's administrative assistant, that Eagleton had indeed been hospitalized for a brief period in 1960 for "fatigue and exhaustion" following a campaign. Frank promised to get the details from Eagleton himself, since they were casual social friends. Overhearing merely the end of the muttered Weil-Mankiewicz conversation, I later snagged Gordon's sleeve as he was leaving and tried to find out about it. He said something like, "We're trying to track down those rumors." That night well-over half the McGovern campaign could profitably have been hospitalized for fatigue and exhaustion.

On Friday afternoon, July 14th, McGovern flew to Washington for the weekend before heading for the Black Hills. Eagleton flew to Kansas City to fulfill a speaking engagement, and then returned to Washington on Saturday night, the 15th, to be briefed by Ted Van Dyk on the key campaign issues before a Sunday "Face the Nation" appearance. Frank headed for the Virgin Islands. I stayed in Miami to help wrap things up, meeting Friday afternoon with several groups, including half a dozen key Chicano leaders, to plan for the fall campaign, and Saturday morning with Doug Bennet and two other Eagleton staff members to brief them as thoroughly as possible on the general election race. The subject of Eagleton's medical record was never raised because, at that point, I knew nothing about it. Late Saturday afternoon, I joined Frank and the others in the Virgin Islands.

That night after dinner Frank mentioned the conversation with Gordon and suggested that he was going to try to get to the bottom of it on the phone. At that point, based on the facts as I had learned them fourth hand, there seemed little cause for concern. At midnight, after his briefing, Eagleton returned Frank's call. At Frank's request, I listened in. In a Friday-afternoon telephone conversation with Bennet before leaving Miami, Frank had learned that reporters had been making inquiries around Missouri about Eagleton's health. Frank's concern was to get all the facts so that if McGovern were asked about it, or if Eagleton were asked about it on the television interview the following day, their answers would be consistent and it would emerge as the inconsequential matter we believed it to be.

Frank: "Tom, I don't know for sure about the integrity of these lines so we better talk in generalities. Now, if a question comes up tomorrow about this fatigue and so forth, how do you think it ought to be handled?"

Eagleton: "Well, it wasn't a big thing. I was just exhausted after campaigning and that's all that needs to be said."

Frank: "You might say, if the question comes up, that you are such an energetic campaigner that you once campaigned yourself right into the hospital, and that's the kind of campaign you intend to run this fall. [Eagleton agreed with that approach.] I'm going to be talking to the candidate sometime tomorrow. In case he gets asked any questions, is there anything else he needs to know?"

Eagleton: "No, that's about it. Nothing very serious."

Frank: "O.K. Tom. Good luck tomorrow. I'll call you back after the program to see how it went."

The conversation left Frank uneasy enough to pursue the inquiry further. The question had not been raised on Face the Nation and, on Sunday, Frank spoke to Eagleton again. There was a polite cross-examination. Was there more than one incident? Yes. All right; a couple of incidents. Treatment the same both times? Pretty much the same, as Eagleton could recall. Both involved exhaustion, fatigue. Any other diagnosis? Would the medical records show any other diagnosis or description? Maybe stuff like melancholy, maybe depression. But it all related to the intensity of campaigning and there have been no recurrences. The conversation dwindled off.

Frank, his wife Holly, and I sat up late in the Virgin Islands' moonlight. I was apprehensive and vaguely ill. Frank spun out some wry, black humor. Holly, clearly frightened, paraded all the horrible possibilities. Three new factors had been added: more than one incident, depression and melancholy, a Vice-Presidential candidate from whom information was coming only very reluctantly. A great deal of time was spent discussing and analyzing the term "melancholy." On one hand, it is a mood which everyone on the real-world side of Pollyanna experiences sometime; on the other, it can be a layman's term for some fairly serious problems. It was difficult to say then which it was.

JULY 17, 1972. Frank phoned the Senator in Washington, bringing him up to date, in general terms, on the limited information we had gathered. Shortly thereafter the Senator left for South Dakota. In the afternoon I called the Washington campaign headquarters to check for weekend messages. Marcia Johnston read several telephone messages and ended with one taken by a volunteer at the switchboard that morning. In effect, the caller, a man, said that Senator Eagleton had been hospitalized three times, for mental illness, and had received shock therapy more than once. He said the information had been obtained from a highly reliable source, a close friend or relative, who had participated in the therapy. He said he was a McGovern supporter and had just given the same information to the Knight newspapers in the hopes of heading off what he was certain would be a vicious whisper campaign against Eagleton in the coming days. He refused to identify himself. Marcia, not knowing what I knew, treated it as a crank call. The volunteer at the switchboard had urged the caller to talk to someone in Eagleton's Senate office.

I told Frank what I had just learned. Because of the circumstances under which the information was given, and probably because my mind rebelled at the implications, I refused to believe it. But if the anonymous caller had indeed contacted the papers, the fat was in the fire.

J U L Y   1 8 ,   1 9 7 2 . Frank and I both checked our messages in Washington. An anonymous caller, presumably the same one, had called that morning asking for Frank or me, had been referred to Frank's assistant, Pat Broun, who was given the same information: several hospitalizations and shock therapy. Frank called Senator Eagleton, a meeting was arranged for Thursday morning, and Frank and I flew to Washington the next night.

J U L Y   2 0 ,   1 9 7 2 . Senator Eagleton, Doug Bennet, Frank, and I met in the Senate dining room from about 8:30 to 10:00 A.M. The exchange was direct. How many hospitalizations? Three. Where were they? The first was in 1960 at the Barnes Hospital in St. Louis. What kind of hospital is that? Private hospital with a special unit called the Renard Psychiatric Division. Then where were the others? Mayo Clinic in Rochester, Minnesota. Two? Yes, 1964 and 1966. Both after campaigns? No, let's see, '60 and '66 were, but '64 was around the holidays, around Christmas. Frank winced visibly. (During the campaign despondency of late December, 1971, I recalled Frank's delivering a homily one night in the office about the Christmas season's being the statistical peak period for psychological and emotional problems and suicide attempts. So now, we were clearly dealing with more than mere post-campaign fatigue, or even post-campaign depression.) What treatment was used? Rest, some medication. But mostly rest. Professional help, psychiatrists? Yes, one or two had been brought in. But they were mostly trying to figure out the reasons for this depression and melancholy, whether it was related to physical fatigue and so forth. Anything else, anything like shock therapy, electroshock treatment? Yes. In 1960 at Barnes and 1966 at Mayo. But not very much on either occasion.

I then brought up the point Frank had made in the second telephone conversation from the islands. We have to presume this information is, or shortly will be, in the hands of the Committee to Re-elect the President. John Mitchell was its chairman. The same John Mitchell who, as Attorney General, had authority over the F.B.I. In any case, it was naive to presume, particularly since Lyndon Johnson had proved so many times to the contrary, that the President didn't have access to every bit of information in the Bureau's records. If the full Eagleton medical history wasn't in those records now, it soon would be, and from there it would go to Nixon's desk. What do those records show? What words are used? What is the diagnosis? What should we expect? Mostly just depression and melancholy. But won't there be some more technical terms that unfriendly experts can twist and turn? The only way to find out, the only way for McGovern to be fully protected, is to know what they say.

Eagleton agreed. He himself had never seen the files, he said, but he would send a staff member to get them. He knew the doctors and he was sure they would cooperate. He would get someone, a name was mentioned, out to St. Louis and to Rochester in the next couple of days. Since McGovern, Frank, and I were headed to South Dakota the following day, it was agreed the files should be sent there as quickly as possible for our evaluation. Eagleton then indicated he would be headed West on Tuesday and planned to stop over in the Black Hills. It was agreed in conclusion that nothing would be done until we got the records and the two candidates met on Tuesday.

Later that morning McGovern held a press conference to announce the appointment of Larry O'Brien as campaign chairman. He had called me on Monday to say that he had talked to Larry at great length the previous evening in Washington and, unless I had serious objections, would like to name him chairman, with special liaison responsibilities to elected officials and party officials. He also thought Larry should travel around the country on behalf of the ticket and act as principal campaign spokesman. I asked what responsibility Larry would want to exercise over day-to-day campaign operations. He said none. He had specifically discussed that with O'Brien and had been assured that he had not the slightest interest in getting embroiled in the details and decision-making. I told the Senator I thought the arrangement was a fine one. O'Brien's experience, reputation, and credentials obviously qualified him to fulfill all those functions.

A great deal of nonsense had been written, particularly by columnists Evans and Novak and Joseph Alsop, about the relationship of McGovern staff members, especially me, to O'Brien. Throughout convention week, Larry had made a number of public statements to the effect that he would not stay on as a Democratic Party Chairman under any circumstances. In the heat of the California challenge, the nomination fight, and the Vice-Presidential selection, he was taken at his word and McGovern started looking elsewhere, specifically toward Jean Westwood, who had worked so diligently and faithfully in our campaign and who had the added advantage of proving the campaign meant what it said about women's rights.

Nevertheless, the Senator was enormously impressed, as were we all, with the resourcefulness, graciousness, aplomb, and good nature with which Larry had handled a potentially explosive convention. He also knew O'Brien represented a great deal to rank and file Democrats around the country. Almost as an afterthought, he called O'Brien Friday morning, the 14th, in Miami, and asked him to reconsider his decision. O'Brien was interested enough to come to the Doral, with several of his staff members, to discuss it. Knowing nothing of all this, I was in the downstairs meeting room conducting an all-day seminar for 200 key campaign organizers on the details of the fall campaign when Marcia brought an urgent message to come to the Senator's suite immediately. I arrived to find O'Brien and his staff milling around in one room, while the Senator, Pierre, Frank, Jean, Fred Dutton, and one or two others sat intently in the other, discussing what to do. Although I didn't realize it at the time, the matter was complicated by Jean's and Pierre's feeling that they had absolutely firm commitments for the two leadership roles in the DNC. I was surprised to find the matter still under deliberation.

The issue, simply stated to me, in hushed tones so the O'Brien people in the next room wouldn't overhear, was that Larry had agreed to stay on as National Chairman *if* he could also run the fall campaign from the DNC. I stated first that I had no problem at all with his staying on as National Chairman—there was a lot to be said for it. But I did object on two grounds to his running the campaign. First was the Jean-and-Pierre objection; I had already been asked at least twice by the Senator to run the fall campaign. Second, I suspected Larry had no interest at all in the daily decision-making and would delegate that to *his* staff. I knew our people in every state well enough to know that they would probably take orders from O'Brien if that were the Senator's wishes, but they would never take orders from people who had not been involved in our campaign before, whom they didn't know and whose first loyalties were to O'Brien, not to McGovern. I made this latter point rather vigorously. I suggested O'Brien be asked merely to be Party Chairman. The Senator said he wouldn't do it. I then said I thought Jean should have the job on the grounds just stated. Although I later bore the brunt of forcing O'Brien out, it seemed to me that everyone around the coffee table at that time agreed with my reasoning, and several of them made similar arguments.

So, when McGovern was able to work out an arrangement with Larry which didn't threaten to alienate our best workers, I readily agreed. The announcement was made within an hour after the completion of the breakfast with Eagleton. I arranged to get together with Larry the following morning at his apartment to give him the same full-dress campaign planning briefing I had given to Doug Bennet a week earlier in Miami. After the press conference, I mentioned to McGovern our breakfast with Eagleton, and said we had picked up additional information. He suggested that we could discuss it the following morning on the plane to South Dakota. He had interrupted his vacation to fly to Washington that morning to cast a tie-breaking vote on a minimum-wage proposal.

J U L Y   21,   1972. After the charter campaign jet was well underway and lunch disposed of, Frank and I moved forward to the front right seats occupied by the Senator and Eleanor McGovern. In direct and comprehensive fashion, Frank and I gave the Senator every bit of information we had gathered about Eagleton's history of mental illness. Eleanor was appalled by the information, the Senator thoughtful. As I recall, Eleanor was the first to raise the question of Eagleton's departure from the ticket. Frank very firmly urged a course which would convince Eagleton to remove himself forthwith, before the story broke in the papers. I was less certain. I advised the Senator that the key was the medical records themselves. If they established beyond a shadow of a professional doubt that Eagleton had surmounted his problem, the brave thing would be to keep him on the ticket. Being something of a traditionalist, I was overwhelmed by the bizarre nature of the problem, as I felt the Senator was. This had never happened before; no one knew the rules. On the other hand, if the records left any doubt in the Senator's mind, then neither politics nor pity mattered; he would have no choice. I tried my best to cast the problem in strictly factual terms. Those records and what they contained could prove to be McGovern's salvation, not his ruin. If the records showed Eagleton to be sound and McGovern dismissed him out of political fear, that fact would get out and McGovern would be ruined. If the records showed any possibility of a recurring problem and McGovern kept Eagleton on the the ticket out of pity or weakness, then the safety and security of the nation were being jeopardized. The records were the key.

I ended my analysis by suggesting that the Senator talk to Eagleton at length on Tuesday, obtain his approval to have the records he would bring with him examined by trustworthy experts who would advise the Senator of their implications, and that the Senator then get together with Frank, me, and whomever else he trusted for political advice to make a decision. As our conversation ended, that seemed to be the course he would follow.

Throughout this 30-minute briefing, the Senator seemed somewhat distracted, even disconsolate. It was the first time I had talked to him at any length since the convention and, I was surprised at his lack of exuberance at his great victory, I asked him about it. "I can't explain it," he said. "Eleanor and I have both been kind of blue since Miami. It's been kind of a letdown emotionally."

JULY 22, 1972. At 10 A.M. about 30 campaign staff members, advisors, and representatives of various party elements gathered in a hall at Sylvan Lake in the Black Hills of South Dakota. This is a national park site with a couple of dozen cabins surrounding a central lodge and dining room. At the base of the peak where these facilities sit is a wash-basin-size pool called Sylvan Lake. I prepared an agenda and chaired the discussion, which covered issues, organization, finance, special groups, media, promotion and advertising, scheduling, electoral strategy, and allocation of resources, as well as a number of other topics. With a brief lunch break, the very productive session went until almost 4 P.M.

During the lunch break, the Senator was shown a *New York Times* article of that date which quoted a "campaign aide" as saying Larry O'Brien's role was merely symbolic and would have little responsibility in the campaign itself. This article came on the heels of dozens of "inside leaks," a problem we had only begun to suffer in the closing weeks of the nomination race. McGovern was furious. He seethingly told me who he thought had done it. When the crowd recollected in closed session that afternoon, the Senator berated the entire group, saying he wanted no more "highly placed aide" or "key McGovern official" statements ever again. He said the *Times* story was untrue and he would tell the press it was untrue. Anyone discovered giving out such stories, he said, would be dismissed from the campaign. He ended by saying that nothing that took place in the discussions that day was to be discussed with any members of the press.

By 6 P.M. the UPI wires were moving a story that McGovern had scalded his staff for leaking stories to the press.

I left the Black Hills Sunday to return to Washington and to finish putting a national campaign organization together. A great deal of work needed to be done very quickly which could not be done from South Dakota. Left behind with the Senator, besides Frank, were all his senior staff and advisors.

Frank had spent considerable time over the previous weekend negotiating with Knight newspaper reporters Bob Boyd and Clark Hoyt to hold off publication of a speculative story on Eagleton's health until the candidates could meet and determine a course. The Knight reporters had been working furiously on the story since the mysterious tip from the anonymous caller seven days before.

J U L Y 2 5 , 1 9 7 2 . At 1 P.M. the call I had been waiting for— Frank's report on the Senator's discussion with Eagleton and the content of those medical records—came through. Now we would know our course of action.

Frank: "You're not going to like this, but we're just going into a press conference."

Hart: "What!"

Frank: "Yeah. I've got a phone here in this hall where they're holding the press conference and there are just a couple of phones and I won't be able to talk very long because in about two minutes every reporter in the Western hemisphere is going to be heading for these two phones, but in the meantime I'm going to stand here talking to you with a smile on my face like I'm very pleased with what is about to happen even though it's really a disaster and I'm sure when you hear what's going to happen you'll agree it's a disaster. . . ."

Hart: "Frank, just tell me what the hell is going on."

Frank: "Well, what's going on is that George McGovern is just now walking up in front of all these reporters to tell them that Tom Eagleton has this problem, but that he's his running mate all the way. . . ."

Hart: "Frank—no, no, can't you stop it? We were going to talk it over. We were going to discuss it."

Frank: "Yeah, I know, we were, weren't we?" He chuckled bitterly.

Hart: "What about the records? What did the records show?"

Frank: "I don't know. He didn't bring them with him. They said the hospitals wouldn't let them out or something like that."

Hart: "What did Eagleton tell him? Why is he so sure?"

Frank: "I don't know. They met by themselves and I wasn't there."

I felt as if the bottom had dropped completely out of the campaign and that more than two years of work had just gone down the drain. And it had, in both cases.

JULY 26, 1972. Now the deluge began. Frank, obviously convinced that he could do more good in Washington than he had done in the Black Hills, returned. And by afternoon the reaction began to set in. The Senator firmly intended to stay with Eagleton when he unqualifiedly endorsed him at the press conference the day before. He meant it when he said a day later that he had no intention of asking Eagleton to leave the ticket, that he was behind him 1000 percent. But it was a serious miscalculation that left no room for movement in response to public reaction. And the reaction was swift.

Two sets of responses occurred simultaneously. The major campaign contributors who had pledged $3 million to $4 million in loans to get the campaign organization off the ground and the direct-mail program underway were calling in to cancel their loans. Within the first 72 hours up to 90 percent of the commitments were withdrawn, or seriously hedged pending the outcome of "the Eagleton thing." In addition, political leaders from almost every major state called in furious at Eagleton for what they considered to be his deception and upset with the candidate for his decision to keep him. If a leader was expressing simply his own point of view, we asked him to conduct a cross-section survey of other Democratic leaders in the state and report back in 24 hours. The headquarters switchboard, in the process of being married to the DNC switchboard, became almost unworkable for certain hours of the day, so many calls were coming in. We asked that a running total of the pros and cons be kept on the random callers.

Within hours after McGovern decreed that he intended to keep Eagleton on the ticket, Matt Troy, the Queens Democratic leader, publicly and loudly called for Eagleton's removal. Since this constituted the first breach in the official posture of Eagleton support, and Matt's statement was attracting press attention out of all proportion to its importance, I called him to suggest that it would be in the best interest of the campaign to line up behind McGovern on this. Matt said he wouldn't take such a public position without first checking it with McGovern.

Rather than continue the debate I let it go, for two reasons. First, we were now into the middle of the awful Eagleton week and, with increasing numbers of McGovern supporters around the country calling for Eagleton's dismissal, the possibility had substantially increased that the Senator might have to back off his initial strong support for him. Second, it was frankly not a matter of enough consequence to bother the Senator about. It was worth one call to Matt to try to calm him down, but it wasn't worth a series of calls to McGovern and then back to Matt and then back to McGovern, ad infinitum. Matt's outburst might have affected a few people in New York, but it certainly wasn't going to move substantial numbers of voters around the country. Besides, the candidate and the rest of us in Washington had many more important things to pursue during that period.

Accustomed to dealing with each other on a daily, year-round basis, the representatives of the national media based in New York and the New York politicians tend to lose sight of the fact that the politicians' feuds, quarrels, ambitions, and opinions are largely inconsequential to the rest of the country. The prevalent opinion that New York sets the political trend for the provinces couldn't be more wrong; it is, in fact, the most provincial of provinces. The key players in the 1972 Democratic drama came from South Dakota, Maine, Minnesota, Iowa, Oklahoma, Indiana, Washington state, and Missouri. Only the beleaguered Mayor Lindsay represented metropolis. Outside Queens, and certainly outside New York City, very few people care what Matt Troy or any of the other political figures in the city think.

By late Wednesday, however, a true national picture was beginning to emerge. Personal understanding, but political intolerance. The consensus from almost every side was: Eagleton must go. From New York, California, Illinois, Massachusetts, Ohio, Wisconsin, and at least two dozen other states, the political leadership was speaking uniformly—we can't win with Eagleton, we can't get a campaign off the ground; Eagleton will be the issue.

Our key state coordinators were digging into their new assignments, reorganizing their states to unify the party and the McGovern campaign. They were calling for money to open headquarters, hire staff, install phones. Time was short. My "patience and time" lecture, used so often in the nomination, wouldn't work. There was no time. If we were to defeat the Republicans, it would have to be done in August. But there was no money either. The campaign's initial financing, for which Henry and Miles had worked so hard, had disappeared.

Eagleton was in Los Angeles on his way to deliver a labor speech in Hawaii. In South Dakota, the candidates and their advisors had adopted a policy of revealing the entire medical problem in a single press conference and then refusing to comment on it further in a sort of "head-in-the-sand" attempt to make the problem go away. Obviously, it wouldn't. It was the hottest news story in years; it was red meat for journalists, and everyone should have realized that. Eagleton ran smack into the issue every time he opened his mouth in California. Finally, pressure forced the policy to be reversed and he began to talk about the problem openly.

Keeping Eagleton on the ticket out of personal sympathy and without first looking at the medical records was a major miscalculation. It was made by the principals on the grounds they could bull it through and hit it head-on once, and that the problem soon would go away; meanwhile, everyone would go on about his business. This led Eagleton off to California, Hawaii, and Missouri before his return to Washington the following weekend. It led McGovern to stay in the Black Hills on some sort of vacation theory. And it led Frank and me, as well as Doug Bennet, to return to Washington to carry out our daily affairs. So the players were spread all over the map. But if the worst possible thing can happen, it will, and, on top of everything else, it did.

Late Wednesday, Washington was alive with rumors about drunken-driving charges against Eagleton. Pursuing the policy, we did our best to beat the rumors down, but failed.

JULY 27, 1972. Any chance, however slim, of salvaging the ticket was destroyed by Jack Anderson's erroneous charges that Eagleton had a record of drunken driving. This was the wedge between the Eagleton and McGovern staffs. In his Hawaii speech to the Retail Clerks Union, Eagleton said he would voluntarily leave the ticket if "people are troubled by my presence on the ticket." At almost the same time, I was talking to Doug Bennet about the Anderson charges, insisting to know if there were any support for them whatsoever. I didn't suspect Bennet of concealing; I just thought he might not know. He scoured Missouri, spoke to Eagleton and found only two inconsequential traffic violations, neither of which involved drinking. I asked if there were any arrests that might have been covered up. Bennet assured me there had not been. But now the Eagleton side, up to this point very much at the pleasure of George McGovern, began to take the initiative. Bennet told me: "This is what we've been waiting for. Now we have the phony charges on the surface. We can prove they are lies and knock the other stuff down at the same time." Eagleton took the offensive on Thursday just as Senator McGovern began to re-assess his own position in the light of the mounting opposition to Eagleton. Anderson had changed the entire picture. While campaigning against the phony charges, Eagleton could somehow lump all the accusations together and present himself as the wronged man, the besieged man, the man against the system.

Faced now with a running mate who only hours before was publicly offering to leave the ticket at McGovern's pleasure but who was now out campaigning to salvage his wronged reputation, McGovern had to recapture the initiative or lose control altogether.

JULY 28, 1972. The Senator phoned Frank or me in Washington several times a day. On this Friday evening he called to say that he had visited with several reporters in an effort to confirm the impression that Eagleton's tenure was still under deliberation by both principals. But the reporters had begun to zero in on an apparent controversy brewing between the two camps. If the matter was still under consideration, why had Eagleton, just shortly before, said that *his* decision (an important new note that had crept into the Eagleton rhetoric) to stay on the ticket was "irrevocable" and that he would "never" withdraw. It didn't sound much like the contrite Tom Eagleton of two days before. The 1000 percent, plus Jack Anderson, had built up great self-confidence.

I also relayed to the Senator the information obtained from Bennet that Eagleton planned to do two network interviews on Sunday in Washington. The Senator, now deeply disturbed by his running mate's public campaign, asked me to call Bennet to see if those couldn't be cancelled. I got Bennet at home later that night and conveyed the Senator's message. We wanted to defuse the public controversy; Eagleton wanted to defend himself and rehabilitate his image. The two goals were absolutely incompatible. Bennet didn't think Eagleton could be turned around, but agreed to relay the message. I also paraphrased for Bennet a portion of a speech McGovern was preparing to make in South Dakota the next day which contained language about not knowing how all this would come out and the necessity of further deliberations on the course ahead. The following morning McGovern would reach Eagleton in San Francisco to read him the exact passage. It later appeared that Bennet was unhappy with me for not stating then that McGovern had made a decision to drop Eagleton. But I could hardly do so when I didn't know about such a decision myself. Indeed, the decision would not be made for 36 more hours, after McGovern's return to Washington.

J U L Y 2 9 , 1 9 7 2 . I told McGovern that Bennet did not think Eagleton would back off the television appearances and the Senator told me to call Bennet back and insist this be done. McGovern, I told Bennet, did not want Eagleton to go on nationwide television the next day. Bennet was bewildered as to why McGovern didn't tell Eagleton himself and said that that was what it would take—McGovern would have to tell Eagleton himself. He told me where Eagleton could be reached in Missouri later that day. Having pressed McGovern on the medical-records matter, and having been authorized by him to take it up with Bennet once more, I asked Bennet how we could get the records. Bennet talked about the reluctance of both doctors and hospitals when they had raised the matter the previous weekend—privileged information, professional ethics, doctor-patient relationship, and so forth. But he agreed to try again and let me know.

J U L Y 3 0 , 1 9 7 2 . The Senator had returned to Washington and a meeting was arranged at his home to reach some conclusions about the Eagleton matter. Earlier that morning, the new party Chairwoman, Jean Westwood, had called me to ask what I thought about her saying on Meet the Press that morning that she believed Eagleton should voluntarily step down. I told her that I thought it was a decision she should make herself, but that if she decided to do it she should notify the Senator beforehand. She did so. I called Bennet again. He said he had been able to reach only Eagleton's St. Louis doctor, and I asked if John Douglas or I could fly out to talk to him. Bennet said only if the doctor received handwritten authorization and a phone call from Eagleton himself, who was then somewhere between stops in Missouri. We discussed at great length the logistics of getting Eagleton to write the note and then transmitting it to the doctor by the time one of us got there in the early afternoon. I had already booked space on every Washington-St. Louis flight that day, and had checked continuing connections to Minnesota. After some more checking in Missouri, Bennet contacted me to say that it would be impossible to communicate the proper authorizations in time and that he doubted the doctor would be cooperative in any case. I pressed for the records further, knowing that only they could prevent the impending tragedy. They couldn't be obtained.

At 11 A.M. an all-day session began at McGovern's home involving the Senator, John Douglas, Henry Kimelman, Frank and myself and, later, Jean Westwood. We each reported and commented. Henry reported a dire financial picture with little hope for improvement so long as Eagleton was on the ticket. The initial lenders necessary to get the campaign off the ground had disappeared.

I gave a national political report. State political leaders, especially in the big states, were almost universally opposed to Eagleton, and each had conducted statewide telephone surveys among local leaders, who supported their judgments. In addition, there was for all practical purposes no Democratic Presidential campaign in the field. The workers, as well as the public at large, were mesmerized by the Eagleton drama and wouldn't come out of their trance until it was resolved. If money to get the organization underway didn't come in soon we would lose one of our few advantages—time—and probably lose the election. Finally, I concluded with my litany—we must see the records. By now I was appalled that so little attention had been paid to the issue of national interest and security. So far all we had was Eagleton's word that he was sound and, as good as that was, under the circumstances, it wasn't good enough. He himself had admitted he didn't know what his diagnosis was. The safety of the nation was involved. The burden was clearly on Eagleton, in strictly legal terms, to rebut the presumption that he might be incapacitated. He alone could do so, if anyone could, by getting the records and/or the doctors to assure McGovern. He had had a week in which to do so, and had not. Indeed, every effort we had made to get him to do so, or to help us get the records, had failed.

Jean's national political assessment was the same as mine. Frank reiterated his view that Eagleton would be *the* issue in the fall, that the Republicans would see to that. He had picked up evidence here and there of all sorts of sophisticated *ad hominem* attacks in preparation.

There was concluding discussion concerning the procedures for selecting a replacement running mate, with some initial suggestions of names. The field had, from our Miami experience, been substantially narrowed. The Senator asked Jean to begin to investigate the procedures in depth, including the earliest possible timetable for reconvening the national committee. He then summarized his thinking of the past week: He had made an initial decision that he had no choice but to stand behind the man he personally had selected; Eagleton should be given an opportunity to take his case to the public without the onus of the Presidential candidate's doubt hanging over him; time was needed to review the "medical situation" and obtain more background information; to prevent initial prejudice to Eagleton's case, he had to say he would have selected him again knowing the circumstances; finally, he had communicated with several prominent psychiatrists, one of whom—an extremely prominent man—had admitted failure in his efforts to educate the public concerning mental illness and had concluded that the public at large was unprepared to accept a potential President with a background like Eagleton's.

McGovern concluded that he saw no other course but to work out Eagleton's departure from the ticket during their meeting the next night.

The Sunday papers contained a re-issue of the first post-convention Gallup poll, which appeared July 21st. It showed Nixon leading McGovern 56 percent to 37 percent, with 7 percent undecided. The poll also measured a three-way race: Nixon, 46 percent; McGovern, 32 percent; Wallace, 18 percent. These were precisely the same figures at this point in 1968, and Hubert Humphrey had almost won that race.

J U L Y   3 1 ,   1 9 7 2 . Eighteen days after Eagleton's nomination, the candidates met alone in a Senate ante-room. Earlier, during a flight that morning to Louisiana for Senator Ellender's funeral, McGovern had asked Gaylord Nelson, a personal friend of both men and one of Eagleton's sponsors on the ticket, to meet with them. After almost 90 minutes, the three men emerged with a brief joint statement which was delivered at approximately 9 P.M.

McGovern, after the decision to remove Eagleton, finally got through to two of Eagleton's doctors by phone. What was said is not known. However, as a condition of his peaceful departure from the ticket, Eagleton insisted that McGovern's statement contain the following disclaimer: "I am fully satisfied that his health is excellent. . . . Health was not a factor." Instead, the Senator continued: "The public debate over Senator Eagleton's past medical history continues to divert attention from the great national issues that need to be discussed."

The events surrounding the selection of Senator Eagleton and his subsequent departure from the ticket cost George McGovern any chance he had to win the Presidency. In retrospect, all that took place thereafter was anticlimatic and politically inconsequential in terms of the final results of the election. The campaign was doomed when Eagleton was selected. We could not win with him or without him. There was no way out. Neither the manner in which the decision was made to keep him on the ticket, nor the negotiations which led to his departure were well handled. For both, I assume my share of blame.

Nor is the answer in a prior investigation of his background before the selection process. The kind of background investigation which a campaign is equipped to make would not have revealed his history of mental illness. The careful manner in which that information had been concealed in his home state for twelve years had succeeded in leaving ignorant Missouri's leading newspapers, including the *St. Louis Post-Dispatch*, distinguished for investigative journalism, and politicians, including Eagleton's colleague, Senator Stuart Symington. Those who claim the McGovern staff could, or should, have uncovered this kind of information about an individual not even under serious consideration prior to the convention don't know what they are talking about.

Nevertheless, all hope of salvaging the Eagleton candidacy vanished without the kind of supporting evidence the medical records or doctors' testimony might have provided. There were three possible bases for a decision on Eagleton's fate—personal, political, or factual. The decision to keep Eagleton was made on personal grounds; the decision to remove him, on political grounds. Both were wrong. The records, the medical evidence, should have been the basis for a decision in either case. The tragedy was in confusing an issue of national leadership and security with personal and political considerations.

MORNING

A U G U S T 1 , 1 9 7 2 . The resolution of the Eagleton matter created the sense of a fresh start, a new beginning. There was considerable feeling that the entire episode was a passing phenomenon, a nightmare from which we had just awakened. And once a replacement was found the campaign would really begin and all else would be forgotten in the all-consuming effort to defeat Richard Nixon.

Following the convention we moved into a much larger headquarters at 1910 K Street, N.W. We tempted fate in the cavalier manner of an under-dog. It was the former Muskie campaign headquarters. Previously the John Marshall Apartments, the tall, lean eight-story structure had been converted some years before to standard, if somewhat seedy, office space. On the top floor Larry O'Brien and his staff resided. The seventh floor contained the issues and research operations. The sixth floor housed the finance and fund-raising personnel. The Vice-Presidential staff was on the fifth floor. On the fourth floor was the campaign management and the political and organizational operations. Press and media and the entire scheduling and advance operations were on the third floor. The second contained a potpourri of printing, polling, special groups, and other activities. On the ground floor were the administrative wing of the campaign, the volunteer operation—including a constantly occupied day-care center for the children of volunteers—and the supply offices.

The building, with its cold, stark, bare interior, and windows barred to prevent burglaries, had the ambiance of an Alcatraz. The two elevators functioned only sporadically, thus causing constant traffic on the dark, narrow stairways. Nevertheless, for the first time, I had an office to myself large enough to hold small meetings in. Staff members had to pass through three doors and get past Marcia Johnston before asking for a raise or asking what I thought of the newest poster. Also, people off the street had a more difficult time finding the campaign management to discuss "the idea that would win the campaign." The small lobby was used as a bicycle parking area and buffet restaurant. Twice a week Joe Pirozzolo cooked lasagna, chicken cacciatore, or some other tasty dish served hot, in some miraculous manner, to staff members having the change. The cuisine was among the best in Washington.

During August's first week, Henry and Miles started trying to resurrect the lost lenders, Morris worked on the direct-mail program, the national political organization was being restructured, and the Senator searched for a new running mate.

The Democratic National Committee was called back into session for August 7th through the 9th. It was the "mini-convention." During this period we were establishing state coordinators in each state, together with headquarters and modest seed-money budgets, so that preliminary organizational work could be completed by the end of August. Also, we were completing the national campaign budget, on both a line item and chronological, week-by-week basis. I had only irregular contact with the candidate, who was talking to a number of his Senate colleagues, once again, about the second spot on the ticket.

A U G U S T   2 ,   1 9 7 2 . We had a discussion at the Senator's home concerning the Vice-Presidency. A number of the campaign people were there. This time the characteristics and qualities stressed most strongly were experience, stability, public exposure, dependability, reliability. Realizing the need to inspire public confidence quickly, the names discussed reflected this awareness: Humphrey, Muskie, O'Brien and Senator Mike Mansfield; Ribicoff again, then somewhat younger men or newer faces, Governor Lucey again, Governor Askew again, Senators Bayh and Mondale again; Senator Lloyd Bentsen of Texas, strongly proposed by Henry, and Sargent Shriver.

McGovern had already talked with Humphrey, who announced his refusal, publicly and elaborately. Several calls were made that night, including one to Mansfield, who, like Humphrey, removed himself from consideration, albeit more modestly. The meeting ended with a decision that the Senator would talk with Muskie the following day.

A U G U S T   4 ,   1 9 7 2 . The Senator called around mid-day to say that Muskie was definitely interested and had asked his staff to meet with our staff. A mid-afternoon meeting was arranged at the Muskie home to include Berl Bernard, fund-raiser Arnold Picker and Senate aide Don Nichol, Henry Kimelman, Frank, and myself. The fact that such a meeting was even taking place struck me as one of the greater ironies of a heavily ironic political season. After some polite minuets, the Muskie people made it clear they were interested in three considerations in return for having Muskie on the ticket: a financial formula for liquidating the lingering Muskie campaign debt, a written apology from Stewart Mott, who had waged his own campaign against Muskie in the spring, and control over the configuration of the Vice-Presidential campaign jet. It seemed to me the whole world had gone mad. This was a Kurt Vonnegut tour through Disneyland, H. L. Mencken's version of *The Making of the President*. There was no discussion of campaign issues, no interest in campaign strategy, little apparent concern for saving the free world. While democracy tottered in the balance, we seriously debated the interior decoration of an airplane!

We returned to report a rather raucous version of the meeting to the Senator only to discover that Muskie had gone off to Maine to ponder what he considered to be a firm offer. We discussed how the offer might still be so conditioned as to make it less attractive, if not outright un-acceptable. Henry contacted Picker to indicate we might have difficulty meeting the financial conditions and a call was made to Maine to indicate reluctance among some of our supporters. These negotiations became comic relief in a period when there was very little to laugh about.

AUGUST 5, 1972. I went to the Senator's home to await word from Muskie. We discussed the choice if Muskie decided not to take it and all agreed—Frank, Henry, and I, as well as the Senator—on Shriver. From the time Shriver's name was mentioned it was clouded by con-tinuing rumors that he had seriously alienated members of the Kennedy family, including Senator Edward Kennedy and Mrs. Robert Kennedy, by not resigning his appointment as U.S. Ambassador to France and return-ing to the United States to campaign for Robert Kennedy in 1968. Like most popular rumors and myths surrounding the Kennedys, this story had taken on the quality of legend over the years. McGovern discussed it that week with Kennedy and found it to be untrue. After the call came from Senator Muskie that he was not interested after all, we tracked Shriver down at Hyannis. Intermediaries had sounded him out on his availability beforehand and found him to be eager. He scrambled up from the tennis court when he heard the call was from McGovern. From my end, I heard:

"Sarge, this is George McGovern. Say, Sarge, we've been going over this Vice-Presidential thing pretty thoroughly for the past few days, as I'm sure you know, and I want you to know that everyone here, in-cluding myself, would like very much to have you on this ticket. [pause] Well, that's great Sarge. I really appreciate it. We've got a lot of work to do, but I know we can win. It's great to have you with us."

The candidate with his second running mate.

Afterwards, I asked the Senator what Shriver's response had been and he related that Shriver said: "George, I want you to know that it's a great thrill and an honor and I'll work my head off. Also, I can tell you there are no skeletons in *my* closet!" We know that to be the case. We had checked Shriver and everyone else out *very* thoroughly.

AUGUST 6, 1972. Shriver swung into action with the energy for which he is famous, filling his Maryland estate with "old Kennedy people" by Sunday morning for all-day planning and organization meetings. After a Van Dyk issues briefing, I came on with the game plan and organizational background. By now we were all getting used to this drill. I thought to myself, if I give this to one more Vice President I'll have it memorized. That meeting was generations encountering each other at a crossroad. I tried to talk about grassroots organization, gypsy-guerrilla advance people, and citizen-volunteer canvassers, while the Kennedy people from 1960 and 1968 barked orders, summoned successful lawyers away from lucrative practices, and negotiated heavy salaries. It was like Che Guevara meeting General Patton.

AUGUST 8, 1972. The mini-convention of the Democratic Party nominated its second Vice President for the first time in its history. Everyone gave very good speeches. To make history, and the occasion, complete, all the caucuses active in Miami showed up again on cue making the same demands and insisting on the same rights. It was difficult to tell whether the oldest democratic institution on earth was becoming a movable feast or a traveling circus.

AUGUST 10, 1972. As part of the comprehensive fall campaign strategy originally discussed with the Senator in late June and ratified in the Black Hills meeting on July 22nd, we proposed that he make three three-day trips in August, each to be a low-profile visit with average voters to listen to the issues and problems they deemed most important. No huge crowds or rallies or speeches, just the candidate out talking to and maintaining contact with the people. We wanted to keep him before the public in the long period between the end of the convention and the traditional campaign opening on Labor Day. We did not want to abdicate media coverage to the Republicans for six weeks.

As a kick-off, the Senator returned to the J. F. MacElwayne Shoe Co. in Manchester, New Hampshire, where, on February 18th, he felt his Presidential campaign first taking off, where the workers had come up to greet him. The return was a sentimental journey and communicated for the first time in too many weeks the real George McGovern out campaigning among and listening to real people. He made stops in Hartford and Providence on that trip, largely to heal the wounds of party regulars and start a unified campaign in New England. The trip ended with a luncheon with editors of *The New York Times,* which later endorsed McGovern.

By the time Senator McGovern took to the road in mid-August, the roles and responsibilities of the key staff members were fairly well defined. The iceberg analogy applies with some accuracy: the visible element of the campaign—the candidates and their traveling parties—represented roughly a tenth of the total activities and energies; nine-tenths was only dimly perceived by the public.

McGovern had decided in June that Frank should travel with him during the fall and that I should remain in Washington overseeing the national campaign operations at the headquarters. It was hoped that some of the issues problems might be resolved with this arrangement and, more positively, that Frank could help translate the campaign's accomplishments to the national press corps. Further, we believed that with tighter coordination of the efforts of the speech writers, press aides, and advisors, confusing and contradictory "insider" leaks could be prevented and a more coherent public image of the campaign presented.

With Larry O'Brien acting as liaison with and ambassador to the leadership of the regular party, I was then free to deal with the daily campaign operations—media programs, field staff and operations, budgets and expenditures, scheduling, and national headquarters functions. In addition, special problems arose with our efforts to relate the campaign to the black community and to the Chicanos, and to respond satisfactorily to the demands of the women's caucus, the farmers, the students, the elderly, or the dozens of other special-interest groups. An immense amount of time was required to solve the problems of particular groups. Often it seemed that the general electorate, if it existed at all, was overwhelmed by the insistent demands of the special-concern groups. Our efforts to beam a uniform message to all voters were unsuccessful. In the short time we had we were unable to discover the formula for a new political cement to replace the glue that had formerly held the old coalitions together.

Contrary to some popular misconceptions, the campaign was not run from the candidate's airplane—except to the degree that a campaign is defined as the candidate's statements. The decisions concerning the allocation of campaign resources—money, time, and manpower—were made from the Washington headquarters. Problems arose from this arrangement when decisions were made on the airplane which contradicted those already made in Washington or which were not based upon all the information available to the national staff in Washington. Although such occurrences were fairly rare, a certain press mythology developed that confusion was constant between the headquarters and the traveling party. It seemed to make good copy. The division of responsibility between the traveling party and the national headquarters was both natural and functional. Confusion was infinitely less than it was made out to be and occurred only in the few instances when those on the plane overlooked the existence of the national headquarters.

A U G U S T   16 ,   1 9 7 2. The Senator was on a mid-Western tour, talking mostly to farmers about their problems, as well as with blue-collar workers. He made stops in Youngstown, Ohio, Springfield, Illinois, visited a farm at Rochester, Illinois, and ended the trip in Milwaukee and Racine, Wisconsin. At Youngstown and Racine, Charles Guggenheim filmed footage for our media program scheduled to begin in mid-September.

As he was emerging from a hotel elevator in Springfield, he was met by reporters, one of whom handed him a UPI wire story saying that Pierre Salinger had just returned after conducting discussions with the North Vietnamese representatives in Paris on behalf of Presidential candidate George McGovern and had recommended to the North Vietnamese that they negotiate a settlement with President Nixon since they could expect no better settlement if McGovern were elected.

McGovern, caught completely off guard by the story, not having talked to Pierre for 30 days, and not knowing the substance of Pierre's actual conversations with the North Vietnamese, denied that he had given Salinger any instructions or authorization to represent his views to the North Vietnamese. McGovern is rarely caught off guard on questions of substance, but nothing aggravates him more than to be confronted with a statement that one of his aides has made and to be asked to account for it. His undoubted pique at Pierre for talking to a reporter before talking to him, plus his uncertainty as to what the facts truly were, led the Senator to resort to a political device he had never felt the need of before—denial. The old political adage, when in doubt, deny. Buy time until you can find out the facts.

The facts in this case were that Pierre *was* operating under authorization to discuss the release of prisoners in connection with a proposal by North Vietnam that a McGovern representative visit Hanoi to inspect bombing damage. To keep these discussions clearly separate from the Paris peace negotiations, Pierre told the North Vietnamese (before leaving, he told John Holum he would do this) that they should not construe any McGovern-related contacts with them as a suggestion that peace negotiations should await the election outcome, or as an indication of more favorable terms available under a McGovern administration and, thus, an invitation to prolong the war.

The fact that Pierre was operating under Senator McGovern's instructions, of course, did come out. Since the specifics of the events never were clearly understood, the net effect of the episode was to make the Senator look duplicitous, even devious. Like the firm resolve to back Eagleton, it appeared on its face to be another serious instance of waffling at best, or political chicanery at worst. In any case, the Salinger affair was a black mark and a serious threat to the candidate's increasingly more fragile credibility.

For two years I had seen McGovern perform occasionally brilliant feats in responding to inquiries from the press and the public. He has one of the quickest minds in American politics. He combines erudition and directness, sophistication and guilelessness. He seldom has to hesitate or calculate. Most of all, he possesses great judgment. Therefore, when a series of events such as the Salinger affair occurred in August, it was impossible not to conclude that the Senator's normally incisive judgment had been temporarily disoriented, like a great ship's compass, by the unprecedented Eagleton misfortune. All the difficulties of August, to my mind, sprang from that.

Except for the few days set aside for that marionette performance called the Republican National Convention, where even the prayers were typed in the script weeks before, the only journalistic game in town was the Democratic campaign. From mid-July until Labor Day and even throughout the fall, McGovern and the entire campaign were subject to more intensive scrutiny than any other Presidential campaign in history. The Eagleton tragedy shattered a myth constructed by the press itself that the McGovern campaign up to and through the convention was a Cinderella political operation: a Henry Fonda prairie statesman, rags-to-riches candidate surrounded by brilliant strategists, cool, calculating organizers, German generals commanding Irish troops. This analysis helped explain a political phenomenon, an event that wasn't supposed to happen. Then, when the prairie statesman turned out to be all too human, and when the "brilliant strategists" made mistakes like everyone else, the errors were amplified a hundredfold. Some elements of the press began to respond to the campaign as if they had been deliberately deceived in July. Minor occurrences overlooked in the rush of pre-nomination success became, during the post-Eagleton period, major blunders and inexcusable mistakes. It was an obvious, documentable shift in treatment, and Richard Nixon was shrewd enough to let it run its course through the fall.

AUGUST 17, 1972. After working in the California primary, Max Factor, his wife, and young child moved to Washington during the pre-convention period to spend full-time on the fall campaign. Max located an apartment in the Sheraton-Park apartment building. Late this night, Max's apartment was forcibly entered by several men who identified themselves, only after considerable questioning, as Secret Service agents. They wanted to know what Max was doing in the apartment. Likewise, Max wanted to know what *they* were doing in the apartment. They told Max he would have to move. He replied that he had a binding rental agreement with the hotel management and had no intention of moving. It was a nice apartment; just exactly what Max and his family wanted. The previous occupant of the apartment had been John Connally, then Secretary of the Treasury.

It turned out the occupant of the apartment immediately above Max was Spiro Agnew. Max would have to leave, the Secret Service agents told him, because his occupancy of that apartment constituted a "threat to the safety of" the Vice President. Max, taking note of the increasing speculation about John Connally's future in Republican politics and the question of succession to Mr. Nixon, said: "Gentlemen, I think the previous occupant constituted a much greater threat to the safety of the Vice President than I do." The Secret Service didn't think that was funny.

A U G U S T   1 9 ,   1 9 7 2 . About the time of the "mini-convention," McGovern announced the appointment of Congressman Frank Thompson, Jr. as chairman of the Democratic voter registration drive. Within days after the California primary, we had begun planning for a massive voter registration drive in the fall. Miles Rubin and Max Factor, who had been so instrumental in the computerized get-out-the-vote drive in the California primary, were particularly determined to see that the statistical and structural background for large-scale registration got underway as quickly as possible. The people in the regional desk operation had begun to collect data, registration statistics and state laws, and Max supplemented this effort during the month prior to the convention. Like other parts of the campaign apparatus, a national voter registration organization was being established during the peak of the Eagleton controversy.

Congressman Thompson was singled out by the Senator out of respect for his demonstrated legislative abilities and for the experience he had gained in 1960 organizing John Kennedy's voter registration efforts. The director of the program on a daily basis under Thompson's guidance was Anne Wexler, who had worked so effectively during the convention. Because voter registration would affect all Democratic races and because we were already crowded at the campaign headquarters, the program was physically housed at the DNC.

As another element in the mix, in late June, Fred Dutton prepared and published through the daily press a lengthy memorandum which analyzed the voting strength of the new, young voters and suggested that therein lay the key to the ultimate McGovern triumph. The memo set the pool of potential voters at 25 million and proposed a figure of 18 million who could be registered. Once in the hands of the reporters it was treated as official campaign strategy and elicited dozens of ponderous news stories throughout the fall. This was the basis of the McGovern campaign strategy; this was how it was going to be done. The only difficulty was that it was *not* official McGovern campaign strategy and had never been adopted as such. It was one man's thoughtful analysis and nothing more. If it had the candidate's official sanction, he managed to keep it rather secret. The fact of the matter was that the registration of 18 million new voters was an impossibility.

Regarding the terms and conditions of Congressman Thompson's involvement in the registration drive, great controversy later developed. I was not party to the Senator's conversation with Thompson. Putting the pieces together afterward, it appears that Thompson told McGovern he would need $2 million to $2.5 million to run a successful registration drive. McGovern apparently said something like, fine, registration is one of our highest priorities, talk to Gary and Henry and the other campaign people and they will see that you get what you need. Thompson took that to mean he would get his money. McGovern meant it to mean that he should work it out with us and, of course, we would give him as much as we could. What I could have told both of them was that under early August conditions we would be lucky to have $2 million to run the *entire* Presidential campaign in the next 30 to 45 days.

In mid-August while out of Washington, I received a frantic call from Anne Wexler who wondered where the quarter of a million dollars was. What quarter of a million dollars, I asked. The quarter of a million for voter registration, she answered. I didn't have the vaguest idea what she was talking about. I told her that as soon as I saw a voter registration budget we could discuss the non-existent quarter of a million. Shortly thereafter, I met with Congressman Thompson and Anne to go over the budget and explain the financial facts of life. We had very little money. Highest priority was to keep the candidate's planes in the air. The payroll had to be met. Rent, phones, and overhead had to be paid. Production money was needed to prepare television and radio spots as well as newspaper and literature layouts. The state coordinators were screaming, not in sequence now, but all at once. There was no money to begin an organization.

I didn't sense much sympathy from the voter-registration people. Since he had negotiated his arrangement directly with the candidate, Thompson believed he had a firm dollar commitment and the money would come from some sacrosanct pot. We analyzed his budget proposal item by item and worked it down to a more realistic $1.2 million. Since registration would close in most states in early October, 30 days before the election, the registration money had to be put into the states in August and September to do any good.

As the August days passed, the voter-registration program was to become an even greater headache. Rather than use the existing campaign structure of regional desks and state coordinators, the registration unit established its own desk system, its own cadre of organizers and its own national network of state contacts, Costly duplication, at best, and empire building, at worst, was the judgment of many in the campaign headquarters. Rather than send the state coordinator one lump-sum each week to be used for organizational activities directed especially toward voter registration, the voter-registration people insisted on a separate budget, which meant that the beleaguered state coordinator got one check which was about half what he needed and that the other half was being spent in the state to duplicate organizational efforts he was making. The national financial people, particularly Miles and Henry, were highly critical of the registration effort and felt I was not being tough enough on Thompson. Thompson, on the other hand, didn't know me and, therefore, like a good politician, didn't trust me. When I told him we could only send over "X" dollars that week, he thought I was holding out on him and circumventing his agreement with the candidate. It was, needless to say, not a happy period. Harsh, bitter, divisive, behind-the-back gossip became a daily occurrence inside the McGovern campaign for the first time in over two years. Adversity was beginning to divide rather than to unite.

AUGUST 23, 1972. We always knew the "Wallace vote" could be critical. If Wallace were to enter the race as a third-party candidate, he would have to draw votes away from Nixon, making the race as close as it turned out to be between Nixon and Humphrey in 1968. If Wallace were not in the race, and it was a foregone conclusion following the May shooting that he would not be, then we had to attract a considerable number of those voters or we would lose badly. The simplest way to attract those voters was to receive Wallace's endorsement. Therefore, when I was contacted in August by Wallace representatives, I made considerable effort to meet with them.

They were Tom Turnipseed and Dr. Peter Beeter. They contrived an elaborate and surreptitious entry to my office to prevent detection. They closed the office door, pulled their chairs against my table-desk, and began a breathless, semi-whispered, discussion. Turnipseed: "Can you be trusted? I mean, can you *really* be trusted?" What kind of a question is that? Of course, I can be trusted. Beeter: "Who do you want to be

President? I mean, who do you *really* want to be President?" These guys used "really" like a secret-society code word. Not knowing exactly what the correct answer was, I played it straight: "McGovern. I haven't spent two years of my life working for Nixon." Turnipseed; tall, coiffured, sartorial, Alabama-to-the eyeballs: "Look, we'd like to make a deal with you right here and now. This Shriver isn't going to make it. Man, they're going to find out so much stuff about him, that it'll make Eagleton look perfect. Believe me. Shriver won't last on this ticket a week. Those reporters are out there now just digging up everything they can find and there's plenty." Beeter, short, unsartorial, Lebanese millionaire: "Do you know what we're saying to you?" No, I don't. These preliminaries, which had now occupied many minutes of leaning-across-the-desk, finger-on-the-chest, hushed-voice, furtive-look-over-the-shoulder, had begun to make the Socratic method look simple. Beeter: "What we're telling you is that pretty soon you're going to need another Vice President and George Corley Wallace is your man." The mind boggled.

I tried to find out if they knew something about Shriver no one else in the Western hemisphere knew. They didn't "really," but the shadows of doubt being cast would have frightened strong men. I knew Shriver to be clean to the very margin of sainthood. His frank and open religiosity made some politicians uncomfortable. No; no skeletons in his closet. How about the other side of Beeter's double bombshell. Had Wallace sent them? Did he know they were there? Which of the byzantine Wallace factions did they represent? What did they "really" want? I got a mish-mash of side-of-the-eye knowing looks, political homily, Cornelia name-dropping, and damn-shame state-of-the-world comedy. Turnipseed delivered a Rabelaisian description of attending the American Party convention as Governor Wallace's representative and getting strong-armed out of the hall by fascist sergeants-at-arms. "By God, I tell you I was scared. I thought those gorillas were going to kill me. I knew they had guns and they got my arm behind my back and one of them got his arm around my throat (here he was up demonstrating) and carried me out of there and if I had resisted they would have killed me right there. By God, it was scary. I thought I was in Hitler's Germany. That's just what it was like. I know now why you liberals are afraid of those people. They're crazy!"

I thought over and over to myself—why can't all the people who want to know what politics is "really" like be in this room?

AUGUST 25, 1972. Despite and amidst the incredible lunacy, the political organization was being welded and hammered back together throughout August. Reporting directly to me were three regional coordinators, Harold Himmelman, with responsibility for fifteen Eastern states and the District of Columbia, Eli Segal, 16 states in the central region, and Rick Stearns, 19 Western states. The regional coordinators had desk systems with an officer responsible for daily problem-solving in five or six states each. In each of the states, a state coordinator operated in much the same fashion as our primary state coordinators—establishing a campaign committee composed of a cross section of Democrats, recruiting staff and setting up headquarters, installing phones, distributing literature, raising money, and generally acting as the state campaign manager.

In late July, a considerable effort was begun to attract seasoned veterans, particularly of the previous Kennedy campaigns, to assume leadership roles in the major states—Steven Smith for New York, John Seigenthaler for California, and others of their caliber—on the ground that they would be better equipped to mediate political gang wars in the larger, more complex states and negotiate with elements of the party recently defeated by our younger organizers. Contrary to the erroneous allegations of some political columnists, substantial and prolonged attempts were made for a number of weeks to attract older, presumably more "regular" leaders. But McGovern was not a Kennedy. He did not evoke the same loyalties in the same people. Their commitment to him was not of the order required to cause these kinds of people to drop their personal and professional obligations and race off to the political wars again. And the same was true, by and large, of key supporters of other former candidates, Humphrey, Muskie, McCarthy, or Johnson. We had learned this through bitter experience in the nomination race and, regrettably, even the spectre of a continued Nixon regime was insufficient motivation to change the situation.

But we didn't suffer organizationally. The McGovern campaign had collected and developed its own generation, its own breed and network of political leaders, and they were the finest in the country. What they lacked in reputation and, therefore, political muscle, they more than made up for with energy, commitment, and raw organizational genius.

Following the Eagleton nightmare, and then through demoralizing rumblings of power struggles and the Salinger incident, the work went forward in the field. Throughout August, hundreds of headquarters and storefront offices were opened, thousands of phones installed, millions of pieces of literature printed, hundreds of thousands of volunteers recruited. Money was raised, strategy was mapped and plans were made. Diplomatic missions were carried out to elements of the regular party to heal wounds and assuage grievances. This massive, monumental organizational effort was the great unreported story of the fall.

Each state coordinator, every local organizer, all McGovern staff members at every level were given the same policy: You *will* cooperate to the fullest with the Democratic Party organization at every level, or you will not work for this campaign. The official and unofficial attitude of the McGovern campaign was intolerance for élitism, arrogance, or disregard for other Democrats. The McGovern campaign was the Democratic Party campaign, and anyone who disagreed with that policy was dismissed. To my knowledge, few disagreed. When a report was received of local conflict between our original supporters and other Democrats, I attempted to deal with it personally through the state coordinator, most of whom will vouch for the fact I resolved disputes against our own people.

On the positive side, all state coordinators knew—few had to be told —that our chances for success were dependent upon our ability to weld the Democratic Party back together. Compared to 1968, this did not seem to be that monumental a task. Given the original 1970 "left-centrist" strategy and the efforts made in the spring to avoid divisiveness and contention with party regulars, the schism can be seen as a result not of the McGovern campaign, but of the "stop-McGovern" effort, which led not only to the bitter California credentials fight but also to the final destruction of a Chicago compromise. In light of that, it is aggravating in the extreme to hear the McGovern campaign criticized as a narrow, fractional element of the party. Our campaign organizers, workers, and supporters earned the title of Democratic "regulars," equals of anyone in party loyalty.

AUGUST 29, 1972. McGovern spelled out the central campaign issues in his Miami acceptance speech. First, he said that Nixon was "the fundamental issue of this campaign." Then he targeted integrity and honesty in government: "this is the time for truth." He traced the pattern of deception, through four administrations, to the Vietnam war, stating that he had "a *public* plan for peace" based upon immediate cessation of hostilities. He urged a foreign policy founded upon "turning away from excessive preoccupation overseas to rebuilding our own nation. . . . The greatest contribution America can make to our fellow mortals is to heal our own great but deeply troubled land." As to our national defense, he promised that "America will keep its defenses alert and fully sufficient to meet any danger," not only for ourselves but for our allies elsewhere, particularly Europe and Israel. But, he added, "National strength includes the credibility of our system in the eyes of our own people as well as the credibility of our deterrent in the eyes of others abroad." Regarding the economy, "The highest domestic priority of my Administration will be to ensure that every American able to work has a job," even if the government must guarantee it. In the area of welfare, McGovern promised to end the "hopeless welfare mess" and substitute a governmental assurance of "an income adequate to a decent life" to those unable to work. He committed himself to an end of economic controls that let profits and prices soar and wages be depressed. He mentioned a system of national health insurance and stricter enforcement of drug laws. Finally, he promised a tax structure where "honest work must be rewarded by a fair and just tax system," one that would close loopholes and tighten taxes on inherited and invested wealth. He closed that speech with the familiar plea, "come home, America." These were the issues and this was the message George McGovern carried to the country throughout the fall of 1972.

After weeks of re-study, review, revision, and slide-ruling, the Senator's economic package, originally presented in January and February and severely criticized in the California primary, was prepared for re-presentation. It was spelled out in a detailed, thoughtful speech before the New York Society of Security Analysts. His proposal, premised upon a "balanced full employment economy," outlined, first, savings to be realized from reductions in present budgetary levels. The Senator promised to cut the military budget by approximately $10 billion in each of the following years by reductions in armaments, missiles, planes and ships (according to the alternative defense budget released in January), and troops, particularly among NATO troops in Europe. Second, the Senator promised a "fair share tax reform" which would raise approximately $22 billion in additional revenue by 1975. The reforms would include ending capital gains preference—"money made by money should be taxed at the same rate as money made by men," closing loopholes relating to unreasonably large inheritances, oil and gas depletion allowances and real estate tax shelters, revising tax provisions relating to tax-exempt municipal bonds, closing farm investment loopholes, and repealing the accelerated depreciation allowances for corporations.

Maximum tax rates would be reduced under the proposal and estate and gift tax provisions would be replaced with a single accessions tax. The Senator calculated the total increase in revenues from the tax reform and defense spending cutbacks would total approximately $54 billion.

With regard to his domestic agenda, he singled out a property tax relief system which would transfer approximately $15 billion in federal funds to local school systems. He also proposed a national income insurance program as an alternative to the welfare mess. This included the guaranteed-job pledge, supported by government-sponsored employment if necessary, at a possible cost of $6 billion. It also included expansion of Social Security at a cost of $3 billion to include complete coverage for the aged, blind, and disabled. Finally, a program costing $5 billion was posed which would guarantee an annual minimum income in cash and food stamps for families with no other income who are unable to work. These programs could all be carried out, the Senator contended, without increasing the taxes of any family which depended on earned income rather than investments.

The economic package met with generally favorable reviews from economists. Indeed, some of the nation's leading economic experts had helped prepare it. But it didn't silence the Republicans from a continuing campaign throughout the fall directed at earlier proposals.

AUGUST 30, 1972. Earlier in the month, after the dust from the move had settled and everyone had occupied an office, we implemented a system of informal staff meetings. Three times a week, the first thing in the morning, the people responsible for the campaign's various departments and functions gathered to report briefly on their respective activities and exchange information necessary to carry out the daily campaign routine. In an effort to keep these sessions informal and brief, I suggested that they be held in a room with no chairs. People tend to hold very short meetings when they are standing up. Most meetings are a waste of time; their only useful purpose is to expedite the exchange of information and to eliminate the need for that other great institutional nightmare, the memo. Decisions are not made in meetings. Individuals make decisions. At best, groups merely ratify them. Finally, most people in an organization to do not need to know everything that everyone else is doing.

The staff meetings were unstructured. That is to say, aside from myself there was no ordained chairman and no fixed agenda. I didn't think, with a 90-day campaign, we had the luxury of wasting three mornings, or even one half day, a week talking to each other. I knew what I had to do and I was certain everyone else knew his or her job. And all of us should have known that none of our duties would get done with all of us sitting around talking. In short, I believed in a highly centralized reporting system and a highly decentralized functional system. Only later did Gene Pokorny conceptualize what this meant and help me realize why it made some people in the campaign unhappy.

AUGUST 31, 1972. The "morning" of the campaign day was over. The first full month of three full months had raced by. We had made considerable progress on the organizational front with very little money. Each of the elements of the body seemed to be healthy—media, issues, political organization, voter registration, the Vice-Presidential operation, scheduling; fund-raising was beginning to pick up, and the candidate had gotten around the country. But we had encountered disastrous luck throughout the month with coordination of statements and recovering credibility from the long night of the Eagleton matter. Too much public attention was still being paid to the internal workings of the campaign, to which person had what authority, to the rumors of internal conflict and controversy.

The headquarters projected the impression of an embattled garrison. In stark contrast to the computerized, sanitized, corporate offices of the Committee to Re-Elect the President (CREEP), our informality and openness, not to say casual messiness, non-plussed most of the reporters, who usually had to dust off their own chairs to sit on. The surroundings were barren, stark, functional, informal—women in jeans, men without coats or ties—and pervaded with an unbounded optimism and wry humor. And the continuing lunacy: bicycles and Joe Pirozollo's portable restaurant in the lobby, children escaping from the day-care center, staff members' pets roaming the halls, screams and table-pounding bursting occasionally from some office, wandering minstrels strumming on the steps, bizarre, ad-hoc, poster-oriented interior decorating schemes in the offices, the conventional Shriver staff seeking shelter from this nuttiness in their offices, volunteers and well-wishers arriving in a steady stream to propose some far-out promotional idea, new slogan, or television spot that would solve all our problems. A human maelstrom. An exquisite madness.

The Watergate affair led us to retain Walter Sheridan, the principal investigator in the Justice Department's organized-crime section under Attorney General Robert Kennedy in the 1960s and an expert in the murky world of information collection, espionage, and detection. It seemed the better part of valor to have our own in-house counter-spy, if for no other reason than to alert us to the range of possible tricks available to those with the financing, manpower, and technology.

Walter Sheridan came and went pretty much on his own and dealt primarily with Frank, his friend from former Kennedy days. Although I am unaware of specific acts of treachery which he prevented or new items of information regarding Republican espionage which he unearthed, Sheridan's very presence was a form of insurance in the weird political atmosphere in which we operated in 1972, and, like most successful acts of self-preservation, proved its worth in the absence of greater harassment.

George Cunningham, administrative chief of the headquarters, supplemented our modest security precautions in the fall by having two or three key telephones, including the private line though which I conducted most of the vital campaign business, electronically "swept" every night to reveal evidence of listening devices.

Although we had no iron-clad means of detecting such things, we assumed that Republican operatives had been insinuated into our headquarters. And although a great volume of information could be accumulated by someone surreptitiously copying documents found on desks or listening outside office doors, there are, in fact, few true secrets in politics. Most of the information a spy might collect in this manner was already in the public domain, or would be soon, and precious little could be used for purposes of subversion or counter-attack.

Out of the post-campaign Watergate investigations did come the information that a special unit in the CREEP specialized in acquiring advance copies of the McGovern and Shriver travel schedules to provide an opportunity to follow up as quickly as possible with a "surrogate" appearance. This may have had certain limited value, although even that is doubtful. If we had spies among us, they were certainly agreeable people, and undoubtedly the best that money could buy.

AFTERNOON

SEPTEMBER 1, 1972. A day earlier, the equilibrium forged from a tempestuous month of campaign uncertainties was shattered by Larry O'Brien's statement to reporters that he was extremely dissatisfied with the campaign's operations and, unless they got straightened out shortly, he would quit the campaign. Upon reading the statements in the papers, I was dumbfounded. I had made a number of trips to Larry's office to brief him on overall plans and activities, media programs, organizational progress, budgets, schedules, and the like. He had received briefings from the regional coordinators. There had been one or two extremely lengthy meetings in his office to discuss media plans particularly. And members of his staff, Stan Griegg and John Stewart usually, were regularly in attendance at our informal morning staff meetings.

After we had worked so hard to bolster campaign morale in Washington and around the country in the aftermath of the Eagleton catastrophe, after we had spent hours on the phone encouraging our workers and supporters in each state, urging them to forget about the past and forge ahead, assuring them that the troubles had passed, and just as we felt the campaign was getting on its feet, Larry's statements came as a crushing blow.

Heartsick, I went immediately up to his office. I told him that the people in the building were shocked and disappointed, that I couldn't understand why we couldn't have talked about his problems before he announced them to the public, and asked specifically what his objections were. I had carried all the campaign budgets, which represented not only weeks of work but also, in financial terms, a complete scheme of the campaign priorities. I spread them on his desk and in five minutes laid out the campaign in as concise and direct a manner as a Presidential campaign has ever been explained to anyone.

Larry professed considerable surprise that his statements had received such attention. He had merely been making some off-hand remarks, he said, and didn't particularly think they would be of any interest to anyone. I swallowed hard on that one. He claimed that his remarks were certainly not directed at me and added, as he had several times before, that he felt the campaign was as fine a political organization as he had ever seen, that we were literally weeks ahead of the 1968 Humphrey effort.

Given all that, I asked, what was the problem. First he claimed he didn't know "what was going on." I reminded him that he was specifically and personally invited to every meeting of consequence in the building. Then, he said, his staff reported that the morning meetings were too informal and unproductive. Allowing as how that description might apply to all meetings, I offered to reduce them to one a week where people could sit down and go over an agenda. Finally, he began to isolate his real grievance, what I suspected had been bothering him all along. It was essentially the candidate himself. Larry couldn't figure out how decisions were made on the issues, on what McGovern was saying.

I laughed, a little bitterly. I gave him a short course in the history of issue development in the campaign, tracing the problems back to the original decision to separate that operation from the principal campaign itself and to the tendency of the issues department to relate itself directly to the candidate. I assured Larry that many of those working on speeches, position papers, and new statements, consequently, felt only passingly obligated, if at all, to notify the campaign management of what they were up to. In other words, if you want to know what the candidate is saying, read the papers, and if you want to know what he plans to say, ask the candidate.

On this score, I was sympathetic to Larry's complaint but I still considered it wrong for him to have made it public and to have made it appear to be a general complaint with overall campaign progress and decision-making, when it was not. Larry O'Brien was upset with George McGovern and just didn't say so. Nevertheless, the damage had been done.

Shortly thereafter, staff meetings went to one a week, with a smaller group sitting down and talking. It didn't solve any problems I had, but it seemed to help others somewhat. Additionally, in the post-convention campaign restructuring, Frank went on the Senator's plane as both political advisor and director of the travel staff. His role was to synthesize the advice McGovern was getting both from inside and outside the campaign and to perform that political screening function of issues and ideas so badly lacking in the nomination race. Frank also attempted somewhat desperately to prevent recurrences of the Salinger episode and some aspects of the Eagleton matter. It was possible to gauge his success only through the absence of mistakes. But, after Labor Day, for the first time the Senator started refusing to answer every random press question thrown at him.

SEPTEMBER 4, 1972. Labor Day, the traditional start of the Presidential campaign. Both McGovern and Shriver started almost uninterrupted campaigning. Shriver had taken himself out on the road a few times in August, to universally good reviews. After an initial few days of shaking down, testing, and weeding-out, he had managed to assemble an excellent staff in short order. My impression of Shriver was extremely favorable. He combined exuberance, humor, drive, wholehearted commitment, movement and motivation, and great self-possession. His most engaging quality was an openness, a readiness to admit ignorance and listen to advice when he encountered some new barrier. He did, however, possess a strong self-will and was hard to move once he reached a conclusion. He could be stubborn to the point of obstinance, and, in contrast to the milder-mannered, gentler McGovern, occasionally quarreled loudly with his staff.

Heading his operation in Washington was the veteran Lee White, a Nebraskan who had served as a White House legal aide to President Kennedy and as Chairman of the Federal Power Commission in the Johnson administration. A philosophical, cigar-puffing, puckish man, cast by these circumstances among hot-eyed political savages, White might well have been a bemused, benign missionary-trader on some foreign island. Working immediately with him were Mickey Kanter and Terch Boasberg. On the road, Shriver had Bill Josephson, former Peace Corps general counsel, and Mark Shields, whose origins were Kennedy, John Gilligan, and Muskie. One or more writers such as Doris Kearns alternated traveling with the Shriver party and working in Washington.

There is a general tendency among Vice-Presidential candidates and some of their staff members to try to create separate political, organizational, or financial operations. Although these potentially troublesome efforts were pretty well avoided with the Shriver people, we did cross swords over the allocation of funds contributed by longtime Shriver friends and ear-marked for his use and over efforts to set up separate Shriver volunteer centers. In each case matters of policy rather than substance were involved and only the most paranoid of the McGovern supporters saw this as a "Shriver in '76" operation. The relationship between the two staffs was overwhelmingly cooperative, thanks in no small part to the imperturbable Lee White.

SEPTEMBER 6, 1972. By early September, a number of fundraising activities were underway to alleviate our chronic financial pressures. Miles Rubin and Henry Kimelman worked on the "special gifts" programs, a euphemism for large contributions and loans. Because major contributions were almost as scarce in the fall as in the spring, the fundraisers made an effort to solicit loans to help get out a massive direct mail, small-contributor program. By now the first of a series of almost continuous mailings had gone out and the results of that effort were beginning to be seen. With the Senator's acceptance speech appeal for a million contributors giving $25 apiece, the "Million Member Club" was also underway. In designing our electronic and print media programs, we also built in fund-raising appeals to help liquidate the substantial costs in both cases. State campaign committees were planning their own fund-raising activities, particularly traditional dinners with well-known speakers. A separate committee was working on special events. although our extremely successful concert series in the spring never was repeated in the fall. Some labor groups, major international unions which had endorsed the ticket, were contributing or lending funds to the campaign. And, finally, under Owen Donley's direction, we integrated a grassroots, door-to-door fund-raising capability into our volunteer canvassing operation. Through these combined means, we hoped to raise the $22 to $24 million necessary to win the election. Although it seemed like an enormous amount of money, it was no more than half what the CREEP would spend.

As in the spring, our campaign budget was prepared along functional lines. The first item was national operations, which included the national headquarters, staff, and overhead, at approximately $1 million. Second was candidate activities, the cost of both candidates' travel, scheduling, and advance, at $1.2 million. Third was electronic media, television and radio time, and production, together calculated at $7 million. Next was print media, newspaper advertising, mailings, literature, and promotional materials and production costs, at $4 million. The largest item, state operations, the cost of maintaining political organizations in the 50 states, was calculated at $10.5 million. And voter registration was budgeted at $1.2 million. The total campaign budget came to $24.9 million. On a cash-flow basis, the budget called for expenditures, for the four major items of state operations, electronic and print media, and voter registration, starting at a level of half a million dollars in the third week in August and escalating to a peak of almost $3 million a week at the end of October.

Morris set his mind to devising plans for mail solicitations in the shortest time possible. Now lists had to be pyramided and funds received as quickly as possible. At least six million dollars had to be raised by direct mail in 100 days. It takes 15 days to produce a mailing and 20 days to receive the bulk of the receipts. The first mailing went to the 110,000 more or less regular contributors to the nomination effort. It was a letter printed on the left side of a computer form with four personal checks printed on the right side. The computer printed the contributor's name in at the top of the letter and on each check. The letter, sent over my signature, asked the recipient to date each check the first of each of the four campaign months, beginning with August, and fill in each check for as much as he could afford. It was an instant monthly contributor club. The mailing, which cost $21,000 to produce and send, raised $1,025,000. Over 35,000 contributors sent in a special label entitling them to a FMBM pin (For McGovern Before Miami).

To expand our contributor lists, on July 1st, Morris had sent a "get-a-friend" letter to our 110,000 contributors asking them to send the names of 10 likely McGovern donors. To the more than 200,000 new names received, a computer letter went out after the nomination saying that their friend, Mr. Jones, had given us their name as a potential contributor, and asking them to join the cause. The letter pulled a more than 10 percent response with an average contribution of $25.

To increase the average contribution from $15 during the nomination period to $25 during the fall campaign, the Million Member Club idea was promoted. An appeal was made every 21 days to the donor list. Since there were no primaries to use as pegs, contributors were regularly asked to support a new project such as a newspaper ad or special television broadcast. Morris described the results as "fantastic." The donor mailings pulled more than 15 percent responses each. During the last three weeks of the campaign Western Union mailgrams and nightletters were sent to contributors of more than $35 seeking funds for special television speeches by the Senator.

More than 15 million letters of all kinds were mailed in the fall. Approximately 700,000 people joined the Million Member Club. Morris estimates that an additional 500,000 people contributed to the campaign at the state level. The average gift in the fall campaign was $24.60. The entire small-donor fund-raising program in the fall, including direct mail, newspaper ads and inserts, television appeals, and door-to-door solicitations, amounted to $16,750,000. There had never been anything like it in the history of American politics.

SEPTEMBER 12, 1972. The lid, dancing precariously on the seething voter-registration pot, finally blew. We met Congressman Thompson's budget requests for four weeks, at increasing cost to the other elements of the campaign, particularly the hard-pressed field operations. Finally, in the second week in September, there was not enough to go around. I notified Anne Wexler several days earlier, while Thompson was on vacation. When Thompson returned, I told him we had $400,000 to cover both state operations and voter registration, the two items totaling $750,000 for that week. Dreading the reaction of the mercurial Thompson, I earlier discussed the matter with the Senator, proposing that the money be distributed proportionately to the state coordinators to keep the campaigns alive and to continue voter registration. Up to then, I had not taken the voter-registration controversy to him, believing that he shouldn't be concerned with it and that he should have an autonomous voter-registration operation if that's what he wanted. But previous stormy confrontations with Thompson led me to fear an abrupt resignation, an event we couldn't afford so soon after the O'Brien scene. So I laid the entire problem before the candidate, presented my recommendation and sought his ratification. I presumed that if it were a McGovern decision, Thompson would not resign.

I was wrong. Thompson returned from vacation, was briefed on the situation, and promptly quit. Like some other McGovern "supporters," he resigned noisily, blazing away in the press, at me, at others, and at the campaign generally. Thompson knew that we had taken the only course open to us and he also knew that McGovern had ratified that decision. Nevertheless, he vented his wrath to the world at large. Once again, a campaign with enough trouble was presented with more. The controversy brewed for two or three full days before dying down. It always interested me that the Senator generated a curious sort of respect which permitted his friends to torpedo his campaign without naming him personally. In any case, Thompson left to resume his own re-election campaign in New Jersey. I recalled a Cervantes line: "Where there's no more bread, boon companions melt away." Cervantes would have felt right at home in the McGovern-Shriver campaign.

SEPTEMBER 13, 1972. The scheduling theory for the fall campaign was evolved by Steve Robbins and Tony Podesta, in consultation with the politicians. Robbins, whose soul nursed grievous wounds—many self-inflicted—from the nomination campaign, had given way to Podesta as chief scheduler and had elevated himself to scheduler emeritus. Podesta had come to us from Muskie and had worked in the California primary with Chicano organizations as Antonio Podesta. Weaned on South Chicago ward politics, Podesta was a match for Robbins in cor-

The hordes of Genghis Khan invade the Safeway.

raling the mad band of advancemen whose uncanny life style managed to liberate them by election day from most of civilization's outward restraints. But Podesta managed also to deal with the balky state co-ordinators, in most cases with less rancor than the thorny Robbins, whose psyche thrived on tension.

Between them, they proposed a travel schedule which would take the candidates (Shriver as well as McGovern) into three major media markets a day to achieve maximum free media exposure. Originally the stops were to highlight "visuals," events with the candidates doing something, touring a plant, visiting a farm or supermarket, demonstrating some concern or highlighting some social problem. But experiments in August showed this strategy to be well-nigh impossible because of the size of the traveling press corps. One trip through a Texas supermarket with 100 trailing reporters, cameramen, soundmen and grips managed to destroy canned fruit displays, terrify early-morning shoppers in their hair curlers and infuriate store managers. It just wouldn't work. To prevent whole fields of ripening crops from being trampled on a tour through a family farm, the Senator was accompanied by a press "pool." But the reporters left behind in the buses felt left-out and useless, and they rebelled. Then the hapless schedulers tried events specifically designed to maximize local media exposure. The traveling national press corps resented that. One after another, plant managers, fearing the reporters like the hordes of the Great Khan, refused us entry.

To compound the problem, the size of the traveling press party forced us to go to stretch Boeing 727s to accommodate everyone and prevent a fleet of airplanes from flying stop to stop. This, in turn, permitted the candidate to visit only those cities with airports having runways which met CAB or FAA requirements for the long 727s. Many middle-size American communities never saw the candidate because his plane couldn't land close enough. On September 18th, we tried a bus trip out of Huntington, West Virginia, back into the Appalachian mountains so the Senator could visit the mines and deliver an "Appalachian manifesto" from the small county courthouse steps. It required hours of travel to get there and hours of driving to get back. That night the Senator called me to say: "I never want another goddamn bus trip for the rest of this campaign. Everybody got car-sick riding for hours around those hills."

Finally, as fatigue set in, three media stops a day were reduced to two. With almost all "visuals" ruled out and smaller communities precluded, by October we were doing standard big-city rallies. The emphasis then shifted to crowds in an effort to show momentum and enthusiasm and to counter the adverse public opinion polls which dropped periodically on the campaign like nuclear bombs on some devastated island.

In September's second week, the Senator campaigned in Houston, Minneapolis, Chicago, Detroit, Cleveland, Pittsburgh, Philadelphia, Albany, New York, Hartford, Waterbury, Portland (Me.), and Baltimore. During the large-city tour in the middle of the week he was joined by Senator Kennedy for a series of noontime and evening mass rallies. The crowds were phenomenal, in several cities, record-breaking. Chicago's lunchtime rally drew 125,000 people in the rain. They weren't all civil servants either, nor were they attracted solely by Kennedy. Much ink was spread that week trying to decipher the popularity—what percent Kennedy, what percent McGovern. But in almost every case, it was McGovern who drew the louder applause and the greater response. Kennedy's contribution was significant and real. Alone among the party leadership, he devoted substantial amounts of time to the campaign and to joint appearances with the candidate at a time when party unity and solidarity as well as enthusiasm were extremely important. His contribution during this period, as well as later, was substantial.

SEPTEMBER 15, 1972. We began our media program, the television spots, during the second week in September. Although the paid radio spots were to start simultaneously, insufficient funds caused them to be delayed by several days. In terms of content, we were using much of the same material used throughout the primaries, as it had been revised and supplemented by new footage produced toward the end of the primary circuit. The spots showed the Senator listening to small groups of citizens—workers, small businessmen, senior citizens, farmers, veterans— discussing their problems with them and offering his proposals to solve those problems. The 60s (one-minute spots) were usually take-outs from the longer five-minute footage, featured one or two succinct citizen questions and the McGovern position statement or response. In September, starting on the 11th, we ran eight five-minute spots on network television and nine 60s. The people in charge of time-buying made every effort to locate our spots as closely as possible to television programs with the highest viewer ratings.

The media program devised by Charles Guggenheim corresponded with our overall political strategy of ranking and targeting the various states. Approximately half the total media budget was allocated to media placement in specific states. In addition to the network buys, in the first week of our media program spots were placed in 52 markets in 16 high-priority states such as New York, Illinois, Pennsylvania, Ohio, Michigan, and Texas. During the second week of the program the number of state markets was increased to 94 and the number of states to 21. Each week, Charles' people consulted with the regional coordinators, Frank, and me to determine the priority states.

Distinguished cheerleader.

Charles much preferred to use longer materials, particularly half-hour biographies and "issues" material. But we were unable to afford it until our direct-mail receipts picked up in October. A continuing controversy inside the campaign centered on the degree to which negative media material should be used. A coalition of O'Brien-Mankiewicz-Van Dyk increasingly favored production of material devoted strictly to criticism of Nixon and the Republicans. Others, particularly Charles, Liz Stevens (who had worked diligently since mid-1971 as a full-time volunteer media coordinator), and to some degree myself, generally opposed it.

The negative media strategy wasn't completely adopted until late October, and, in the meantime, Charles produced some simple, straight-forward, highly effective, spots critical of the Nixon administration in such areas as Vietnam, unemployment, inflation, crime and, particularly, corruption. One brief spot ran as follows:

Alfred C. Baldwin, a former FBI agent, has stated this:

He was hired by James McCord, Security Chief for both the Republican National Committee and the Nixon Campaign Committee.

Mr. Baldwin was assigned to listen illegally to over two hundred private telephone conversations—calls made by Democratic Chairman Lawrence O'Brien and others from tapped telephones in Democratic Headquarters at the Watergate.

He sent reports on these conversations to William E. Timmons, Assistant to President Nixon for Congressional Relations at the White House.

In 1968, Mr. Nixon said: "The President's chief function is to lead, not to oversee every detail, but to put the right people in charge, provide them with basic guidance, and let them do the job."

The question is do we want the system to continue to work this way for the next four years?

Another brief, but devastating, spot directed at campaign financing read as follows:

President Nixon has received $10 million in secret campaign contributions from men and interests whose names Mr. Nion refuses to reveal to the American people.

Who are these men, and what do they want?

We never did find out, did we?

SEPTEMBER 16, 1972. Corruption in government and political espionage, constituted a dominant theme throughout the fall. On the 16th, a grand jury in Washington indicted the "Watergate seven" for illegal wire-tapping, breaking and entering, burglary, and related crimes in connection with the "bugging" of the Democratic Party headquarters in

Washington. As the facts slowly filtered out during the summer, it became evident that the entire scheme had been carried out under the explicit direction, guidance, and control of the Republicans, some combination of CREEP and the Nixon administration, the White House, the very building where the President of the United States lives and works. High-level officials—former Attorney General Mitchell and former Secretary of Commerce Maurice Stans—were implicated, and other names were mentioned, up to and including that of H. R. Haldeman, the Presidential chief of staff whose desk is very near Mr. Nixon's. A search of the desk of Howard Hunt, one of the seven burglars and spies, who worked in the Executive Office building next to the White House, revealed a gun and a telephone tapping device. Frank had said it: "These are desperate men and they will stop at nothing."

The official posture of the administration, when confronted with evidence that it was involved in the greatest and most serious political espionage undertaking in the history of the Republic, was: "Boys will be boys." They couldn't be faulted for lack of chutzpah!

Only slowly was it revealed that these desperate men had, indeed, not stopped at wiretapping and burglary. In the depth of May 23rd's dark night, two carloads of these villainous clowns had sought to break into our previous headquarters at 410 First Street, presumably to work their skills on our telephones and file cabinets. As fate would have it, dire poverty had forced us into quarters having no windows and only one usable door. On this particular night the door happened to be occupied either by our guard, hired from a private company which specialized in sleeping guards, or by a drunk. Whichever, the body in the doorway managed to dull the competitive appetites of these hardy Republican mercenary burglars. Nor did we hear until later that Republican money had been used to hire infiltrators to gather information inside our headquarters, such as about the layout of my office and Frank's office, that an equally clownish figure named Segretti was scurrying around the country recruiting additional spies and saboteurs from his law school class, that members of the White House staff may have been involved in the infamous "Canuck letter" which led indirectly to the Muskie-*Union Leader* confrontation.

Only after this pattern of conduct began to emerge did other unaccountable incidents begin to make sense.

For example: the call placed from New York on June 20th, ostensibly by me, to AFL-CIO President George Meany's office in Washington, practically demanding that Meany travel to New York for a meeting with then frontrunner George McGovern. What the Republicans couldn't calculate, however, was my father's sudden illness, which required me to leave New York before the call was made.

For example: the call placed to Walter Cronkite one night following the evening news, ostensibly by Frank Mankiewicz, to congratulate Cronkite on the favorable treatment being given by CBS to McGovern according to some "deal" between the network and the Senator's campaign—a call, naturally, which infuriated Cronkite almost as much as the call from "Gary Hart" had infuriated Meany.

Frank managed to straighten Cronkite out when he heard about the mysterious call, but Meany's secretary apparently is still convinced I called from New York that day.

In 1972 the American people had their worst fears about politics confirmed. They learned more than they ever wanted to know about the lengths to which corrupt men will go to preserve power. They learned that money contributed by Texas oil interests was "laundered" in Mexican banks before being surreptitiously hidden away in CREEP's bank accounts, making it more difficult than ever to find out where it came from and what political debts it represented. They learned that such "laundered" money could be used to hire desperate men who would wiretap, spy, sabotage, steal, and generally disrupt the political process. They learned that great amounts of money would be spent on such operations, at least $100,000 and perhaps three-quarters of a million dollars.

The McGovern-Shriver campaign did its best to keep these facts before the American voters. But it wasn't enough. The tragedy of these oafish, sophomoric political conspiracies wasn't that they were directed at us, the Democrats. The real tragedy was that they lent credence to the native American suspicion of politicians and the political process. They justified and rationalized a grassroots conviction that all politicians are corrupt and venal, that they lie, cheat, and steal, that they would stop at nothing to obliterate their opponent. These events deepened the suspicion and distrust of the people for their leaders at a time when lack of credibility and confidence in government has become a way of life. These selfish, power-lusting little men, in their greedy struggle for self-preservation, ruined decades of effort to restore the stature of public service, to exalt the role of government, and to inspire in men and women the highest aspiration of political involvement.

There are those throughout America still puzzled that the magnitude, the sheer weight and dimension, of these blatant political crimes didn't make a greater impact during the election. But for an electorate which anticipates corruption it isn't a question of whether, but of how much. And once that attitude is confirmed, there isn't much difference between the Hughes Tool loan and the Russian wheat scandal, or even the sabotage of the American political system. That is the tragedy of 1972.

SEPTEMBER 19, 1972. Staff difficulties generated by the O'Brien statement continued like aftershocks from an earthquake. Once analyzed, the essence of Larry's grievance was the seeming lack of coordination of issue statements, the public announcements of the campaign positions. But one of the steps taken was to establish a screening process to prevent statements from being issued or positions taken until they had been thoroughly reviewed inside the organization.

A number of observers have attempted, with no apparent success, to account for the seeming pattern of discontent inside the fall campaign. Every campaign, by its very nature, invites the kind of personality conflict which feeds on tension and pressure. The miracle of the McGovern campaign was that it went so long with almost none of this. Kennedy campaigns, the McCarthy campaign, Humphrey campaigns, and every political operation Lyndon Johnson ever touched, had more than their share of personal clashes and jealousies which went largely unreported, presumably on the ground that they were inconsequential and of little interest. Why, when the adversities of the fall brought minor troubles of this sort to our door, it was suddenly news, I cannot say.

In part, honest differences did result from personal relationships established between the candidate and individuals in the campaign. Many people had direct access to the candidate, few felt constrained in approaching him and not enough felt responsibility to respect a chain of command. If you can report your views, ideas, or complaints to George McGovern, why feel the necessity of letting the campaign manager handle it? Consequently, the candidate involved himself in all sorts of decisions—media, financial, structural, personal—which he needn't have, decisions which sapped his energies and took his time. Gordon Weil, for one, believes that the Senator resisted absolute delegation of responsibility to any individual because he knew it would upset his friends, that he was unable to create a powerful, dictatorial figure through whom all problems must pass because it would make some supporters unhappy, and that he found it extremely difficult to say no to certain people. I think, rather, that it was a product of years of running his own campaigns, of keeping his fingers on all operations, of never really having a single person in whom to place absolute reliance.

By now it was clear we had introduced some revolutionary concepts and methodologies to American politics that would continue to have an impact regardless of the outcome of this campaign. There had been the emergence of the massive volunteer army. There had been a high degree of technical skill combined with ideological commitment and motivation. We had introduced democracy to political campaigning. We had decentralized authority and decision-making, encouraging local authority and control. There was also our program of popular, broad-based campaign financing. And we had brought into positions of organizational leadership a new generation of young, tough, pragmatic, effective, disciplined politicians—the best of several decades of political organizers in this country.

During a telephone conversation one day, Gene Pokorny told me we had developed a concentric matrix. I didn't know what he was talking about. He explained that most institutions and political campaigns were organized along hierarchical lines, defined as "a body of persons organized or classified according to rank, capacity, or authority." According to this traditional organizational concept, titles and lines of authority were of paramount importance in establishing relationships and the decision-making process. On paper, a hierarchy is represented as a pyramid.

According to Gene, in the late 1950s emerging think-tank-type institutions experimented with an organizational concept called the concentric matrix. It was designed to adapt an organization's functions to a group of peers, people having essentially equal abilities, backgrounds, and talents and, therefore, egos—people whose background and experience made them resent someone "over" them. Thus, an organizational chart was devised which was horizontal, rather than vertical like a pyramid. It was a series of concentric circles running from the center outward. The "matrix" suggested lines bisecting the circles running from the center outward, making a web-like figure. Each segment of the circles, each slice of the pie, represented a campaign function running from the center outward according to the centrality or importance of the function performed.

In the pyramid hierarchy, command flows down and response or information flows up. In the concentric matrix, command flows out and response or information flows in. The important distinction is that in the old structure some people are "higher" than others, they dominate and control. In the new structure, everyone is on the same plane, but some are closer to the center than others. All information is at the center, and since information is power, the closer one gets to the center of the organization, the more powerful he is. The individual at the very center, in a political organization the campaign manager, is the theoretical recipient of all information and alone is in contact with all campaign segments.

Now this distinction is upsetting to those accustomed to a hierarchy. Throughout the fall, McGovern was besieged on all sides by advice to appoint a dictator, a person "with a big whip." The advisors were pleading, in effect, for a return to an outmoded organizational device. The reason we accidentally stumbled onto the newer concept was that the McGovern campaign appealed to highly motivated, intelligent, resourceful people who didn't require a politician with a big whip to tell them what to do or how to do it; they would have rebelled against that kind of old-fashioned dictatorial domination. They required guidance and direction, not authoritarianism. The glue that held the McGovern organization during the difficult, often bitter, months was respect, appreciation, and goodwill. The respect for leadership was reciprocated, and discipline was not sacrificed.

SEPTEMBER 24, 1972. The public opinion polls had not been friendly to us since the Eagleton matter. Since the late July Gallup poll showed us starting about where Humphrey did, with Wallace in the race, things had gone downhill. In mid-August, Harris had the race at 57 percent for Nixon, 34 percent for McGovern, with 9 percent undecided. On August 20th, Gallup had the race at 57 percent to 31 percent, with 12 percent undecided. Yankelovitch, polling for *The New York Times,* showed the margin to be 56 percent to 28 percent, with 16 percent undecided. By August 30th, Gallup had figures showing Nixon leading 64 percent to 30 percent, with only 6 percent undecided. By mid-September, the Harris figures were even worse: Nixon, 63 percent; McGovern, 29 percent; undecided, 8 percent. Then, on September 24th, the bottom was reached. Yankelovitch published a poll which showed a 39 percent difference, 62 percent to 23 percent, with 15 percent undecided.

In the 60 days between early July and early September, a winnable election had become virtually unwinnable without some sort of dramatic breakthrough, and in the third week of September Pat Caddell stated that the hinge upon which voter attitudes toward McGovern—and therefore the election—swung was Eagleton. In overwhelming numbers the voters felt that McGovern had either "acted like a politician" in getting rid of Eagleton, had somehow personally wronged Eagleton himself, or had handled the matter badly by first keeping Eagleton and then removing him. Many believed a combination of all three.

It was apparent that most voters had not considered the possibility that McGovern had genuinely sympathized with Eagleton at the outset in determining to keep him on the ticket and had only reluctantly bowed to the overwhelming political pressure to remove him or consider the national welfare, as opposed to Eagleton's personal welfare, in resolving to change his course. Obviously, the great mass of voters had not even contemplated that McGovern might have been sufficiently disturbed by the absence of concrete medical evidence regarding Eagleton's condition to lead him to act in the national interest in changing his mind and deciding to ask for Eagleton to remove himself.

It was an impossible situation for the Senator and the campaign. McGovern was the goat, Eagleton the hero. If McGovern attempted to justify his decision further, he would appear to be treading on Eagleton's reputation and future to his own political ends. Yet, if the public continued to feel that he had acted politically—and even then in a fumbling manner—he would certainly lose the election. The depths of the moral dilemma have not even begun to be explored. As we contemplated the alternatives, they seemed insuperable.

SEPTEMBER 25, 1972. Harris published his figures: 59 percent to 31 percent, with 10 percent undecided.

The time had come to break precedent. Pat Caddell had been surveying continually throughout the fall and his latest results showed a continuation of the narrowing trend and a somewhat closer race. We called a press conference in Washington to release his results, hoping to boost morale and overcome the devastating effect of the other polls. Pat's figures showed Nixon with 56 percent, McGovern with 34 percent, and 10 percent undecided. His study showed that fully one-third of the voters had changed their minds since early July, that there was, in other words, unprecedented volatility among the electorate. Further, with the southern states, except Texas, out of the sample, the race narrowed to 55 percent to 36 percent.

These figures achieved, at least for the time being, their purpose of encouraging the workers and supporters. They definitely verified a trend upward from the grievous lows of August. We felt at that time that the margin could be closed by election day. I could see no defeatism anywhere in the campaign.

SEPTEMBER 28, 1972. Larry, Henry, Miles, Frank, and I had breakfast in Washington with the Senator. The purpose of the meeting was to discuss media proposals, but it wandered into aimless generalities. The Senator was alert and attentive after little sleep, but he seemed extremely fatigued. Larry read portions of a memorandum concerning the concept of a television "debate" between the Senator and selected film clips of President Nixon addressing himself to various issues. We had kicked the idea around at some length and, with the Senator's approval, pursued it further. It was later abandoned, however, after a review of the available film footage showed the idea to be unprofitable. There was some rambling discussion of campaign finance, but since nothing special was resolved I considered it a waste of the Senator's time.

Anne Wexler had assumed responsibility for completing the voter registration drive. By the end of September more than four million new voters had been registered through our efforts, obviously in the most heavily Democratic areas of the most heavily Democratic states. Anne predicted that this figure would be doubled by the close of registration a couple of weeks hence. If we could register enough people, and get all of our voters out on election day, and just get that gap narrowed in the polls, we could still win.

Only in retrospect is it clear that most of our efforts in the fall campaign were futile. But the absence of signposts, of visible signs of progress, produced all sorts of manifestations of energy—diverse attempts to demonstrate purpose and direction. In the midst of the fall campaign, the volunteers—under the direction of two artists—redecorated the headquarters lobby with vivid posters of the candidate against a raven-ebony background. And startled commuters, flooding down Washington's K street one morning in late September saw the drab national headquarters adorned with a mostrously large stylized rainbow fixed like a gleaming cyclopean eye in the middle of the building's facade.

Even as symbolic acts of self-improvement and psychic healing occurred, however, there were occasional moods of helplessness, which, with the announcement of each new poll, tended to make all efforts seem futile and useless. At the lowest points, since nothing seemed to work, nothing seemed to matter. It was as if we were on a monstrous deterministic train whose speed and route we were unable to alter.

It led me to conclude that the political mechanisms are much less important in a national election than in a nomination race. Although the great bulk of the campaign work went on outside the public view, it could have only a limited effect on the public mood; it would be crucial only in a close election. Only the candidate and the public perception of him mattered, and very little could be done organizationally to alter that. It was how he appeared, through his public campaigning and through the media, that mattered. And when nothing seemed to work, solace was sought in giant rainbows.

SEPTEMBER 30, 1972. The afternoon of the campaign had come to a close. We now had only 38 days left in the campaign. We had to close in the polls at the rate of almost a point a day. But we always believed that we could get the margin down to about 15 percent by October 10th, to 10–12 percent no later than October 20th, that Nixon would respond to the narrowing gap by coming out to campaign, and that we could then defeat him in face-to-face campaigning in the final two weeks.

McGovern and Shriver were campaigning as hard as they could, maintaining a merciless schedule. Organizational activity was underway in every state; we were on the air with a substantial radio and television program; mailings were beginning to rescue the campaign from back-to-the wall desperation; a host of speakers was traveling the country for the ticket. Yet there was nothing tangible, nothing concrete, nothing to show movement and progress. At the headquarters, the staff and volunteers grasped at straws for encouragement, cheering each appearance of one of the candidates on the evening news, savoring each favorable

editorial or report of some new administrative malfeasance, longing for
some proof that victory lay ahead.

EVENING

OCTOBER 1, 1972. The Presidential campaign day had entered its evening hours. Soon the campaign would be measured in hours.
But the immediate sensation during this period was of endless, ceaseless
motion, of constant problem-solving, of swirling, pressing demands from
all sides.

There were daily conversations with "the plane," meaning the Senator's
traveling party. Jeff Smith, now the Senator's personal assistant, was con-
scientious about calling me to see if there were any vital messages for
the Senator, calls to be made or late-breaking news. He also relayed
word of activities on the road—contacts made with key politicians, successful or unsuccessful events, changes in schedule, and so forth. Frank
occasionally called in with organizational problems that could be spotted
on the road but not from Washington. On matters of campaign policy,
or major decisions such as the Senator's desire to make a number of
"fireside chat" type speeches in October, a flurry of calls took place
concerning arrangements to be made and events to be cancelled. Generally, the communications between the traveling party and the headquarters were good, particularly after Jeff joined the Senator. But occasionally, some momentous decision would be made by the Senator which
we would find out about only third-hand, hours after the fact. That
sprang from a feeling which one gets traveling on the plane with the
candidate, traveling staff, and reporters, that the entire campaign is
there and that everything else is at best secondary and will follow along,
like the camel's body following its nose, wherever it is led.

In general, the mood of the campaign, both in Washington and on
the plane, entering its evening hours, was one of determination, conviction, pragmatic, reasoned optimism, and hope. We were, if anything,
tempered by adversity, not easily discouraged, and not readily defeated.
But through the determination and seasoned pragmatism was the lingering, haunting desire for certainty, for some hard evidence which reason
could grasp and hang onto in the stormy political seas. People in the
field looked to Washington for hope and certainty, thinking, as we are
led to think, that the fount of political knowledge and information was
somehow flowing in the nation's capitol. Even if that were true at other
times of the year, it is not true during national elections. The truth of
politics lies with the people—the constituents, the electorate—during a
campaign. Thus, the people in Washington looked to the states, the

communities, to tell us what truly was happening. The daily canvass results, the results of the phoning, the response of the people who took leaflets, the housewife at the door, the worker at the plant gate. What were they saying? What were they thinking?

The answer was hopeful. They haven't decided. They are still making up their minds. They can still be moved by the need for change in the country, by the need to end the endless war, by corruption in government, by Nixon himself. The election still seemed winnable.

Throughout these days our workers were contacting millions of voters in every state. In planning the fall campaign, it was my judgment that we could raise a million volunteers to work in the general election race. This was based upon the calculation that there must be an average of 20,000 Democrats in each of the 50 states who would be willing to work at least a few hours on this campaign if properly contacted and organized. Such a massive political organizational effort had never been done before, but we had proved in California, the most difficult state of all to organize, that it wasn't impossible. Although this tremendous citizen-volunteer effort wasn't designed for pure publicity purposes, it would demonstrate widespread political support for the McGovern-Shriver ticket and would provide, as during the primaries, an impressive manpower pool for a campaign unable to pay for political labor. The key to raising this massive volunteer army was motivation. The kind of dedication and commitment present among our primary workers had to be sustained and increased.

It is impossible to document the number of volunteers who did participate in the fall campaign effort. Nor is it possible to calculate accurately the effect on morale of the Eagleton controversy, the Senator's alleged "changing of positions," or continued attention to troubles at the top. The only evidence of the success of our volunteer effort is the ability of the local organizers to raise workers for canvass drives, leafleting, phoning, and general organizational activities. There were few reports of the failure of such activities for lack of workers. The people were there and they were used as effectively as possible.

OCTOBER 7, 1972. McGovern, in the first week of October, traveled to Newark, New York City, Boston, Niagara, Buffalo, Cleveland, Chicago, Des Moines, Kansas City, St. Louis, and Baltimore. The Kansas City rally was typical. Scheduled for the cavernous Union Station, the hub of the mid-Western rail network, the night of October 6th, the event drew a crowd estimated at 25,000. The people came from both sides of the Kansas-Missouri line, neither state being especially strong for the Democratic ticket in 1972. Less than half the crowd could be jammed into the station building, and the remainder packed around the building outside covering the parking lots and spilling into the streets. While waiting for the candidate, who was about an hour behind schedule, the throng was entertained by a dozen of their heroes, the Kansas City Chiefs football team, led by Ed Podolak and Bob Stein who delivered campaign speeches. At 10 P.M., the Senator arrived, to be greeted by a roaring welcome from the perspiring thousands who had raised the temperature in the vast stone structure to summerlike levels by sheer body-heat alone. After delivering his standard stump speech, the Senator and his party were off for the next day's campaigning.

OCTOBER 9, 1972. On October 9, 1968, Richard Nixon, then campaigning for the Presidency against Hubert Humphrey and the Johnson administration said, "Those who have had a chance for four years and could not bring about peace, should not be given another chance." We sought to resurrect those words to haunt him. In September, a special committee was created within the campaign to organize activities around the fourth anniversary of that remarkable Nixonian boomerang. To a certain degree our efforts were coordinated with similar activities being undertaken by church groups and peace organizations supported by Stewart Mott and other contributors.

Special literature and buttons were prepared for distribution. Statements were prepared giving the factual details surrounding the cost of the war during the Nixon years. But the principal activities were major addresses by McGovern and Shriver, as well as speeches scheduled for a host of political leaders and key campaign supporters around the country. Speakers included 23 Senators, a dozen mayors, ten Governors, state legislators, entertainers, labor leaders, military people, and a number of the McGovern children. The October 9th activities were coordinated by the National McGovern-Shriver Labor Committee to orient this effort toward working men and women, to make it as broadly based as possible and prevent it from becoming just one more peace demonstration. More than 50,000 pieces of literature were distributed in Michigan, Wisconsin, and Connecticut. Carl Wagner projected a quarter of a million leaflets to be distributed in Detroit alone. All together, these efforts had a substantial impact in reminding voters of the administration's failure of performance on the bitter issue of the war.

OCTOBER 12, 1972. Ted Van Dyk, after several days on the road with the candidate, came into my office completely unnerved. "I can't tell what's happening out there," he said. "There is something strange going on and I can't put my finger on it." He was severely disoriented by an incident at the University of Minnesota where the Senator interrupted his own speech to play a tape recording of an anonymous Vietnam veteran giving a firsthand description of the war's devastation, particularly among civilians. The tape came from a Boston radio talk show and was given to the Senator by the announcer, Jerry Williams, the previous night. As the tape was played in Minnesota, 20,000 students and scores of reporters sat stunned at its contents and the dramatic circumstances in which it was introduced. Ted couldn't decide whether it was high drama or elaborate bad taste. Further, he couldn't evaluate the absence of public response to McGovern, whether it was a result of a complete malaise or McGovern's diffident, low-key style. Troubled all day by his experience, he marched into my office that evening to announce in his staccato style: "I've figured it out. We're going to win!"

To track the movements of the candidates, their wives and campaign principals such as Larry O'Brien and Jean Westwood, in August we established a campaign "clearinghouse." The clearinghouse also was the focus for communications between the headquarters and the candidates' planes. Its third major function was to digest the news from the major papers, wire-services, and networks each day and distribute these news summaries to the campaign management. All in all the clearinghouse functions were carried out by a staff of a half-dozen under the disciplined eye of Max Factor, the campaign's human computer. Besides supervising all these activities, Max also established and monitored a region-by-region system of measuring the campaign's quantitative progress. An informal structure was set up to tabulate, week-by-week, and state-by-state, the number of pieces of literature distributed, the number of offices opened, and the number of canvassers operating. Although, some of the organizers in the states resented Washington's intrusion into their activities, it was one of the few means of measuring any kind of campaign movement. Max, who seemed never to sleep, and his assistants, did a remarkable job of centralizing communications and keeping the campaign from disappearing in a dozen different directions.

OCTOBER 17, 1972. In September, Ohio industrialist and former Senate candidate Howard Metzenbaum proposed a series of statewide telethons which would provide an opportunity for the Senator to appear on television hook-ups in the key states in a format in which he excels, answering individual citizens' questions. During October and early November, almost a dozen of these hour-long telethons were produced in the larger states. The Senator enjoyed doing them more than giving rally speeches, and Eleanor McGovern was able to participate in the responses. In most cases, the fund appeals contained in the telethons brought in sufficient proceeds to liquidate their costs.

In addition to the speakers blitz put on for the October 9th activities, a wide-ranging speakers bureau operated throughout the fall. It was of considerable help to state campaign committees requiring celebrities for special events and fund-raising activities. Our very earliest group of speakers included Pierre Salinger, Shirley MacLaine, Dennis Weaver, Marlo Thomas, and Warren Beatty. They, of course, were joined by dozens of others as the campaign gathered steam.

Pierre's contribution to the campaign was enormous. He was one of the first political "names" to join us, starting in the desperate pre-New Hampshire days. Under the circumstances of his background and experience, Pierre might have been expected to be domineering and overbearing. To the contrary, he was compliant and cooperative. He gave speeches in places others wouldn't go. He made no demands and attached no conditions to his appearances. He required no coaxing and no coaching. He knew the arguments to make and he made them forcefully and engagingly. Whatever inclinations he felt, and they must have been considerable, to tell us how to run the campaign or to run it himself, he resisted. His political judgment was consistently sound. He was, in short, a pro.

Toward the middle of October, the campaign began to take a turn which some, including myself, found disagreeable. The candidate began to place more and more emphasis on the corruption issue. In his honest and sincere efforts to communicate the threat to the national fiber, to somehow awaken the voters from their indifference, he pressed harder and harder. Due particularly to his fatigue and to the increasing personal toll the campaign was taking, it seemed that his attacks began to border more and more often on harshness and stridency. More and more of the people in the campaign, both in Washington and around the country, reported their disturbance.

There developed a definite conflict of opinion on this subject. Frank particularly thought the Senator should become even tougher on the corruption issue, demonstrating through wrath and indignation, an ability to feel and project the same kind of strength on this matter that he did on the war. Frank's interpretation of the national mood was that it was one of volatility and anger, that people wanted an angry leader who would say "no" to his friends and "look out!" to his enemies. To a large degree it seemed that many saw the campaign in highly moral terms, good versus bad, right versus wrong. And as the campaign continued into its evening hours, the candidate shared that view more and more. The greater the danger seemed and the less the people responded to that danger, the stronger became the inclination to heighten the contrasts, to deepen the blacks and lighten the whites, and to turn up the volume.

The danger in this strategy was that it personalized the campaign. It did indeed make the issue Richard Nixon, as the Senator had promised in his acceptance speech. But it also made the issue George McGovern. And both were taken for good and for ill. Richard Nixon may have been seen as the man who winked at spying, who took care of his friends and contributors, who might sell the Republican Party and chunks of the government out to the highest bidder, who, in short, was a politician of the most political order. But he was also the politician who bombed the hell out of the North Vietnamese without Russian or Chinese retaliation. He was the politician who first set foot on Chinese communist soil. He was the politician who went to Russia and signed a lot of agreements which seemed to make that problem go away for awhile. But most important in the voters' minds was what didn't happen. What didn't happen was nuclear war. Nixon was the politician who had kept the lid on ultimate warfare for another four years. And that is the most important accomplishment a President can make in the minds of most voters. We survived a while longer under his administration.

McGovern, on the other hand, was the more decent, honest, honorable man. You believed him when he talked. You knew he meant what he said. You *would* buy a used car from him. You might not agree with him, but you knew where he stood. And he would sure make a better brother-in-law. Most of all, he didn't seem like a politician.

But to many, he seemed to have changed his mind on Eagleton. To others he seemed to have turned around on Salinger. Still others couldn't understand how he could criticize Johnson for so many years and then say such elaborate things about him. In the minds of those many millions who think seriously about the Presidency for a few hours every four years, the whole thing got down to trust and confidence. You couldn't trust Nixon to hold your wallet, but you seemed to be able to trust him to keep us from greater harm. You could trust McGovern to hold your wallet and everything else you owned. But, when the hard bargaining started, when the missiles appeared in Cuba, how would he react, what would he do? All that was required to lose the election was for that shadow of a doubt to be created. And it was.

OCTOBER 20, 1972. The search continued for an effective means of communicating the message of the Democratic ticket. During the second and third weeks of October, McGovern traveled to 27 cities between Boston and San Diego, between Fargo and Austin. At each stop, at almost every appearance, the crowds ranged from good to spectacular, in both size and enthusiasm. In spite of the mileage covered and the number of speeches given, the Senator still did not believe that his message was getting across. He still searched for some more effective means of communication with the voters.

His instincts were right. In 1972, the whole idea of crowds was an anachronism. In the past, candidates held rallies and gave speeches before large audiences to place themselves and their issues before the people. But television made campaigning to live crowds no longer an effective way to reach the most people. One television appearance can contact more people than a month of rally speeches.

The question then is, why not simply campaign from a television studio? Nixon tried that in 1968 and almost lost the election, an election which he began with a wide margin. The American people can perceive phoniness. In 1968, they perceived that Nixon was giving phony answers to phony questions from phony audiences. Furthermore, the tradition of American elections is that the leaders are supposed to go to the people— literally. They are expected to present themselves before representative groups around the country, to be seen and touched and heard, to be examined outside the protectiveness of the nation's capital or a television studio. And even if they are only seen by a fraction of the electorate, that fraction, those relatively few thousands, are held to be the surrogates for all the others. They look the merchandise over and approve it or reject it for all their fellow citizens.

Realizing each of these principles to a greater or lesser degree, we attempted to construct a visual campaign which would combine public appearances with maximum media exposure. As detailed previously, we tried to put the candidates before as many voters as possible—via television—in the context of doing things. Not lecturing or haranguing, but visiting with people representative of a particular interest or problem, listening to their problems, and informally discussing possible solutions.

Because the network news broadcasts could not give these informal discussions adequate coverage, we tried to schedule these events in as many local media markets as possible. Local news shows would give heavy coverage to such meetings between the candidates and area farmers, shopkeepers, students, housewives, older people, minority groups. But it didn't work in practice, largely because of the resistance to "pool" reporting, and we didn't have adequate time to solve that problem. This led us to fall back on the standard rallies in an effort to make major media coverage simpler and to demonstrate crowd enthusiasm.

I still believe the concept is not only sound, but inevitable. Presidential candidates will not continue to speak day after day to large, somewhat manufactured, crowds. On the other hand, they will not isolate themselves in television studios. Before the next Presidential campaign, some canny scheduling strategist will develop a means to combine maximum media coverage with face-to-face, informal campaigning.

In the meantime, the Senator's solution was to schedule five major television addresses, three on Vietnam, one on corruption, and one on the economy. The first speech, on October 10th, dealt specifically with the failure of the Nixon promise to end the war, the deception of the 1968 "secret plan," and the cost to the nation in the four years that followed in terms of lives—almost 20,000, money—almost $60 billion, and priorities —a deteriorating domestic scene.

The second speech, on the 20th, dealt with the economy. Although not one of the more exciting subject areas, the speech itself was one of the best the Senator ever gave. In introduction, the Senator declared that "the Nixon administration has given us the highest inflation in two decades . . . the highest budget deficits in three decades . . . and a deficit in our international trade for the first time in the 20th century." He stated further that "every single time this administration has faced an important economic choice, they have picked a policy that is right for the few and wrong for you." The administration raised interest rates, a move favoring investors and bankers and harming the average borrower. Nixon also fought inflation with higher unemployment as a deliberate decision. "No President has the right to destroy your livelihood for the sake of an economic game plan," he stated. Finally, the policy of wage and price controls had failed because the system was being used to dictate wages but had defaulted on prices.

In addition to these three wrong moves, the Nixon administration had increased the welfare rolls dramatically even while preaching the work ethic and had refused to propose meaningful tax reform even while the poor lost their homes to taxes and many wealthy corporations paid essentially no taxes.

A McGovern administration, the Senator promised, would "guarantee a job opportunity for every man and woman in this country who is able to work." It would "adopt a tough, even-handed system to curb the cost of living." And it would "fight to reduce the tax burden" on average taxpayers, requiring all citizens and corporations to pay a fair share by the closure of $22 billion in tax loopholes. He concluded by contrasting his campaign, funded by hundreds of thousands of small contributions, to the Nixon campaign financing methods:

The special interests have given Mr. Nixon a $40 million campaign fund. They know I mean what I say and they don't like it, and they are trying to stop me. The Nixon public relations experts . . . are using every technique in the book to persuade you that the administration is acting in your best interests. But how many of you can really say that your life has improved in the last four years? How many of you can say that your city streets are safer, your tax burdens fairer, your grocery bills lower, or your sense of security and well-being stronger? Do you really want four more years of these policies?

This and other speeches closed with straightforward, low-key appeals for contributions to make further broadcasts possible. The total amount of money received from all five speeches exceeded one and a half million dollars, more than double the cost of the program.

Symptomatic of the difference between the pre- and post-convention campaign was the sharp contrast in staff attitudes toward work in the field. During the nomination race, we often had figuratively to chain Washington staff members to their desks to keep them from escaping into the next primary state. At every opportunity the Washington staff bolted for the excitement and participation of the intense primary campaigning or caucus/convention organizing.

In the fall, when a plan was developed for moving all but a skeleton Washington staff out into the key states to help with scheduling, press, organizing, canvassing, and other campaign activities, few people wanted to leave Washington. They all believed their headquarters jobs were vital. It was a drastic turn-around in mood and attitude. Now the headquarters offered safety and security from the harsh world. It should have been seen as an omen.

OCTOBER 23, 1972. In spite of the successes of the television speeches the warmth and size of the crowds greeting the candidates and their wives, and the increasingly favorable reports from our canvassing efforts, the polls had leveled off with a twenty-point margin between Nixon and McGovern.

Late at night on the 23rd, the Senator called to discuss a major black rally under consideration for the first of November. At the end of the conversation, he said in a rather dour, ironic way: "You got any secrets back there in Washington for closing a 20-point gap?" And then he chuckled.

I tried to point out that we only had to carry about a dozen and a half states to win and that the margin in the twelve most important states was nearer ten points in each state. Still, he seemed baffled that he was not getting through to people with his message. The truth was so clear to him that he couldn't understand why it wasn't clear to everyone.

Contrary to some impressions, throughout the fall and into the closing days of the campaign we were receiving substantial help from almost all elements of the regular Democratic Party in each state, as well as from the labor movement. Although AFL-CIO President Meany had decreed official labor neutrality back in August, more than 45 international unions endorsed the Democratic ticket. These included many of the large unions, the Communications Workers, the United Auto Workers, the Machinists, the Municipal Employees, as well as the unions most successful at fund-raising and general political support. A National Labor for McGovern-Shriver Committee was formed and its many members worked hard at producing literature and media programs, as well as at educational and money-raising projects. More than half the American labor movement, both its leadership and rank and file members, supported the Democratic candidates, in most cases with great enthusiasm. Even in instances, such as with the Steelworkers, where the official union policy at the national level was neutrality, many locals and rank and file members joined our cause and worked effectively within the state campaign organizations.

OCTOBER 26, 1972. "The dream of every person in direct mail solicitations," says Morris Dees, "is to receive more mail than you can open." Morris had described his operation as a pump, in the summer. He said that proceeds from initial mailings had to be put back into more mailings, to prime the pump, to build the small-contribution pyramid. But he predicted that by the end of October the pump would continue to pour by itself for two or three weeks under the influence of all the combined mailings. Added to this eventual river of contributions was the rather unexpected success of the television speeches as fund-raising instruments. The Vietnam speech on October 10th alone brought in almost one million dollars.

But in the last week of October, it happened. We received more mail than we could open. Increasingly large groups of volunteers were being used to open and sort the letters. But finally they were overwhelmed. We had sacks and sacks of mail sitting on the headquarters floors unopened for lack of manpower. Henry Kimelman and Owen Donley organized a crash program of late-night "opening parties" for staff members. Although almost everyone in the headquarters worked extremely hard day-in and day-out there was almost 100 percent response. For two straight nights, a large front room whose walls had been knocked out to accommodate the crowd was used by 200 people opening and sorting the contribution letters.

It was an incredible sight. Tens of thousands of dollars poured from the envelopes. And from reading the letters, it was clear the offerings were coming from all age groups, from all parts of the country, from various races, and from all kinds of people—rich and poor, professionals and laborers, shopkeepers and students, policemen, truck-drivers, and housewives. It was an inspiring outpouring of hope for this country, of belief in its processes, of determination to make it better. The longings,

The money came in faster than it could be counted.

aspirations, and dreams of millions of Americans found expression in the notes and letters that accompanied those contributions. It was the first chance many of us chained to Washington desks had to read the public mood, to sense the feelings of the people, to renew our faith in the effort we had undertaken so many months before. It was indeed a moving experience. Those dozens of people who stayed to the morning hours at the headquarters will not soon forget it.

Eleanor McGovern had campaigned throughout the fall on a fairly independent schedule. She had been scheduled and her trips advanced separately from the Senator. She had, as before, created a tremendously favorable impression, very successfully projecting herself as a potentially active and astute First Lady. She did not limit herself to repeating a "party line" or set speech, but insisted upon writing much of her own material and varying from city to city. Her particular interest was the welfare, care, and development of children, an interest that was not lost on the voting mothers of the nation. Not only was she able to address herself articulately to those and other issues, she also projected a sincere interest and concern for the people she met during her travels. She made a contribution wherever she went, and was particularly helpful in moving into those areas of the country where the Senator was unable to go. In the campaign's closing days, she joined the Senator for his concluding appearances.

Eunice Shriver has been described as the most Kennedy of the Kennedys and the best politician in the family. Although that might be considered too potent a distillation for anyone to achieve, her performance during the fall campaign tended to support both descriptions. She seemed inexhaustible. Like Eleanor, Mrs. Shriver carried out a heavy independent travel and appearance schedule. She also was articulate, but laced her political speeches with anecdotes, improvisations, and spontaneous humor. She also seemed unintimidatable. She would go almost anywhere in search of voters and was not easily put off by precedents or tradition. She attended a traditional Maryland bull roast sponsored by a badly divided local party organization. After being invited by the pro-McGovern-Shriver faction, she was met at the door by the leader of the "anti's," who disinvited her. Deciding she would not make the trip in vain, she entered anyway and managed to get out a rudimentary speech before the startled old-line party leader could physically recapture the microphone from her.

OCTOBER 30, 1972. Those inside the campaign favoring "negative" television spots won out in the final week. John Stewart of Larry O'Brien's staff worked hard with a New York media consultant, Tony Schwartz, to produce half a dozen one-minute spots highly critical of

WIDE WORLD PHOTOS

Too bad they couldn't vote.

the administration on the war, the economy, and corruption. A screening of the spots caused two or three to be discarded on grounds of excessive hostility and a potential backlash effect. The remaining two or three were placed in the final week's network spot rotation. Whether a media strategy favoring longer-running negative material would have materially affected the ultimate vote totals, I cannot say. But I don't think it would have. Everyone knew Nixon well-enough; they didn't need to be reminded. Our job was to reveal the true McGovern, a leader who offered hope and promise, who was constructive, not destructive. The negative stuff ran counter to the basic McGovern character.

OCTOBER 31, 1972. The evening of the long campaign day had come to a close. Only a few night hours remained. It was almost inconceivable, after two and a half years, to think that in one week there would no longer be a campaign. No more worries about money, staff, television, schedules, literature, telephones, personalities, morale. No more shrieking or moaning state coordinators no more phone calls in the middle of the night bringing some new crisis, no more insomnia, no more fatigue.

But in one more week there would be no more campaign to win, no more cause, no more goal. Some of the best political talent in a century would dissolve into an administration or disappear back into society. There would be no more laughter at the ridiculous comedy of it all, at our own incredible audacity at having challenged the political system and won. Like everything else, it had to end, and everyone realized that and was ready for it. It had been too long.

That mood of desperation common to all political campaigns set in during those final hours. Have we done enough? Let's buy more television, let's put the candidates into an extra city or two every day, let's put in more phones in Pennsylvania, more literature in Ohio. What if—a horrifying, gut-wrenching, cruel thought—what if we lost by only a few electoral votes and those few electoral votes represented one single state that itself was narrowly lost? What if we had made a little extra effort in that state? But which state might it be? It might be any one of a dozen and a half. How do you know where to make the extra effort? Better make it everywhere, or risk going through the rest of your life feeling personally responsible for another Nixon term, wondering "what if?"

The days and nights were crowded with pressure, tension, and palpable anxiety. The responsibility of the undertaking began to be felt, and the consequences of defeat. The hopes of millions of Americans, as well as the obligation to them, which began to weigh on me so heavily, must have descended on George McGovern a hundred-fold. And the clock was drawing on toward midnight.

NIGHT

NOVEMBER 1, 1972. We had begun planning for the change of administrations. In September, names had been solicited from a number of sources for a special task-force to conduct the planning. One of the people highly recommended to coordinate the effort was Washington attorney Harry MacPherson. Having met Harry a few weeks previously, I asked him in October and he willingly accepted the responsibility. He had a number of suggestions of good people to help and other names were supplied by a friend, Dean Peter Krogh of the Georgetown Foreign Service School.

Harry is an unassuming, witty Texan who was a White House aide to President Johnson and who wrote a perceptive and engaging book on his experiences in government. He is one of the few men in Washington who seems to be held in high regard by almost everyone.

In the several weeks toward the close of the campaign, Harry and others were working both on transitional procedures—how exactly does governmental power change hands?—and on finding the talent available to assume command—who are the most capable people available? Anticipating, to some degree, the David Halberstam thesis that the "best and the brightest" might not always be the most capable or have the best judgment, I specifically had asked Harry and his group to search out the hidden talent, young, unknown, potential achievers. That work was underway as the campaign came to a close. (True to the McGovern campaign fashion, the Senator had, in the meantime, made similar requests to Clark Clifford *and* Theodore Sorenson. But, better to duplicate in such matters than permit the matter to slip by.)

NOVEMBER 2, 1972. Many hours were spent toward the end in discussions related to the final media effort. The networks had each set aside blocks of prime time during the final weekend in the anticipation that the campaigns would want them. Although we now had more money than ever, great amounts of it would have to be put into the get-out-the-vote push. Besides, we didn't want to saturate the airwaves and drive the voters away from the polls. Finally, concluding speeches by the Senator were scheduled for Friday, the 3rd, and Sunday, the 5th.

As it turned out, both would deal with Vietnam. After never seeming to strike fire during the campaign, the sudden, "peace-is-at-hand" Kissinger announcement at the end of October brought this issue right back to the front pages and the front of everyone's mind. A few days passed while we tried to evaluate the bona-fides of the promise. It was either a long-awaited fulfillment, the timing of which just happened to take place on the eve of the American elections, or the ultimate in cynical, political deception. If it were the former, we could only applaud it; if it were the latter—and if that fact could be proved—it might cost Nixon the election. We were not caught by surprise. We had picked up a variety of rumors during October that something of this magnitude was afoot. But the problem remained of handling the announcement in the proper way.

Kissinger's October 26th statement had emphasized that only six or seven details had to be worked out before the peace agreement. Peace did, indeed, seem to be at hand. But on the night of November 2nd Nixon went on nationwide television in effect to reject the agreement his own chief negotiator had announced a week earlier. Nixon seemed to indicate that the agreement would sacrifice our national "honor" and was unacceptable. The Senator immediately decided to go before the national cameras himself the following night.

NOVEMBER 3, 1972. The Senator opened his remarks with the observation that Nixon had withdrawn the latest promise of peace and had not suggested when to expect another one. This was so, he stated, because "it is not the details, but the central issues, that are still in dispute." The hope of peace was betrayed. It was, he said in the strongest language possible, "a deception designed to raise our hopes, before we went to vote on Tuesday." He pointed out that the purported terms of the agreement were the same as those which administration representatives described as "surrender" when proposed by McGovern. The remainder of the speech referred in very personal terms to the continuing price of the war and to the failure of the Nixon administration to live up to its four-year commitment to end the war. He concluded by calling election day "a day of reckoning for America . . . a day when we decide between war and peace."

The final week of the campaign for the political organizers was devoted to election day planning and preparation. Meetings were held almost around the clock with the regional coordinators, Eli Segal, Harold Himmelman, and Rick Stearns, concerning amounts of money needed in their states for get-out-the-vote activities, phones, leaflets, sound-trucks, materials, workers, mailings. In the major cities, some party leaders and minority groups demanded and got substantial sums to compensate their ward and precinct workers for devoting election day to turning out the vote.

Endless hours were spent evaluating the qualifications and background of the people to whom this money was to be entrusted. Rick and Eli made a swing around the country at the end of October, visiting our state coordinators and state party leaders to determine where our election money should be placed. Yancey Martin and Paul Cobb, our two principal black organizers, also went into two dozen cities to determine the location of the most effective black political organizations and the identity and reputation of their leaders. Our fund-raisers were on the phone throughout the day and night raising more money for the last push.

From the reports of those who had traveled, we developed a final get-out-the-vote budget completely drying up the treasury, getting every last ounce of financial resource out into the field. It wouldn't do any good in Washington on election day. In the case of one or two of the big-city Democratic leaders, bitter arguments broke out over the weekend over the sums they should receive to turn out the traditional Democratic vote. There were threats of sit-downs, of staying home, of no vote. In each case, one group of people in the campaign said that we should not deal with the party bosses, that they were weak and ineffective and couldn't deliver a vote even if they wanted to. There was doubt whether some of them wanted to. Others in the campaign didn't think we could take the chance. Remember that haunting loss-by-one-state theory? The stakes were too high to bet that the bosses' power had long since departed. The pressure of such decisions was grueling.

But money or no money, our committed workers were going to turn out. In the many states and cities where our political operation was built upon the faithful, there was no question of performance. The suggestion of paying money to turn out the vote would have been considered callous and offensive. They were in this because they believed in McGovern, Shriver, and the Democratic Party's traditions. They wouldn't have to be coaxed or paid to work. They disliked Nixon too much.

Elaborate security precautions were laid out for the headquarters on election day. The same kind of precautions were implemented in each state election headquarters. We had every reason to believe there were dozens of Howard Hunts, hundreds of Gordon Liddys, and thousands of Donald Segrettis (his name meant "secrets" in Italian, someone said). Our phone system was secured. The number of people to be permitted in the headquarters on election day was restricted, the doors and all floors were placed under guard, and special badges and passes would be required. There was no way to know how many of the staff members might be on the Republican payroll. Marginal paranoia abounded. But election year had been like that since June.

In the final days, the Senator traveled to New York for a garment center rally of over 50,000, to Chicago for a torchlight parade and rally with Mayor Daley which drew tens of thousands, to Cincinnati, Battle

WIDE WORLD PHOTOS

"Don't worry about Illinois."

Creek, Grand Rapids, Waco, Corpus Christi, Little Rock, St. Louis, Moline, Philadelphia, Wichita, Long Beach, and finally back home, Sioux Falls, South Dakota. Since Labor Day, George McGovern had visited 64 cities and traveled 51,465 air miles.

Early one morning toward the end—it must have been 5 or 6 A.M. wherever he was—the Senator called me at home. He sounded tired and frustrated and his voice was hoarse and cracky. He said: "I sure can't figure out why the people around the country are so apathetic. Do you have any ideas about what we might do? Can you think of anything else that might stir them up?" I said: "No, Senator, I think you're doing everything you can. I still think we can win this thing. All we have to do is win the right combination of states to get an electoral majority, and I think we're going to do that. Everyone is working very hard." I felt guilty and inept. I felt somehow responsible for letting him down. I didn't have any secrets or tricks. I didn't know what else to do.

NOVEMBER 7, 1972. Election day. Judgment day—it was like final exams in school. There was a dazed quality about the day, as if it weren't really happening, as if it were all a dream. It was all ending too suddenly. It was as if the psyche's 100 mile-an-hour train were being stopped on a dime.

If we won five big states—California, New York, Illinois, Pennsylvania, and New Jersey—we would get 158 electoral votes. If we won Texas or Ohio, plus Massachusetts, Minnesota, and Wisconsin, we would have 60 or 61 more electoral votes. Then if we won Maryland, Connecticut, West Virginia, Iowa, Oregon, Hawaii, Rhode Island, South Dakota, Alaska, and the District of Columbia, we would have 60 more electoral votes. Added up, that would give us 278 or 279 electoral votes and the Presidency. There were perhaps half a dozen to a dozen other states where we thought we had a chance, so if one or two of these didn't come through we could make it up somewhere else. In the absence of a dramatic political breakthrough, it seems to us that we would lose most of the southern states, some mid-Western states, and a number of mountain states rather badly. For that reason, the possibility existed that we might lose the popular vote and still win the election with the electoral vote. We hoped it wouldn't be that close.

McGovern was in South Dakota, together with Eleanor and the family, the traveling party, and the national press. Arrangements had been made for a victory celebration there. Frank remained in Washington throughout most of the day and, with Miles Rubin, Henry Kimelman and others, flew to South Dakota that evening.

At the headquarters, the only activities were monitoring the voter turnout and making sure the voters were being brought out all across the country, but particularly in the crucial cities and states. Although interpretations were made during the day of the projected turnout in this or that area, it all seemed to be grasping at straws. The campaign was democratic to the end. In the closing hours the eastern advance people caucused in Philadelphia and voted on which state to work in on election day. But they always were a renegade bunch. Even their Rasputin, Steve Robbins, couldn't control them at the end.

It all got down to the Wallace vote in the key northern states. If Nixon got the votes Wallace got in 1968, we would lose by a landslide. If we could carry most of the states Humphrey carried in 1968, add California and win some other states, which he narrowly lost, by picking up the alienated northern Wallace voters, we could win. They had to believe that McGovern represented responsible change, that he was not part of the political establishment which they felt so distrustful of. They were tired of all the big guys getting the breaks from government while they paid the bills. Things had to change.

So now it was a matter of wait and see. The hours dragged on. The voter turnout, though heavy in spots, was lighter than expected across the country. It was impossible to know what that would mean. Everyone worked in every state. There was no letdown.

Finally, the evening hours came. The networks came on the air with their computers and tabulation boards. As the polls began to close, results were posted. Everyone knew that the earliest states would not be particularly good for us. It would take results from some of the larger states, where we expected to do well, before the story could be told.

The first indication was Connecticut. The earliest returns did not look good. Then in mid-evening the first figures from Ohio were very troublesome. Within a few minutes, Connecticut, and then Ohio, were projected for Nixon. I knew it was all over.

I called South Dakota and found the Senator asleep. About an hour later he called back. He wasn't surprised that we had lost. He remembered telling Eleanor on the Saturday before that his instincts told him we would lose. He was surprised at the proportions of the vote. He couldn't understand it. It made no sense to him at all. But we will have to keep trying, he said, our time will come.

Later that night he addressed the crowd in South Dakota:

The presidency belongs to someone else. But the glory of these devoted working friends, and their dedication to the noble ideals of this country, sustains us now and it will sustain our country. We will shed no tears because all of this effort, I am positive, will bear fruit for years to come.

* * *

So I ask all of you tonight to stand with your convictions. I ask you not to despair at the political process of this country because that process has yielded much valuable improvement in these past two years. The Democratic Party will be a better party because of the reforms that we have carried out. The nation will be better because we never once gave up the long battle to renew its oldest ideals and to redirect its current energies along more human and hopeful paths.

After watching the Senator's speech, I walked out of the headquarters into the black, rainy night thinking: still no rest. We still have miles to go before we sleep—miles to go before we sleep.

One Man Can Make a Difference and Every Man Should Try

Edmund Burke said that the march of the human mind is slow. Any evaluation of the 1972 McGovern phenomenon must finally decide whether it was marching a half-step faster than the collective national mind or marching to the beat of a different drummer—whether the McGovern campaign was simply ahead of its time, or out of step. That evaluation cannot be made outside a historical context.

In the life of every nation, change is as inevitable as the passage of time itself. Even if principles and purposes remain constant, the very process of life and death dictates that leadership must change. The old must give way to the new. The ineluctable tide of new generations is our most certain protection against stagnation. As each new generation emerges, it assumes the power and responsibility previously assumed by its predecessors from an even earlier generation. But it is a myth that power is passed, like a torch, from one generation to the next. While one generation has power, it also has strength, and some fleeting claim to immortality. It relinquishes that power only under duress, because the loss of power is a blunt reminder of mortality. If, in primitive times, the chief caveman was also the keeper of the fire, he fought to prevent younger, stronger cavemen from taking the fire, for it was not only the key and symbol of his power, but also his defense against obsolescence.

In his inaugural address, John Kennedy said: "Let the word go forth from this time and place, to friend and foe alike, that the torch has been passed to a new generation of Americans." The torch had been passed all right; but only after John Kennedy and the people of his generation had wrested it, by organizational force and political skill, from the men of Roosevelt's, Truman's, and Eisenhower's generation. There should be no mistake. Power is won, grasped; it is never handed over willingly. That is a good part of what politics is all about.

John Kennedy's emergence on the national scene was almost inevitable. After 15 years of post-war stewardship by pre-war leaders, the national mood was ripe for promise, for hope, for excitement. "Let's get this country moving again!" The country was ready for a change, if not of direction, at least of pace. Those now busily discounting the Kennedy Presidency and leadership are largely missing the point. The people understood why New Frontier legislation might not get passed. It is always simpler to change Presidents than to change Congresses. The important fact was that the political windows had been thrown open, new leaders were in charge, *an effort was being made* to change things. The mood of a nation is not much different from the mood of an individual. In times of trouble and distress, we seek security and protection. Once the siege is lifted, then we feel expansive, ready for innovation and experiment. That was very much the mood of the country at that turning point in 1960.

But then, one of history's aberrations—assassination—struck to upset political nature's timetable. That tragic act of unpredictable circumstances put the country back in the hands of the previous generation. Although not that much older chronologically than John Kennedy, Lyndon Johnson was very much a man of the former era. His political antecedents, his ties to Roosevelt and Sam Rayburn, his respect for the traditions of a Richard Russell, his security in courthouse and clubhouse politics, cast him, particularly in the minds of the young, in the mold of "politics as usual." For millions, it was as if they had successfully willed the nation toward the future, toward change, and then suddenly, literally overnight, found themsleves back with Eisenhower, or, farther back, with Jim Farley. That wasn't what they wanted. That wasn't what the nation wanted.

If an assassin robbed the country of the hope of progress, the Vietnam war robbed Lyndon Johnson of any chance he had to prove he could carry out that hope. As the war gradually escalated, as national priorities began to warp and twist, as hope for the future gradually faded, a mood of gloom, suspicion and fear settled over the land. Deprivation led to racial violence, which set white against black and black against white. A new affluence, based in part on an economy invigorated by military spending, brought increased crime—like a neat social irony. The young, out to blame someone for the screwed-up world, turned against their elders and much of society's establishment. And across the land 100 million middle-Americans sat brooding in their mortgaged shelters.

But even as the people themselves became increasingly embittered by the hope that failed and longed for new leadership and guidance, their leaders grew older, more institutionalized, and more out of touch. The country grew more divided over the war. The young became more angry at the old. The old became increasingly less patient with the young. The generation gap grew wider.

Then, strangely came a voice seeking to capitalize upon this discontent, the voice of George Corley Wallace. For a time, that voice followed its own natural instincts. It sought to capitalize upon the common fear through demagoguery. The basis of the discontent was believed to be race. But soon even Wallace realized he had stumbled, like a native in search of game happening on an incredible ancient ruin, on much larger things. Then he began to see a broad-based teeming unrest stretching far to the north and from coast to coast. These people were angry not only at blacks, they were angry about a lot of things. Wallace began to try a new, much larger, lever—government. And that rang more bells than even race. Wallace had his finger on or near the problem. But he picked the wrong villain. He sent his "message" to the wrong address.

For the anger, frustration, and alienation weren't directed simply at government. *Nothing* worked anymore. All the institutions were failing. None could solve the problems of crime, of drugs, of the war, of taxes. Worst of all, none of the traditional institutions could return a sense of direction and purpose to America, or restore the ruling values by which our national life had always been gauged. Offered only two alternatives out of the past in 1968, the frustration of the people only deepened. Thus, we entered the 1970s. A sundered nation, an alienated citizenry, our prospective leadership in near-rebellion, our existing leadership badly out of touch, and a system of failing institutions. The people wanted change. The leadership didn't bring change, but rather exploited fear and apprehension to avoid it. And the country drifted along.

Then came 1972 and Edmund Muskie. By all traditional political measures, Muskie should have been his party's nominee and should have had a reasonable chance at defeating Nixon. But Muskie failed because he offered nothing new. He offered more solidity and stability, when for ten years people had longed to recapture energy and movement, direction and purpose. You can't out-solid Nixon. Nixon is solid to the point of immobility. If the voters are given a choice between solidities, they will inevitably stay with the solidity they have. Between the two of them, the American people might as well have been offered two concrete men.

No, in those early primaries, the voters showed they knew something that their leaders didn't. It was a measure of the leadership's lack of understanding of the nation's plight that the leadership lined up strongly behind Muskie. The leaders merely proved they didn't know what was happening in the country. The political leadership thought the country still wanted protectionism, the status quo. They thought the issue was stewardship, rather than leadership.

George McGovern then entered the scene. He had come to national prominence on that great divisive issue, the war, the issue which contributed more to the social fragmentation than any other. McGovern's genius was both in correctly reading the longing for change and in realizing the only hope for its success was in a leader who could bridge the national divisions—the generation gap, the racial distrust, the bitterness over the war. He spoke of himself and his campaign as "a bridge over troubled waters." He used phrases like "healing," "reconciling," "bringing together," and "restoring."

His principal effort to reconcile, aside from ending the war, was through party reform. He sought to open and democratize the rules and procedures by which the Democratic Party operated. If one of the major institutions for change could be opened up, and people could be made to feel there was still hope through working in the system, they might draw encouragement and inspiration. Further, they might come to believe that the dead hand of old office-holders could be put aside without the violent protests of 1968. In most states, the reforms proposed by the commission which McGovern chaired were carried out by party activists who were not necessarily supportive of a McGovern Presidential bid and even, in many cases, by those who came to support other candidates. The myth that McGovern rigged the rules to his own advantage, completely unsupportable in fact, was created after his successes by those who resented his emergence and who could otherwise not explain it.

Unquestionably, McGovern did threaten established institutional leadership, particularly that of the Democratic Party. That leadership, in many states old and angry at the increasing pressure for change, saw him as an even greater threat than John Kennedy twelve years earlier. For Kennedy was forced to deal with them to construct his coalition; McGovern achieved his success by working harder and more effectively than anyone else, and was able to by-pass the aging power brokers. Seeing the threat of imminent loss of power, the old-line leadership made desperate last-minute attempts to halt McGovern by an unprecedented theft of legitimately elected convention delegates. Although the flags of fairness and justice were flown by the stop-McGovern forces, they merely concealed the fundamental motivation—power.

Even after this final obstacle to the nomination was surmounted, there were still more millions of voters to convince that the gaps could be bridged, that the country could be healed, that change could be brought about. The mass of voters wanted desperately to build that bridge, to close the gap, but the distance frightened them. They could be brought to the point where they were ten years before only by a most skillful and competent leader. Most of all, that leader had to be able to instill utmost confidence in the people; confidence not only that he truly meant what he said about the changes he proposed, that he was not merely another politician, but also confidence that he had the competence and political skill to govern the country, bridge the troubled waters, and move toward the future—all at once.

All the while, McGovern perceived the demands being placed upon him and his candidacy and the dimensions of the task which he had taken on. The test of his skills would not await assumption of office.

While campaigning, during the very process of seeking the Presidency, he was called upon to bridge the gaps in his party—an effort constantly frustrated, not by his supporters, but by the opposition forces. He was called upon to bridge the generation gap, to relate the traditional national values and political system to a generation of young people who had become deeply suspicious of both. He was expected somehow to use his very campaign as a mechanism to solve complex and profound problems of society brought to him by activist women's organizations, by minority groups, by young people. The burden of the undertaking was immense. Because so few shared his understanding of the almost superhuman task he had to perform to win the election, there were few in national leadership capacities who could help or share the burden.

He was encouraged to adopt a 1968 Robert Kennedy approach of challenging the institutions, of confronting outmoded and unworkable elements of the system head-on. He was advised not to seek leadership and control of the institutions, but to question their very existence. But 1972 was not 1968, and the confrontation approach seemed harsh, divisive, and frightening to most people. One couldn't bridge the troubled waters by pouring gasoline on them and setting them afire. In the closing weeks of the campaign, when the Senator resorted to this confrontation approach, he seemed strident and angry. The people are not angry; they are frustrated and troubled. They reject those who seek to challenge the structure, to destroy and replace their institutions.

The times cried for a leader who could heal and transform our nation. Of all those considered for the Presidency in 1972, only George McGovern had the necessary qualifications. He had read the public mood correctly. He had to demonstrate that he could provide the necessary leadership. Of all the Democrats, only McGovern could have defeated Nixon. A status quo candidacy was bound to fail. But if he were unable to instill the necessary confidence, and demonstrate the necessary competence, his campaign would fail the most miserably. He stood the only chance to win, and the only possibility of losing badly. His campaign was, indeed, a dangerous mission.

Contrary to the revisionists who descended upon the McGovern candidacy within hours after the election, the McGovern campaign was not a political aberration representative only of a radical Democratic fringe. McGovern, his key staff members, and his closest advisors all spring from the mainstream of Democratic Party traditions. They represent the present and future of the Democratic center. The "stop-McGovern" forces are the leaderless, directionless fringe representing, at best, a Democratic Party of some forgotten past.

Through that political marathon which were the primaries, George McGovern managed brilliantly and all alone to survive the hazards and to forge, accurately in the public mind, the impression of an honest, determined, trustworthy leader for change. The two pillars of success were confidence and competence. But even in the closing hours of the nomination race, one of those two pillars, confidence, was beginning to show faults. Some of the proposals he had chosen to feature in his campaign appeared to be vulnerable at best and ill-conceived at worst.

In recent decades, progressive ideas and innovative proposals have sprung in large part from the liberal wing of the Democratic Party. The Democratic Party, and the progressive thinkers in its liberal wing, have provided most of the grist for the governmental mill since the days of Roosevelt. Liberals propose and conservatives oppose. Although McGovern himself had excellent insights into the general mood of the electorate, it was apparent throughout the campaign that the fount of specific proposals and programs was running dry. The traditional sources of invigorating, inspiring and creative ideas were dissipated. The best thinkers of the 1930s, 40s, and 50s and even the 1960s were not producing. Whether this resulted from age, depression, frustration at the nation's ponderous rate of progress, or lassitude, the results were crystal clear: by 1972, American liberalism was near bankruptcy.

The more effectively the organizational side of the campaign performed, the more crippling were the blows from the substantive or issues side of the campaign. McGovern somehow brought to the surface a whole new generation of political organizers, the best the country has seen for many years. But he did not bring out a new generation of thinkers. He did not because it isn't there. Our campaign received a deluge of erratic, worthless ideas and proposals, but it received very few creative ones. This criticism is not directed at other McGovern staff members. The issues staff of the campaign labored long and hard, but it never had the support from the traditional centers of liberal thought that Roosevelt or John Kennedy had. The fact that one of the most detailed, well-thought-out McGovern positions involved a negative—proposals to cut defense spending—proves the thesis. The fact that one of the principal domestic proposals—a plan to eliminate the present welfare system (another negative)—was abandoned due to internal inconsistencies is another proof. The fields of liberalism failed to provide a crop in 1972. The soil is worn out.

Further, the bastions of organizational liberalism and progressivism— Massachusetts, New York, Minnesota, Wisconsin, Oregon, California— are populated by quarreling, feuding, bickering factions. The effort required to hammer together McGovern's natural base in some of these states defies description. The liberal leadership in many states has become so severed from the problems of the working man, that ordinary foot-soldier of the Democratic armies, that it skirts obsolescence and irrelevance. Democratic Party liberals better pull their socks up and get back in the game, or very soon no one will give a damn. New ideas must be found to solve old problems and those ideas must be related to ordinary working men and women. The only reason the Democratic Party has survived in any kind of leadership role this far is because the Republican Party died a long time ago and its death has gone unnoticed.

Even as the cracks began to appear in the pillar of confidence, the public opinion of the Senator's ability to propose sensible programs, the other major pillar, competence, began to weaken. A candidate is judged both on what he says—his "platform"—and on what he does—his ability to handle problems.

The tragic Eagleton affair shattered any chance McGovern may have had to emerge as a competent leader. Every measure we had of voter attitudes—canvassing, phoning, polling—showed, from late July on, that "the Eagleton thing" was the insurmountable barrier of our campaign. Once the impression was dimly created in the public mind that the Senator had vacillated, had wavered under pressure, then incidents such as the Salinger matter merely reinforced that impression. From the minute McGovern received the nomination the millions who had not yet formed an opinion began to scrutinize him closely. Overnight, the Eagleton incident created a monumental test of the candidate's competence. And the solution and then re-solution met with immense dissatisfaction.

With competence eroded by issues so subject to frightening characterization, and confidence weakened by a freakish human confrontation, victory was hopeless.

But to analyze further matters which will be analyzed by all the experts for years to come does not solve the long-range problem. How and when can peaceful change be brought about in this country? How shall the power necessary to implement change be restored to the forces of progress?

The troubled waters are still to be bridged. Indeed, after another Nixon term, they will undoubtedly be more troubled. Yet change is inevitable; it is as certain as the transition of generations themselves; it can be brought about, and it can be brought about more expeditiously than by waiting for the dinosaurs to pass into eternity.

First, the forces of change and progress must organize themselves. They must literally get together. To organize means merely to "pull or put together into an orderly, functional, structured whole." The very term organize derives from sources meaning "instrument." An organization is not an end in itself, it is an instrument to be used. It is a tool to accomplish a result. That instrument must be forged and honed, like the finest steel.

Second, the organization must relate to people. All kinds of people.

An exclusive organization is a useless, ineffective organization. Those who would bring change and progress to this country must get back in touch with everyday people, working people, people of all colors, of all ages, of all economic backgrounds. Somehow the organizational techniques employed must insure the most relevant, inclusive organization possible.

Third, to recapture power, the forces of change and progress must develop a new generation of leaders who can instill confidence and demonstrate competence. The Democratic Party, under penalty of irrelevance and extinction, must bring forward a new generation of thinkers who are in touch with the real world and a new generation of leaders who can inspire enthusiasm, hope, and energy in the people.

All this can be done, and it can be done in very little time. It will require men like George McGovern to continue to exercise an influence. His candidacy brought new hope to millions. It was the first step in forging a new political "center," a movement consecrated to change and progress. It was the occasion for the emergence of new activists. Unlike those who have gotten into politics for an individual candidate and then disappeared after his defeat, the thousands of people who came into the McGovern campaign will stay active in party affairs all across the nation. They are joining the staffs of Senators, Governors, and Congressmen. They are seeking party positions at the state and local level. Some will undoubtedly seek office themselves.

Just as the campaign became a test for McGovern, that campaign itself became a bridge over troubled waters for those who supported him. His courage, his refusal to accommodate to "the establishment center" and to become simply another politician, restored faith and hope for the disillusioned. It won for him not only the nomination but, more enduringly, the respect and admiration of millions of Americans. His campaign became a way out of the disillusionment of the 1960s with their assassinations and their war. It became a reason to continue, to keep trying.

And to pick up the torch of change which has flickered sometimes only dimly since 1963, the forces of progress and hope must keep trying. As Winston Churchill told his people, and the people of the world: "Never give up, never give up, never, never, never give up." Those who supported George McGovern will not give up. They are not that kind.

George McGovern said it all when he accepted his party's nomination. "American politics will never be the same again."

INDEX

Oakland, California	9/4	Detroit, Michigan	10/9
Seattle, Washington	9/4	Battle Creek, Michigan	10/10
Portland, Oregon	9/5	Chicago, Illinois	10/10
Los Angeles, California	9/5	Erie, Pennsylvania	10/11
San Diego, California	9/6	Boston, Massachusetts	10/11
Dallas, Texas	9/6	Minneapolis, Minnesota	10/12
Houston, Texas	9/6	Fargo, North Dakota	10/12
Peoria, Illinois	9/7	Seattle, Washington	10/12
Rockford, Illinois	9/7	Portland, Oregon	10/13
Duluth, Minnesota	9/8	San Francisco, California	10/13
Des Moines, Iowa	9/8	San Diego, California	10/13
Albuquerque, New Mexico	9/8	Los Angeles, California	10/14
Houston, Texas	9/10	Austin, Texas	10/16
Minneapolis, Minnesota	9/10	Houston, Texas	10/16
Chicago, Illinois	9/12	San Antonio, Texas	10/16
Detroit, Michigan	9/12	Ft. Worth, Texas	10/17
Cleveland, Ohio	9/12	Washington, D.C.	10/17
Pittsburgh, Pennsylvania	9/12	Detroit, Michigan	10/18
Philadelphia, Pennsylvania	9/13	Cleveland, Ohio	10/18
Albany, New York	9/14	Toledo, Ohio	10/18
New York, New York	9/14	Philadelphia, Pennsylvania	10/19
Hartford, Connecticut	9/14	New York, New York	10/19
Portland, Maine	9/15	Washington, D.C.	10/19
Baltimore Maryland	9/15	New York, New York	10/20
Washington, D.C.	9/16	Scranton, Pennsylvania	10/21
Huntington, West Virginia	9/17	Allentown, Pennsylvania	10/21
Cincinnati, Ohio	9/18	Reading, Pennsylvania	10/21
Carbondale, Illinois	9/18	Johnstown, Pennsylvania	10/21
Chicago, Illinois	9/18	Pittsburgh, Pennsylvania	10/21
Milwaukee, Wisconsin	9/19	Washington, D.C.	10/21
Flint, Michigan	9/19	Philadelphia, Pennsylvania	10/23
Columbus, Ohio	9/19	New York, New York	10/23
Newark, New Jersey	9/20	Dayton, Ohio	10/24
Philadelphia, Pennsylvania	9/20	Milwaukee, Wisconsin	10/24
New York, New York	9/21	Cleveland, Ohio	10/25
Detroit, Michigan	9/21	Detroit, Michigan	10/25
Rochester, New York	9/22	Cedar Rapids, Iowa	10/26
Pittsburgh, Pennsylvania	9/22	Sacramento, California	10/26
Cleveland, Ohio	9/23	Los Angeles, California	10/26
New York, New York	9/23	San Diego, California	10/28
Sioux Falls, South Dakota	9/24	Spokane, Washington	10/28
Billings, Montana	9/24	Seattle, Washington	10/28
Seattle, Washington	9/25	Baltimore, Maryland	10/28
San Francisco, California	9/25	Washington, D.C.	10/29
Los Angeles, California	9/26	Hartford, Connecticut	10/29
Washington, D.C.	9/26	Pittsburgh, Pennsylvania	10/30
Baltimore, Maryland	9/30	Syracuse, New York	10/31
Atlantic City, New Jersey	9/30	Newark, New Jersey	10/31
New York, New York	9/30	New York, New York	11/1
Baltimore, Maryland	9/30	Chicago, Illinois	11/1
Washington, D.C.	10/2	Cincinnati, Ohio	11/2
Newark, New Jersey	10/2	Battle Creek, Michigan	11/2
New York, New York	10/3	Grand Rapids, Michigan	11/2
Boston, Massachusetts	10/3	Chicago, Illinois	11/3
Niagara Falls, New York	10/3	Waco, Texas	11/4
Buffalo, New York	10/4	Corpus Christi, Texas	11/4
New York, New York	10/4	Little Rock, Arkansas	11/4
Cleveland, Ohio	10/5	St. Louis, Missouri	11/4
Chicago, Illinois	10/5	Moline, Illinois	11/5
Des Moines, Iowa	10/6	New York, New York	11/5
Kansas City, Missouri	10/6	Philadelphia, Pennsylvania	11/6
St. Louis, Missouri	10/7	Wichita, Kansas	11/6
Baltimore, Maryland	10/7	Long Beach, California	11/6
Washington, D.C.	10/9	Sioux Falls, South Dakota	11/6
New York, New York	10/9	Washington, D.C.	11/8

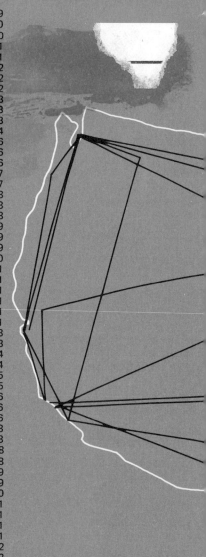